FORENSIC SCIENCE

Edited by

JOSEPH L. PETERSON
John Jay College of Criminal Justice

FORENSIC SCIENCE

Scientific Investigation in Criminal Justice

AMS PRESS, INC.
New York

Library of Congress Cataloging in Publication Data

Main entry under title:

Forensic science.

    1. Criminal investigation — Addresses, essays, lectures. 2. Crime laboratories
— Addresses, essays, lectures. 3. Criminal justice, Administration of — Addresses,
essays, lectures. I. Peterson, Joseph, 1945-

HV8073.F59	364.12'1	75-11812

ISBN 0-404-13139-5
0-404-13145-X (pb.)

Manufactured in the United States of America

TABLE
OF
CONTENTS

ACKNOWLEDGMENTS

Acknowledgement is made to the authors and publishers below who have granted permission to reprint material and who reserve all rights in the articles appearing in this anthology.

Benson, Stacy, and Nicol, "Systems Analysis of Criminalistics Operations," *Journal of Forensic Sciences,* 1972, pp. 25-49.

Borkenstein, "The Administration of a Forensic Science Laboratory," from *Methods of Forensic Science*, edited by A.S. Curry, New York: John Wiley & Sons, 1964, Vol. III, pp. 151-168.

Bowman, "The Indigent's Right to an Adequate Defense," *Cornell Law Review,* Vol. 55, No. 4, April 1970, pp. 632-645. Copyright © 1970 Cornell University.

Cowan, "Decision Theory in Law, Science, and Technology," *Science*, Vol. 140, June 7, 1963, pp. 1065-1075.

Curry, "Chemistry and Crime," *Chemistry in Britain,* Vol. 5, November 1969, pp. 501-504.

English, "Forensic Science in Criminal Prosecution," *Analytical Chemistry* Vol. 42, No. 13, November 1970, pp. 40A-48A.

Fitzsimons, "Science and Law — A Lawyer's Viewpoint," *Journal of The Forensic Science Society*, Vo. 13, 1973, pp. 261-267.

Fong, "Criminalistics and the Prosecutor," Vol. I, Section B, Chapter XIV from *The Prosecutor's Sourcebook*, edited by James George and Ira Cohen, New York: Practicing Law Institute, 1969.

Goddard, "Scientific Crime Detection Laboratories in Europe," *American Journal of Police Sciences*, Vol. 1, 1930, pp. 14-37.

Grant, "The Problems of the Defense Expert," *Journal of The Forensic Society*, Vol. 9, No. 2, 1969, pp. 191-198.

Gunn and Frank, "Planning a Forensic Science Lab," *The Police Chief*, January 1972, pp. 36-41.

Kalven and Zeisel, "The Anatomy of Evidence," from *The American Jury*, Boston: Little, Brown & Co., 1966, pp. 134-148.

Kingston, "The Law of Probabilities and the Credibility of Witnesses and Evidence," *Journal of Forensic Sciences*, January 1970 pp. 18-27.

Kingston and Kirk, "The Use of Statistics in Criminalistics," *Journal of Criminal Law, Criminology and Police Science*, Vol. 55 1964, pp. 514-521. Copyright © 1964 Northwestern University School of Law.

Kirk, "Criminalistics," *Science*, Vol. 140, April 1963, pp. 367-370.

Lassers, "Proof of Guilt in Capital Cases — An Unscience," *Journal of Criminal Law, Criminology and Police Science*, Vol. 58, No. 3, 1967, pp. 310-316. Copyright © 1967 Northwestern University School of Law.

Law Enforcement Bulletin, "Forty Years of Distinguished Scientific Assistance to Law Enforcement," November 1972, pp. 2-6, 24-28.

Levitt, "Crime Labs Expand as Business Flourishes," *Chemical and Engineering News*, January 3, 1972, pp. 16-18.

Nicol, "Criminalistics," from *Municipal Police Administration*, edited by George D. Eastman, Washington, D.C.: International City Management Association, 1969, pp. 305-316.

Ormrod, "Evidence and Proof," *Medicine Science and the Law*, Vol. 12, January 1972, pp. 9-20.

Parker, "The Status of Forensic Science in the Administration of Criminal Justice," *Revista Juridica de la Universidad de Puerto Rico*, Vol. 32, No. 2, 1963, pp. 405-419.

Parker and Peterson, "Physical Evidence Utilization in the Administration of Criminal Justice," Washington, D.C.: U.S. Government Printing Office, 1972.

Thomas, "Milestones in Forensic Science," *Journal of Forensic Sciences*, April 1974, pp. 241-254.

Tribe, "Trial by Mathematics," *Harvard Law Review*, Vol. 84, April 1971, pp. 1329-1344. Copyright © The Harvard Law Review Association.

Turner, "Technical Evidence: Its Availability in the Justice Process," in *Law Enforcement Science and Technology*, edited by S.A. Yefsky, London: Academic Press, 1967, pp. 247-249. Copyright © 1967 The Thompson Book Company.

Walls, "What Is Reasonable Doubt?" *Criminal Law Review*, August 1971 pp. 458-470.

Walls, "Whither Forensic Science?" *Medicine Science and the Law*, Vol. 6, 1966, pp. 183-189.

Williams, "Forensic Science," *Analytical Chemistry*, Vol. 45, November 1973, pp. 1076A-1089A.

Wilson, "Crime Detection Laboratories in the United States," from *Law, Medicine, Science, and Justice*, edited by Larry Baer, Springfield, Illinois: Charles C. Thomas, 1964, pp. 464-475.

Wilson, "Forensic Science and the Analyst," *Pure and Applied Chemistry*, Vol. 21, 1970, pp. 513-526.

PREFACE

Forensic science, the application of science to the law, is emerging as a major force in the attempts of the criminal justice system to control crime and to ensure a high quality of justice. Forensic scientists possessing a wide array of analytical skills direct their expertise to problems of reconstructing criminal acts, identifying physical evidence, linking offenders with their victims, as well as exonerating falsely accused people. In many cases the forensic scientist, through the application and interpretation of various scientific tests, supplies valuable information which cannot be determined by other conventional methods of investigation.

At present, however, the potential impact of forensic science is unrealized. Although the number and sophistication of forensic laboratories have advanced markedly in the past decade, laboratory performance has not reached a level of consistency, and mismanagement and underutilization are still unsolved problems. Professionals in this field have taken a passive position with respect to issues such as the proper role of the laboratory in the overall law enforcement structure. Generally, forensic scientists have restricted their creative efforts to problems at the laboratory bench.

This collection of articles focuses upon the growth and delivery of forensic science services in the past fifty years. The philosophical foundations of law and science serve as a fitting introduction to a more pragmatic discussion of present conditions in forensic science laboratories throughout the world today. Several

PREFACE

noted scientists describe proper techniques for interpreting the meaning of scientific tests and include suggestions for managing and evaluating large scientific operations. The various applications of science to the administration of justice are reviewed in another section which documents the unfortunately minimal involvement of science in the legal process. Finally, the issue of availability of scientific evidence to both the prosecution and defense during the course of a criminal investigation and trial is debated.

This anthology is unique because it deals exclusively in the forensic sciences with seldom researched areas of philosophy, management, and utilization. The questions asked by the contributors will, it is hoped, lead to a reconsideration by students and experienced professionals of what forensic science is and can be.

The British hold a position of high respect in the world community of forensic scientists. For this reason, many of the articles in this collection were originally published in Great Britain. The reader will note that the British spellings of certain words have been retained as they appeared originally.

—Joseph L. Peterson

I.

The Role of Science in a Legal System

INTRODUCTION

The institutions of science and law touch and profoundly shape the lives of all citizens. While the law serves to direct society's actions by enforcing prescribed rules of conduct, science has systematized the accumulation of knowledge through the observation and classification of facts. Although the ancient Greeks considered the two to be inseparable, law and science have now assumed quite different roles in society; each reflects its own unique historical developments. The men and women who are trained as natural scientists and attorneys are required to acquire basic knowledge, methods of procedure, and codes of conduct which have evolved over the past several hundred years. When the two professions do come into contact, as in forensic science, it is important to understand how people in each profession engage in fact-finding, make decisions, and translate their findings into action.

A fundamental process shared by scientists and jurists is decision-making: the making of critical choices based upon various forms of information. In the initial article Thomas A. Cowan explores the types of decisions required of scientists and lawyers and discusses several important differences about them. He observes that law is fundamentally interested in *feeling* and arriving at a just verdict, while the scientist strives to divest himself of all feelings and prejudices which may bias his results. Mr. Cowan suggests that a closer alliance between scientists and attorneys in their study of decision-making would result in significant benefits to society.

Evidence and proof are two terms widely utilized by scientists and lawyers in describing the components and conclusions of their investigations. Sir Roger F.G. Ormrod, past President of the British Academy of Forensic Sciences, acknowledges the differences in meaning of each term, depending upon the discipline which is employing it. Observing that fact-finding is an activity shared by both scientists and lawyers; Professor Ormrod examines the decision-making process used by lawyers, scientists and doctors within the context of forensic science. He presents a particularly interesting discussion of how each discipline collects facts and uses or excludes such information in the making of formal decisions.

The address by H.J. Walls offers an equally informative perspective on the role of natural sciences in the adversary system of criminal justice. He focuses on many of the problems in communication between the forensic scientist and the attorney. How should the court interpret and decide among the opinions of several experts who may disagree on the meaning of certain evidence? As the forensic sciences become more sophisticated and specialized, and as experts recognize that they must express their conclusions in quantitative or statistical form, the courts may have an even more difficult time in understanding and using the testimony of experts. The author also explores the meaning of "beyond reasonable doubt" and considers whether such a degree of proof can be translated into statistical terms.

The final selection in this section highlights the views of a lawyer on the role of science in the detection and adjudication of crime. J. Fitzsimons suggests that eyewitness testimony is inherently unreliable due to its subjective nature and that courts should be eager to use objective scientific evidence as often as possible. The use of science is not without imperfections as illustrated by cases in which experts are used by adversaries in supporting only one side of a legal controversy. J. Fitzsimons would prefer a system which would be a combination of both adversary and inquisitorial systems of law, in which an expert would be permitted to read his full report to the court and to be cross-examined.

DECISION THEORY IN LAW,

SCIENCE, AND TECHNOLOGY

Thomas A. Cowan

The aim of science, traditionally put, is to search out the ways in which truth may become known. Law aims at the just resolution of human conflict. Truth and justice, we might venture to say, having different aims, use different methods to achieve them. Unfortunately, this convenient account of law and science is itself neither true nor just. For law must know what the truth is within the context of the legal situation; and science finds itself ever engaged in resolving the conflicting claims of theorists putting forward their own competing brands of truth. In the face of this obvious dialectic, can we still cling to our device of the two ways of thinking? I believe we can, for a while at least. For if we were to ask a scientist to make a cool appraisal of legal methods for ascertaining truth, whether in decision, legislation, or executive order, we might well expect him to throw up his hands in despair and call for the aid of the anthropologist as a specialist in primitive folkways, if indeed he did not go immediately to the paleontologist. On the other hand, the scientist's *apparently* irresponsible attitude toward the destructive monsters he creates—what is often taken to be his wholesale disregard for or even downright antagonism toward art, morality, and religion—strikes many members of the legal profession as callous. Worse than that, there is strong evidence at hand that the scientist, in league with the businessman and the soldier, intends to rule the world of tomorrow—and intends to make both businessman and warrior as scientifically knowledgeable as they will need to be in order to fulfill their function in a world grown monstrously technological. For many scientists, the lawyer is merely a necessary evil—necessary, that is, for sweeping away archaic legal obstacles in the path of scientific enterprise. The lawyer, it needs hardly be added, is often suspected of creating these obstacles in order to remove them later for a fee. The two antagonistic ways of thinking then, if they do exist, certainly have sufficient reason for having come into being. Do they in fact exist?

A lawyer is taught early to look for the human *interest* behind all phenomenology. It is not expected that a plaintiff's account of a series of events will be in agreement with a defendant's account of the same series. More than that, plaintiff's attorney's account is not expected, or certainly not always expected, to be the same as defendant's attorney's. On the other hand, not only is a scientist's account of a set of events expected to be the same as that of another scientist's, but an elaborate methodology exists and must be followed to assure that all competent to undertake the investigation will arrive at relatively similar results. What the scientist is expected to avoid, as *scientist*, is preferring his own biases over those of his fellows. These biases must wash out in the course of the work, leaving results that are public, verifiable, general, and in accordance with truth, as current scientific methodology sees that commodity. The lawyer deals with human interest, bias, greed, falsehood, or just plain temperamental difference. The scientist, when he comes to deal with the same material (as psychologist or sociologist) proceeds to process it by taking out the bias. The lawyer does not do this and usually does not believe that the scientist can do it either.

The scientist *generalizes*; the lawyer *individuates*. It would take a lifetime to substantiate this bald assertion, but since none of us has a lifetime to give to it, I shall confine myself to a summary statement: *Litigation aims to individuate, and the judicial process is most at home when it disposes of a unique conflict situation uniquely.* What then of precedent? What of the universal or at any rate the general rules of law that govern human conduct? What of standards to which "all or almost all" must adhere? Worse still, what of legislation that may fall upon 180 million people at one time? And finally, what of executive order, decree, or ruling that may be addressed to one, many, or all subject to the jurisdiction? I know about these objections. I know them only too well. All I can say now is this: somehow or other a generalization such as "Every one who breaks and enters the dwelling, etc., shall be guilty of burglary" is different, vitally different, from a generalization such as, "Masses attract each other directly as their product and inversely as the square of the distance between them." Both are laws, both are general laws, but whereas the first is addressed to unique individuated subjects in such a way as to preserve as much as possible their unique individuality, the other subsumes the particularity of the *objects* concerned in the grand sweep of its generality. You will notice that I resisted the temptation to say of the first that it was a "prescription" and of the second that it was a "description." I happen to believe that both are prescriptions, the legal one being addressed to all subject to the law; the scientific, to all scientists "whom it may concern." The second, that is, is not really a *description* of nature but rather a *prescription* for scientists to act in certain ways rather than in others(1).

One way of putting the matter of *individuation* is to say of it that individuation invokes that autonomous function of the human mind which, following Carl Gustav Jung, we call *feeling*(2). The law is primarily interested in feelings—for example, feelings of justice; the *right* disposition of the dispute; the *best* ordering of human relations so as to attain a minimum amount of pain, suffering, loss; and the *optimal* procedures for attaining these results. And I believe that the law will warp and twist the facts, sometimes in an apparently shameless manner, if necessary, to obtain what it thinks of as the *just* result. To be sure, justice for one is justice for all. To discriminate unfeelingly is unjust. But equality before the law is not the same as uniformity for the scientist. True equality in law might almost be said to consist in the maxim: *no two cases are ever really alike.*

If you will allow me now to assume as established what you might have been willing to grant at the outset—namely, that there really are two ways of thinking—perhaps I can get on to what I think the lawyer might do about it.

In the first place, I believe that the legal community has little to gain from emphasizing existing differences between the scientific and the legal ways of life. Indeed, I believe that the two ways are different in a peculiarly helpful fashion; that is, I believe that they complement each other. Each is strong where the other is weak. This does not necessarily assure us that they will get along together. It is rarely the two individuals who perfectly complement each other who get to the altar. Therefore, a nudge from the shotgun may eventually be necessary. But first, let us see how far patient inquiry may take us.

Suppose we begin by admitting that the law's own scientific endeavors are woefully archaic—for example, that its fact-finding process is a relic of the childhood of Western culture. Should we not blush to say that our jury system is designed to find facts? This does not mean that our juries do not serve a vital function. It means that we can hardly call that function "fact-finding" in an age whose scientific devotion to sophisticated methods of experimental fact-finding is so steadfast. Fact-finding as a preliminary to executive order is still less apt to be "scientific"—that is, controlled, impartial, dispassionate, objective. And when we come to the methods by which legislators find facts, it is best to draw the curtain and move silently away from the mess. Fact-finding, the scientific side of law, is evidently nothing for law to be proud of.

On the other hand, law is highly skilled in making value judgments or, as I shall call them here for sake of greater precision, *feeling-value judgments*. By "feeling" (2, p.64) I very definitely do not mean emotion, for emotion colors all mental states and functions. I mean the process by which the distinctive worth of an individual is brought into view—the focusing or concentrating on a special object, or the selecting of one among a group of alternatives (decision making). This mental function is the opposite of the function by which the human mind sees similarities and generalizes from them.

Law discriminates on the basis of such feelings. It follows the great tides of community feeling and channels them by rules and processes whose purpose is to lessen conflict between man and man. In this massive undertaking, law uses of necessity a fact-finding process, but that process is subsidiary to the main great undertaking, the peaceable ordering of human relations according to principles based on feeling. Equity, equality, reasonableness, good faith, due process, mutuality, form, the speedy and efficient disposition of conflict, and the rest are principles based on feeling. To be sure, if they are based on misconceptions of fact, or, worse still, upon perversions of fact, the law finds itself perpetuating injustices. For indeed the right ascertainment of the facts upon which a legal disposition rests is itself a prime feeling-value of all advanced cultures. And if the culture in question also happens to be highly advanced in technological and scientific ways, the conflict may become intolerable. Still, the strength of the law lies in its feeling life.

How fares science in this respect? Feeling is precisely the area in which modern science is weakest. I should not like to have to press this delicate issue too hard. It is one which the scientific community scarcely needs to be reminded of. Put in the form of a question it is this: Do scientists have any responsibility for the power which they create, power which today may easily destroy all life on earth? Put it another way: Is science responsible for the apparent fact that modern technology causes the sources of artistic inspiration and of craftsmanship to dry up; that it aborts the instinct for workmanship by automating and thus trivializing the efforts of myriads of working people? What of the great surges of human feeling, inchoate and suppressed, which well up in protest at the technological way of life? Are all these overwhelming problems to be dumped into the lap of law to be solved?

Religion and morality seem slowly to be marshaling their immense forces against the technological juggernaut. But law seems to be standing aside, unwilling to adopt an antiscientific attitude, and apparently unable to lend science any aid in its disastrous slide toward the abyss.

I am not sure that any rising sector of humanity (the so-called power elites) can pause to consider what may happen to them if they attain to a full power position. Certainly, science and scientists, even the social scientists, the lawyers' nearest scientific neighbors, seem to lawyers to show little concern for this danger. This is not surprising. Law created and guided the great revolutions of the 18th and 19th centuries without a moment's concern for the help that science could give it. For instance, one can search the Constitution of the United States in vain for even a reference to science, beyond the patent clause. However, now that the great legal revolutions of the 19th century seem somewhat spent, and the vast world-wide impetus to change is scientific rather than legal, perhaps it behooves the legal community to take stock and to search for ways and means to understand, if not actively to co-operate with, the new scientific society. If the mountain of technology will not come to the law, perhaps the law should consider going to the technological mountain.

I end this section with the correction of its theme. There are not two ways of thinking, the legal and the scientific, but there are two fundamental and, I hope, complementary modes of orientation to human problems—that is, to think one's way into them or to feel one's way out of them. Each needs the other.

LAW AND SCIENCE IN HISTORY

In the beginning of Western culture, law and science were one. The great cosmogonies of the pre-Socratic philosophers were not only bold scientific speculations on the physical nature of the universe which directly challenged the old sacred myths of the gods as world-builders. They were also reaffirmations of the timeless conviction that justice rules the world.

Socrates himself, though the focus of Greek interest had shifted from the physical universe to the nature of man, proclaimed that to know the good is to do it. Science and morality have identical aims. Vice and injustice are ignorance.

It is not necessary for me, in this brief sketch, to dwell upon Western man's increased preoccupation with religion in the centuries before and after Christ. In order to create his new religion, Western man apparently found it necessary to turn away from the physical universe. A result was the collapse of Greek science. And Roman civilization, with empire-building as its object, raised the arts of law and administration to heights scarcely ever to be attained by later European cultures. The break-up of the Roman world brought with it the thousand-year task of Christianizing the barbarian peoples. This meant not only teaching them the tenets of the common religion but also inculcating in them the principles of law and order. When, at the Renaissance, attention was once more turned to the physical universe, it seemed necessary for the new scientists not only to break with established religion but also to turn resolutely away from the study of man and the ways by which he governs himself in order to concentrate attention on the physical environment and the ways in which it is governed. *It became necessary to challenge the very meaning of the word Law.* Henceforth, for the scientist, the word *law* would come to mean a law of physical nature. And the laws of nature were once more thought not only to be independent of man's will but also to be the rules by which man's destiny is governed. Western science, emulating the pre-Socratic models, issued the fiat that, far from being the very pinnacle of the universe and the only reason for its existence under God, man is among its lowliest creatures. His true nature and that of all other things is to be explained by the blind ordinances of a vast machine, the whole physical universe itself. These conceptions were and still are in direct opposition to the idea that, by the exercise of his free will, man gives laws to himself and determines his own destiny.

It would be too much to say that the conception of law (legal law) remained uninfluenced by the ideas or motifs of Western science. After all, science was clearly remaking the world. Its interstitial effect upon law was immense. Roscoe Pound has devoted much time and attention to the rise and development of "mechanical jurisprudence." It will suffice here to call attention to his studies and to the vast literature upon which they are based.

More important even than this was the fact that these developments forced a split between science and law. When, therefore, the philosopher Kant followed this with the bold assertion that the domain of existence is separate from that of obligation, that the "is" is separate from the "ought," it seemed to many that that separation was the most natural thing in the world.

We know that law did not long remain shackled even in theory to the "mechanical ideal." A century ago, jurisprudence became openly and avowedly a "teleological science"—that is, law came to be recognized as a consciously contrived mode of social control. This not only completed the emancipation of law from religion, it also put law in direct opposition to the mechanical science of the day. Henceforth law was to be sharply distinguished not only from religion and morality (by reason of law's secular emphasis) but also from mechanical science (by reason of law's insistence that it is a conscious product of human wit and endeavor).

What is the present prospect? Science has not yet won through to the Kantian insight that laws of nature are human necessities. Scientists still purport to be describing, or at least to be attempting to describe, the overall general principles by which the cosmos governs itself. It is not yet good form to call these laws the products of human invention. To do so seems to contemporary scientists to be running the risk of ascribing to the scientist the power to make into a "law of nature" anything which idle fancy might dictate. Yet it does not occur to the lawyer to maintain that, because he recognizes that law is consciously made, therefore anything may be made law which "idle fancy" suggests. This madness is reserved for the absolute dictator.

I have now given reasons why law and science are not one. I have not of course attempted to justify this state of affairs. Indeed, I feel that I should not be at all justified in setting out the differences if there were no possibility of lessening them. It is therefore encouraging to note that newer developments in science lead to the belief that the two disciplines may be able at long last to draw a little closer together.

THE SCIENTIST AS DECISION MAKER

The origin of modern science seems almost to coincide with the invention of instruments of precision, notably the telescope and the microscope. These instruments multiplied man's power of observation, bringing into his ken objects hitherto beyond the range even of his imagination. After the first phase of sheer wonderment and joy at the new toys, it was realized that what these instruments really meant was that man could now perform the act of *measurement* with an accuracy not possible to him in the past. And when more accurate measurements became possible they also became, *ipso facto*, necessary. *The grand enterprise of science was seen to be the perfection of the art of measurement.* Carefully and still more carefully to measure the speed at which metallic balls roll down an inclined plane, at which a pendulum swings, at which planets revolve about the sun—this and kindred operations are to be the means by which the scientist is to wrest from nature her secret laws. With measuring, of course, goes counting, but it was necessary to wait for contemporary instruments to demonstrate how sophisticated that latter art could become. At any rate, the Renaissance ideal was clear: to measure the measurable and to reduce the hitherto unmeasured to the measured.

It is by no means unanimously agreed by the scientific community that the ideal of measurement has lately undergone subtle and far-reaching modification. In the first place, the ordinary working scientist pays little attention to the implications of this ideal. For, if the legal community is able to do its daily work without regard to the philosophical implications of law (leaving legal philosophy to a small group of specialists), scientific, as distinct from philosophic, participation in the development of the philosophy of science is still less in evidence. I do not mean to say that the part which measurement plays in the scientific process is not the object of current investigation. I do mean that the focus of scientific inquiry is seen to be shifting, and that the shift is in a direction that has exciting possibilities for rapport between science and law. *The scientist, in brief, is being recognized as a decision maker.* The body of lore currently called decision theory represents an attempt to understand how a scientist does and should make scientific decisions. This is not the present avowed major concern of decision theorists. If you ask them what they are doing they are very apt to say that they are studying the ways in which decisions can be made rationally, and, in the broader framework, that they are interested in the way decisions are actually made, whether made rationally or not. This learning, though new, is proliferating rapidly. And it is only a matter of time before the process turns to the work of science itself, at which time it will be perceived that scientists, too, spend their time making decisions.

It might surprise anyone but lawyers to find that current effort directed toward investigation of the process of decision making almost ignores the vast body of legal learning on the decision process. The fact is that law, and particularly judicial administration, does possess this body of knowledge, and the realization that the very essence of law is decision is just barely breaking through the consciousness of the present-day decision theorists.

Perhaps it would be helpful at this point to interpolate a brief account of the research activity which calls itself decision theory. The movement can be said to have started in this country with the appearance in 1944 of a book by John von Neumann, mathematician extraordinary, and Oskar Morgenstern, mathematical economist. The book was called *Theory of Games and Economic Behavior* (3). In it the authors worked out a proposal for studying conflict situations in a highly formalized and rigorously mathematical manner. Sophistication consisted in reducing the conflict elements to a skeletonized formal model (their mathematically most simplified structure) and then in working out in detail and in strict mathematical fashion the way the players of the game must play if the outcome is to have the best possible chance to conform to an ideal of rational behavior accepted by the players in advance. It will be noted that the simplicities and sophistications of this game are exactly the opposite of those attending the "games" the legal community plays. For with lawyers, sophistication lies primarily in the complexities which the fact situations present. Human temperament in all its intricacy and human conflict in all the variegated shapes it may take are the *matter* of the lawyer. His formal model—the body of his principles, rules, precepts—and his ways of processing this rich conglomerate are themselves relatively simple. Consider the "fundamental principles" of negligence law: one must act with reasonable care; contributory negligence bars recovery. Consider attractive nuisance, last clear chance, voluntary assumption of risk, *res ipsa loquitur*. These are metaphors, allegories, catch phrases. But the manifold forms in which they come up are often enough to break the hardest judicial head.

Lawyers have no body of first principles from which the solution of specific cases can be deduced by rigorous rules of procedure. In fact, they consider the very ideal of rigorous deductive processes in law to be outmoded. The whole burden of 20th-century legal realism was taken to be the dismantling and junking of the system of "legal certainties" upon which, from time immemorial, law had been thought to rest. And yet, game theory prides itself precisely upon its claim to deductive rigor. Conflict, we have been told, is fitted into a mathematical mold distinguished from earlier attempts at formalizing conflict situations by virtue of its mathematical rigor.

Thus, law and science are curiously out of phase respecting one of the most important aspects of their methodology. Law can only regard the scientist's pursuit of formal rigor as outmoded and unsophisticated. This means that the hard-headed American legal realist instinctively dismisses the claims of modern scientific decision theorists as naive. And naive they do look, it must be admitted. Yet, it is also undeniable that the wonders of modern contemporary culture rest precisely upon such scientific naiveté. It may turn out that this is the kind of naiveté which eventually shows itself to be a deeper sophistication.

In any event, scientific decision theory is not irrevocably aligned with game theory, anymore than it is necessarily tied to game theory's analog in the realm of hardware, the computer. Decision theory is more general than either game theory or computer technology. There is a great deal of experimental work going on in an effort to learn how and why people make the everyday decisions they do. This work is broad enough to cover every aspect of the decision process. It encompasses learning theory, because it views the process of learning as a course of decision making. It has invaded foreign policy making because it sees this activity as primarily a series of decisions. In fact, once one puts on decision-theory glasses he sees decision making in all phases of human behavior. And if the glasses are turned upon the behavior of scientists, it is seen that the practice of science is itself a long and complicated process of decision making.

LAW AS A DECISION PROCESS

So thoroughly immersed is law in the business of decision that one might easily be tempted to say that decision is its sole activity. Passing over the administration of justice for the moment, we might examine legislation briefly to see what part decision plays in it. The major part, we might be tempted to say. Legislative law is the reconciliation of competing pressure groups in formulas that aim to reduce tension and compromise differences, and that represent the best interests of the subjects, as the legislators see and weigh these interests. And when judicial and legislative law presents itself for execution, the executive action under such law is one long series of decisions to enforce or not to enforce.

The body of learning on the subject of decision in the legal process staggers the imagination. If, to the literature on how agencies of the law do decide, one adds the stupendous quantity of literature on how legal decisions *ought* to be made, and then if one buries the mass in the avalanche of reports on decisions actually made, it becomes necessary to forget the whole nightmare in the simple interest of self-preservation. Needless to say, since so much of the law's variegated life consists of decision, there exists no *authoritative* body of learning or generally agreed upon ideas on the subject of how legal decisions are actually arrived at, to say nothing of how they ought to be arrived at. Still, it is possible to see that much of the dispute revolves about one overall subject. This is the question of *whether and to what degree the legal decision is based upon rational considerations.* If we were to adopt the lingo of the system theorists for a moment we could put the matter this way: There is an immense and complicated Input into the judicial Decision Maker which we can observe. We also can observe the Output in the form of the Decision and all its effects that we care to observe. The judicial Decision Maker is the Black Box between Input and Output. Does the Black Box operate according to rational principles, and if so, what are they?

A century ago many thoughtful observers of the judicial process would have said that the Black Box is indeed governed by rational principles. In reply to the question of what these are, the answer would have been: "Logic." The principles themselves which form the basis of the legal system are rational intuitions of the nature of justice, revealed to our minds by a merciful and just God, or analyzed out of the nature of the mind itself by the process of reason. These, when supplemented by the facts of the particular case to be decided, then yield valid conclusions, provided the rules of logical reasoning are adhered to.

Curiously enough, something like the above description lies at the foundation of contemporary game theory and indeed of much of general decision theory to boot. But a century of jurisprudential theory in both Europe and America has subjected the above *rational* account of the nature of judicial decision to searching criticism, in the course of which almost all elements of the explanation have been superseded. The first element of the theory to go was the assumption that the processes of logic govern the course of judicial decision. German jurists of a century ago, following the lead of the early sociologists and Marxian economists, began to construct a theory of law as a consciously chosen and purposefully devised agency of social control. This imposed on the theory the first important element of nonrationality. The decision need no longer be *consistent* (a logical demand) with the set of rational principles that furnish the body of existing law. Social necessity may dictate a change, however irrational the change might appear in the light of existing rational principles of law. Not the rational principles of the mind but the wholly nonrational demands and interests of society came to be recognized as the foundation of the decision.

We know how, in the 20th century, theories of the irrational nature of judicial decision grew. Sociological jurisprudence and then the new American legal realism purported to expose the contents of the legal Black Box. It turned out that the Black Box operates irrationally, or at least nonrationally. The decision maker appeared to be subject to the manifold influences of a hopelessly complicated Input. In addition, the Box could add on its own irrationalities. The judgment was seen to be the result of completely unpredictable intuition, or even of blind chance. Currently, a reaction against these excesses has set in. Jurists once more reaffirm their faith in the ultimately rational character of judicial decision. But this present rationality or "reckonability" is itself a fearfully complicated thing, vastly different from the few simple, general principles which our forefathers took to be the rational bases for the decision of cases.

Lawyers might well hesitate to suggest to modern scientific decision theorists that they take a look at the jurisprudential literature of the past century if they want to see what *can* happen to a rational theory of decision making. It seems entirely too cruel. Yet if the theorists *did* happen upon this body of learning they could easily conclude that perhaps the nonrational elements of decision making are at least as important as the rational ones. They could learn that the decision maker is more interested in the *effects* of the decision than in its form: that the teleology of decision making is more powerful than its logic in shaping the course of decision; that intuition has a more important role to play in even simple and apparently trivial decisions than the rational constraints of present-day decision procedures allow. I should add, for myself, that since it seems to me that every true *decision*, as distinct from an *inference*, involves an element of individual choice, the constraints imposed by general logic and generalizing mathematics upon decision procedures virtually rule out the study of truly creative decisions and tend to restrict decision science to mechanical, and therefore dull and repetitive, instances of decision making—to those which allow themselves to be bunched together and processed in accordance with the generalizing demands of logic, set theory, probability, and the universalizing effects of randomized processes. How these processes can be remade to deal with the individual event, I of course cannot say. But unless they can be, they will not handle the interesting cases of decision—which is precisely what the legal decision process does. It might therefore be appropriate to close this section with the suggestion that the scientific decision makers have available to them a sophisticated body of learning on the making of highly consequential individuated decisions which are explained and defended by "reason," a process that has had a fairly consistent history since the time of Roman law. For a starter, they might try the late Karl Llewellyn's *The Common Law Tradition*. Study of the manifold ways in which the relatively highly controlled doctrine of precedent (itself a rational constraint on the decision process) may differentially influence decision should be most enlightening.

At any rate, whether the scientists do or do not study legal decision making is hardly the lawyer's responsibility. It is enough for him at present to try to understand the scientists. If, following the tenets of realistic jurisprudence, he watches these scientists in action instead of listening to their theories, he finds that, like other artisans, they are constrained more by the nature of their tools than by poverty of the imagination. In the case of law, much of what happens is due to the limitations of political institutions rather than to any narrowness of legal vision.

NOTES

(1) "[The] logic of contemporary science is the logic of imperatives."—C.W. Churchman, in E.A. Singer, *Experience and Reflection* (Univ. of Pennsylvania Press, Philadelphia, 1959), introduction, p. ix.

(2) C.G. Jung, *Psychological Types* (1938).

(3) J. von Neumann and O. Morgenstern, *Theory of Games and Economic Behavior* (Princeton Univ. Press, Princeton, N.J., ed. 2, 1944).

EVIDENCE AND PROOF:

SCIENTIFIC AND LEGAL

Hon. Sir Roger F.G. Ormrod

The words I have chosen as the title to this address are common to the vocabularies of the three disciplines which comprise the British Academy of Forensic Sciences, although the meaning attached to each word varies with the discipline which uses it. The fact that they all use these two words is, however, significant because the common use of such words as 'evidence' and 'proof' implies, despite the apparent diversity of meaning, an underlying activity which is common to all three. In contrast, and no less significant, each discipline uses quite different words to describe the results of its activities. The scientist speaks of the 'results' of his experiments, builds up a 'hypothesis', hopefully evolves a 'theory', which, if successful may give rise to a new scientific 'fact' and, occasionally, to the formulation of a new scientific 'law'. The doctor makes a 'diagnosis' and proceeds to 'therapy' or 'treatment'. The lawyer calls his conclusion an 'opinion' or an 'advice', and the forensic process leads to a 'verdict' in the case of a jury, or to 'findings of fact' by a judge sitting alone, which in turn leads to a 'sentence' or a 'judgment'. These words are remarkably precisely chosen and if closely examined, will be found to reveal accurately the differences which characterize the conclusions of each discipline. [*Hypothesis* from the Greek meaning a foundation or provisional supposition; *theory* meaning a hypothesis confirmed by further observation; *diagnosis* from the Greek meaning to distinguish or discern; *verdict* from the French *ver* and *dit* meaning to speak the truth; *sentence* from the Latin *sententia* meaning opinion; *judgment* from the

Latin *judicare* literally to speak the law (*jus* and *dicere*). This secondary usage meaning an estimate, as opposed to an observed measurement, e.g., 'I judged the distance to be 100 yards' is interesting.]

The use of common terms with widely differing connotations is a prolific source of misunderstanding and confusion and a serious obstacle to communication between scientists, doctors, and lawyers. If the first step to knowledge is awareness of ignorance, the first step to mutual understanding is awareness of a lack of understanding and of the reasons which underlie it. But the common use of words obscures the lack and causes frustration. Understanding seems so close yet proves elusive; to each profession the others appear to be wilfully obscurantist, retreating into a jargon of their own just when understanding is about to be achieved, or worse still, criticizing his expertise in terms of their own, using the common words in *their* senses to demonstrate *his* errors in *his* field. It seems, therefore, an appropriate exercise of the prerogative of the President of this Academy to examine these matters in some detail, first identifying the common ground, and then exploring the differences to elucidate and clarify them.

The fact that this Academy exists at all indicates that there must be a real body of interests and activities which are common to the three constituent disciplines. The fact that the words 'evidence' and 'proof' are used by all of them points to the nature of these common interests and activities. All share the same fundamental objective, the discovery or ascertainment of the truth to the greatest extent which their techniques permit and their functions require. The highly complex but very different intellectual structures, which each discipline has elaborated in its own field, all depend for success upon the establishment of reliable bases of fact. The most elegant scientific hypothesis, the most brilliant intuitive diagnosis, and the most penetrating analysis of the law are futile if they are not firmly rooted in fact. 'Finding the facts' is, therefore, the basic and essential activity of all three disciplines and is their common bond. All of them inevitably are deeply concerned with 'evidence' and 'proof' but because the function which each has to fulfil and the materials which each is obliged to use are different, they attach widely different shades of meaning to these words.

FUNCTIONS OF INDIVIDUAL DISCIPLINES

The three professions can be arranged in a sequence using a time-scale. Speaking generally scientists are under little or no external pressure to arrive at their conclusions within a given time. This is certainly true in the field of pure science or basic research but is less so in the case of the applied sciences which may have to produce answers comparatively quickly. In medicine, the necessity of establishing a diagnosis is more pressing: the patient is ill and in need of relief of symptoms and treatment so that decisions cannot be indefinitely deferred. In many cases, however, symptomatic treatment may be started immediately on the basis of a provisional diagnosis, to be reviewed later as further evidence is collected. In such cases 'proof' may be deferred for variable periods of time. The law, however, has no such elasticity. In our system of jurisprudence courts are required to make decisions, unequivocally, one way or the other at the end of the trial; the 'facts' must be found on the evidence which is available and the question of proof decided then and there. The findings are, of course, subject to review on appeal but the scope for revision is limited by the application of the general principle, which cannot be seriously disputed, that justice deferred is often justice denied, and that accordingly litigation must not be allowed to drag on indefinitely. Appellate courts, therefore, impose stringent restrictions on the introduction at that stage of fresh evidence.

These fundamental requirements influence the standards of proof demanded by each discipline and the nature of the decisions which each can make. The pure scientist can wait indefinitely while he accumulates his evidence and tests each link in the chain. Proof to him means, ideally, proof beyond all possibility of demonstration of error. The applied scientist may have to act on something less irrefragable. The doctor must often act on evidence which falls short, sometimes far short, of proof in the scientific sense but as evidence accumulates he can, usually, adopt or change his therapeutic measures when his 'proof' is complete. Courts of law are in the unenviable position of having to make decisions which affect people's lives, and often liberty, under sub-optimal conditions, sub-optimal not in the sense that better decisions could be made by modifying the trial process or devising some different kind of process but in the sense that they arise from the very nature of the task itself. This accounts for their very cautious and often conservative approach. The concept of the 'burden of proof' is an essential part of the lawyer's technique for dealing with these difficulties. Courts, unlike doctors, can at least decide to take no action. Thus the prosecution is required to prove the case against the accused and the claimant in a civil action is required to prove his case against the defendant. Failure to discharge this burden of proof leads to a refusal by the Court to act; the accused is acquitted or the action dismissed. (In consequence, many cases, both civil and criminal, are not brought to court at all because the difficulties of proof cannot be overcome.) On the orthodox view, the standard of proof in a criminal case is 'proof beyond reasonable doubt', whereas in a civil case it is 'proof on the balance of probabilities' but these are little more than convenient aphorisms. In practice, judges and juries in criminal and civil cases subconsciously adjust the weight of the burden of proof to the gravity of the consequences which will flow from their decision. It is only natural to demand a high standard of proof, amounting even to certainty, before imposing a sentence of imprisonment whereas a lesser degree of certainty is acceptable in deciding which of two drivers in a running-down case was responsible for the accident. But the limitations of this technique of avoiding positive errors by taking no action are obvious, for much negative injustice can result from it; a dangerous criminal may escape conviction or a meritorious plaintiff may fail in his claim if the burden of proof is set too high or courts become too cautious.

MATERIALS OF INDIVIDUAL DISCIPLINES

It is not only their functions which oblige the disciplines to accept different standards of proof; the material with which each must work exerts a similar influence. Science is essentially measurement; as new techniques of measurement are introduced, new fields of enquiry and of knowledge develop. The introduction of the mass-spectrometer and the techniques of chromatography have enabled minute quantities of substances to be detected and measured. Other techniques have enabled the chemical processes in single cells of the body or in bacteria to be followed step by step and measured. The story of the double helix is the story of the discovery of complex chemical processes taking place in the nuclei of individual cells and of the unravelling of the structure of DNA and RNA, and of the means by which cells produce identical reproductions of themselves, all of which was made possible by the introduction of increasingly refined methods of measurement. The validity of scientific conclusions depends to a considerable extent on the accuracy of these measurements. Medicine, using the advances of scientific knowledge, now has a great many parameters by which it can measure bodily functions and so detect significant deviations from the normal. Some of these are sufficiently reliable in themselves to permit a diagnosis to be made—obvious examples are the white cell-count in leukaemia, or the red cell-count in anaemia—but in many cases the so-called 'normal' cannot be precisely defined so that conclusions can only be drawn from the measurement if the deviation is gross. In the case of the United States astronauts, on the other hand, measurements were repeated regularly and frequently enough for the doctors to establish precise norms for each man so that it was possible to predict from a slight rise in the white cell-count the onset of a febrile illness a few days before any symptoms were observed. But generally speaking, medicine is dependent still for its decisions on the evidence of the history, symptoms, and physical signs elicited from the patient. Its raw material is still the patient whose personal idiosyncrasies and unreliability as a witness may confuse and distort the other evidence.

The law is in an even worse case. It has, practically speaking, as yet no parameters, although a beginning has been made with the *Road Safety Act* 1965, which introduced for the first time a scientifically measurable test of fitness to drive after taking alcohol. By making it an offence to drive with a blood-alcohol exceeding 80 mg. per 100 ml., Parliament has introduced an objective measurable standard into the law. There are, of course, a number of other objective standards to be found in the Food and Drug legislation and in some aspects of Factory law but these are of small importance in the daily work of the courts. The law's raw material is made of even more unreliable stuff than medicine's. Lawyers have to contend not only with the fallibility of human observation and memory but, unlike their scientific and medical colleagues, with self-interest and dishonesty. Science (although not the social sciences) is spared the problem of the unreliable witness. Medicine has to contend with the 'neurotic' or 'functional' case but rarely with the malingerer.

These reflections seem to point to a paradoxical conclusion. The scientist with the most reliable material has the most time in which to reach his findings whereas the lawyer, with the least reliable material, has the least time in which to make his decisions. The doctor's position lies mid-way between these two extremes. It is not surprising that 'evidence' and 'proof' mean something different to each of them or that they have evolved different methods of handling their data.

COLLECTION OF INFORMATION

All three disciplines are faced with the fundamental problems of collecting their data and evaluating them. Evaluation is now probably more important and critical than collection in medicine, the law, and in the physical sciences, but it was not always so. The newer sciences, in particular the behavioural sciences including criminology, still face serious and unresolved difficulties of collection. Similar difficulties confronted the physical sciences as well as medicine and the law at earlier stages of their development. In fact, all of them owe their development to the evolution of methods of data collection and as new techniques of collection are invented new branches of science emerge.

Historically speaking, the collection and classification of facts is a surprisingly late development in all three disciplines. Although used by the Greeks to some extent, particularly by Hippocrates who began the process of recognizing and describing medical syndromes, it fell into disuse for all practical purposes until the seventeenth century. Up to that stage scientists and doctors collected the opinions of earlier writers and piled speculation upon speculation. Burton's *Anatomy of Melancholy*, published in 1621, amply illustrates the point. It is impossible to disentangle any factual observations from it. But in the seventeenth century scientific observations as we know them, began and the age of experiment started. The work of Newton, Boyle, and Harvey was the dawn of a new era. Men began to make observations, evolve hypotheses, and test them by experiment. The eighteenth century was the age in which men began to collect and assemble data on a large scale and attempt to classify them. Linnaeus carried out his vast studies in the early part of this period and scientists such as Sir Joseph Banks amassed data in enormous quantities about all kinds of natural phenomena: but it was not until the nineteenth century that the systematic organization of data began on a large scale which led to the rapid discovery of knowledge of all kinds. It was the capacity to organize as well as to collect data which enabled Darwin and the early geologists like Lyell to make their great contributions. At the beginning of the nineteenth century medicine had advanced very little from the Middle Ages but there then began a process which has been of great importance, painstaking clinical observation and careful classification of these observations which gradually led to the identification of specific diseases. Sometimes, as we now know, the observations were misleading or the classifications faulty but in the main this work laid the foundations of modern medicine. It was the age of the eponymous disease, such as Paget's disease, Bright's disease, and many others. With the development of pathology in its various forms, the era of scientific medicine began and rational, as opposed to empirical, therapy became possible.

An analogous situation existed in the law, which may be a surprise even to lawyers. The fact-finding process is a relatively late development in all legal systems. For centuries the courts were preoccupied with formalities rather than fact. Success in litigation depended much more upon precise compliance with the strict rules of procedure than upon the facts or merits of the case. An error by the pleader in the form of his written pleading was fatal to his case and a vast mass of technical learning was built up out of previous rulings or precedents which resembles quite closely the enormous accumulation of wholly unrealistic medical writings about the four 'humours' and similar artificial notions. Rights and obligations depended almost entirely upon formalities. The law simply ignored a transaction which was not in the appropriate form. A failure to comply with the strict formalities of signing, sealing, and delivering a deed would invalidate a transfer of land. It took a long time for the law to accept the evidence of witnesses as its main source of data and it is still trying to develop techniques for collecting and evaluating them. The reasons for this slow development are not difficult to understand. The fact is that the law has been faced for far longer than science or medicine with the intensely difficult problem of evaluating its data which is inherently less reliable than that of either of its sister disciplines. Legal procedure and the laws of evidence can only be properly understood in this context.

EVOLUTION OF LEGAL SYSTEMS

The Western World in its attempt to solve these problems has evolved two different legal systems, that which is in force on the continent, and to some extent in Scotland, which is often called the Civil Law because it is founded in the *jus civile* or the law applicable to Roman citizens, and the Common Law which was developed in England from Anglo-Saxon origins and has spread throughout the Commonwealth and the United States (with certain exceptions such as Scotland, South Africa, Quebec, and certain states, such as Louisiana and California, whose legal systems were established from continental origins before the Common Law reached them and still retain to a greater or lesser extent their Civil Law characteristics). These systems are sometimes contrasted as the Inquisitorial and the Adversary systems, each based on the belief that its methods are best suited to the attainment of justice, although both are becoming increasingly conscious of their own defects and the merits of the other.

In the past both systems have attempted to solve, or rather to evade, the problems of evaluation by the widespread use of the principle of exclusion, that is, types of data or evidence regarded as inherently unreliable were excluded from the legal process altogether, rather than admitted for what they were worth. This accounts very largely for the obsession of the law with formalities. By insisting that transactions to be legally effective must be accompanied by certain formalities or rituals the law achieved two things. In the first place, it created a permanent record of the transaction and helped to fix the event in the minds of observers, and in the second, it excluded any other evidence or data bearing on the event, so eliminating the necessity to evaluate conflicting versions. Many other illustrations can be given. For example, it was a rule of the Civil and Canon Law that the evidence of a single witness was of no value in legal proof. *Testis unus, testis nullus.* Napoleon is said to have observed that the effect of this rule was to provide that while the evidence of one honourable man could not prove a single rascal guilty, the evidence of two rascals could convict an honourable man! The Common Law always refused to accept this rule but it is still a fundamental principle of Scots criminal law that a jury may not convict on the evidence of a single witness, however reliable (Smith, 1961). One vestigial trace of it, however, survives in English law in the rule that two witnesses are required to the execution of a will. The explanation is that until 1857 probate and matrimonial causes were dealt with by the ecclesiastical courts which applied Canon and Civil Law principles. The rule results every year in a considerable number of people dying either legally intestate or with an effective earlier will which they clearly wished to supercede. Whether the rule is effective in preventing or discouraging forgery or undue influence may be doubted, but it effectively excludes any other evidence of the fact that the contents of the will represents the last wishes of the testator. The court only enquires into that question if the will has been duly attested by two witnesses and then only in cases in which lack of testamentary capacity or undue influence is alleged.

The Civil and Canon Law seem to have been rather less mistrustful of the value of witnesses than the Common Law but it adopted a method of dealing with them which strikes one today as almost perverse. The tribunal entrusted with the task of finding the facts did not at any stage see or hear the parties or their witnesses. The parties themselves were not permitted to give evidence but set out their cases at length in writing, the complainant in what was called the 'Libel' (or little bill) and the respondent in the form of an Answer. Both parties swore to the truth of their allegations. Each then submitted lists of witnesses who were examined, not by counsel and not in the presence of a judge, but by an official examiner to the court who put questions to them in private, based on the libel and answer. The opposing party was permitted to submit lists of questions or interrogatories to the examiner who put them to the witnesses, but neither party had any means of knowing at that stage what evidence the witness had given. The examiner recorded the answers in the form of a deposition of each witness and the court or judge decided the issues of fact entirely upon the basis of these depositions and other supporting documents. This technique at least made certain that the judge was not influenced by the appearance, personality, or attitude of the witnesses! It is almost impossible for us to imagine how a matrimonial case could be tried in this way but what Lord Stowell would say about our present method of trying divorce cases I shudder to think!

The common lawyers regarded trial by Common Law with bitter disapproval. They thought that it was wholly unreliable and susceptible to every form of deception. In the primitive days the Common Law used a variety of methods of trial most of which placed more faith in Divine intervention than in evidence. Trial by ordeal when guilt or innocence depended upon whether the accused could thrust his arm into boiling water without being scalded, or trial by battle when the result depended on the prowess of one's champion were scarcely exercises in fact-finding. Another method was by compurgation in which the parties swore that their claim was just and brought a number of other people to swear, not that the respective stories were true, but that the oath of the party they were supporting was a good and reliable oath. This may also have its roots in the idea of Divine intervention in favour of the honest man. The technique of the oath has persisted but in a different form, originally no doubt with the idea of enlisting the fear of damnation as an aid to honesty, but now regarded more as a way of impressing upon witnesses the seriousness of the occasion and the necessity for care. There is, however, still an element of fear about it as a way of discouraging the marginally dishonest from lying.

In the Middle Ages the jury appeared as an alternative mode of trial but only at first with the consent of the defendant. Judges found it a much better method but frequently had to resort to extreme measures to extract the necessary consent. Reluctant defendants were subjected to considerable pressure, with progressively increasing weights until they consented to be tried by a jury! At this stage the jury had no judicial function. They were summoned to court as a body of people who had personal knowledge of the facts in dispute and were required to swear that their account was true. Hence the word 'verdict' which is derived from the French *ver* and *dit* and means literally 'a speaking of the truth.' Gradually this jury evolved into a body of men who decided the facts on evidence provided by the witnesses but until the seventeenth or eighteenth century they were expected to use their own knowledge and steps were deliberately taken to include some people on the jury who would be likely to have some prior knowledge of the facts of the case. Some people still maintain that it is important that criminal cases should be tried in the county where the crime was committed and by a jury drawn from the county. (But they would unhesitatingly reject the idea that such a jury should have prior knowledge of the case it is trying.) One faint trace of this older concept of the jury survived until quite recently in the City of London Special Jury which was chosen from people in the City with special knowledge and experience of business and commerce and was asked to try difficult civil cases involving complex financial and accounting problems.

When trial by jury in its present form had become established judges were faced with the difficult task of trying to ensure that this body of twelve, usually in the past illiterate and uneducated, men should come to the right decision as often as possible. Such juries were not well equipped for weighing nice points of evidence and naturally were liable to be unduly influenced by the advocates. The method used to solve this problem was once again to apply the principle of exclusion. The prisoner was not permitted to call any witnesses until the seventeenth century although Queen Mary, of whom Blackstone remarks that her 'early sentiments till her marriage with Philip of Spain seem "to have been humane and generous" ', begged her judges to permit it (Blackstone, 1766). In 1607 the House of Commons insisted, contrary to the practice in England and the express law of Scotland, that Englishmen tried in the three northern counties for felonies committed in Scotland, should be permitted to call witnesses in their defence. This was extended to all cases of treason in 1696 and felonies in 1702.

In Blackstone's own day (mid-eighteenth century) prisoners were still not allowed to be represented by counsel except upon a point of law, although he himself said that 'it seems to be not all of a piece with the rest of the humane treatment of prisoners by English law.' Some of the judges apparently felt the same and, as he records, 'seldom scrupled to allow a prisoner "leave to stand by (them) at the bar and instruct him what questions to ask, or even to ask questions for him." ' The advantages of cross-examination to which we, rightly in my view, attach great importance as a technique for testing the reliability of our data, had obviously not yet been appreciated.

Up to 1843 the principle of exclusion was carried to the extreme length of excluding the evidence of any person who was 'interested' in the issue which was in dispute. Much learning accumulated round the meaning of the word 'interested.' It included not only the parties but any one else who fell within the definition of 'interested.' This, of course, solved most of the problems of evaluation of evidence by the simple process of preventing them ever arising, but at the cost of excluding most if not all of the really relevant data from the court's consideration. This rule was partially abrogated by the *Evidence Act* 1843 which permitted interested persons who were not parties to the dispute or their spouses, to give evidence. The evidence of those most vitally concerned and therefore most likely to know the facts, was still regarded as so unreliable or so difficult to evaluate that it was excluded altogether. Accused persons were, of course, parties to the proceedings and therefore, forbidden to give evidence in their own defence.

A system so much out of balance was obviously fraught with the danger of causing grave injustice. The only way of dealing with such a situation was to apply the 'fail-safe' principle in an attempt to ensure that when the system failed the injustice did not fall on the accused individual. The method adopted was to place a heavy burden on the prosecution to prove beyond reasonable doubt all the facts necessary for a conviction and to give the accused the benefit of any doubt. In such a situation it was impossible at any stage or in any circumstances to call upon the defence to explain or disprove anything. Hence, presumably, the rule which still governs our criminal practice that the burden of proof never (or hardly ever) shifts from the prosecution to the defence, a rule which in these days when all defendants are or can be legally represented and are free to give evidence themselves and call any witnesses they wish, sometimes leads to absurd results.

The *Evidence Act* 1857 further relaxed this rule by permitting the parties in civil cases and their spouses to give evidence, but another 50 years had to elapse before the rule excluding the evidence of accused persons was finally and completely abolished by the *Criminal Evidence Act* 1898. But we have not yet succeeded in eliminating the exclusion principle altogether. The hearsay rule still operates in a virtually unmodified form in criminal cases to exclude evidence of statements made in the absence of the other party although it has been mitigated in civil cases and is in practice often ignored by consent of both sides.

Until the *Evidence Act* 1938 statements, no matter how relevant, made by persons who could not be called as witnesses to give oral testimony in court were, speaking generally, excluded because the makers had not been sworn and were not available for cross-examination. This Act, however, harked right back to the ideas which were prevalent a hundred years earlier by resuscitating the rule about persons 'interested' in the dispute, and excluded statements made by the parties or other persons 'interested', and another crop of cases on the meaning of 'interested' grew up. These restrictions have now been removed by the *Civil Evidence Act* 1968 but highly complicated procedural rules governing the admissibility of such statements have been laid down. Fortunately, in most cases counsel seem to be willing to waive these rules and agree to such statements being 'let in'.

As a consequence of these relaxations of the exclusion principle the amount of data available to the Court in certain cases has been considerably increased and difficult problems of evaluation arise. It is easy, but not very courageous to cling to the old principle that little weight should be given to statements which have not been tested by cross-examination. This is not in any event an infallible test but it is to the law what the controlled trial is to medicine—a way in which the risk of error due to bias or inaccuracy in the maker of the statement may be diminished. So far the courts have not had enough experience of this type of evidence to develop a technique for dealing with it, but as time goes on they are likely to be faced with more and more of it. I have already discovered one aspect of its value. A party or a witness who knows that the other side has certain statements of this kind which can be put before the court is faced in cross-examination, if the statements are true, with the dilemma of either admitting the facts wholly or in part, or boldly denying them. The latter course is highly dangerous if no motive can be suggested for the maker of the statement to lie, or no explanation for mistake on his part suggested. This tends to produce valuable admissions.

This Act has also made it possible to use statements made by the parties themselves at or soon after the events which are in issue. The other side, of course, could always use such statements if it suited its case. For example, what the plaintiff said to the police-officer after the accident could always be used by the defendant to prove that the plaintiff was not telling the truth in court, but the plaintiff could not use it to show that the account of the accident which he was giving in the witness-box was the same as that which he gave immediately after the accident. In some cases this type of evidence may be very valuable, in others it may merely establish that the plaintiff's powers of invention came into play at the earliest possible moment! Under the 1968 Act, and subject to the procedural rules, this kind of evidence may now be given and the court will have to evaluate it. This Act does not apply to criminal cases but the former strict rules have been relaxed in other ways.

In criminal cases evidence of previous convictions, even if directly relevant in the sense that the accused has actually been found guilty in the past of very similar conduct, is excluded because of its 'prejudicial' quality. This is another way of saying that such evidence is so difficult to evaluate accurately in any individual case that it is too dangerous to attempt it. Nevertheless, it sometimes results in highly relevant data being kept from the court.

Another important source of data is excluded by the rule that a man should not be required to incriminate himself and is, therefore, entitled as of right to refuse to answer questions the answers to which might incriminate him. The origin of this rule is obscure. Dr. Granville Williams regards it as a piece of race-memory from the evil days of the Star Chamber when people were brought before the court and compelled to take the oath and answer questions. Undoubtedly this rule is one of the crucial differences between the inquisitorial and adversary systems of trial. To compel a man to answer questions and perhaps convict himself, seems to conflict with the basic theory of the adversary system which rests on the belief that justice is most likely to be done if each side puts its case as strongly as it can be put before a court which is required to reach a decision exclusively on the material which emerges from this process. It is difficult to find any other logical justification for this rule but it is deeply embedded in the history and customs of our culture. The admission of such evidence is felt to be 'unfair' and there would be jealous resistance to any change. But what is meant by 'unfair' is not easy to define. Ideas of fairness are apt to differ according to whether one is a victim, an accused, a police-officer, counsel for the prosecution, counsel for the defence, or a detached bystander. It would be interesting to know what the 'man on the Clapham omnibus' (if the opinion polls could find him) thinks about these matters, but it will not be a simple matter to make radical changes in these rules or in the rule excluding previous convictions. Such changes are apt to produce unforeseen consequences. However, at a time when crime rates are rising rapidly, and sophisticated crimes are becoming increasingly frequent it may be appropriate to reconsider both rules. There is nothing inherently objectionable in the notions that an individual around whom suspicion has accumulated should be asked to explain the circumstances or that a man's past conduct may throw light on his present. In civil cases, the process of discovery, either of documents or by the administration of written questions in the form of interrogatories, before trial, sometimes compels a party to provide conclusive evidence against himself. This is one of the law's techniques for collecting its data and is not objected to. Similarly no one would complain in a civil case if relevant evidence of past conduct were given. It would be useful to review the present rules of procedure and evidence in order to define those which are really survivals from the past when accused persons were gravely handicapped and which can no longer be justified in these days when many, if not all, the old handicaps have gone. Is it, for example, still necessary in all cases to preserve the rigid rule that the burden of proof is always on the prosecution, or ought there to be some relaxation so that during the trial when the prosecution has proved enough to raise serious suspicions the burden should shift to the defence? Two different attempts to solve this kind of problem in very restricted contexts have been made recently. The *Road Safety Act* 1965 makes it an offence in certain circumstances to refuse to provide a breath or urine sample; the *Family Law Reform Act,* 1969, s. 23., provides that the court may draw such inferences 'as appear proper in the circumstances' from a refusal to submit to a blood test. The latter technique has considerable advantages over the former. It has elasticity which enables the court to evaluate the refusal in the light of all the surrounding circumstances and is free from undue technicality. The former, by making refusal an offence and therefore punishable *per se,* stimulates the ingenuity of the advocate to find technical defences, with the result that a collection of decided cases quickly accumulates and nice distinctions clog the working of the procedure. There would be very little hardship or risk of injustice if courts were free to draw inferences adverse to the accused from a refusal or a failure to provide an innocent explanation of facts which raise a strong suspicion but fall short of proof of guilt.

The changes in the rules of procedure and evidence, which I have described have a parallel in the recent history of the jury system in civil cases. The two are certainly inter-connected. In England during the last 40 to 50 years jury trial has become virtually obsolete in civil cases, although it still survives in actions for defamation. It survives also, virtually unaltered, in the Republic of Ireland and in the United States. In England it has been gradually replaced by trial by a single judge, largely on the initiative of the lawyers. For a long time there was a genuine option. A party could choose judge alone or judge and jury. Over the years it became increasingly common for judge alone to be chosen, until trial by jury became the exception rather than the rule and it was correspondingly more difficult for the party asking for a jury to overcome his opponent's objection and the court's own reluctance to order trial by jury. The change has taken place so gradually that its implications have scarcely been noticed but they are profound. The role of the judge and with it the expertise which he must acquire has changed. From being essentially an umpire whose task it was to control the trial and sum up the evidence to the jury, he has become the fact-finder and decision-maker. For the judge there are many subtle differences between these roles. It is one thing to sit and listen to evidence, note it, analyse the impact of one piece of evidence upon others, and lay the results before a jury in a summing up, and quite another to listen to evidence, study the witnesses, evaluate the data, and *decide* whether this or that piece of evidence is reliable and therefore whether the plaintiff has proved his case or not. Moreover, in contrast to the jury, the judge must expose his reasoning processes to the world. In some cases, perhaps in all, he will also, wittingly or unwittingly, expose some part of himself. No longer protected, except marginally, by the exclusion principle he must, to an increasing extent, evaluate evidence of different types with little but experience to guide him. The jury serves several functions. It is at once the oldest and the most extensive practical example of what is now called 'participation'. It also acts, to some extent, like the scientist's control samples, providing something like a norm and submerging personal idiosyncrasies in a group decision. It also reduces the influence of the judge's 'persona' by which I mean the complex which results from up-bringing, training, experience, attitudes, and adaptation to life which make a human personality. The judge sitting alone has to deal with his own persona as well as with those of the witnesses and with the objective data which are put before him. This is, of course, not a unique phenomenon. Everyone who has to make decisions about other people faces the same problem in varying degrees. In the extreme case of the psychoanalyst it is necessary for him to undergo a training analysis in order to understand his own persona as far as possible. Other people who have to perform functions of this kind learn about themselves to varying degrees, from their training and cumulative experience.

The task of evaluating evidence in a legal setting is not, however, as difficult or indeed as hazardous, as this description implies. Although there are no parameters, there is in nearly every case an area of common ground between the conflicting stories. This varies in extent from case to case. In the rare cases where the conflict is absolute, one side at least must be lying and the problem is simplified to that of finding which of them *must* be lying. In other cases, the area of common ground provides a solid foundation on which to build.

Admissions, if made in the witness-box, even if partial and reluctant, are extremely helpful. Unlike confessions made out of court to the police, or to enquiry agents, there can be no argument about what was said or why it was said. Contemporary documents, particularly letters and accident reports, are invaluable. The more letters there are, the more the court can infer about the facts and the writers. Even false or dishonest letters help. There are few dishonest geniuses about and only they can maintain a false story without a flaw for a long time. Then there is the objective evidence such as marks on the road, damage to vehicles, and so on, which provide a check. At least they set the limits within which the truth must lie. At a more subjective level, the impression which witnesses create in the witness-box can be helpful. The identical set of facts deposed to by a witness in the box and in an affidavit settled by counsel can produce quite different impressions. Counsel, if he is clever, can introduce subtle little glosses which make a most compromising witness sound the epitome of understanding. All these factors help to narrow down the area in which the judge must perform his evaluation but he is always left with a problem. He has to decide the probabilities of the case and may have to draw a line between saying to himself 'I am satisfied that on the present material the only reasonable conclusion is so and so', and 'I am pretty sure the facts are so and so but I cannot say "it is proved"'. All these matters have ultimately to be assessed in terms of probability, another word which breeds interdisciplinary misunderstanding. Legal probability is not the same as statistical probability which measures the difference between two events occurring by chance or of there being a causal connexion between them. Legal probability is closely connected with experience and is essentially a conclusion based on experience that one set of events is more likely to have occurred than another. Where statistical techniques can be used, as in blood groups, they can add to or correct what are otherwise empirical impressions but over most of the field statistical techniques cannot be applied.

It is within this frame of reference that expert or scientific evidence must operate in the trial process. Scientific proof, if it can be given, of course resolves all difficulties. Evidence of blood groups again is a good example but scientific evidence, falling short of proof, may be conclusive when it is added to the other ingredients of the case. Handwriting evidence which can go no further than a guarded opinion that 'A' could have written the disputed document becomes almost conclusive when set by the judge against the other evidence in the case which establishes that if 'A' did not write it nothing short of an extremely elaborate plot would have enabled 'B' to have done so. The one essential of all expert evidence is a frank statement by the expert of the limits of accuracy within which he is speaking, and a readiness to indicate, whether asked or not, what his evidence does *not* prove or suggest as likely. Just as counsel is under an obligation to call the judge's attention to points of law which are against his case, so the expert should be under an obligation to make sure that the court does not, unwittingly, use his evidence without realizing its scientific limitations.

CONCLUSION

In the end, therefore, evaluation is a process which combines analysis of fact with experience. Legal training is a good way of learning how to analyse and correlate facts. The experience of advocacy is sometimes regarded as an unsuitable preparation for the apparently different role of a judge. This apparently tenable view is based on a misapprehension of the advocate's technique. Every advocate has to begin every case by evaluating it rationally and judicially, if only to identify its weaknesses. He must also try to anticipate his opponent's case in order to determine his own tactics. What he does with these evaluations when he comes to present his case depends on his skill as an advocate. The good advocate sees both sides of the case but presents only one. The experience acquired in the life of an advocate is very wide although there is a prevalent idea that barristers and judges have no experience of real life. No one sees more criminals and hears more about crimes than a man who has worked as advocate or judge in the criminal courts for many years. No one hears more about the sex life and the family life of more people and of a wider cross-section of the public than the person who has practised in the divorce court for many years. Certainly not psychiatrists who see only the really disturbed. Social workers and probation officers and marriage guidance counsellors obtain their experience from different angles which suggest an explanation for this notion that lawyers have little or no experience of real life.

It is not so much experience which is lacking as knowledge of how to use it and apply it to the full in the light of the findings, experience, and theories of other disciplines working in the same field. This is where postgraduate courses could be so helpful and valuable. This too is the primary function of the British Academy of Forensic Sciences and it is of paramount importance for there is no other organization at present in Great Britain which is in a position to fulfill it.

REFERENCES

Blackstone, W. (1766), *Commentaries on the Laws of England, Book* 4, pp. 349, 352.

Cross, R. (1967), *Evidence,* 3rd ed. London: Butterworths.

Smith, T.B. (1961), *British Justice. The Scottish Contribution (Hamlyn Lecture,* 1961), p. 118. London: Stevens.

WHITHER FORENSIC SCIENCE?

H.J. Walls

I expect that you have all at some time been exposed to the schoolboy conundrum about the lily in the pond: the lily doubles in size every day, and at the end of forty-nine days fills half the pond. How long till it fills the whole pond? The answer is, of course, fifty days, though even educated people have been known to pause before giving it. Science today is that lily in the pond. Like the lily, it is growing at an exponential rate. It is an index of its rate of growth that scientific librarians reckon they have to provide for a mass of technical literature which doubles in bulk about every fifteen years. That means, put in another way, that, if the present trend continues, in the next fifteen years as much new scientific knowledge will have been published as in the whole of history up to now.

That is why I said science was like the lily in the pond. The space for its expansion is not infinite. There is a limit to the amount of scientific effort that is possible. We have also to eat, and it would, to say the least, be a somewhat unbalanced world if everyone not engaged in food production was a practising scientist.

I am not saying all that as a prophet of woe—anyway, I never qualified in prophecy—I am only pointing out the obvious. I understand that at the present time the number of electrical engineers in this country is growing so fast that, if the present rate of increase continues, every employed worker in Britain will be in electrical engineering by 1990. Well, that obviously won't happen and I have no doubt that science will some time or other stop growing at its present rate. Read, for example, Lord Bowden's speech last year to the European Institute of Business Administration, which was reported in full in *The New Scientist.*

However, it might be admitted that for us, caught right in the middle of this expansion, it presents some problems, and I would like here today to look at one or two aspects of them a little more closely. I will certainly propound more questions that I answer. In particular, I would like to explore a little our common problems of organisation and communication—the organisation of scientific effort to make it as serviceable as possible to the cause of justice, and the useful communication of our, the scientists', results to those who have to evaluate their significance.

Forensic science, which is after all a pretty obscure and esoteric sort of profession, is frankly small beer in the world of science. It is in fact so small that it is only now becoming aware that it *has* any problems or organisation. It is, as you all know, only a couple of generations or less since it started as the hobby, or at least sideline, of a few talented scientists, or doctors with a scientific bent, who like getting mixed up with the police and enjoyed the kind of problems this association brought them. (I am, of course, talking about science as distinct from medicine.) They could still in those days without being geniuses cope with all the science the job demanded. *Now,* most people realise that that is no longer true. If forensic science is to grow as it should—and what doesn't grow dies—or is even to use all the scientific knowledge which even now it could, it just has to be a collaborative affair. No one can now be an expert in all its branches.

That brings us right up against our very first difficulty. Since our law takes a very unfavourable view of second-hand scientific evidence, that means that we are more and more going to have to use two—or eventually perhaps three or four—scientific witnesses where one general-purpose one did before. This is already beginning to put a strain on our limited supply of expert witnesses. Also, with the increasing complexity of the laboratory tests used, it is becoming more difficult to combine the proper performance of them with being ready to dash off to court, sometimes at very short notice. As a servant of the Crown I think I may dare to state the obvious fact that, in respect of both of the points I have just made, our work would be a good deal easier if the law was satisfied with a comprehensive report issued by a laboratory after considered, unhurried and, if need be, collaborative work on the particular problem.

Any busy forensic science laboratory can be considered in one light as a factory. Its raw material is the exhibits brought to it, these are processed according to what the investigator wants to know, and the finished products are the reports issued. Now it is a fact too obvious to need any words wasted on it that in any efficient factory there must be division of labour. The ultimate of that is, of course, the motor-car or similar production line. The last thing we want is that our staffs should become simply production-line operatives, but at least we do not expect each member of them to do everything with his own hands—write down every measurement made, make up his own reagents, type his reports and so forth. At the same time, and whatever form laboratory reports take, we cannot abandon personal responsibility for all scientific work done in the pursuit of justice—which, after all, concerns people and is not just the lady on the Central Criminal Court. To satisfy the claims of justice and simultaneously achieve economy of effort is already a problem and is likely to remain so.

To go back to our factory analogy for a moment, the most efficient processing of the material would demand several things. First, we should prepare a flow sheet in which the separate operations are defined and their most efficient sequence laid down. It would be necessary at this stage to decide on what constitutes a separate operation. To use our motor-car analogy, is one man both to insert the bolt and screw on the nut, or do we have one man inserting bolts and another screwing on nuts? Secondly, the necessary staff would have to be allocated to each operation. Thirdly, the smoothest and speediest changeover between operations would have to be devised.

Well, I need scarcely say that there can be no question of carrying the production-line idea to its logical conclusion in the organisation of a forensic laboratory. After all, it is a fact which we frequently stress to intending entrants, to reassure them that they will not get bogged down in dull routine work, that almost all our jobs are "one-off" ones. But even one-off jobs utilise in various combinations a number of basic operations.

In more complex cases, if a whole battery of tests has to be done, their efficient ordering may have to be consciously planned and explicitly stated—especially if several people are involved, and even more especially if they are not all there all the time.

The increasing complexity of the work also brings us another difficulty—or perhaps it would be fairer to say the same difficulty in another guise. To know all that there is to be known about one new technique or one complicated analytical box of tricks is already quite a task and is certainly not going to get easier. But forensic science cannot safely be left to a group of people each of whom is master only of his own limited section of the necessary science. Someone needs to take a synoptic—in plainer English, if you like, broad—view of each big case and decide both on what needs to be done and on the best way of doing it. An experienced member of a laboratory staff can still do this, but it is becoming more difficult. And as people get more specialised, we have to face the fact that someone who has made some particular complex technique his speciality would be more than human if he did not want to use it, even in circumstances in which it was not necessarily the best for the purpose in hand. It may not be too fantastic to look forward one day to computerised laboratory programming, with which the man in charge feeds into the computer, suitably coded, both all the questions asked and details such as sensitivity and specificity of the possible techniques, and the times needed to get an answer by them; the computer would then tell him the optimum procedure to yield the greatest amount of useful information with the minimum consumption of time and material.

I did not come here to alarm you by projecting a science-fiction sort of future for our business, but I am honestly trying to look at the way things are shaping. And before I leave the question of organisation there are several other things I would like to say about it. The first also concerns a difficulty to which we ourselves, the scientists, must find the solution. It isn't a new one—the whole scientific world has been painfully aware of it for some time. It is the difficulty of coping with the spate, flood, Niagara, tidal wave, or any other metaphor you like, of new information, to which I referred in my opening remarks. The bulk of this I am talking about now is that pouring from the world's scientific presses, but we must add to that the working information which each scientific worker collects in the course of his everyday duties.

I think that we in forensic science can reasonably claim that for us this problem is a particularly acute one. Many scientists today are after all very specialised—you all know, and are reminded everyday, about the expert who knows more and more about less and less and ends up by knowing everything about nothing. In spite of what I have just said about increasing specialisation in our field, it is and is likely to remain a relatively unspecialised one as fields of sciences go. As I mentioned a few minutes ago, someone has to take a broad view of each problem presented to us, and in taking this the range of different sciences and branches of science and twigs of branches of science which we may need to use or to borrow from is tremendous. Now, it is bad enough keeping up with the literature in one limited field; to do so in all the fields which might be useful is already impossible and will get more so, if linguistic purists will allow me degrees of impossibility. Commercial abstracting services exist, but I don't think I am being unfair to them in saying that only someone with knowledge of and experience in forensic science knows *what* to abstract. The dilemma is that the man who knows can't spare the time, and anyone with the time can't really know. If we bracket with this large problem the lesser but still considerable one of keeping our own stock of accumulated information usefully classified and accessible, we have a very large problem indeed. I am, I am ashamed to say, much more ignorant about computers than I ought to be, but it seems even to my ignorance that it should be a fairly simple operation to store in the instrument all the relevant facts which one has gradually accumulated, and to programme it to deliver all of those, but only those, which have a bearing on any particular set of circumstances.

The application of this to published information is too obvious to need elaboration. But as I have just said, I think it could also be applied to our own accumulated data. For example, everyone working in a forensic science laboratory knows that, in the examination of material submitted in connection with breaking offences, one finds large numbers of multi-layered paint fragments which one rejects because they have clearly nothing to do with the case in hand. But if one had stored in a computer memory the layer structures of *all* painted surfaces associated with *all* breaking offences over the past twelve months, say, what a tempting prospect of linking Bill Sikes, whose clothing we have been examining, with some of his earlier jobs. Some people have in fact already tried to do this on a limited scale. If you quite reasonably object that the examination and codification of all these paint fragments would be an impossibly laborious task, I will counter by agreeing that for us now it almost certainly would be, but that I see no theoretical reason why the job should not be automated by using an automatic reflecting micro-spectrophotometer, which would simply count the layers and note their colours and feed the answers into the computer. We should be able to plan *that* relatively simple operation if we can send off instruments to analyse the surface of the moon.

To return to sub-lunar matters, and forgetting computers for the moment, the ability to take a broad view of new developments is particularly important in the sector in which new analytical methods are being developed by our academic and theoretical colleagues. The rate of this development is also increasing more or less exponentially, so that it becomes more and more difficult to keep up with it. New developments come faster and faster and we use them sooner and sooner. We are soon, like the Red Queen, going to have to run as hard as we can to keep in the same place. But we fall out of the race at our peril.

There must admittedly be some time lag between the first appearance of a new analytical tool and its use by us. Before its results can be taken into the witness-box it must be proved reliable. But this time lag should be no longer than necessary. The only way to keep it short is for us to keep a broad view of what is happening in the outside world of science—progress in which, as I have repeated probably *ad nauseam*, gets more and more difficult to follow. And, unfortunately, the inventor of or expert in a new technique is by his very expertise rarely able to take the broad view. He is almost inevitably blinded, or at least blinkered, by what it can do to what it cannot do, or to what it does no better but much more expensively than older techniques. That responsibility rests fairly and squarely on our own shoulders. It is a buck we cannot pass.

I would like to turn now to my second general topic—the problem of communication. Again this is a problem that has always been with us—but again the exponential growth of science is making its difficulty increase at a similar rate. Law and science are uneasy bedfellows.

The part of the problem which is probably easiest both to describe and to deal with is that consequent upon the sheer increasing technicality of scientific evidence. I believe the only way to overcome this difficulty is for both sides to make the effort to bridge the gap and meet in the middle. The scientist must not only know his subject, he must know or learn how to explain it to the non-scientist. This is an exercise which is very good for him in any case. The so-called popularisation of science is quite unjustly looked down upon by some too academically minded persons. Anyone who has ever tried to do it without sacrificing scientific precision of thought knows that the exercise is a merciless revealer of any patches of woolliness or ambiguity in his own ideas. The lawyer for his part must, I am afraid, learn something about the science he is dealing with—not necessarily its details, but certainly its general principles.

That brings me to the other part of the problem of communication, about which I shall have rather more to say. I hope the lawyers in my audience will forgive my saying that I have found their profession on the whole rather ignorant of what science is all about. So—even without dragging in Sir Charles Snow and the second law of thermodynamics—I trust that I will be forgiven a few general remarks on this.

It is a great pity that the same word "law" has come to be used for two completely different things—the regulations made by a society for the conduct of its members, and the abstract natural principles discovered by science. The fundamental difference between them is, of course: the government's laws are prescriptive instructions, which lose nothing in validity however often they are disobeyed—many of our traffic laws, for example. Scientific laws are descriptive generalisations from observation, and any one is completely destroyed by a single disobedient fact with which the law proves to be stubbornly inconsistent. If the law will not fit some well-attested fact, it must be scrapped and a new one found.

All that may be so obvious that you are wondering why I bother to say it. But I do believe that the power of the word may confuse our minds; our ineradicable habit of verbalisation has its dangers.

Now these laws of theirs are what scientists are really concerned about. The vast body of scientific factual information has—as mere data—no particular significance except in so far as it relates to them. I have sometimes formed the impression that learned counsel thought of science simply as a corpus of facts established for all time by measurements of absolute accuracy. If they did, their idea of science could hardly have been more wrong. I have just said what the significance of the facts is. As for their being established for all time, they may or may not be—that is unimportant. New facts are discovered which make us look at the old ones in a different light, or new theories give a simpler and more satisfying picture of the old facts; science changes, though the facts may not.

As for the accuracy, there is no such thing as *absolute* accuracy. All scientific measurements are subject to error. The great thing is to know how large the error is likely to be. All we can really do is to give a figure for whatever we are measuring, and another for the probability that its true value lies within some prescribed range on either side of that—and the wider we make the range, the greater the probability. I know that the law doesn't like the word probability, but I shall have to come back to that.

However, as I was saying, it is its so-called laws—or theories—that are the real business of science. Bertrand Russell says somewhere—I forget his exact words—that the true function of science is the confirmation or disproof of hypotheses. Now, if we hold on to that proposition, we find that law and science are not nearly so unlike each other as both sides—but may I respectfully say, especially lawyers—think they are. (Perhaps I should explain that by "law" I mean now the use of evidence in the British criminal codes.) I suggest that we can apply Bertrand Russell's proposition *in toto* to a criminal trial, simply making our hypothesis, not the truth or falsity of a scientific generalisation, but the guilt or innocence of Bill Sikes. Even our British accusatory system fits into that. Scientific facts are of no value in a vacuum. To be useful they must tell for or against some hypothesis. Let me quote Darwin on that. "How odd it is," he said, "that anyone should not see that all observation must be for or against some view if it is to be of any service."

Perhaps I should there digress again for a moment to allow that that is, of course, true only of a science which has developed far enough to formulate hypotheses. Many sciences—botany or astronomy, for example—start with an unorganised mass of observed facts from which general principles may emerge by induction. This, of course, is the method dating back to the *Novum Organum* of Francis Bacon—a lawyer, by the way. But as far as we are now concerned, even sciences which have not developed far enough to have produced their own internal hypotheses can be used to test the hypothesis of a criminal trial. Take serology, for example. As a science *per se* it is still in its primitive Baconian stage, with a mass of data still awaiting illuminating generalisations. But I need not tell you how often evidence about blood groups derived by its techniques can be crucial in disproving or supporting an hypothesis of guilt.

Any criminal trial indeed must—or at least should—be an example of scientific method. An hypothesis is advanced—the guilt of the accused—and the truth or falsity of this is considered unemotionally in the light of the evidence which has been collected. In a sense, when the investigating officer asked people questions, not knowing what the answers were going to be, he was conducting scientific experiments.

And still another parallel with science emerges here. It is well known that it is logically, at least, easier to prove innocence than guilt. Whatever the mass of suspicion, an alibi based on one single piece of wholly credible testimony is sufficient; innocence has been proved conclusively. Guilt, on the other hand, is proved only by the accumulation of evidence pointing to it, and then only "beyond reasonable doubt"—which means, by implication, never absolutely. It is just the same with scientific hypotheses. Modern philosophers of science, chiefly Professor Karl Popper, have pointed out that a scientific hypothesis can, logically, never be proved, only disproved. However often the result of an experiment supports an hypothesis, we cannot be logically certain that some unknown and unexpected cause will not produce a contrary result the next time, and if that does happen, and if the unexpected result cannot be explained in some way consistent with the hypothesis, then the hypothesis is in strict logic disproved. If all the evidence supports it, it is provisionally accepted, but, as I have just said, it is never free from the risk of being upset by one reliable incompatible observation, which may send us looking for a new and better hypothesis. That, of course, is why the scientific world picture, instead of being the firmly established body of data I mentioned earlier is always provisional, never final, always changing.

As a matter of fact, scientific laws, so-called, always have been of this type—statistical probabilities rather than prescriptive absolutes—but it is only recently that scientists as a whole have begun clearly to realise this fact themselves. The change is no doubt due to the revolutionary developments in the physical sciences at the beginning of this century.

By "statistical," on the other hand, I mean the kind of scientific principle that can be used to predict the behaviour of large numbers of individually random and indeterminate objects or events. You cannot predict whether your next toss will land heads or tails, but you can predict with confidence that in a long series of tosses there will be an approximately equal number of heads and tails, and the longer the series the more nearly perfect the equality. No one doubts that if you made as many tosses as there are molecules in a cylinder of gas, the law of equality of heads and tails would be observed as precisely as Boyle's Law of gases. As far as we know at present, it is quite impossible to predict whether any given atom of radium will undergo radioactive disintegration five minutes or 5,000 years hence, yet we can predict with great confidence that, of a large assemblage of such atoms, half will have disintegrated within 1,620 years. That is, any given atom stands a fifty-fifty chance of disintegration within that time.

You may be wondering what on earth all this has to do with forensic science. The answer to that is: communication from science to law, which was never easy, is being made more difficult by this developing trend towards scientific results being expressed as probabilities—not just as something that might be so, but as something that has a definite numerically expressible chance of being so. The law, of course, wants yes or no, black or white, this or not this. In fact, if I may make the observation in passing, I have sometimes thought it looks on "probability" as a dirty word. On the other hand, I have found it will accept "odds," which is only the same thing differently expressed. Is that because we are a betting nation?

I am convinced that the law will have to recognise this fact and come to terms with it. I am referring now to the kind of scientific conclusion where the probability is measurably less than 1. But, as I said a short time ago, *all* scientific conclusions are really matters of probability. Sometimes, of course, this is so near 1 (that is, certainty) that it is for all practical purposes indistinguishable from certainty, and the residuum of "reasonable doubt" is vanishingly small. The principle, however, remains valid. For example, nothing is more conclusive than fingerprint evidence, but there is no prescriptive law of nature that prohibits two fingerprints from being identical. There is merely a descriptive one that two never *are* identical. That, of course, is quite easily explained: the number of possible different fingerprint patterns is so large that there aren't enough fingers in the whole world over many generations to give a reasonable outside chance of two identical ones turning up.

We have indeed already seen the thin end of the wedge go in. Courts accept evidence about glass fragments in which all the scientific witness can say is that they are indistinguishable to within certain limits of accuracy, and the odds against—that is, the probability of—that happening by chance are so and so.

There is some very interesting work going on now on the characterisation of human head hair by means of the neutron activation analysis of the trace elements on it. As you probably remember, rather bold claims were made some years ago across the Atlantic that in this way a hair could practically be tied to the head from which it came. The present, much more systematic, work has shown that these claims were undoubtedly premature and over-stated, but that considerable significant differences between hairs from different heads do undoubtedly occur. We are not yet ready to use the results of this work routinely in evidence, but when we are they will be meaningful only if they are given as statistical probabilities. Some quite sophisticated statistical mathematics have been developed in connection with this work, and its use will enable us to give precise estimates of probabilities instead of, as at present, vague statements such as "similar to," "could have come from the same head" and so on. And it would obviously be quite wrong not to be precise instead of vague if the known facts make that possible.

Indeed, there is really no reason why in certain fields that sort of evidence should not now be used more than it is. The distribution of blood groups within the various blood-group systems which we can now determine on dried bloodstains is known, at least for the population of this country. I may perhaps point out in passing that lawyers tend, if I may respectfully say so, to take insufficient account of conjunctive probabilities. The conjunctive probability of a series of independent events occurring—or, in this case, results being found—is the product of their individual probabilities when they occur separately. The punter who backs a double where the odds are twenty to one for the horse in the first race and ten to one for that in the second race knows that the odds against his double coming off are 200 to one. Suppose, to come back to forensic science, that a specimen of blood is grouped according to four independent systems, and that it belongs to the commonest group in each, and suppose, for the sake of argument, that each of these groups occurs in half the population. Half the population is a large number of people, but when four independent systems are in question, that means in this case that the blood could only have come from half of half of half of half of the population—that is, one-sixteenth. That is already a considerable lengthening of the odds. If we could use eight systems, on the same assumption we would have come down to one-256th part of the population. And if the groups to which the blood belongs happen to be among the rarer ones, it is quite on the cards that we can say that only one person in several thousand has this combination of groups. As a matter of fact, we do say that sort of thing now when the opportunity to do so arises. But there is no reason why we should not carry it a little farther. It should not be impossible in some cases to make an estimate of the number of persons from whom, on other evidence, the blood might have come. Suppose this were 100. The important question then is: if the bloodstain and the person from whom the prosecution alleges the blood came, and who is one of that 100, are of the same rare combination of groups, what is the probability of more than one person in that 100 having it? If, to take a figure more or less at random, one person in 5,000 in the population as a whole shows that particular combination, then, according to my arithmetic, the probability of two people out of our 100 showing it is one twenty-five hundreth—that is, the odds against the event are 2,500 to one—and the probability of more than two people out of the 100 having it is quite vanishingly small. And, obviously, the smaller the number of persons from whom the blood *might* have come, the smaller the corresponding probability. If instead of 100 it was, say, twenty, then the odds against more than one person in that twenty having the same combination of groups are over 60,000 to one. Does that sort of figure constitute proof "beyond all reasonable doubt?"

We as scientists often wonder indeed just what "beyond all reasonable doubt" really means. Can we give it a quantitative connotation? I have already suggested that a criminal trial is really a scientific process. I am not going to suggest to you that juries will eventually be replaced by computers. I value my neck too highly, and anyway I admit that there would be difficulties in translating the credibility of a witness into computer language. But law and science would at least make a more harmonious marriage if we could put some sort of figure on "beyond all reasonable doubt." Does it mean with a probability of .99, or .999 or .999999 or something even higher? Should it be a higher probability in a trial for murder than in one for petty larceny? I leave the thought with you.

I have carried out my promise of saying something on the two general topics which concern us all of organisation and communication. Whether I have said anything of any value is another matter of which I leave you to be the judges. I have asked a good many questions and answered practically none. But I hope that I have at least given you some idea of what I think are the kinds of questions we will have between us to answer if our joint endeavours in the cause of justice are to continue to be fruitful.

SCIENCE AND LAW—

A LAWYER'S VIEWPOINT

J. Fitzsimons

The last 25 years or so have seen a revolution in the application of scientific method to crime detection, and the modern-day criminal is himself, of course, well aware of this. The clever criminal will make every effort to remove all obvious traces of his presence, but he cannot remove what he cannot see, and it is impossible for him to vanish without trace. There is always some trace if it can be found, and modern science is helping, with more and more sophisticated techniques, to find and identify such traces, whether they be fingerprints, bloodstains, particles of skin, or strands of hair; and it must always be remembered that the developments in scientific knowledge and instruments may be applied to the purpose of obtaining information not only to point the finger at the guilty but also, and just as importantly, to remove suspicion from the innocent.

One cannot stress too much the role of science in the detection of crime as an important element in the law's attempts to curb the growing menace of crime, particularly organized crime, in our society. One hears a great deal of talk nowadays about the effect of punishment as a deterrent to crime, whether in fact it is or should be a deterrent. I have always been of the opinion that there must be a deterrent, but to talk of punishment as a deterrent (or as the only deterrent) is putting the cart before the horse—one cannot consider punishment until *after* the criminal has been caught and convicted—and I do not believe that the criminal will have much regard to the possible prospect of punishment so long as he has a good chance of not being caught or convicted. I firmly believe that the greatest deterrent to crime would be the certainty (or near certainty) of detection, and the law (and the government for that matter) should therefore ensure that all necessary assistance is given to developments in detection methods, scientific or otherwise.

THE RECEPTION OF SCIENTIFIC EVIDENCE

The law must also be prepared to give proper weight to scientific evidence and to endeavour to keep up with scientific developments. The courts have tended in the past to be rather conservative and to lag behind science but one can, I think, detect a more enlightened, forward looking attitude over the last few years. To take one obvious example: a big step forward was taken in 1968 by the Scottish High Court in the case of Gordon Hay, an approved school boy who was convicted of the murder of a young girl in a cemetery in Biggar. The court allowed the most detailed scientific evidence linking bite marks on the girl's body with the highly unusual dental characteristics of the accused boy. If one looks at the very detailed account of the case (*J. Forens. Sci. Soc.*, 1968, 8, 4) one can see an excellent example of the value of sound scientific evidence, carefully investigated and prepared, and presented in such a manner as to survive a very searching cross-examination. Possibly the most important aspect of the case from the point of view of the relationship between law and science was the fact that the court sanctioned the granting of a warrant *before* the boy was arrested to compel his submission to dental examination (measurement and photographing of his teeth). In sanctioning this unprecedented procedure the court undoubtedly recognized not only the importance of scientific techniques in investigation but also the importance of allowing the investigator the facilities to preserve possible vital evidence required for such investigation.

In the Hay case, the accused was in effect convicted on the scientific evidence alone but, as you well know, such cases are few and far between. In the majority of cases the scientific evidence does not by itself effectively decide guilt or innocence, but is more likely to form one of the links in a chain of circumstantial evidence, e.g. by putting the accused at the scene of the crime because of fingerprints. But no matter how it is used, one of the important aspects of such evidence is that it is objective, as distinct from the subjective evidence of the eye-witness.

THE FALLIBILITY OF PAROLE EVIDENCE

Perhaps you would allow me to say briefly something about this. Ever since becoming a lawyer I have been struck by the rather touching faith which the law has in parole evidence—the evidence of witnesses to facts given in open court (in most cases some months after the event) and, despite the increasing use of objective scientific evidence, a significant proportion of trials depend almost entirely on parole evidence. On the other hand, anyone familiar with the courts (indeed anyone who reads reports of trials in newspapers) cannot fail to be aware of the frequency of very wide discrepancies between various witnesses' accounts of the same event. Some of these discrepancies may of course be due to deliberate lying, but the deliberate perjurer is probably a much rarer animal than most people, even lawyers, imagine. The honestly mistaken witness, according to psychologists, is much more common. It must always be remembered that a legal trial is inevitably a backward-looking affair; it is an attempt to reconstruct a series of events which occurred often months in the past. The court has to depend very largely on the perception and recollection of witnesses, and psychological studies and experiments over the past 50 or 60 years have demonstrated that errors in perception and recall are much more common than is usually appreciated, so much so that Professor Glanville Williams concludes that "error in testimony is the rule rather than the exception." (Williams, 1958)

Psychologists have shown that there are two main sources of error in recollection—errors in perception and errors in memory, and the two combined tend to make our recollection of events extremely unreliable (Williams, 1958; Blom-Cooper and Wegner, 1968; Tube, 1971). Experiments going back more than a century, but particularly over the last 50 years, have shown that an individual surrounded constantly by thousands of stimuli (sights, sounds, colours, odours) can assimilate only a limited number of such stimuli at any given moment, so that he is forced to select some and reject others. This process of selection may be affected by external factors, such as the size or novelty of an object or happening, or by internal factors such as emotion, fatigue, even hunger or thirst. It has been demonstrated that a statement by a person in a highly excited or disturbed emotional state—because, for example, he has just been attacked or been in an accident—is particularly likely to contain inaccuracies. This is probably at least part of the reason for the relative frequency of wrong identifications by persons who have been robbed or assaulted.

Witnesses may also be in error because of what psychologists refer to as a "state of expectance." A condition of expectancy serves to facilitate the entry of certain stimuli and to inhibit the entry of others—it is those elements of a total situation for which we are prepared that are most likely to trigger off the perception. In other words we tend to see what we expect to see, or what we desire to see. (The mother who sleeps through a thunderstorm but wakens at her baby's first cry, the nervous child who sees a ghost in every corner, are familiar examples.) Besides defects in perception, psychologists also lay stress on the fallibility of our memories. They have provided convincing evidence over the last half century that little of what we remember remains unchanged for long. The memory is not a simple storage system and it too can become distorted by passage of time, our emotions and the psychological and physiological needs of the moment. One of the greatest dangers in the trial process arises not so much when a witness forgets something but when, through a trick of memory, he genuinely believes that he saw or heard something he did not. One well recognized mechanism, for instance, affecting the memory is the process of transference, an event being remembered as belonging to a different occasion from the one on which it actually happened.

An illustration of the tricks memory can play may be seen in the case of Patrick McCloy (Petitioner, 1971, S.L.T., (notes) 32), a boy aged 13, who was charged, along with his brother and another boy, James Sutherland, with theft. All three appeared in court on December 1, 1969, when Sutherland admitted the charge and was fined. Patrick McCloy stood trial with his brother on February 9, 1970, and was convicted. An appeal was lodged and in the stated case the magistrate stated that "the accused James Sutherland, having been dealt with at a previous diet was called and gave evidence for the prosecution", and went on to state that she had preferred the evidence of Sutherland to that of Patrick McCloy. In fact Sutherland had not given evidence at the trial but the magistrate refused to accept this at the adjustment stage of the procedure. McCloy's conviction was eventually quashed after a special petition to the High Court. If, by some quirk of memory, one can have a fairly experienced magistrate convinced only weeks after the event that she has heard evidence from a non-existent witness, how much more likely is a witness' memory of events months in the past to be affected, particularly when he is being questioned in the strange and often (to him) hostile, atmosphere of a courtroom?

Scots law has always, to a certain extent, recognized the existence of this problem of the fallibility of witnesses by insisting as one of the basic rules of criminal law that no person may be convicted on the evidence of a single witness; there must always be supporting evidence as corroboration. By insisting on this rule the law helps to provide its own check on the credibility of the evidence of each witness since discrepancies will alert the court to the existence of potential errors. On the other hand one cannot necessarily say in this context that there is safety in numbers. This was brought home to me in one of my first cases in which I was prosecuting a man on several charges of indecent exposure. The point at issue was identification, probably one of the most common sources of error in criminal trials. No less than seven witnesses positively identified the accused at the trial and could not be shaken in cross-examination. However, as a result of further information given to me during the trial, I visited the "locus" of the offence and became convinced that the witnesses could not have seen the man's face clearly in the situation they said he was in. On questioning the witnesses further I discovered that they had all seen the accused person being arrested and had simply presumed that he must have been the man. The accused was acquitted and the real culprit was caught some time later, but that trial could easily have resulted in the conviction of an innocent man on the evidence of witnesses who honestly thought they were telling the truth.

I hope I have said enough to make my point that the testimony of witnesses to an event being investigated by a court is not always as accurate as we tend to assume, and it is the subjective nature of such evidence which makes it so unreliable. The courts should therefore be eager to seize on objective scientific evidence, whenever possible, as a valuable method of checking or corroborating other evidence. Leaving aside the question of interpretation, objective physical evidence cannot perjure itself and can be of immense value in providing checks and setting limits within which the truth must lie.

LAWYERS AND SCIENTISTS—AN IMPERFECT ALLIANCE

I think that for the reasons outlined most scientists and lawyers would agree that science has a vital role to play in the investigation of crime and the legal process. If this is so, then I ask myself why there is still evident in modern times a certain discord, one might almost say mutual distrust, between lawyers and scientists; what Sir Roger Ormrod has described as the "credibility gap" between lawyers and experts; what I would prefer to call a "communication gap." The gap has undoubtedly been narrowing over the years, and gone are the days when cross-examination of an expert witness was more like an attempt at character assassination, but there does remain a problem of communication between the disciplines. One reason may be that to a certain extent the lawyer subconsciously resents the entry into the court arena of an expert on any subject. (Belli, 1968; Eaton, 1968) Lawyers undoubtedly tend to surround themselves, particularly in court, with a sort of mystique which is accentuated by the tradition, the ritual, the robes, the legal jargon and so on. The lawyer is familiar with such surroundings; this after all is his natural "habitat." The ordinary witness is out of place in such surroundings, so the lawyer has the upper hand; but he may resent not having the upper hand when dealing with a witness whose knowledge on a particular subject is greater than his own, especially if he feels unable to grasp and therefore to test the evidence being given. The problem is compounded by the fact that the expert is privileged as a witness in that he can give evidence not only of facts but of opinions based on the facts. Lawyers may tend to feel uneasy in such a situation.

Conversely, of course, the expert may feel "put out" that his firmly held professional opinion should be disbelieved or questioned by "some fellow in a gown and wig" who knows little, if anything, of the subject in question.

Sir Roger Ormrod (1968) has pointed out, and this may have a great deal to do with the situation, that until relatively recently most of the confrontations between lawyers and scientists occurred in murder trials. The author points out that the threat of the death penalty led the defence in such cases to attack expert evidence in detail, and the pressure put on the expert witness tended to poison relations between lawyers and experts. It should of course be appreciated that the defence would attack other witnesses just as vehemently in such cases, but perhaps the expert was more able and ready to react against such questioning which he might well regard as a slur on his professional standing.

THE DEGREES OF PROBABILITY

However, I would suggest that the major reason for the discord lies deeper and is based simply on lack of understanding and communication. The course of a scientific investigation and of the legal trial process are probably much more alike than lawyers or scientists often realize (Walls, 1971). Both science and the law work on the basis of probabilities—and both share the same fundamental objective—the discovery of the truth to the greatest extent which their techniques permit.

In the process of trying to "find the truth" each discipline must work with raw data which is tested and analysed in accordance with well-tried techniques used in that discipline; and what many scientists possibly do not realize is that the raw data of the legal trial process is the evidence given by the witness and the technique which the lawyer uses to test his data is the well-tried technique of cross-examination. If the expert witness could appreciate this he might not be so prone to treat a close and detailed cross-examination as a personal attack on his integrity; the lawyer is simply testing his data in the only way he knows how—a way in which the risk of error due to bias or inaccuracy in the maker of the statement may be diminished. Once all the evidence has been tested, the court has to reach a decision based on the data presented, and it does this by giving a decision based on the balance of probabilities. This word "probability" is used in both disciplines but because it does not mean the same in each context, its use may lead to misunderstanding.

Scientific probability may be based on measurements, on statistical probability, as for example where the fingerprint expert can use statistics to show that the chance of two persons having identical fingerprints is so small as to be not worth considering; he is talking of the highest degree of probability—what Lord Clyde called, in the first Scottish fingerprint case, "practical infallibility".

But legal probability is not the same as statistical probability—it is in fact rather a nebulous concept, a conclusion based on experience and intuition that one set of events is more likely to have occurred than another. In civil law, the courts require proof on the balance of probabilities, but in the criminal sphere the law goes one step higher on the ladder of probabilities and requires proof beyond reasonable doubt. The law is not infallible and does not claim to be so; when a court finds a man guilty, it is not necessarily saying he is guilty—it is saying that it has been proved beyond reasonable doubt, on the evidence presented to it, that he committed the crime. The two are not necessarily synonymous. Probability in this sense is a degree of rational belief but it is not necessarily measurable or quantifiable. In the same way, the scientist does not prove everything with certainty—he also hopes to establish facts beyond reasonable doubt; the difference between the scientific and the legal situation is that the scientist is able to calculate the probability of the doubt.

I realize that I need not point out to you, as scientists, that the importance of scientific evidence based on, say, fingerprints or bloodstains does not rest on certainty but on a very high degree of probability. I am not at all sure, however, that all lawyers appreciate this. In the case of blood analysis we have not yet arrived at the state of probability of identification that has been reached with fingerprints. However, through painstaking research and development of techniques, scientists will no doubt one day be able to "identify" individual blood in the same way as fingerprints, and will be prepared to present to the court statistical data to support their case. On the other hand the courts, in evaluating evidence, cannot undertake painstaking research of this nature. At the end of a trial the court is obliged to make an immediate decision, one way or the other, on the evidence presented to it (and only on that evidence), and the judge or jury must decide whether guilt has been established beyond reasonable doubt. It is impossible in the legal situation to quantify this reasonable doubt, to express it as a mathematical probability as the scientist may do (Tribe, 1971).

I would like now to turn finally to another problem facing the scientist in the legal process—the problem of communication between the expert and the court, i.e. judge or jury, in the actual giving of evidence.

The expert, in giving evidence, is engaged in the very subtle art of communication from one mind to another, and a scientist, if he does not prepare properly, may experience great difficulty in communicating to the court, to the lay mind, particularly when it has to be done in answer to questioning. The scientific evidence, often highly complex, has to be assessed by a judge and by a jury with probably no experience of such matters at all. The scientist must therefore present his evidence in language which is capable of being understood by the lay mind. The evidence of a brilliant scientist may be lost to a jury if presented in highly technical language. One of the problems here of course is that although we call the scientist giving evidence an expert witness, he may be anything but expert "as a witness." He may be an expert in his field, but be very inexpert at giving evidence.

Even assuming the expert *could* be a good witness, in the sense of being able to put his opinions across effectively to the lay mind, is he in fact able to do this efficiently under the system of questioning to which he is subjected in the witness box? Many scientists would say "no", and I as a lawyer would agree (though I may be in a minority here).

As you probably know, there are, in the Western World, two types of procedure for the questioning of witnesses. First there is the system in use in Continental countries, called the Inquisitorial System, in which basically the witnesses, including the accused, give evidence in narrative form but subject to interrogation by the judge. Only then do opposing counsel ask questions, and cross-examination as we know it does not occur. The judge carries out the investigation and calls the witnesses.

The system in use in England and Scotland is the accusatorial, adversary system, a partisan system under which each side calls its own witnesses to support its case. The prosecution and defence take sides, as in a game, and each side presents its evidence to an impartial tribunal which decides the case on that evidence and nothing else. The judge therefore may be regarded as no more than a referee or chairman with power to see "fair play" but not to interfere with the partisan nature of the proceedings.

Although the criminal trial procedure is supposed to be a search for the truth, it is my view that the adversary system is neither designed for nor suited to the finding of the whole truth. The judge in general cannot call witnesses, and neither "side" is bound to call particular witnesses, and the court may therefore be required to decide a case, not on the whole evidence, but on a carefully selected assortment of the evidence. A trial may degenerate into a contest to find out which side is telling the better story or, as Oliver Wendell Holmes once put it, to decide which side has the better lawyer!

How does the expert witness, in particular, fare under this procedure? Not very well in my opinion. Lawyers tend to pay lip-service to the independence of the expert witness—we trot out the well-worn statement that "the expert is not a witness for the prosecution or defence but is a witness of the court." But what do we do in practice? We allow one side to call the expert as "their" witness in this "game" and subject him to this partisan type of questioning. The witness is controlled by the questions asked; the questioner is dominant and the effect of the evidence on a jury may depend as much on the skill of the questioner as on the knowledge of the witness. Under the rules the witness cannot volunteer information not encompassed by the language of the question. In this way the evidence is brought out in coherent and orderly fashion, but it may also be brought out selectively. I wonder how many experts leave the witness box with the feeling that they have not really been allowed to put forward all their findings, reflected in the rather cynical statement that the expert witness should take the oath in the form "I swear to tell the truth, nothing but the truth, and so much of the truth as I am allowed to tell!"

There may also, under the adversary system, be danger of greater accent being put on the witness himself and his "performance" under cross-examination than on what he says, and this is particularly true of one of the worst aspects of the adversary system in relation to expert evidence; what is often referred to as the "battle of the experts"—the big names of the medical or scientific world ranged on each side at a trial. A jury may have difficulty digesting scientific evidence given by one expert, but how much more difficult must it be for them to choose between experts who disagree on some complex theory or, for instance, on the cause of death in a murder trial. The jury's choice in such a case may well be based largely on the witness' personality, his performance in the witness box or even on his reputation.

This type of situation arose in the trial of John Donald Merrett in Edinburgh High Court in 1927 for the murder of his mother. Mrs. Merrett died of a gunshot wound and the boy claimed his mother committed suicide. The prosecution produced as expert witnesses Professors Littlejohn and Glaister who said that accident or suicide were so highly improbable as to be almost inconceivable. The defence produced Professor Robertson, Robert Churchill and the famous Sir Bernard Spilsbury, who maintained the wound was consistent with suicide or accident. Faced with this conflict of opinion among some of the most famous experts of the time, what was the jury to do? Is it any wonder resort was had to what Sir Walter Scott called "that bastard verdict," the not proven? (Twenty-seven years later John Merrett, after a long criminal career, murdered his wife and mother-in-law in England. By that time he had changed his name to Ronald Chesney.)

THE ACCUSATORIAL AND INQUISITORIAL SYSTEMS

It is all too easy, of course, to criticize a system without suggesting alternatives or improvements. In conclusion, therefore, I would put forward suggestions to avoid some of the problems mentioned. The answer certainly does not lie in abolishing argument by simply restricting scientific evidence to one witness; nor in my view should there be a single "court expert" as in the German system where a court expert carries out tests and investigations, may examine witnesses, and makes a report to the court. The danger in such a situation is that the expert may tend to gather an aura of infallibility around him. One of the problems in arriving at a solution is that lawyers in particular tend to plump either for the adversary (accusatorial) or the inquisitorial system. Why cannot we have a compromise, an amalgam of the best elements of each type of procedure? (Scottish criminal procedure historically reflects such an amalgam although the inquisitorial part of the procedure, the judicial examination has fallen into disuse in practice.) My suggestion would be (and I would not necessarily limit this to expert witnesses) that the witness should be called by the judge on application by either side; the expert should read his full report and be questioned on it by the judge; only then should he be subject to cross-examination by each side. In case of disputes the judge should have power not only to call other experts as witnesses, but to appoint an expert (or even a panel of experts) to act as assessor to the court.

Perhaps, however, the basic problems of communication between law and science can best be overcome by a true dialogue between the disciplines, particularly at the stage of training of students. It is to be hoped that the exchange of lectures in the Law and Forensic Science courses at the University of Strathclyde will go some way to overcome any such barriers by giving budding scientists and lawyers at least a basic working idea of the concepts and techniques used by the other discipline.

REFERENCES

Belli, M., 1968, *Med. Sci Law*, 8, 15.

Blom-Cooper L., and Wegner, J., 1968, *Med. Sci Law*, 8, 31.

Eaton, A., 1968, *Med. Sci Law*, 8, 78.

Ormrod, R., 1968, *Criminal Law Rev.*, 240.

Tribe, L.H., 1971, *Harvard Law Rev.*, 84, 1329.

Walls, H. Jr. 1971, *Criminal Law Review*, 459.

Williams, G., 1958, *The Proof of Guilt*, Stevens and Sons Ltd., London.

II.

The Development of
Forensic Science Laboratories

INTRODUCTION

To understand a particular professional discipline it is helpful to examine significant historical events from which the present discipline evolved. In forensic science it is particularly revealing to review the progressive uses of the natural sciences in the criminal justice system. Although legal codes and various forms of justice date back centuries before Christ, science was still in its infancy prior to the sixteenth century, and important contribuitons to the legal system were not made until the nineteenth century. What began as isolated cases in which an interested doctor or scientist assisted a magistrate in interpreting evidence has evolved into a far reaching system of forensic science laboratories serving the major law enforcement agencies in this country and abroad. An examination of the slow, sometimes frustrating efforts of scientists to introduce their findings into court highlights the great progress made during the last decade when the number of forensic science laboratories in the United States alone has more than doubled.

In the first selection Frederic Thomas presents a personal description of selected "milestones" which mark the gradual acceptance of scientific procedures and proof by the criminal courts. Being a Belgian, the author is able to present a particularly interesting and detailed account of European scientists who were early pioneers in forensic science. Dr. Thomas, while noting the outstanding successes of many forensic scientists, concludes his paper with a discussion of miscarriages of justice precipitated by untrained or overzealous experts.

Calvin Goddard, the firearms expert who investigated the St. Valentine's Day Massacre in Chicago in 1929, authored the next selection on the status of crime laboratories in Europe in 1930. The United States was decades behind the European countries in the use of scientific methods for crime detection. Mr. Goddard was dispatched to Europe to survey crime laboratories there in order to organize and administer one of the first scientific laboratories in the United States. The scope of the work undertaken by European laboratories in the 1930's is truly remarkable, even by today's standards. Although not included in this particular selection of readings, Part II of this article appeared in the next issue of the old *American Journal of Police Science* and described all the major European forensic laboratories in considerable detail.

The final selection written by the late Charles M. Wilson, an early criminalistics pioneer, is based upon his personal recollections of the early development of laboratories in the United States.

Although other fine books discuss the contributions of individual forensic scientists, such as Jurgen Thorwald's *Century of the Detective* and *Crime and Science*, the selections here are drawn from resources not always found in the forensic scientist's library.

MILESTONES IN FORENSIC SCIENCE

Frederic Thomas

Rather than presenting a static picture of the history of the forensic sciences and more particularly of legal medicine as the textbooks tend to do, I think this is an opportunity to show to what extent progress in these fields has been linked to the forward march of the basic sciences generally.

In this paper my primary concern will be to repair as much as possible the harm caused by the two world wars—especially the first—to the diffusion of information, and to give their due to men who have outstanding achievements to their credit but who, nevertheless, have remained as unknown as the proverbial "unknown warrior." Science was surprisingly well under way when the first upheaval occurred in 1914 and brought about such chaos that much work had to be started all over again.

Though one can never sufficiently underline the merits of pioneers of centuries gone by, it is undoubtedly wiser to entrust this task to professional historians conversant with Latin and, accessorily, other classical languages. I can, however, safely recall a few giants.

My compatriot Andries van Wesel, better known in the United States by his latinized name of Andreas Vesalius Bruxellensis (1514-1564), is the founder of modern anatomy (1,2). He was well familiar with the legal medicine of his time, since his research depended entirely on cases of violent death. He was on excellent terms with judges and hangmen alike and attended capital executions(3). In that golden age for anatomy executions could occasionally be scheduled to meet the needs of the master and his students(4).

Ambroise Paré (1510-1590) was the surgeon of kings and the king of surgeons of his century and the father of French legal medicine(5). He was self-taught, having begun the hard way, as apprentice to a barber, when still a boy, before becoming a skilful "chirurgien barbier" and, later, the greatest surgeon of his time. When one explores his monumental treatise in three volumes totaling 2499 pages, one is dumbfounded by the universality of his knowledge of medicine(6). He was apparently the first to describe firearm wounds scientifically, to deduce the location of a bullet in the body by asking the victim's position when he was hit, and to find a bullet by palpation of the surface of the body. He accomplished sundry other diagnostic feats which implied an astonishing knowledge of what we now call forensic ballistics(7). He posited the problem of the so-called crib death but gave the wrong explanation, namely that of "overlaying" or smothering (Vol. III, p. 658 of Ref 6). In his description of Caesarian section on a dead woman, he describes in a few sentences with extraordinary lucidity the breathing mechanism of the fetus (Vol. II, pp. 716-717 of Ref 6). He was not far from the truth concerning carbon monoxide poisoning. In his description of a double accident with recovery, on the 10th of March 1575, he attributed the cause to: "La fumée maligne du charbon ardent" (Vol. III, p. 663 of Ref 6). He was also the first to teach his contemporaries how to write a medicolegal report properly (Vol. II, pp. 651-675 of Ref 6). A humanist in the full meaning of the word, he was terribly conscious of the incredible sufferings of his fellowmen in those somber days. He took the considerable risk of pleading the cause of many a poor woman who had resorted to abortion and would otherwise have incurred the death penalty, by involking the authority of St. Augustine (the latter had laid down the doctrine of the *foetus animatus* as opposed to the *foetus inanimatus*) (Vol. II, pp. 652-653 "De L'Ame" and Vol. III, p. 658 of Ref 6). His writings not only bear witness to his outstanding technical skill but also make him the pioneer of modern medical ethics. In 1550 his famous motto—"soigner souvent (attend often), guérir parfois (heal sometimes), consoler toujours (comfort always)"—provided an unsurpassed lesson of ethics for the generations to come.

Paolo Zacchias (1584-1659) occupied a key position as the personal physician of two successive Popes, Innocent X and Alexander VII, and as first medical expert of the Holy Catholic Church Tribunal or Rota Romana. The author of the monumental treatise *Quaestiones Medico-legales*, he is considered by most to be the mastermind of the legal medicine of his day(8).

Another Italian, Giovanni Lancisi (1654-1720) deserves a special mention because he was the first to manifest scientific interest for the all-important problem of sudden death. With the full approval of the Church in the person of three successive Popes (Innocent XI, Innocent XII, and Clement XI), an indispensable prerequisite in those insecure times, he actually performed systematic postmortem examinations of the Rome cases. Thus, he succeeded in unveiling at least one cause for sudden death—cerebral hemorrhage—a noteworthy achievement(9).

In those days, a lot of pluck was needed to dare question the accepted dogmas and what the Germans call "Autoritätsglauben." Johann Schreyer, a German physician of the 17th century, possessed the necessary audacity. When, in 1681, he threw a newborn's lungs into a basin of water to determine if the child had been born alive, he was asking for trouble and got it. This simple gesture led to Court proceedings which lasted many years and caused him no small amount of unpleasantness, but the battle was won and the method, from then on, joined the meager armory of the medical expert of those days. The reader will find the story in Zeldenrust's textbook(10). Though written in Dutch, it is a little more accessible than Schreyer's paper in Gothic German(11).

At the turn of the century, another giant made his appearance on the scene: Giovanni Battista Morgagni (1682-1771), pupil of Valsalva. He is considered to be the father of modern morbid anatomy. His classic work *De sedibus et causis morborum*(12) has been translated into English(13) and is a gold mine for the historians of legal medicine.

From this time forward it becomes easier for the layman interested in the history of sciences to reach a personal opinion regarding the work of past scientists, since these men had begun to write in their mother languages. They have left us masterpieces.

With the end of the 18th century, chemistry made its definitive entry on the scene. With Scheele's (1773) and Priestly's (1774) approximately simultaneous discovery of oxygen, the way was open for Lavoisier to unravel the mystery of combustion (1776) and, in one stroke, to clarify completely the mechanism of respiration, thereby putting an end to centuries of obscurity. May I remark in passing that there was a time when arteries were considered to be simply pipes ensuring the distribution of air in the body! The role of the lungs had actually been largely unraveled more than two hundred years earlier, by the Spanish-born anatomist Miguel Serveto (Servede) (1511-1553). In 1553, he described the pulmonary circulation and proved that the blood becomes red in the lungs by mixing with the inspired air. The unfortunate man, who was at cross-purposes with Calvin, was arrested that same year in Geneva and burned at the stake on the charge of heresy.

Though Lavoisier's momentous discoveries were ended by the French Revolution, which bears the entire responsibility for his untimely death (the French Revolutionaries condemned him to death and refused his reprieve on the extravagant grounds that France had no need for scientists: "la France n'a pas besoin de savants"), he had succeeded in his short life in opening unlimited horizons to science. From the forensic point of view his discovery provided the key to the whole problem of asphyxia. It may be necessary to remind the reader that, until then, death by drowning, for instance, was attributed to the excessive penetration of water into the gastrointestinal tract (hence, the German word "Ertrinkung" and the Dutch expression "verdrinking," meaning too much absorption of drink). The poor creature who was unfortunate enough to be recovered alive underwent the ordeal of enemas destined to evacuate the water from his gastrointestinal tract.

From this point onwards, it is not an exaggeration to speak of the permanent fireworks of major discoveries in all fields of endeavor. The forensic sciences, until then in the cradle, received their share of the booty. Fortunately, from this time on we can keep track of the discoveries, thanks to the new textbooks and journals. They bear testimony to the amazing skill and foresight of the men of science of those days. Major trials usually provided them the opportunity of giving the full measure of their genius.

The first spectacular murder by poison which was the occasion for a major advance in forensic toxicology took place in Belgium, in the middle of the 19th century. It is the *Visart de Bocarmé* case, the first "scientific" crime on record to my knowledge(14-16). The personality of the culprit, as well as the remarkably high standard of the scientific evidence for the Crown, give this case a place of honor among famous trials. Before examining the facts, one should remember that chemical toxicology was then in its infancy. Nothing worthy of mention existed before the appearance of M.-J.-B. Orfila (1787-1853). Orfila, a Spaniard endowed with exceptional gifts, had come to France in 1807. He succeeded in overcoming the difficulties of pursuing his medical studies in Paris all through the Napoleonic Wars and graduated brilliantly in 1811. He was the first to prove that metallic poisons are not only absorbed by the gastrointestinal tract, but that they then reach other organs, where their presence must be detected and their amount assessed.

Only a few years before the *Visart de Bocarmé* case Orfila had been summoned to give evidence for the Crown in a notorious poison trial in France—*l'affaire Lafarge*(17)—where, for the first time in history, convincing scientific testimony was given. It was the first occurrence, to my knowledge, in which the defense attempted to rebut the scientific evidence for the Crown by calling in its own expert. The accused was an attractive young widow who, after the death of her husband, married a certain Monsieur Lafarge, by the intermediary of a matrimonial agency. Their union was an unhappy one. In December 1839 Lafarge, who was alone on a business trip in Paris and who was in perfect health, ate a cake which his wife had sent him. He immediately became very sick and complained of symptoms consistent with arsenic poisoning. His condition worsened after his return home, where he was within easier reach of his wife, and he died on 13 Jan. 1840. It was proved that, as far back as 15 December, Madame Lafarge had bought arsenic at a chemist's. The postmortem having been followed by unconvincing chemical investigations, the court consulted Orfila and ordered an exhumation. The exhumation led to analyses, the results of which were again contradictory, so that at last Orfila was called in personally from Paris to Tulle, 300 miles to the south. He demonstrated arsenic in the viscera by the Marsh test, which was performed, as was then customary, on porcelain plates and he assured the jury that the earth of the cemetery was free of it. The accused, who had in the meantime fallen in love with one of her lawyers, was condemned to penal servitude by the assizes before the unfortunate expert for the defense, F.-V.R. Raspail (1794-1878), whose mad rush to Tulle had been retarded by a fall from horseback, reached his destination. Raspail is supposed to have contended at the time that he could have extracted arsenic from the President's own chair. I recount this to depict better the vivid controversial background peculiar then, as now, to trials for murder by poisoning: from the start these have always tended to become tournaments. There is no field which lends itself better, in my experience, to the avenging of old feuds between forensic experts than a case of criminal poisoning.

Orfila's figure was to loom in a most unfortunate fashion in the Bocarmé case. Count Bocarmé, a ruthless man facing ruin, decided to save himself from imminent bankruptcy by murdering his wealthy brother-in-law. With extraordinary perseverance and cunning he first studied chemistry and thus learned, by reading the 1843 edition of Orfila's treatise, that nicotine was unidentifiable in the dead body. He thereupon grew tobacco, acquired the necessary equipment, and attempted to extract pure nicotine out of it. He failed. A persevering man by nature, he then actually applied for private tuition in chemistry in Ghent and ultimately succeeded in his purpose. The stage was set. He then invited his unfortunate brother-in-law, an invalid, to dinner on 20 Nov. 1850. Having sent the servants away, he suddenly threw himself on the victim, overpowered him, and then, when his brother-in-law lay on the ground, poured (with or without the help of the Countess) the nicotine into the victim's throat, thereby bringing about fulminant death but nearly causing the Count's doom, some of the poison having spilled in his own face. The Crown was fortunate enough to obtain the services of one of the greatest chemists of the day: Jean-Servais Stas (1813-1891). Stas not only accomplished the feat of detecting the nicotine in the dead man's body, but worked out the whole method for the identification of alkaloids, by the process which now bears his name. Stas's evidence was so overwhelming that Orfila, though he attended the trial, declined to give evidence for the defense.

This major discovery by Stas led to a painful incident which has since been entirely cleared up by the historians of medicine(18-22). Orfila, who had heard of the sensational murder in Belgium shortly after its committal and knew of the identification of the poison by Stas, wrote to the latter immediately, pretending he wanted to obtain technical information destined for the fifth edition of his treatise on toxicology. Once in possession of the information, he hastily published a modified version of Stas's method, taking advantage of the fact that the latter was tongue-tied by the forthcoming trial. An unpleasant polemic ensued which was given much publicity at the time. Orfila having been caught redhanded, so to speak, had his great reputation somewhat tarnished at the very end of his career. Stas's discovery of the method for the detection of alkaloids is no doubt one of the major contributions of the nineteenth century to forensic toxicology.

Another outstanding man in that remarkable period of scientific advance, was Lambert-Adolphe-Jacques Quetelet, citizen of the city of Ghent (1796-1874). Quetelet was one of the greatest statisticians of the 19th century(23). A great friend of England, he was a member of the Royal Society and belonged, in fact, to the group of young Turks who founded the Royal

Statistical Society of Britain(24). Two great achievements have immortalized his name. The first is his treatise entitled *Physique Sociale*, the first edition of which appeared in 1835. It is a quantitative study of man and of human activities, heralding the new science of sociology of which he was the founder. As far back as 1828(25) and 1831(26) he also published statistical studies on crime, and the second edition of *Physique Sociale*, which was published in 1869(27), embodied a wealth of information on this subject. This treatise inspired no less a person than Florence Nightingale(28). Her letters to Quetelet are now much treasured relics, as are also those he himself wrote to H.R.H. the Duke of Saxe-Coburg-Gotha, the future husband of Queen Victoria (of whom he had been preceptor) on the theory of probabilities applied to moral and political sciences. It is, however, his monumental work entitled *Anthropométrie ou mesure des différentes facultés de l'homme*(29) which has the most direct bearing on forensic sciences. It is to Quetelet that the credit goes for having applied, to biology in general and to anthropometry in particular, the law of Laplace-Gauss and for having made an attempt to develop an archtype of the human being, the famous "homme moyen" or "average man." The so-called Law of Quetelet was to be the keystone on which Bertillon later based his classic system of identification(30).

In the meantime, the study of asphyxia had made giant strides from both the chemical and the morbid anatomy approach, with such outstanding men as the chemist Felix Leblanc and the medicolegalist Tardieu. To the former we owe the description of carbon monoxide poisoning as early as 1842(31). Ambroise Tardieu (1818-1879), a pupil of Orfila, curiously enough immortalized his name by the description of the petechia which bear his name, notwithstanding the fact that they had already been fully described by H. Bayard in a case of infanticide in 1847(32), as Tardieu himself reluctantly admitted(33).

From this time on the story of the forensic sciences, at least on the continent of Europe, identifies itself increasingly more with a very few Schools which rose progressively, so to speak, from the ground up in large cities such as Paris (1795), Vienna (1804). Berlin (1850), etc—the places where they were most needed. Their prestige was ensured from the start by their total intellectual independence and their universally accepted reputation of absolute integrity under all circumstances, thanks to which they successfully survived a succession of political upheavals and much clashing of swords. I will not attempt to retrace their respective histories, a task which has already been achieved by men better placed to do so, such as L. Dérobert and V. Balthazard(34). F. Reuter(35), L. Breitenecker(36), and W. Krauland(37).

Special tribute must be paid to Austria at this stage which, by its fundamental contributions, must be considered as the cradle of the forensic sciences. Humanity owes a tremendous debt of gratitude to that country for the outstanding achievements of so many of its citizens—Carl von Rokitansky, E. von Hofmann, A. Kolisko, A. Haberda, J. Wagner Jauregg (Nobel prize in 1927), Hans Gross, Sigmund Freud, K. Landsteiner (Nobel prize in 1930), S. Jellinek, and others—whose names have now become household words and who each, directly or indirectly, brought a major contribution to the advancement of the forensic sciences.

I cannot refrain from dwelling a little longer on the special merits of the mastermind of the Vienna School: E. von Hofmann. ["von Hofmann" is written with one "f" only, since he was Czech by birth and not German (personal communication of Professor W. Holczabec to the author).] Because of his exceptional qualifications he had been wisely called from Prague to Vienna in 1875 and appointed to the leading chair of legal medicine of the Empire. It is quite unnecessary to dwell on the overwhelming responsibilities often imposed upon the forensic expert at a moment's notice and when least expected. That is precisely what happened to von Hofmann when, on the 30th of January, 1889, the heir to the throne of the Austro-Hungarian Empire, Archduke Rudolf, took his own life at Mayerling after having shot his mistress, Baroness Maria Vetsera. It is superfluous to evoke the story in detail, since it has been excellently retraced in D.A. Crown's recent paper(38). I differ with the latter author when, on p. 339, he casts aspersions at von Hofmann and his colleagues for having expressed the view that the abnormalities of the skull of the Prince justified the conclusion the latter was mentally disturbed at the time. I don't see why this explanation should necessarily be presented as nonsense. That, of course, is a matter of opinion. And I would like to seize this occasion to remind the reader that the implications of premature closure of sutures and other causes of intracranial hypertension at present know a renewal of interest. The Mayerling affair had far-reaching consequences. The Catholic Church, through Cardinal Rampolla, at first denied the prince a religious burial on consecrated ground, only changing its mind belatedly. The Emperor remembered this terrible slight when, at the death of Pope Leon XIII, in 1903, Rampolla was on the point of being appointed his successor. The Emperor actually availed himself of his right of veto and another candidate had to be sought.

The incredible sufferings of the ill-fated imperial family of the Habsburgs could easily fill a chapter of a textbook. One now tends to forget that they were to have incalculable political repercussions and, in fact, actually changed the face of the world. On 4 May 1897 the princess of Alenson, sister of Elisabeth, Empress of Austria, perished in the historic fire of the "Bazar de la Charité" (a fancy fair) along with the flower of French nobility. This was the occasion for O. Amoëdo (1897)(39) to lay the basis of "forensic odontology." The victims, it must be remembered, were among the few in those days who could afford dental care. On the 10th of September, 1898, in Geneva, Empress Elisabeth herself was stabbed by an anarchist, when she was about to step aboard one of the picturesque white steamers which cruise the peaceful Lake Leman. The wound, caused by a shoemaker's awl, seemed only superficial. The Empress went aboard. The ship departed but, to everybody's amazement, it soon after turned round and made for the harbor at full speed. Elisabeth was already dead. She had succumbed to a hemopericardium. This drama nearly led to war between Austria and Switzerland. Finally, on 28 June 1914, Archduke Franz-Ferdinand, who was to succeed to Franz-Joseph who was left without an heir by the death of his son

Rudolf, was shot dead at Sarajevo. This tragedy was to have incalculable consequences, as it triggered World War I.

The merits of von Hofmann, however, are not limited to the unraveling of what we now call headline cases. His major claim to gratitude of his contemporaries is that of having clarified once and for all the tragic subject of sudden death. He himself wrote a fundamental paper on its causes in 1884(40), thereby clearing the way for A. Kolisko, whose monumental treatise (it covers 795 pages) remains the most authoritative book ever written on the subject(41). This breathtaking piece of work never received the recognition it deserved, simply because it was published on the eve of World War I.

Professor Holczabec informed me that von Hofmann mentioned coronary occlusion in his routine autopsy procedures, a fact which seems to have escaped the attention of the historians of medicine. I have not found it mentioned in Leibowitz's recent monograph (42). Von Hofmann also described death from rupture of tubal pregnancy as far back as 1888, suggesting then the possibility of salvation by surgery.

I would like, at this stage, to put on record parenthetically a number of spectacular discoveries which, during the second half of the 19th century, were to have providential repercussions for the welfare of mankind. If, in 1873, E.K. Abbe of Iena(43) had not, at the initiative of Carl Zeiss, invented the condensor of the microscope and, in 1878, with Stephenson, given it its finishing touch by the added improvement of oil immersion, biology would have had to wait much longer before unraveling the well-guarded secrets of nature and the hygienists would have had to grope in the dark still further in their search for the causal agents of infectious diseases. The interdependence of scientific disciplines was becoming more obvious from day to day. Abbe's discovery had opened unlimited horizons to modern bacteriology and Robert Koch rightly paid tribute to this great physicist, his compatriot, when he underlined the immense debt of gratitude science owed him. Hence, as was to be expected, famous Schools rose in Paris, Berlin, and other centers.

Because of this 1894 proved, in its turn, to be a very fruitful year for science. Jules Bordet (1870-1961), who had just finished his medical studies in Brussels and was only 24 years old, was sent to the Pasteur Institute of Paris with a Belgian Government Fellowship and entrusted to the tutorship of E. Metchnikoff. In only one year a series of breath-taking discoveries in the field of fundamental immunology ensued, among many others the discovery of the *complement system* (1895), which heralded the entry of the test tube in the biological laboratory and the ultimate triumph of *in vitro* techniques, for which Bordet shares the honor with a handful of his contemporaries. His subsequent discoveries of the specificity of hemolytic sera and of the biochemical specificity of proteins in the different species (1898) led straight to the introduction of the serodiagnosis in forensic medicine, to which Paul Uhlenhuth was to dedicate his whole life. Uhlenhuth(44) expressed himself in the following terms on the subject: "Bordet fand dann weiterhin, dass sich auch nach Einspritzung von *Kuhmilch* im Blutserum Vom Kaninchen *Präcipitine* bilden, welche das Casein der

Kuhmilch ausfällen." (Bordet further discovered that, after injection of cow's milk to rabbits, a precipitin is formed in the blood serum, which has the property of precipitating cow milk casein.) Bordet, whose centenary has just been commemorated, was awarded the Nobel prize in 1919(45).

To measure at their real value the merits of these pioneers, it is indispensable to bear in mind the appalling conditions in which they had to work. Dr. R.B.H. Gradwohl actually told me that Metchnikoff, who needed monkeys for his experiments but could not afford to buy them, relied on the friendship of sailors for his supply.

Among the flow of discoveries which marked the end of the 19th century, yet another one deserves being rescued from oblivion. When, in 1894, P. Mégnin published his classic monograph entitled *La Faune des Cadavres*(46) in which he proved convincingly that the onslaught of insects on human remains tends to occur in a definite sequence, he provided a valuable new means of assessing the time of death. Though it was, in fact, not his discovery, Orfila having already noted the phenomenon, Mégnin provided the first comprehensive study of the subject. Mégnin's contribution undoubtedly inspired my compatriot M. Leclercq, when he wrote the chapter on the entomology of the cadaver in his excellent book in English(47).

It was at this time (1895) that Bacillus botulinus was discovered in my native country by one of my predecessors, E. van Ermengem, in the course of a purely medicolegal investigation(48).

Among the many citizens of Italy who contributed to the greatness of their fatherland in those days, I will only select one, Cesare Lombroso (1836-1909), the founder of criminal anthropology(49). As is the case for most pioneers, his life was a constant uphill struggle and he did not live quite long enough to be awarded the laurels he so richly deserved. Among the many criticisms leveled at him was the reproach that his doctrine was solely based on anatomical characteristics. His detractors ignored the fact that the basic knowledge one had to rely on in those days was very limited indeed, and that the time had yet to come when, for instance, the laws of Mendel would at last take their place in the panoply of biological sciences and help to clarify many problems. The state of mind which then prevailed is exemplified by the discourteous exclamation (recorded by Lombroso's nephew) by his arch opponent, the Franciscan A. Gemelli, after Lombroso's death: "I funerali di un uomo et di una dottrina" (the funeral of a man and of his doctrine)(50). Times have, however, changed for the better. The chromosomes now have their say in the matter and such feelings belong to a distant past. The name of Lombroso now again shines in the firmament of the criminological sciences.

The forensic sciences in Holland have always been reduced to the role of poor parent, in sharp contrast to the other forms of scientific endeavor, which have permanently flourished. A noteworthy contribution from that country must, however, be put on record. In 1899 the Dutch free lance, M.L.Q. van Ledden Hulsebosch, published his classic atlas(51) on human excrements, a mine of information for the criminalist on the microscopical structure of all imaginable nutriments during their transit through the gastrointestinal tract.

In passing, I would like to put on record that Christiaan Eijkman, who shared the Nobel prize in 1929 with Fr. G. Hopkins for their fundamental work on vitamins, was professor of hygiene and *forensic* medicine from 1898 to 1928 at the University of Utrecht, and that H.F. Roll, a Dutch pupil of A. Kolisko, is the author of one of the best treatises on legal medicine ever written. It is entitled *Leerboek der Gerechtelijke Geneeskunde voor de Scholen tot Opleiding van Indische Artsen* and, as the title emphasizes, was more particularly destined for the native doctors of the Dutch East Indies. The first edition was published in 1908-1912, in Batavia(52), and covered 1056 pages. A revised second edition was published in Holland in 1918-1927(53), and is a classic in that country.

One would be tempted to think that events in the field of the forensic sciences would, from now onwards, move quickly. Actually this was not the case. The reason must be sought in a certain reluctance on the part of forensic scientists to trust any spectacular discovery before they were absolutely convinced of its reliability. This is probably the reason why the stupendous discovery of the blood groups in 1900, by K. Landsteiner, only found its real forensic echo nearly a quarter of a century later, although it had long since triumphed in clinical medicine. Perhaps it is because of the first world war that the so-called forensic serology only started getting under way so late, notwithstanding the fact von Dongen and L. Hirschfeld had already provided the proof of the Mendelian heredity of blood groups in 1910, thereby definitively opening the way for the scientific investigation of disputed paternity. World War II likewise retarded the beneficial consequences for mankind of the momentous discovery by Landsteiner and Wiener, in 1940, of the Rhesus factor, which in due course was to ensure further headway in forensic serology(54, 55).

It may be wise to remember that scientific firearms identification also came into being soon after the turn of the century. It was the outcome of magnificent research by a handful of pioneers whose respective merits have been duly recalled by the present author in a previous paper(56).

I will not dwell on the more recent advances in the field of the forensic sciences in general, since information is readily available in all textbooks and journals and the subject will be dealt with by colleagues much more qualified than I to acquit themselves of the task. Suffice it to say that, whereas the underlying basic principles laid down in the past remain unchallenged, progress nowadays is essentially linked to the staggering improvement of equipment, which has completely changed the outlook of our laboratories.

Before ending, I will review briefly a few notorious trials, some of which turned into deplorable miscarriages of justice. The events narrated now belong to the histories of the nations where they occurred. Some undoubtedly convey a message to the forensic expert of today. I will not examine in detail the trial of Socrates, in 399 B.C. The scanty information available reached us mostly through Plato and may be distorted. All we know for certain is that Socrates was condemned to death by poisoning and forced to drink a concoction of hemlock. He accepted the verdict with exemplary resignation. Before dying he presented characteristic symptoms which have been described with remarkable precision by Plato(57).

We are better informed about the trial of Galileo in 1633. He was then nearly seventy. That poor astronomer was severely condemned by the Tribunal of the Inquisition on the serious charge of having confirmed, in his writings, the Copernican theory of gravitation!

Quite involuntarily Marc-Antoine Calas, of Toulouse, when he committed suicide by hanging on 13 Oct. 1761, contributed directly to the atmosphere which was to trigger the French Revolution a few years later. The tragedy which ensued originated from the family having committed the classic, if understandable, mistake of attempting to disguise a typical suicide, precisely the sort of situation with which every forensic expert is conversant nowadays. Jean Calas, the youth's father, a Calvinist, confessed under torture to a crime he had obviously not committed, and was condemned to the wheel on the charge of having killed his own son because the latter intended to abjure his father's religion. This scandalous miscarriage of justice provided Voltaire, exiled at the time in Geneva, a unique opportunity to exercise his redoubtable talents as polemist in the defense of a just cause, thereby helping to dig the grave of the French monarchy(58). The abridged story can be found in Ref. 59.

The execution of the Duke of Enghien at Vincennes, after a mock trial, on the night of 20-21 March 1804 (he had been kidnapped by the emissaries of Napoleon five days before), has always been considered a major political blunder on the part of the Emperor. At the end of his life, Napoleon was aware that this incident would tarnish his legend in the eyes of posterity and, on his deathbed in St. Helena, he took great pains to justify it in a codicil to his will. To my knowledge this sordid crime has never raised any forensic problem whatsoever and I will leave it at that.

The notorious "Affaire Dreyfus," at the end of the nineteenth century, was, on the contrary, to put the forensic sciences of those days very much in the foreground but to do them grievous harm(60). The drama is universally known. For our purpose it can be summed up as follows. In September 1894 a secret message, the historical "bordereau," was recovered from a wastebasket at the German Embassy, by French counterespionage. Amateur handwriting experts came to the conclusion it had been written by Captain Alfred Dreyfus, a probationer on the General Staff. The document was therefore submitted to a commission of three "qualified" experts. Alphonse Bertillon, who had already been entrusted with making some photographic enlargements of it in his position as Head of the Criminal Identification Department, was invited to join the group. Whereas the first three experts disagreed in their conclusions, Bertillon surprisingly enough (see further) imputed the handwriting to the unfortunate officer. He was never to change his mind at any moment throughout his life. Only much later was it discovered that it was not Dreyfus at all but a certain M.C.F.W. Esterhazy who was the culprit but, in the meantime, Dreyfus had been condemned to imprisonment for life in a fortress, deprivation of rank, and degradation and he was deported to Devil's Island accordingly. His sufferings there have been put on record by others. Under incessant pressure of public opinion, Dreyfus was retried in 1899, to be again condemned, though more lightly. Only in 1906, on the basis of new evidence, which included this time the confession of Esterhazy himself, was Dreyfus fully rehabilitated.

Practically the entire responsibility for this historical miscarriage of justice rested on the shoulders of Bertillon. The latter had resorted to probabilistic methods, probably inspired by Quetelet's treatises, but he had applied them in the wrong way. In 1904 the High Court had, in despair, turned to the "Académie des Sciences" which, at the Court's request, picked out three of its most eminent members, one of whom was no other than Henri Poincaré, the greatest French mathematician of his century and professor of the calculus of probabilities at the Sorbonne. Their evidence was absolutely devastating for Bertillon. The reader will find the dramatic story in Locard's(61) fascinating appraisal of Bertillon's report and of his true role in the "Affaire" and how the unfortunate pioneer of identification got involved against his better judgment. We know Bertillon had warned, in all honesty, that he had no personal experience with questioned documents. He apparently changed his mind in due course, thus becoming the principal artisan of a historical tragedy that brought his country to the brink of revolution and that had, moreover, incalculable long-range consequences. It is universally recognized today that this unbearable iniquity and the hostile state of mind towards Jews in general prevailing at the time in France, triggered Zionism, of which Theodore Herzl was to become the mastermind and the symbol. It is indeed reassuring for the welfare of humanity that civilized people should always have been infinitely sensitive to any form of injustice!

Regrettably enough, the masterly report of Henri Poincaré and his colleagues(62), which covers 123 pages, was never given the attention it deserved. The page was turned and, with World War I in the air, everybody in France was beginning to realize that still graver issues lay ahead. As a matter of fact, only the conclusions were ever produced in Court. Now that passions are subdued, it would be well worth while to give this historic forensic monument the dissemination it deserves, so as to make available the many teachings it conveys. With the help of our colleague, Miss Suzanne Hotimsky of Paris, I recently raised it from its dusty lair in the French Ministry of Justice, where it was safely tucked away. It is now at everyone's disposal.

The tumultuous course of the "Affaire" was highlighted by a number of tragedies (including two suicides) in true Italian operatic style for which Brouardel, professor of legal medicine in Paris, or one of his colleagues, had to be called in(63). The events culminated on the evening of 16 Feb. 1899 with the sudden death of the President of the French Republic, Felix Faure, who was 58 years old, from an attack during a gallant rendezvous with a young lady who uttered a loud scream and thereupon fled by the back door. Public opinion wrongly connected his demise with the Dreyfus case. That same afternoon the President had received the reigning Prince of Monaco, Albert, who had come to speak to him in favor of Dreyfus. Dreyfus's enemies went as far as insinuating that Albert had presented the President with a poisoned cigar. The story makes fascinating reading(64).

Mathematical probability was used for the first time in evidence on striation matching in a Belgian court in a 1929 headline case(65,66). Basic data, mostly from the USA, have now ensured everywhere the entry in Court of probabilistic methods in the evaluation of legal evidence.

A feature common to nearly all miscarriages of justice or alleged ones is that the catastrophe could have been so easily avoided. Prevention in general, however, postulates the firm conviction that, when a case turns up, one never can know beforehand in what one is getting involved and whether or not it will be easy going; hence, it is an imperious necessity to call in the right man at the right time, that is, from the very start, and not when irretrievable harm has already been wrought. But mankind is incorrigible by nature. This sort of thing has been going on for ages everywhere, with eternally the same consequences (sometimes of stupendous magnitude), as is borne out by the examples cited above. There is no reason to think it will stop.

Among the more recent examples, the first which comes to one's mind is the notorious Marie Besnard case, which caused so much commotion in France some twenty years ago. The widow Besnard was accused in 1949 of having poisoned, by means of arsenic, most of the members of her family and also some friends, 13 persons in all, including her mother. She underwent five years of preventive imprisonment, three successive trials, and was eventually acquitted in 1961. The investigation had promised in the beginning to be easy going because of the number of victims. Unfortunately, the wrong people were called in to deal with it. By the time competent experts took over, the case was hopelessly lost, with most damaging and undeserved consequences for the reputation of French toxicology. Perhaps the only consolation was of a scientific character, namely that the case shed new (if disquieting) light on the possible behavior of arsenic in bodies buried in the earth. Much has been published since in France on this important subject, mostly in the *Annales de Médecine légale* and in the *Annales des Falsifications et de l'Expertise Chimique*.

The same slovenliness marked the beginning of the Montesi investigation in Italy and led to the same disastrous consequences. The body of Wilma Montesi, an Italian girl of sixteen, was discovered on the beach of Tor Vaianica, near Rome, on the morning of the 11 April 1953(67). The cause of her death was never satisfactorily determined because the first autopsy had been bungled(68). The case became irretrievable and the whole affair degenerated into a notorious political scandal which shook the country and caused much ill feeling.

Our English friends also had their troubles recently with the Evans case, which is still in everybody's mind. If one can give credence to the four books successively dedicated to it, one cannot but help fearing the worst(69-72). The case has all the appearances of a grievous miscarriage of justice and led to the abolishment of the death penalty. It is worthy of notice that at no time did pertinent criticism bear on its forensic implications. This is in no way surprising. Legal medicine, chemical toxicology, and the forensic sciences in the more restricted sense of the word have always been at their best in Great Britain. Such outstanding scientists as A.S. Taylor, Thomas Stevenson, H. Littlejohn, Sydney Smith, J. Glaister, B. Spilsbury, W. Wilcox, L.C. Nicholls, and many others, only to speak of the dead, all deserved well of their country and, though a biographer has from time to time recorded their achievements—accomplished, so to speak, with their bare hands—there still is a need for a more ambitious survey of their contributions considered collectively. This task, however, should preferably be undertaken by an English historian of medicine.

The list of alleged miscarriages of justice and other forensic muddles is interminable but I will stop here. The reader will find a whole array in Thorwald's books(73,74), which are an inexhaustible mine of information.

At a time when it seems the most normal thing in the world that events should move fast, I end by expressing the hope that those who do me the honor of reading this paper will measure the magnitude of the effort it cost our forefathers to lay the foundations on which we ourselves are now building, with less suffering than was theirs. I apologize if, in my endeavor, I have laid too much stress on the contribution of my own country and of its neighbors. As a matter of fact, as I understand, it was part of my mission.

SUMMARY

In this paper I have attempted to review, in chronological order, the respective merits of the men of science who, in the past centuries and more particularly from the Renaissance to the second world war, in 1939, have played a significant part in the advancement of the forensic sciences. Some of these pioneers are giants whose immortal names are landmarks in the memorial of mankind. Their contribution to the forensic sciences, it must be emphasized, was often completely overshadowed by their great discoveries. Others, less fortunate apparently, are now entirely forgotten, though they, too, have major contributions to their credit. Not all of them were, by any means, primarily interested in our field of endeavor; their participation in forensic work was sometimes of a purely fleeting character.

My primary concern was to repair, as much as possible, the harm wrought by the two world wars—especially the first—to the diffusion of information, and to give their due to men who deserve much credit for their achievements. To measure the real value of the extent of their merits, it is indispensable to keep in mind the precarious conditions in which they had to work.

The paper ends with comments on a number of historical tragedies and more or less recent miscarriages of justice, some with far-reaching consequences. The features the cases have in common are stressed and the message they convey to the forensic expert of today is discussed.

NOTES

(1) Burggraeve, Ad., *Etudes sur André Vésale*, C. Annoot-Braeckman, Gand, 1841.

(2) Ad Quartum Centenarium Annum Andreae Vesalii Defuncti, Commémoration solennelle du quatrième Centenaire de la mort d'André Vésale, Académie Royale de Médecine de Belgique, Brussels, 19-24 Oct. 1964.

(3) Fredericq, L,. "André Vésale" *Mémoires de la Societé Royale des Sciences de Liège, 42 série*, Vol. 6, 1942, p. 350.

(4) Heger, P., "Notes sure André Vésale," *Revue de l'Université de Bruxelles*, December 1903, pp. 24-25.

(5) Muller, M., "La Médecine Légale au temps d'Ambroise Paré," *Archives de l'Institut de Médecine Légale et de Médecine Sociale de Lille* No. 1, 1954, p. 33.

(6) Paré, A., *Oeuvres complètes*, J.-F Malgaigne, Ed., Vols. I-III, J.-B. Baillière, Paris, 1840-1841.

(7) Michelet, L., *La vie d'Ambroise Parè* Librairie Le Francois, Paris, 1930, pp. 38-39.

(8) Zacchias, P., *Quaestiones Medico-legales*, Vols. I-III, Germani Nanty, Lugduni, 1674.

(9) Hoffman, M., "Die Lehre vom plötzlichen Tod in Lancisis Werk 'De subitaneis Mortibus'," *Abhandlungen zur Geschichte der Medizin und der Naturwissenschafte*, No. 6, 1935, pp. 1-62.

(10) Zeldenrust, J., *Gerechtelijke Geneeskunde* Stafleu's Wtenschappelijke Uitgeversmaatschappij N.V., Leiden, 1966, p. 237.

(11) Schreyer, J., *Erörterung und Erläuterung der Frage: Ob es ein gewiss Zeichen, wenn eines todten Kindes Lunge im Wasser untersincket, dass solches in Mutterleibe gestorben sey?*, Chr. Hendeln, Halle, 1745.

(12) Morgagni, G.B., *De Sedibus et Causis Morborum per Anatomen Indagatis Libri Quinque*, Remondiana, Padua, 1761.

(13) Morgagni, G.B., *The Seats and Causes of Diseases*, B. Alexander, Trans., Vols. I-III, Millar & Cadell, London, 1769; abridged and elucidated by William Cooke, Vols. I and II, Longmans, London, 1822 (cited by J.O. Leibowitz).

(14) Bouchardon, P., *Le crime du chateau de Bitremont*, Albin Michel, Paris, 1925.

(15) *Procès du Comte et de la Comtesse de Bocarmé*, Deghistelle, Charleroi, 1851.

(16) *Procès du Comte et de la Comtesse de Bocarmé devant la Cour d'assises du Hainaut*, Leroux, Mons, 1851.

(17) Fayol, A., *La vie et l'oeuvre d'Orfila*, Albin Michel, Paris, 1930.

(18) Stas, J.S., "Recherches médico-légales sur la nicotine, suivies de quelques considérations sur la manière générale de déceler les alcalis organiques dans le cas d'empoisonnement," *Bulletin de l'Académie Royale de Médecine de Belgique, I^e série*, Vol. 11, 1851-52, p. 202.

(19) "Lettre de M. Orfila, Discussion," *Bulletin de l'Académie Royale de Médecine de Belgique, I^e série*, Vol. 11, 1851-52, p. 362.

(20) Stas, J.S., "Réponse de M. Stas à la lettre adressée par M. Orfila à l'Académie Royale de Médecine de Belgique concernant la découverte de la nicotine dans le cas d'empoisonnement. Discussion," *Bulletin de l'Académie Royale de Médecine de Belgique, I^e série*, Vol. 11, 1851-52, p. 369.

(21) Pasquier, V., "Dela priorité entre MM. Orfila et Stas. Des moyens de deceler la nicotine dans les empoisonnements," *Bulletin de l'Académie Royale de Médecine de Belgique, le série*, Vol. 12, 1852-53, p. 579.

(22) "Discussion du rapport de la Commission chargée d'apprécier le différend qui s'est élevé entre MM. Stas et Orfila à propos de la recherche de la Nicotine dans les organes humains," *Bulletin de l'Académie Royale de Médecine de Belgique, I^e série*, Vol. 12, 1852-53, p. 990.

(23) Mailly, E., *Essai sur la vie et les ouvrages de L.-A.-J. Quetelet*, J. Hayez, Imprimeur, Brussels, 1875.

(24) Martin, L., *Journal of the Royal Statistical Society, Series A*, Vol. 124, 1961, p. 540.

(25) Quetelet, A., "Recherches statistiques sur le royaume des Pays-Bas," *Nouveaux mémoires de l'Académie des Sciences*, Vol. 5, 1828, p. 90.

(26) Quetelet, A., "Recherches sur le penchant au crime au différents ages," *Mémoires de l'Académie des Sciences*, Vol. 7, 1831, p. 87.

(27) Quetelet, A., *Physique Sociale ou essai sur le développement des facultés de l'homme*, 2nd ed, Vols. I and II, C. Muquardt, Brussels, J.-B. Baillière, Paris, and J. Issakoff, St. Petersburg, 1869.

(28) Martin, L., "Notice sur une lettre écrite par Florence Nightingale à Adolphe Quetelet en 1872," *Revue de l'Association des Médecines sortis de l'Université Libre de Bruxelles*, 1951.

(29) Quetelet, A., *Anthropométrie ou mesure des différentes facultés de l'homme*, C. Muquardt, Brussels, Gand, Leipzig, 1871.

(30) Bertillon, A., *Identification anthropométrique. Instructions signalétiques*, 2nd ed, Imprimerie administrative, Melun, 8°, 1893, p. XXXV of the Introduction.

(31) Leblanc, F., "Recherches sur la composition de l'air confiné," *Annales de Chimie et de Physique*, Tome 5, Series 3, 1842, pp. 223-268.

(32) Bayard, H., "Considérations médico-légales sur l'avortement provoqué et sur l'infanticide," *Annales d'hygiène publique et de médecine légale*, Vol. 37, 1847, pp. 455-456.

(33) Tardieu, A., *Etude médico-légale sur la pendaison, la strangulation et la suffocation*, Librairie J.-B. Baillière et fils, Paris, 1879, p. 266.

(34) Dérobert, L., "Petit historique de la Médecine légale en France et à Paris," *Paris Médical*, n°s 44-45, 1941, pp. 158-165; Balthazard, V. and DéRobert, L., *Histoire de la Médecine légale*, Vol. 3 in *Histoire Générale de la Médecine, de la Pharmacie, de l'Art Dentaire et de l'Art Vétérinaire*, Albin Michel, Paris, 1949 (published under the direction of Professuer Laignel-Lavastine).

(35) Reuter, F., "Geschichte der Wiener Lehrkanzel für gerichtliche Medizin von 1804-1954," *Beiträge zur gerichtlichen Medizin*, Vol. 19, Supplement, 1954, pp. 1-78.

(36) Breitenecker, L., "160 Jahre Lehrkanzel für gerichtliche Medizin in Wien," *Beiträge zur gerichtilichen Medizin*, Vol. 23, 1965, pp. 21-43; "Osterreichische Hochschulzeitung, 16. Jahrgang Nr. 13, 1 July 1964, pp. 1-2.

(37) Krauland, W., "Zur Geschichte der deutschen Gesellschaft fur Gerichtliche Medizin," *Beiträge zur Gerichtlichen Medizin*, Vol. 27, 1970, pp. 16-26.

(38) Crown, D. A., "Historical Research, Document Examination and Crown Prince Rudolph of Austria," *Journal of Forensic Sciences*, JFSCA, Vol. 11, 1966, p. 339.

(39) Amoedo, O., "The role of the dentists in the identification of the victims of the catastrophe of the 'Bazar de la Charité,'" *Dental Cosmos*, Vol. 39, 4 May 1897, pp. 905-912.

(40) Von Hofmann, E., cited by Reuter, F. (Ref 35), *Beiträge zur gerichtlichen Medizin*, Vol. 19, Supplement, 1954, p. 18.

(41) Kolisko, A., *Plötzlicher Tod aus Natürlicher Ursache, in Dittrich's Handbuch der Arztlichen Sachverständigen-Tätigkeit*, Vol. 11, Urban & Schwarzenberg, Berlin and Wien, 1913, pp. 701-1496.

(42) Leibowitz, J. O., *The History of Coronary Heart Disease*, Wellcome Institute of the History of Medicine, London, 1970.

(43) Abbe, E., "Ueber einen neuen Beleuchtungsapparat am Mikroskop," *Archiv für Mikroskopische Anatomie*, Vol. 9, 1873, pp. 469-480.

(44) Uhlenhuth, P., "Uber die Entwicklung des biologischen Eiweissdifferenzierungsverfahrens im Dienste der gerichtlichen Medizin unter besonderer Berücksichtigung eigener Forschungsergebnisse (Persönliche Erinnerungen)," *Deutsche Zeitschrift für die gesamte gerichtliche Medizin*, Vol. 39, 1948-1949, p. 312.

(45) "Célébration du Centenaire de la Naissance de Jules Bordet (1870-1961)," *Mémoires de l'Académie Royale de Médecine de Belgique*, Vol. 7, No. 6, 1972, pp. 317-453. (The bulk of Bordet's research is to be found in the *Annales de l'Institut Pasteur* of the turn of the century.)

(46) Mégnin, P., *La Faune des Cadavres. Application de l'Entomologie à la Médecine Légale*, Masson and Gauthier-Villars, Paris, 1894.

(47) Leclercq, M., *Entomological Parasitology—The Relations between Entomology and the Medical Sciences*, Pergamon Press, New York, 1969, Chapter 7, pp. 128-142.

(48) Thomas, F., "Milestones in Forensic Medicine: The Belgian Contribution," *Medicine, Science and the Law*, Vol. 4, 1964, pp. 155-170.

(49) Lacassagne, A., "Cesare Lombroso (1836-1909)," *Archives d'Anthropologie Criminelle*, Vol. 24, 1909, pp. 881-894.

(50) Lattes, L., "Retour à Lombroso," *Revue médicale de Liege*, Vol. 12, 1957, p. 42 (footnote).

(51) Van Ledden Hulsebosch, M. L. Q., *Makro- und mikroskopische Diagnostik der Menschlichen Exkremente*, Verlag von J. Springer, Berlin, 1899.

(52) Roll, H. F., *Leerboek der Gerechtelijke Geneeskunde*, Landsdrukkerij, Batavia, 1908.

(53) Roll, H. F., *Leerboek der Gerechtelijke Geneeskunde voor de Scholen tot Opleiding van Indische Artsen*, Ter Algemeene Landsdrukkerij, 's Gravenhage, 1927.

(54) Prokop, O., "Karl Landsteiner zum Gedächtnis," *Beiträge zur Gerichtlichen Medizin*, Vol. 26, 1969, p. 141.

(55) Holzer, F. J., "Persönliche Erinnerungen an Karl Landsteiner," *Beiträge zur Gerichtlichen Medizin*, Vol. 26, 1969, p. 147.

(56) Thomas, F., "Comments on the Discovery of Striation Matching and on Early Contributions to Forensic Firearms Identification," *Journal of Forensic Sciences*, JFSCA, Vol. 12, 1967, pp. 1-7.

(57) Brouardel, P., *Les Empoisonnements criminels et accidentels*, J.-B. Baillière et fils, Paris, 1902, p. 19.

(58) Voltaire, *Traité sur la tolérance à l'occasion de la mort de Jean Calas, nouveaux mélanges philosophiques historiques*, 1772 edition, Tome 32, Part 2, p. 30.

(59) Thomas, F. and Cleymaet, G., "Introduction à l'Histoire de la Médecine légale plus spécialement envisagée du point de vue belge," *Revue de Droit Pénal et de Criminologie*, 1947, pp. 406-430.

(60) Charpentier, A., *The Dreyfus Case*, Geoffrey Bles, London, 1935.

(61) Locard, E., *L'Affaire Dreyfus et l'expertise de documents écrits*, J. Desvigne et Cie., Lyon, 1937, pp. 17-66.

(62) *Affaire Dreyfus, Rapport de Messieurs les Experts Darboux, Appell, Poincaré*, Archives Nationales, Paris, 2 Aug. 1904.

(63) Reinach, J., *Histoire de l'Affaire Dreyfus, Vol. 3, Procès-verbal d'autopsie*, Librairie Charpentier et Fasquelle, Paris, 1903, pp. 643-651.

(64) Reinach, J., *Histoire de l'Affaire Dreyfus*, Vol. 4, Librairie Charpentier et Fasquelle, Paris, 1904, Chapter 7, "Mort de Felix Faure," pp. 546-554.

(65) De Rechter, G., "Affaire de Beernem. Identification du marteau ayant servi d'instrument du crime," *Revue de Droit Pénal et de Criminologie*, 1929, p. 1121.

(66) Remy, M. and Sintair, *Le crime de Beernem*, S. Vancampenhout, Brussels, 1929.

(67) "Affaire Montesi (Indictment)," *Archivio Penale*, Vol. 11, Part 2, 1955, p. 342.

(68) Pellegrini, R., *Il Caso Montesi*, Casa Editrice Guanda, Parma, 1954.

(69) Eddowes, M., *The man on your conscience. An investigation of the Evans Murder Trial*, Cassell and Company Ltd., London, 1955.

(70) Tennyson, Jesse F., *Trials of Timothy John Evans and John Reginald Halliday Christie*, William Hodge and Company, Ltd., London, Edinburgh, and Glasgow, 1957.

(71) Kennedy, L., *Ten Rillington Place*, Victor Gollancz Ltd., London, 1961.

(72) Kennedy, L., *Ten Rillington Place*, Panther Books Ltd., London, 1971.

(73) Thorwald, J., *Das Jahrhundert der Detektive. Weg und Abenteuer der Kriminalistik*, Droemersche Verlagsanstalt A. G., Zürich, 1965.

(74) Thorwald, J., *Die Stunde der Detektive. Werden und Welten der Kriminalistik*, Droemersche Verlagsanstalt A. G., Zürich, 1966.

SCIENTIFIC CRIME DETECTION

LABORATORIES IN EUROPE

Calvin Goddard

When in the summer of 1929, the establishment of the Scientific Crime Detection Laboratory of Chicago had become a fact, and its affiliation with Northwestern University duly consummated, the question arose as to how it should be patterned, i.e., just what fields of activity it should enter, the staff necessary to exploit these fields adequately and efficiently, their qualifications, the tools they would require in the form of supplies and equipment, and the space needed to house such an organization.

This being the first time that a really comprehensive attempt to combat crime in all its phases by scientific laboratory methods had been undertaken in the United States, we had no precedent to go upon—at least on this side of the water. There existed, in Europe, and had existed for many decades, however, a number of institutions engaged in work of the character we contemplated, whose activities we wished to duplicate more or less closely. The obvious thing, then, was to visit them and see what they were doing, and how.

As Director of the Laboratory I was given this mission, which carried me in all to some thirteen countries, during a period of about eighty days. My resulting observations and recommendations are recorded in the following, detailed report. In this, conditions in Europe and America are contrasted, and an idea of the scope of the scientific investigations undertaken overseas, presented.

My studies were carried out in the capitals and principal cities of England, France, Spain, Switzerland, Italy, Roumania, Hungary, Austria, Germany,

Denmark, and Belgium, visited in the order named. The institutions were in general of two groups—i.e., Scientific Police Laboratories and Medico-Legal Institutes. The character of the work undertaken in the former differed, sometimes slightly, sometimes very materially, from that of the latter, yet both always had something of value to offer. In addition, I called upon individual experts in their homes and offices, including Mr. Gerald Gurrin, handwriting expert to the London Police; Major H. B. C. Pollard, firearms expert to the London Police; Pierre Foury, firearms expert to the Paris Police; M. Flobert, firearms expert to the Paris Police; M. Gastine-Renette, firearms expert to the Paris Police; Dr. Robert Heindl, author of treatises on fingerprinting, etc., and Editor of the "Archiv für Kriminologie" Berlin; and Dr. Heinrich Poll, medico-legal expert and fingerprint authority, Hamburg.

ITINERARY

Since my work along the line of scientific crime detection had, up to the date of my appointment as Director of the Laboratory, been confined entirely to studies of firearms and ammunition as they figured in criminal cases, I was naturally anxious to add to my fund of information bearing upon their manufacture overseas. I therefore visited and studied manufacturing processes at Woolwich Arsenal, London, England (small arms ammunition); Imperial Chemical Industries, Birmingham, England (pistols and revolvers): Orbea & Company, Eibar, Spain (pistols and revolvers); Gabilondo & Co., Elgoibar, Spain (pistols and revolvers); Armas de Placencia, Spain (field guns and shell); Proof House, Eibar, Spain (proof tests of small arms); Manufacture Francaise d'Armes et Cycles, St. Etienne, France (pistols and rifles); Small Arms Collection, Municipal Museum, St. Etienne, France; Proof House, St. Etieene, France (proof tests of small arms); Versuchsanstalt für Handfeuerwaffen in Wansee, Germany (small arms tests of all kinds); Fabrique Nationale, Liége, Belgium (small arms and small arms ammunition); Proof House in Liége, Belgium (proof tests of small arms); and Small Arms Collection at Musée des Invalides, Paris.

Itinerary: New York, Cherbourg, Paris, Brussels, London—Birmingham—London, Paris, Madrid, San Sebastian—Eibar—San Sebastian, Lyon—St. Etienne—Lyon, Lausanne, Rome, Trieste, Bucharest, Budapest, Vienna, Dresden, Leipzig, Berlin, Copenhagen, Berlin, Hamburg, Kiel, Cologne, Liége—Brussels—Liége, Paris, London, Southhampton, New York.

Countries visited: England, France, Spain, Switzerland, Italy, Jugo-Slavia, Roumania, Hungary, Austria, Czechoslovakia, Germany, Denmark, Belgium.

EUROPEAN AND AMERICAN CONDITIONS, CONTRASTED

My provisional opinion that the United States is, for the most part, immeasurably behind Europe in scientific methods of crime detection was completely confirmed. Some of the causes for this condition are:

1. The European Police are commanded by men chosen for high education and marked ability, every one of whom is alive to the importance of employing all possible scientific aids in crime detection. (On the contrary, only too many American police officials are quite satisfied with the "good old fashioned methods" and turn up their noses at anything that savors of science.) Practically without exception, they hold degrees as doctors of law, science, philosophy or medicine. Their tenure is commonly longer than in the United States, appointments being more or less for life, hence they do not look upon their work as of a transient character, as do our Police Commissioners, and go into it more wholeheartedly—and more successfully.

2. European Detective Departments are ordinarily a national rather than a State organization. They do not suffer from the restriction of their activities within circumscribed borders, but are free to work anywhere throughout the country, unencumbered by variations in laws and regulations from province to province (or state to state). This permits the establishment of standards of instruction, practice, and cooperation which the United States will probably never know.

3. The European detective who, as with us, is commonly promoted to this status after a period in the uniformed service, is thoroughly schooled in the importance of the complete search of the locality of a crime for the traces or clues from which the events that there transpired may be reconstructed. He is also alive to the importance of a multiplicity of things which may serve as clues—things we commonly disregard. This is accomplished through the medium of a course of training more or less extended (a year or longer) and usually quite rigorous. Even the uniformed patrolman is ordinarily required to possess and be familiar with an instruction booklet devoted largely or wholly to a description of what to do and what not to do at the scene of a crime.

4. The public in general has become educated in the importance of avoiding the locality of a crime until the Police have examined it, and do not despoil the area before they arrive, as in the United States.

5. Crime is relatively less frequent (in ratio to population) than in the United States, hence the Police Expert has more time to devote to the individual case.

6. The ratio of trained police investigators to population is higher than in the United States, thus increasing the proportion of number of men available to investigate each crime.

7. Every Police Department of any size commands the services of one or more experts at all times.

8. Lastly, the staff expert must be a qualified individual, duly recognized as such by the State, before he can be employed in his expert capacity. This ordinarily means that he must hold a degree as doctor of medicine, *plus* a diploma in legal medicine, which involves from one to three years of intensive additional study after acquiring his regular medical degree. So armed, he may

apply for appointment to the official roster of qualified experts, from which the Court appoints individuals as necessity arises, to conduct investigations in cases that require expert services. The defendant may ordinarily ask permission to employ his own expert but if, in the opinion of the Court, the State expert can adequately handle the situation, this application may be denied, and the Court's ruling is final. Furthermore, if the defense applies for, and is granted, permission to retain its own expert, he will command no respect before the jury unless he be from the "Qualified" list—which will probably not be the case, since those listed do not care to assist a defense when their constituents are already serving the State. [In some countries (e.g., Germany) the defense expert, if any, is *paid by the State*, when the defendant is unable to meet the expense himself.]

Thus, instead of permitting mere pretenders to give "expert" testimony, as often happens with us, only those actually qualified as a result of arduous training, are called upon. The result is that the word of an expert, rather than being a subject for jest, as a commodity always to be controlled by the highest bidder, is given most respectful consideration. The career of an untruthful or careless expert comes to a quick and permanent end as soon as his delinquencies are evident, and, as a matter of fact, such a thing as a dishonest or badly trained expert is practically unknown.

To summarize, Europe leads the United States in the science of crime detection because:

1. Police Departments are commanded by men of a caliber able to appreciate the all-important part which science can play in crime detection if given the opportunity, and anxious to employ scientific aids whenever such employment is indicated.

2. The Investigation (Detective) Department is a national, not a state, or provincial, organization, and the criminal cannot delay or inhibit pursuit by flight into the next province (state) as he may in America.

3. The individual detective knows what to do, and the individual policeman what *not* to do, when at the scene of a crime. The former recognizes the importance of many traces and clues which his American contemporary completely disregards.

4. The Public is educated to leave the premises about the crime scene alone until the Police have made their examination.

5. There is relatively less crime in Europe than in America.

6. There are relatively more detectives in ratio to the population in Europe than in America.

7. Experts are always available to assist the European Police.

8. In Europe an expert *is* always an expert, *not* an imitation.

THE EUROPEAN LABORATORIES

To supplement the activities of the Detective Department experts, who are commonly functionaries of a Scientific Police Laboratory, we usually find a state-controlled Medico-Legal Institute. Sometimes other special institutes are also available for investigations in the fields of Toxicology, Biology, Chemistry, and Pharmacology. The staffs of these institutes ordinarily cooperate with that of the Scientific Police Laboratory in the instruction of candidates for the Detective or "Criminal Investigation" Department. There is of course a line of demarcation, sometimes vague, sometimes very definite, between the duties of the Scientific Police Laboratory, the Medico-Legal Institute, and any other institutes in the locality. Grouping the Medico-Legal and other institutes under the single heading of "M-L. I.," and designating the Scientific Police Laboratory as "S. P. L.," we may well consider at this point some of the types of official investigations carried on abroad, the agencies by which they are handled (M-L. I. or S. P. L.) and the equipment necessary in each instance.

ABORTIONS

When illegal abortion is suspected as a cause of death, the matter is always gone into by officials of the M-L. I., who conduct the autopsy, preserve the uterus and appendages when criminal acts are evident, and report findings to the police and prosecutor for appropriate action.

Apparatus Required (hereinafter referred to as A. R.). The usual equipment (refrigerating) for the preservation of the body pending autopsy; trained pathologists; the ordinary furnishings of a properly equipped pathological laboratory.

ADULTERATIONS (food, chemicals, etc.)

Study of this subject is not ordinarily within the province of the Police, being relegated to the M-L. I., but in some cities, notably Paris and Berlin, the work done in our "Health Department" laboratories, is a Police function. The advantage here is that the Police may personally purchase food samples, analyze them in their own laboratories, and report findings to the public prosecutor when indicated. (It must be constantly borne in mind, now and hereafter during the course of this report, that abroad the police are servants of the Central Government, *not* of the local municipality.) Thus these matters may be handled without passing from the jurisdiction of a single department, providing a continuity of action which makes for speed and efficiency.

A. R.—The usual equipment of a well fitted chemical and bacteriological laboratory.

ANTIQUES—GENUINE OR SPURIOUS

The study of the authenticity of antiques is sometimes gone into by the S. P. L. (e. g., Paris and Vienna)—never by the M-L. I. Offhand it would seem that this subject opens so large a field that one would hesitate to enter it without due and prayerful consideration. But as a matter of fact, the investigator who knows *where to go* for information along lines on which he is poorly informed personally, can usually achieve success in cases of this kind. Thus, in the Paris S. P. L. there stands a porcelain altar piece depicting the Virgin and Child, cherubs, etc., enamelled in colors. It had been sold to a collector as a fifteenth century product for 30,000 francs ($1,200). He became suspicious of it and sent it to the laboratory for study. Analyses of a rod of iron embedded in the back of the piece by way of reinforcement showed it to be of a composition not developed until the eighteenth century! The fraud exposed, the dealer made complete restitution to his client and, being informed that the cartage charges for returning the treasure to his shop would be 400 francs ($16), told the police to keep it! So there it stands today, in its dimensions of some 3x6 feet a decided menace to navigation through that portion of the already overcrowded laboratory.

Now Mr. Bayle, Laboratory Director (shot and killed by an assassin at the entrance to his office during my stay in Europe), was not an expert on the history of ironworking, but he knew where to go to find someone who was—hence the successful termination to this particular investigation.

A. R.—Varies with each case considered.

BIOLOGICAL STUDIES

When these do not go further than the precipitin test for human blood, they may be and frequently are carried out in the S. P. L. When other serological reactions must be gone into (e.g., Wassermann test for syphilis: blood grouping for paternity), they ordinarily become the province of the M-L. I., more rarely of the biological department (when it exists) in the local University. These tests must be carried out by persons trained in serology, involving either a medical degree or an apprenticeship in a serological laboratory. They also require considerable laboratory paraphernalia. They are indicated, e.g.: when blood stains are to be analyzed to determine whether of human origin or not; when, in a prisoner, the question of an abnormal mental or physical condition due to syphilis, is involved; and, when it is desired to settle the paternity of a child through a study of its blood and that of the supposed parents (see *PATERNITY*).

A. R.—Electric refrigerator, incubator, fresh-serum, blood cells, antigen, etc., for Wassermann test, laboratory reagents, glassware, etc.

BLOOD—TEST FOR PRESENCE OF

Apart from precipitin tests to distinguish between human and animal blood (already discussed under *BIOLOGICAL STUDIES*), it is often important to determine first whether certain stains are of blood *of any kind*. For this, various tests, microscopic (haemin), chemical (guaiac and benzidin) and physical (spectroscopic) are employed. The last is especially satisfactory, but requires expensive apparatus and trained operators. In some cases they are carried out in the S.P.L., in some in the M-L. I. Occasionally they are undertaken by both agencies.

A. R.—Microscope, spectroscope, simple chemical reagents and glassware.

BOMBS

These are studied in the S. P. L. In but one of those, however (at Bucharest), did I find a special room fitted for bomb study. Strangely, its walls are not reinforced in any way, and an explosion therein, besides eliminating the inmates, would be disastrous to those in the adjoining chambers.

According to my lay mind, the ideal method of studying these playthings is by preliminary radiography when, if the outer container be not too thick and dense, the nature of any metallic contents will be at once revealed (as illustrated by photographs in the S. P. L. museum in Berlin). The location of the firing mechanism, to produce detonation upon opening or inverting, may thus be demonstrated, as well as the clockwork, if it be a timed affair.

A. R.—X-Ray outfit: ordinary mechanics' tools (for disassembling); wall protection; life insurance.

BONES, ORIGIN OF

Cases arise where there are indications that a murder has been committed and an attempt made to destroy the body by fire or other consuming agency. Charred or otherwise damaged bones are recovered. Are they human or animal? This is purely a medical problem and is handled by the M-L. I.

A. R.—Knowledge of comparative anatomy.

BULLETS—STUDIES OF

These are made by the S. P. L., M-L. I. or both. They are for the most part crude, though in a few instances good work is being done. Four departments (London, England; Cairo, Egypt; Lyons, France and Edinburgh, Scotland) have adopted for this work comparison microscope to be employed in bullet and shell by Gravelle of South Orange, N.J., in 1925 and used by me constantly since. This was the first comparison microscope to be employed in bullet and shell identification, and its application to this field has removed these investigations from the realm of uncertain conjecture to that of a real science. Of the two adaptations that I had an opportunity to examine personally, the first (at London) was badly designed (although its author had studied my own instrument in my laboratory in New York), as it places the bullet images with their axes in a vertical, instead of a horizontal plane, and has rigid lighting fixtures, permitting no modifications according to conditions, while the second (at Lyon), was hopelessly wrong in design, so wrong as to render a bullet identification with it absolutely impossible (since it fuses the images nose to nose, or base to base, instead of employing the nose of one bullet and the base of the other). This microscope had been prepared for the commercial market by a student working in Locard's laboratory, from a study of an illustration in a reprint sent him by me in 1927. Of the third (at Cairo), I had an opportunity to study an illustration only. It too, was patterned after a photograph reproduced in one of my articles and appears to be correct in principle and detail. The fourth (at Edinburgh), presumably copies that in Cairo, having been installed by the same man, Dr. Sidney Smith.

The fact that Europe is imitating us in methods of bullet identification is flattering. Indeed, it was in this field alone (if you can receive with credulity an expression on this subject by one whose known personal interest might readily arouse suspicion of bias) that I found the United States more advanced than Europe. Everywhere, certain photographs which I was carrying with me, showing the comparison microscope designed by Gravelle for my laboratory, and of the results achieved through its use, were studied with marked interest, and requests for copies of the photographs and reprints of articles describing the instrument and method of operation, were almost universal. In Vienna, indeed, I was persuaded to loan my prints to the S. P. L. long enough to permit them to reproduce all of them for their own records—which they did most expeditiously.

In general, European methods of bullet identification are hopelessly antiquated. In Paris, for instance, they still roll the fatal and suspected bullets on a lead foil surface, in an effort to register thereon common characteristics. The method is adequate when major abnormalities are present, hopeless when the diagnostic points are microscopic, as is commonly the case.

A. R.—Comparison microscope, helixometer (instrument for studying interiors of barrels), micrometers, chemical balances, reference collections of rifling statistics, specimen arms, ammunition, bullets, unfired and fired shells, powders, etc.

CERUMEN

The fact that cerumen ("ear wax") may play a part in crime detection has but recently been recognized. It is based upon the discovery that samples of this secretion from the ears of a man who has been in a dust-laden atmosphere will show an admixture of the preponderant dusts. Thus, a flour mill worker, wishing to conceal his identity following a crime, might change his clothes and disguise his face as much as he pleased—a sample of cerumen from his ears would still show plenty of flour dust incorporated in it! These studies are made both by the S. P. L. and M-L. I.—the main requirement being that the individual conducting them be familiar with the appearance of the commoner types of dust particles.

A. R.—Microscope plus practical knowledge of the microscopic characteristics of various dusts.

DUST

This figures prominently in many difficult cases. Apart from its admixture with cerumen (see above), it may be recovered from the pockets, seams, and fabric of a piece of clothing, and reveal the occupation of its owner or the nature of the surroundings which he has lately frequented. Dust from bags, boxes, trunks, and other containers may tell us what they formerly contained. Such studies are usually the work of the S. P. L., but occasionally the M-L. I. undertakes them.

A. R.—Practical knowledge of the appearance of dust particles of different origins; a good microscope.

ELECTRICITY—EFFECTS OF

Electricity (man-made) when out of its proper channels may produce myriad effects, now leaving death and destruction in its wake, now playing but harmless pranks. The study of these phenomena is a science in itself. It has been attempted in a large way at but one of the cities which I visited (Vienna) where Professor Jellinek of the M-L. I. has been at work upon it for 30 years past.

A. R.—Varies with each individual case. (A fund of experience is the most important requirement.)

EXPLOSIONS AND EXPLOSIVES

A careful examination of the premises following an explosion may uncover the presence of fragments of bombs or infernal machines, physical and chemical studies of which may reveal some special characteristics which will prove a clue toward the detection of the makers. Again the investigation may show the explosion to have been due to gas or oil leakage, explosive dusts, etc. Such work is done by the S. P. L.

A. R.—Varies with the case. Usually the ordinary equipment of a physico-chemical laboratory is adequate.

FECES

The importance of the examination of feces, both of suspect and victim, in criminal investigations is steadily receiving greater recognition. (In the case of the victim, fecal specimens are secured at autopsy.) In this way we can determine in large measure the character of the foods constituting recently eaten meals, thereby often placing victim or suspect in a certain locality at a given time, with the upsetting of otherwise perfect alibis. In those instances where the criminal has left a fecal movement at the scene of the crime—an act not infrequently committed through the superstitious idea that good luck will follow—the fecal analysis may reveal the presence of parasites, ova, or other abnormal constituents which will help to fix the identity of the culprit if he be subsequently captured. This work is done by the M-L. I., though the directors of some S. P. L. undertake it as well.

A. R.—Microscope, chemical reagents, glassware, experience.

FINGERNAILS, SCRAPINGS FROM

Some European experts (e.g., Locard) advocate the taking of scrapings from beneath the fingernails of *every person suspected of a crime*—immediately after arrest. A study of the material thus collected may reveal clotted blood; bits of skin, tissue, hair, etc., clawed from victim during struggle; and paint, dirt, wood splinters, cloth fibers, etc., fixing the suspects's occupation or presence in a certain locality within a recent period.

Scrapings from the fingernails of the *victim* may produce similar interesting data. In the presence of negative microscopic findings, the material may still be extracted with salt solution and subjected to the precipitin test for human blood. This work is done sometimes by the S. P. L., sometimes by the M-L. I.

A. R.—Microscope, chemical reagents, glassware. (Special sera for precipitin test.)

FINGERPRINTS

Here again is another distinct science, which lies commonly within the province of the Police alone, yet the average European M-L. expert is at least fairly conversant with it. Systems of classification and other practices vary in different countries, and the subject is one which can be gone into only at great length if it is to be discussed with any degree of satisfaction. In my opinion, the Scientific Crime Detection Laboratory of Northwestern University (hereafter referred to as the "S. C. D. L.") should concern itself with fingerprints only to the extent of keeping abreast of the latest and most approved methods of searching for and making permanent records of "latent" fingerprints, i.e., those found on objects at the scene of a crime, and of keeping the Police with whom it cooperates fully informed of all recent progress in this field.

FINGERPRINTS AS GUIDES TO PATERNITY

This subject is a rather abstruse one, but it suffices to say that fingerprints, like blood grouping tests (see below), yield very valuable information in paternity studies, but within definitely circumscribed limits.

FIRE ARMS—STUDIES OF

All European S. P. L. and M-L. I. Museums contain numerous specimens of firearms that have figured in crimes, and studies of varying scope are made of the parts played by these weapons. But I saw, save in one case, no instance of a systematic effort to prepare a reference collection of arms of all available types, such as exists in my laboratory in New York, or of any other of the data which are necessary to make possible a comprehensive grasp of this subject. This was in Budapest, where attempt had been made (in the M-L. I.) to catalogue the variations in width and angle of grooves in the rifling of a few of the different makes of automatic pistols most commonly used. True, many S. P. L. and M-L. I. had made collections, more or less extensive, of *cartridge types*, but none had done this with respect to the loose bullets and empty shells which are the really important factors.

The one phase of firearms investigations where I was able to profit from European ingenuity, was with respect to tests of arms made at varying distances from a fixed target, to determine, if possible, the distance from which a certain fatal shot was fired. The London Police arms expert, Mr. Churchill, employs squares of tanned *pigskin* as his targets, thus more nearly reproducing the color, texture and resistance of the human skin than I (or others with whom I am acquainted) have been doing. This seems an excellent practice, and worthy of more general adoption.

Firearms investigations are, in Europe, about evenly divided between S. P. L. and M-L. I.

A. R.—Reference collection of arms, powders, bullets, shells, etc., also (See *BULLETS*).

FIRES, ORIGIN OF

Study of the premises immediately after a conflagration may yield clues which will make it possible to determine whether the fire was accidental (due to human carelessness), caused by lightning, or of incendiary origin. Thus a bit of fused glass adhering to a wire in the ruins of a farmhouse which had burned during the night, caused the release of two discharged employees whom the farmer had accused of burning his home, for glass fuses only at a temperature higher than that developed in an ordinary blaze of this kind, but is readily fusible by lightning, which produces arcs of tremendously high temperature. (It developed on investigation that there *had* been a severe electrical storm during the night.)

A. R.—Experience—ability as investigator.

FOOTPRINTS (UNSHOD)

These human traces are constantly furnishing the police of Europe with the information necessary for identification and conviction in crimes of all types. Means for preserving (pending photography), photographing, and permanently recording them by molds of wax, plaster, etc., have been elaborated without number. When the clue is sufficiently fresh, tracking is undertaken, as in the United States, with dogs. Expert human trailers are of course a memory of the past, save in certain semi-civilized areas.

A. R.—Materials for making molds, and for taking specimen impressions from suspects for purposes of comparison: photo equipment. A. S. P. L. function.

FORGERIES

See *HANDWRITING—GENERAL.*

GASTRIC CONTENTS

Apart from toxicological studies (see *POISONING, CHEMICAL*) on these materials, they may assume an importance similar to that of the *Feces* when a determination of the nature of the most recent meal becomes a matter of significance. Specimens for analysis may be secured from a suspect by use of the stomach tube, from the victim by autopsy.

A. R.—Usual chemical laboratory equipment. This work is done exclusively by the M-L. I.

GLASS, FRACTURES OF

Glass panes, fractured by missiles of varying shapes and velocities, shatter in different fashions. A pane perforated by a bullet traveling at very high speed may show a small round hole and nothing more. It often becomes important to determine the nature and velocity of the projectile which has passed through a given piece of glass, and from which direction it was traveling. Comparison tests, with glass of identical composition, are then in order. These are done sometimes by the S. P. L., sometimes by the M-L. I. (more frequently by the former, naturally).

A. R.—Varies with the individual case.

HAIR, IDENTIFICATION OF

In some cases it becomes necessary to determine whether strands of hair found in connection with a crime are of human origin, whether or not they belong to a certain individual, what parts of the body they grew upon, and so forth, much scientific investigation has been done along these lines, and valuable findings recorded. This work is usually done by the M-L. I., sometimes by the S. P. L.

A. R.—Microscope, simple reagents, knowledge of appearance of hairs of different types.

HANDWRITING—GENERAL

Here is another field so large as to constitute an art in itself. For, as in medicine, although science may be employed in our studies, the arrival at the correct conclusion can never be reduced to the certainty of a mathematical formula. The commonest reason for studying a specimen of handwriting is, of course, to determine whether it be authentic or forged. Here not only a careful examination of the *form* is important, but also a consideration of the *text* (which, in a forgery, may contain references to events happening *subsequent* to the date which it bears) and of the paper and ink, either or both of which may be of a type introduced after the purported date of the instrument.

For detecting alterations, additions, and erasures, numerous chemical and physical aids are employed, including photography, heat, ultraviolet rays, microscopic study, various reagents, etc. To ascertain whether two specimens are from the same *hand*, various graphometric systems are available which give excellent results when employed by properly trained investigators. This work is carried out in the S. P. L., and the *A. R.* has already been touched upon.

HANDWRITING—OF CRIMINALS

A new science has arisen in Germany (although I am informed that it was first worked out in America). It concerns the identification of a criminal by his handwriting. "Modus operandi" files, covering various types of criminals, have been established in which authentic specimens of the handwriting of each of the professional gentlemen under observation, are kept. Thus, specimens of the handwritings of Hotel Thieves will be in one drawer, of Blackmailers in another, etc., sub-classified under such general listings according to the way each man forms the individual letters of the alphabet. Suppose, then, a hotel robbery, an "inside job," is reported. The registry slips filled out by the guests at that hotel, as required by law and on file with the local police, will be secured and compared with the specimens in the "Hotel Thief" file. One of them may show handwriting characteristics identical with such a filed specimen. The author is apprehended—and the loot recovered!

It might appear that this would be a difficult means of "registering" criminals and that the results would not be commensurate with the effort involved. But I am assured that this is by no means the case—that the system has definitely proved its usefulness, and passed the experimental stage. (One identification per week by this method is the average in Dresden and Berlin, the two cities where I saw it in operation.) It is of course purely a police enterprise, carried out in the S. P. L.

A. R.—Special filing cabinets, folders, and index cards: trained graphologists as operators.

HANGING

The determination of whether a person found suspended in air came to his death by suicide, accident, or murder, is ordinarily a M-L. I. function. These cases are sometimes very perplexing, as when a man has been murdered and later suspended in simulation of suicide, and autopsy may be necessary to establish the facts.

A. R.—Trained investigators; pathologist to do autopsy; usual pathology laboratory equipment.

HEELS, RUBBER (See SHOE PRINTS)

HEMOGLOBIN

When searching for blood, a garment showing no stains (having been washed by the murderer), may, on soaking in salt solution and concentrating the resulting extract by evaporation, yield positive results when tested for hemoglobin. Such tests are conducted both by S. P. L. and M-L. I.

A. R.—Chemical reagents; a spectroscope.

INDUSTRIAL ACCIDENTS

European M-L. I., being State-controlled, are frequently charged with the examination of persons injured while at work, to determine the extent of their disabilities. This is medico-legal work in a sense, but not in that in which we commonly employ the term. The S. C. D. L. will certainly not be concerned with it.

A. R.—The usual diagnostic aids employed by physicians and surgeons.

INFANTICIDE

The means of producing the death of an unwanted infant are legion, but strangulation and fracture of the skull by a blow appear to be the two most often employed. A properly conducted autopsy will ordinarily disclose the fact if death has occurred as the result of violence. Strictly a M-L. I. function.

A. R.—Pathological laboratory equipment.

INFERNAL MACHINES (See *BOMBS.*)

INKS

Before we can become experts in the study of documents, we must be familiar with inks—their composition, history, and methods of manufacture. This is a S. P. L. function.

A. R.—Reference library; chemical reagents.

INVISIBLE WRITINGS

In Europe, where myriad political propagandas are always at work, and police agents are constantly scrutinizing the mail of "suspicious" persons, invisible writing is very often used for communication. It is also frequently employed by incarcerated individuals for communicating with the outside world. Thus a letter from a penitentiary inmate to his brother, in heavy black ink, may read, "Thanks for the candy and cigarettes. Please bring my overcoat when you come next Sunday. The days are getting pretty chilly. Your unlucky brother—Bill," while between the lines, penned in some readily available medium such as fruit juice or urine, and absolutely invisible in ordinary light, we find, when we subject the document to the ultra-violet rays: "Got the gun O.K. Have car and rope outside west wall at noon Tuesday. Throw rope when I whistle."

These writings are studied in the S. P. L.

A. R.—Various chemical reagents; ultra-violet ray lamp.

JEWELS, GENUINE OR SPURIOUS

Differentiation may be made through studies of the physical and optical properties of the suspected stone as compared with one known to be genuine.

A. R.—Microscope, ultra-violet ray lamp, means for testing hardness, specific gravity, etc. Such work is done in the S. P. L.

LARVAE—IDENTIFICATION OF

The discovery in clothing of larvae of certain animals may be most important. The Paris S. P. L. determined that the body of a certain man had, prior to its discovery in a vacant lot, lain for a time in a dark cellar, from the presence on the clothing of the larvae of a certain blind beetle living only in such localities, and eventually solved the mystery of his murder thereby. These studies are undertaken by the S. P. L. with the assistance of entomologists.

A. R.—Means for agitating clothing in a closed receptacle and collecting the resulting dust for study; consulting entomologist.

LIGHTNING, EFFECTS OF

These, like the aberrant effects of man-made electricity, appear in countless forms, and long experience is required to establish familiarity with them. Yet it is often extremely important to be able to differentiate between death from lightning, murder, natural causes, etc., and knowledge of the commoner phenomena attending lightning strokes becomes very necessary in such cases. As for artifically made electricity, the only place where a comprehensive study of these has been made is the M-L. I. at Vienna.

A. R.—Experience, gained by observation.

METALS, ETCHING

Serial numbers, letters, symbols, etc., erased from metal surfaces by filing, etc., may be brought out by etching with special acid solutions. A. S. P. L. function.

A. R.—Chemical reagents.

METALS—OTHER STUDIES

Gold bricks, metallic dusts, etc., sometimes require scrutiny. The composition of a "brick" can be revealed by tests as for coins (see below—*MONEY,*

METALLIC). Dust may be studied microscopically and chemically (when secured from clothing, fingernails, etc.) to determine its nature and origin. This also is a S.P.L. function.

A. R.—Microscope; chemical reagents.

MONEY–METALLIC

There is much coining of counterfeit money abroad. Apart from chemical analysis, spurious coins can be told from the genuine by variations in color, weight, milling, and in perfection of detail. Photography with enlargement will always bring out clearly the last named discrepancy.

A. R.—Microscope, photo equipment, chemical reagents (for qualitative analysis). Handled by the S. P. L.

MONEY–PAPER

Counterfeiting of paper money is also very common over-seas. The means employed include photography, lithography, engraving, freehand drawing and painting, etc. Comparison with genuine specimens under ultra-violet rays will show variations in color of paper. Enlarged photographs will demonstrate differences in detail, which can first be noted with a low power microscope. The work is done by the S. P. L.

A. R.—Photo and ultra-violet equipment; microscope.

"MOULAGE"

There has been developed in the S. P. L. in Vienna a method, which is being adopted elsewhere (Berlin), of making permanent records in wax of inanimate objects, human features, organs, etc., when these will be useful for police or medical purposes. Thus, the marks of teeth upon a half-chewed apple may be recorded by making a moulage cast of the exhibit, using materials colored so naturally as to give the impression that we are gazing upon the original and not a reproduction. The materials devised for this purpose have a much wider field of application than has plaster of paris, and, as already noted, the added advantage that objects cast in them can be given an absolutely lifelike appearance. This work, which is done only in the S. P. L., would well merit the attention of the S. C. D. L.

A. R.—Special materials for making positive and negative casts and molds.

OCCUPATIONAL DEFORMITIES

In many parts of Europe, where standardized production has not yet reached the stage in which it exists in the United States, the individual artisan, working in his own shop, is still a familiar figure. Over a period of years, the oft-repeated performance of certain manual and pedal operations peculiar to his trade produces hypertrophy of the muscles most employed, atrophy (relative) of others, callouses here, indurations there, etc. The deformities, especially of the hands, so resulting have been studied and photographically recorded. Collections of such photographs may be found in various M-L. I., where such researches are conducted.

A. R.—Photo equipment.

OCCUPATIONAL DISEASES (See remarks under INDUSTRIAL ACCIDENTS.)

OVA (See remarks under LARVAE which apply equally here.)

PAINTINGS

Examination with X-Rays, ultra-violet rays, analysis of pigments, fabrics, etc., will ordinarily fix the approximate age of a painting, and thus assist us in deciding whether or not it be the work of him to whom it is attributed. Such studies are done in the S. P. L., with the assistance of outside experts.

A. R.—X-rays; Ultra-violet rays; chemical reagents.

PALM PRINTS

Are treated in the same manner as FINGERPRINTS.

PAPER

A general knowledge of the various methods of paper production and of the history of paper manufacture, is an indispensable adjunct to a proper study of handwriting and of false documents—printed, typewritten, engraved (bank notes), lithographed, etc.

A. R.—Photo apparatus; ultra-violet ray lamp; chemical reagents. These investigations are carried out by the S. P. L.

PAPER—FINGER PRINTS ON

It is not generally known among the laiety that fingerprints may readily be developed upon paper, and valuable clues derived therefrom. Toilet paper left at the scene of a crime by one who has defacated there always shows prints—and I saw in Copenhagen a sample of paper secured under such circumstances which caused the arrest and conviction of the criminal. The work is done in the S. P. L.

A. R.—That usually found in fingerprint laboratories.

PARASITES (See FECES and LARVAE.)

PATERNITY

All human bloods fall into four specific groups according to certain properties of agglutination which they possess. These are (according to one classification) numbered simply 1, 2, 3, and 4. A child whose blood falls in a certain grouping—say group 2—*can* be the issue of parents with bloods of certain group combinations and *cannot* be born of parents of certain other groupings. The determination of the group status of bloods of parents and child, when paternity is questioned, thus becomes very important, and this test may give very helpful information. It is commonly done in the M-L. I.

　A. R.—Usual serological laboratory equipment.

POISONING—CHEMICAL (homicidal)

This is handled by the M-L. I. The technique of such investigations (analyses of organs following autopsy) is pretty well standardized everywhere.

　A. R.—Usual toxicological laboratory equipment.

POISONING—FOOD (accidental)

Investigated also by the M-L. I.

　A.R.—As for toxicological studies.

POSTAGE STAMPS

Forged stamps for postage, documents, internal revenue, etc., may be recognized by comparison with genuine specimens, from which they will vary in color, texture of paper, perforation count, details of engraving, etc. This work is done by the S. P. L.

　A. R.—Microscopes, ultra-violet ray lamp, perforation gauges, chemical reagents, photo equipment, etc.

POST MARKS

Criminals sometimes produce alibis supported by letters postmarked under a certain date, the postmarks being forged. Such forgeries are detected by comparison with genuine marks made by the official stamp of the office in question.

　A. R.—Microscope; photo equipment.

POWDERS—GUN

M-L. authorities have made extensive collections of specimens showing the effect of powder burns on the human skin, clothing, etc. Sections of skin about 4 inches square surrounding the entrance wound are dissected away, mounted on glass, and preserved in fixing solutions in specimen jars. While interesting, they are of doubtful value for comparison purposes in subsequent cases, since rarely if ever do exactly similar conditions prevail.

A. R. —Pathological laboratory equipment. Function of the M-L.I.

Another phase of powder investigations is the search of clothing, skin, etc., of the victim for the individual unburned grains always present in cases of shooting at close range. These may exist in great numbers on the surface of a garment with a woolly nap—where they may be photographed in situ (enlarged), and compared with grains taken from other cartridges found on the person or premises of the accused (for size, shape, color, etc.).

A. R.—Photo equipment: microscope. Work done by S.P.L.

PRINTING—DATE OF

The date of a printed document may be roughly fixed by a study of the paper, ink, and kind of type employed. Outside assistance is usually necessary. A. S. P. L, function.

A. R.—Microscope; photo equipment; chemical reagents; experience.

PSYCHIATRIC EXAMINATIONS

Legal Medicine in Europe includes psychiatry, so the staff of the M-L. I. is called upon to make psychiatric studies of criminals (to determine their degree of responsibility, etc.), persons considered for commitment to institutions, etc. This is of course strictly a M-L. I. problem and presumably the S. C. D. L. will never be troubled with it.

A. R.—Experience in psychiatry.

SEALS, EMBOSSED

The die used may be forged. This may be demonstrated by comparing the suspected seal (photographed and enlarged) with one from a die known to be genuine.

A. R.—Photo equipment. A S. P. L. function.

SEALS, WAX

Seals in wax on letters or documents may be forged. It then becomes necessary to study the material (wax) used, in addition to the character of the imprint (see, above—*SEALS, EMBOSSED*), for the forger will rarely have wax of the same composition as that used at the authentic source. Though the color may be correct in daylight, when the two (false and genuine) are compared under the ultra-violet rays, a difference in shade will be at once apparent.

Sometimes a genuine seal is removed and replaced, additional wax of the same color being used in the resealing. Here again, the ultra-violet rays will show which portions of the final seal are original and which have been added. This is of course a S.P.L. function.

A. R.—Ultra-violet ray lamp; photo equipment.

SERUM (See *BIOLOGICAL STUDIES.*)

SHOE PRINTS

The procedure is the same as for *FOOTPRINTS*. In Europe, it has been found worth while to make specimen collections of the different types of hobnails employed in various localities, because of the characteristic impressions left by them. In the United States, it would probably be well to prepare such collections of the various patterns of rubber heels produced by the several manufacturers of this commodity, and to have them available for reference purposes. The work is done by the S. P. L.

A. R.—Photo and molding equipment; reference collections.

SHOT-GUN

In homicides with bird shot, the recovered pellets are weighed, measured (for diameter) analyzed chemically if necessary, and compared with others removed from unfired cartridges taken from the person or property of the suspect in an effort to determine whether they are of identical origin. A S. P. L. study.

A. R.—Chemical balances, reagents, micrometer.

SOIL

Soil adhering to the shoes, hand, property or clothing of a person suspected of a crime, or of the victim, may, on chemical and microscopic study, reveal the nature of the terrain they passed over immediately before the crime.

A. R.—Microscope; chemical reagents; equipment for photomicroscopy. This is a S. P. L. function.

SPIDER WEBS

Since spiders of different types spin their webs in certain more or less fixed localities, the presence on the clothing of a suspect of a bit of the web of a spider known to frequent, say, bushes and hedges, may help us in ascertaining the terrain he has passed over. This is usually a M-L. I. function.

A. R.—Knowledge of the habits of different species of spiders.

SPOTS AND STAINS

These must first be photographed in situ at the scene of the crime, then secured by scraping (from walls), by removal of sections of wood, stone, linoleum, etc. (furniture and floors), or by confiscation of any garments, draperies, etc., on which they appear. They may then be studied at leisure in the laboratory (S. P. L.) to determine whether they are of animal, vegetable, or inorganic origin, and their exact nature.

A. R.—Photo equipment; microscope; chemical reagents.

STAMPS, RUBBER, FORGED

The remarks under *POSTMARKS* apply here.

TEETH, PRINTS OF

These may exist at the scene of the crime in foodstuffs of firm texture (apples, pears, cheese, chocolate bars) or on the persons of criminal or victim, following a struggle. They must be photographed at once, since the original exhibit will usually soon deteriorate, then put into permanent record form, through casts by moulage, plaster, etc. Other casts are then taken from the teeth of suspects—or from impressions left by them in materials similar to those found at the scene, and comparisons are made. The work is done in the S. P. L.

A. R.—Photo equipment; moulage materials.

TEXTILES

A thread, ravelled from an article of apparel, may be the deciding clue in a murder case. Hence a knowledge of the microscopic appearance of fibres used in textile manufacture is an important element of the fund of information which the Police Expert should have at his command.

A. R.—Mounted specimens of sample fibres of every variety possible to obtain; microscopes. A S. P. L. function.

TIRE PRINTS

These may be found at the scene of an automobile accident, or even stamped upon the skin or clothing of a victim over whose body a wheel has passed. By keeping a reference collection of tread patterns as used by various tire manufacturers, the brand of tire involved in a particular case may be ascertained. Further, a careful study of the roadway will usually reveal the direction of travel of an automobile the tracks of which we come upon without knowing offhand its destination. This is essentially S.P. L. work.

A. R.—Reference collection of illustrations of standard tread types; power of observation; photo equipment—for recording findings at the scene; materials for making casts.

TOOL MARKS

Marks left by tools or weapons on wood, metal and even bone (the human skull) may often be identified to a particular tool. The procedure involves photography, moulage or casts of the marks made and comparison of these with the serrations or irregularities on the edge of the tool, study of the dimensions of the tool and of the marks discovered, etc. A. S. P. L. function.

A. R.—Photo equipment, moulage materials, etc. (At Lausanne I saw a human skull split by a hatchet, the surface of the sectionalized bone showing a series of parallel striations that registered exactly with serrations on the edge of the hatchet that had delivered the blow!)

TYPEWRITERS

The make of typewriter on which a given document was written, the exact machine used, and even the identity of the typist, can often be determined from the study of the paper in dispute, and comparisons with other products of the same typewriter, from the same hand. This is another S.P.L. function.

A. R.—Reference collection of letters written on various machines of known makes and models; photo equipment; special protractors; measuring scales, etc.

URINE

Urine specimens discovered at the scene of a crime should be analyzed to discover, if possible, abnormal constituents which will assist in determining the identity of the person passing them. (This particular clue caused recently an arrest and conviction in Germany.)

A. R.—Simple chemical reagents; microscope. Such work is done both by S. P. L. and M-L. I.

WADS, GUN

When found at a crime scene, these must be compared with others removed from ammunition found on the person or property of the suspect, to determine identity, if such exists. In the absence of a suspect, comparison with a reference collection of wads of known makes will reveal from what ammunition factory they came.

A. R.—Photo equipment; reference collection. A S. P. L. function.

WATER, ANALYSIS OF

This is done by the M-L. I. or the Police Chemistry Laboratory when such exists. Does not concern the S. C. D. L.

A. R.—Usual chemical and bacteriological laboratory equipment.

WEAPONS—VARIOUS

Already discussed under *FIREARMS* and *TOOL MARKS.*

WOUNDS—GUNSHOT

Purely a medical problem, handled by M-L. I.
A. R.—Pathological laboratory equipment; experience.

In the foregoing list, I have presented an outline by no means complete, of some of the activities in which the Police, Medico-Legal, and other laboratories which I visited, are engaged.

CRIME DETECTION LABORATORIES

IN THE UNITED STATES

Charles M. Wilson

The historical picture of crime detection laboratories in the United states is rather discouraging when viewed factually.

Proper perspective requires first a definition of the effort, or the work product, of the technician in the crime laboratory. The author knows no better description than that which was provided many years ago by Dr. William Sauder, former senior physicist at the National Bureau of Standards in Washington, D.C., and an early pioneer in this area of laboratory applications to the problem of crime and the determination of guilt or innocence. He defined this work product as that of "the technician in the laboratory who attempts to study the cause or combination of causes which either did or could produce the given result." The inferences in that statement demand careful contemplation. For the laboratory technician to be successful, he must not only be provided with the proper *equipment* with which to work but also with the proper *evidence* with which to work. His efforts may later become an essential part of a fact finding inquiry, a judicial area, or, if he is unable to form definite decisions and conclusions, they may become a directional aid to the investigator by suggesting areas of interest. We can see that the technician has a dual role, both roles having crucial importance.

This brings us to the critical consideration of the relationship between the technician and the investigator. If the technician is unable to arrive at a conclusion because the evidence given him is inadequate or the information given him concerning the event under investigation is inadequate, it is a disappointment to him and it is a disappointment to the submitting investigator. The relationship, then, involves responsibilities on the part of both parties. A laboratory must provide the investigator, the line officer, with knowledge of what the technician needs in order that he be of greatest assistance in an investigation. Such knowledge is provided by a training program and the circulation of laboratory subject matter to all levels of law enforcement, such as: what material to recover, how to mark it, what quantity is needed and generally what can be done with it. This general information is supplemented by considering individual types of evidence material with relation to its recognition, proper recovery and marking for purposes of identification. With this type of education, the investigator knows what a properly staffed and equipped laboratory can do if given certain materials and thereby can meet his own obligations to recognize, recover and mark properly physical evidence of any nature.

The circulation of this basic information to all levels is extremely important for another reason. As the result of experience in training courses established at Northwestern University's Crime Laboratory in 1930, we found that students returned to their respective departments and jealously guarded the information for their own personal advancement. Obviously, this result defeated our purpose, in these all too short courses, of spreading the information to other investigators and, in that way, increasing the overall departmental efficiency. The answer to this problem was to make available, in very fundamental and simple form, the proper information concerning recognition, recovery and identification to all levels of a department. This puts the highest administrative or policy making officer in competition with the lowest recruit in carrying out the investigative responsibility.

Now, with this understanding of the responsibilities of the laboratory technician and the field investigator, we can examine the history of crime detection efforts in the United States.

We started approximately a hundred years behind the British system. Our system was born as a result of syndicated crimes and violence in Chicago. The birth was triggered, in 1929, by the infamous St. Valentine's Day massacre in which several hoodlums and a couple of their supporters were lined up against a brick wall on the north side of Chicago and several executed in a matter of minutes by an execution squad which used machine guns, shot guns and .45 automatic pistols. Witnesses to this horrible crime reported that the perpetrators escaped from the scene in what appeared to be a squad car and that they were in a uniform of some kind. The responsible members of the community were so enraged by this act that a blue ribbon coroner's jury was empaneled.

Mr. Bert A. Massey, a member of that panel, was financially able, fortunately, to go beyond the facilities that existed locally in 1929. Since the evidence in that case revolved around questions of firearms exhibits, Mr. Massey went to Col. Calvin Goddard, an independent consultant, who maintained his own laboratory in New York. Col. Goddard was asked to come to Chicago and assist the coroner's jury in their inquiry into this crime in which seven people had been executed. The rather complete account of Col. Goddard's evaluation of the physical evidence in that case is a model of competent work.(1)

Mr. Massey was so impressed by this work of Goddard and his associates that he asked Goddard to consider coming to Chicago and establishing a crime laboratory. After he prevailed upon Goddard to come to Chicago for that purpose, he provided financial assistance of about $125,000 for the establishment of the laboratory which also enabled Goddard to examine facilities abroad. Col. Goddard visited and studied, first hand, some 100 medico-legal, psychiatric, and crime laboratories in Europe during 1929 and 1930. Goddard's review of these facilities was excellent.(2) His contrast between what he observed in Europe and what existed in the United States was not very complimentary to the American system as of 1930. There was very little organized training in this area, and any serious effort in the United States was usually the result of personal interest and avocation of independent specialists and consultants.

The laboratory, with Col. Goddard as its first director, was established at the Law School of Northwestern University, in 1929-30. John Henry Wigmore, Dean of the Law School, was responsible for this site. As early as 1915, Dean Wigmore envisioned the utilization of an objective scientific laboratory as an aid to the dispensers of justice—the lawyers and the jurists. In 1915, in the plans for the new law building, he provided the third or top floor as space for such a laboratory because of his convictions. Wigmore was the moving force, along with Massey, in bringing into being Northwestern University's Crime Laboratory.

Goddard sought out, as his full-time staff, people who had attained some stature in their respective fields of specialty. Backstopping this staff were some outstanding individual practitioners who served as consultants when requested by the permanent members. To name a few staff and consultant individuals: Leonarde Keeler, one of the pioneers in polygraphy; Col. Seth Wiard, firearms identification; Dr. Clarence Muehlberger; Albert S. Osborn of New York, who is considered to be the father of handwriting identification in the United States; J. Fordice Ward of Chicago, document examination expert; Herbert J. Walter of Chicago; Dr. Emmons of the University of Wisconsin; P.H. Knuckles of the Underwriters Laboratory in Chicago and, lastly, a man who, in 1930, was one of the leading exponents in the United States of modern police systems and modern police methods: Professor August Vollmer of Berkeley, California.

The caliber of these men might well be pointed out through a discussion of one of them. The author, as a young boy going to high school in Berkeley, California, knew of August Vollmer. At that time, Vollmer was maligned, ridiculed and publicly abused by the newspapers because he had the audacity to suggest that policemen should be university trained (Vollmer, himself, was a self-made man). The author grew up to know him and love him. It is submitted that the efforts of August Vollmer, as Chief of Police at Berkeley, California, evolved and developed the modern police system in that state. To the foresight and the determination of this man can be attributed, in large measure, the fact that even today, there is more know-how on the subject of police administration and records, in the United States, between the Pacific Ocean and the Nevada line than there is between the Nevada line and the Atlantic seaboard. No less than seventy-five or eighty men worked their way through the University of California as patrolmen in the Berkeley Department. These individuals later became located in key administrative positions in corrections, police administration, police records and the handling of information throughout the country. Several years ago, the author reviewed the results of police training in the State of California, at the secondary level. Through their integrated system of training and police administration,(3) there were no less than 600 people taking secondary school courses for credit who, at the time, were associated with an enforcement agency or were shortly to be affiliated with either enforcement agencies or correctional institutions at the state, county or city level in California. The wisdom and foresight of August Vollmer turned theory into sound practice. He was one of the consultants to the Northwestern Laboratory.

There were other early workers in 1930: Captain Edwin Crossman of Los Angeles, a west coast pioneer in firearms identification; Dr. William Sauder, Bureau of Standards; Dr. Israel Castellanos of Cuba, a very close friend of Col. Goddard; Inspector J.A. Churchman, later director of the Canadian Mounted Police Laboratory in Ottawa; Raymond Pinker, Director of the Los Angeles Police Department Laboratory started in the 20's and Professor J.H. Mathews of the University of Wisconsin. Dr. Mathews started his own laboratory before 1930 when he was Chairman of the Department of Chemistry at the University. Since his retirement, a few years ago, he has devoted his time to the preparation of a rather excellent book on firearms identification.(4) This monumental work, in two volumes, is the greatest collection of authorative information on weapons, investigation and identification ever brought together. The work contains photographs and measurements of rifling characteristics of nearly 3,000 specimens originating in twenty-three countries. It discusses new techniques, methods of restoration and numerous related subjects and contains 2684 illustrations in its 928 pages. Here is an example of another pioneer.

Now, thirty-two years after Goddard established this laboratory, and forty-seven years after Wigmore envisioned this establishment we need to ask ourselves what our objectives are and how we are going to achieve them. At the present time, today, in the United States there are fifty or sixty so-called crime laboratories. These vary from one man organizations up to the very excellent coroner's laboratory maintained at Cleveland by Dr. Sam Gerber, or to Dr. Milton Helpern's excellent medical examiner's laboratory in New York. While some of the one man organizations have given good service, others leave a great deal to be desired. When you say laboratory you should, first of all, know what constitutes a laboratory.

Without a doubt, the laboratory, as it exists in the United States, is an appendage of a quasi-military operation of an enforcement agency. As in the military, the laboratory technician in the quasi-military operation is subordinate to the administration, which is usually not technically trained. The technician, therefore, does not have the freedom of decision nor the opportunity for research that would exist if he were a dedicated, well-trained scientist acting as a civilian in the proper framework. The author feels that he is privileged to make this distinction as he has served in both capacities, administrative and technical, with a laboratory that must answer civil and criminal questions arising from the administration of justice. This concept was discussed in 1957 at Camp Zona in Japan, where it was the author's privilege to be on a consulting assignment for the United States and Philippine governments. The commanding general of the Eighth Army, and his laboratory administrative officers, there, were complaining about the lack of personnel for their laboratories. This discussion led me to suggest that this military operation in the laboratory was inconsistent in itself. Theirs was an attempt to depend upon military personnel to staff the laboratory. When a qualified man was found and trained, they would freeze him in rank which would result in a personal sacrifice to the individual. No longer able to advance, the man would leave the service. I suggested that they staff their laboratory with civilian personnel and use military officers as the administrative personnel. In this way the military officers would be educated by the laboratory personnel without the foolish situation developing of a non-technical person trying to direct the professional work of the qualified technician. The administrative officer could then be rotated as the occasion demanded and both he and the laboratory he would then administrate would benefit. This has application to fundamental thinking about the police department operation.

This same unhappy situation that existed in the military laboratory referred to, exists today in law enforcement agencies which attempt to maintain laboratories in the United States. Some of these agencies which are so eager to have a laboratory have demonstrated to the author's satisfaction that they don't even know what a laboratory is for. Even worse, they have little or no conception of the proper use of a laboratory. This observation is reflected in the fact that practically every case originating with an enforcement agency is tagged with a top priority label: this is the most important case we have! Of course that may be true to the person referring the case, but there are many such referrals to a laboratory. Obviously the laboratory personnel can not operate with top priority labels on every case. The technician, then, must have the authority—and sufficient information—to determine intelligently whether or not a priority really exists. In Wisconsin, our determination is made on this basis; those cases which do carry top priority are the ones involving a crime of violence against the person—murder, assault, sexual assault where force is used—and those which involve crime against property are relegated to later examination when time is less pressing.

For the most part, the present situation exists because many leaders in police administration have become overly conscious of the use of kits, of gadgets. While such kits have made many contributions in the areas of police administration, police traffic control, administration of detective boards and the like, this over emphasis has reached the point where if one department has a kit then every other department wants to have one, too. It does not make any difference whether it is a marijuana detecting kit or a slide rule which gives the distance that a car, weighing so much and traveling at such-and-such a speed, must have skidded on a dry street. Everybody wants to have one! This oversimplified approach to technical procedures, this placing of technical materials in the hands of people who are completely uninitiated in the subject matter, is a serious concern.

The proper conceptual use of a laboratory requires some fundamental thinking about economics. At what level can the expense of a laboratory be justified? This depends, to a great extent, upon the ability of the people involved to pay for the service, and upon their interest in receiving such a service. It is submitted that the proper place to maintain a laboratory will depend upon the number of people it is going to serve. Not every little town hamlet can expect to maintain a laboratory. On a state or provincial basis, the work effort of the laboratory can be utilized at almost every enforcement level by simple administrative procedures. In addition to the basic expense, it must be realized that development of new techniques and new applications requires further expenditures. This is, in part, related to the training of investigators. California first set the pattern to aid these training activities by setting aside 15% of all fines and forfeitures as a special fund for law enforcement training.

The Wisconsin State Crime Laboratory, of which the author is a part, is a technical service agency operated at the state level as a small separate state department. We participate in criminal matters only when requested to do so by a specified enforcement official or when the person charged with a crime obtains, through his counsel, an order requesting our services from the judge who will hear that criminal matter. The privilege which ordinarily attaches to the materials submitted to us by the prosecution, also attaches to the results of any examination undertaken for the defendant under such an order. This provision was incorporated into our statutes at the suggestion of the District Attorney's Association, because they did not want the laboratory work-effort to be a one-way street. The statutes also provide for certification, by the presiding magistrate, of laboratory results at preliminary hearings and their admission into evidence when offered by the prosecution or the defense. A demand by either party to examine the expert whose findings are so certified will adjourn the hearing until that technician appears. Now, this is *only* at preliminary hearings. At the trial, the technician who did the work must be present. The laboratory is prohibited by statute from engaging in civil matters unless a state official, acting in an official capacity, becomes a party to the civil action. As an illustration: the Assistant Attorney General handles highway matters and, if he has a bridge that has been collapsed by a truck, he then becomes an official party to a potential civil action. The Wisconsin State Crime Laboratory can enter, as a tax supported agency, under those conditions, when requested to do so by the Attorney General's office. This is the only way in which the laboratory can officially become involved in civil matters. The writer, as Superintendent, has discretionary power regarding the release of findings of the laboratory in a criminal matter for use in civil proceedings, once advised that the matter is no longer of interest to the proper state authority. We have always adopted the policy of releasing the findings to all interested civil litigants at the same time so that we will not be accused of partiality.(5)

It is submitted that there is a danger in depending too heavily upon a national agency to do laboratory crime detection work. This has the tendency to produce sterility at other levels. The attitude is taken "Let somebody else do it" or "Send it in for analysis." We hear that word "analysis" so often we begin to wish it did not exist. The people, who demand that this be examined and that that be looked at for "analysis," have no conception of the meaning of the word. Furthermore, our laws are the products of our habits and customs, determined in large part at the local level where most matters are adjudicated. Let me cite an example. A hundred and fifty years ago, in Massachusetts, to deprive a man of livestock was to deprive him of life itself, thus that act was a capital offense. Today, in Massachusetts, it is a misdemeanor. Fifty years ago, in Texas, if you deprived a man of his stock you deprived him of his food and a means of transportation. Today, in Texas, the theft of livestock is still a capital offense and probably will continue to be for many years. This is a good example of the evolution of our laws which reflect the habits and customs of our people. Now, if we take the "Let somebody else do it" attitude, we will not be carrying through with our responsibilities in the adjudication of these matters.

In the United States, the training of crime laboratory specialists leaves much to be desired. So does the quality of work. There are actually only two schools, in the author's judgment, which provide more than a smattering of formal training in this specialty at the secondary educational level. There are, of course, many secondary schools for training in the natural sciences but this is merely the starting point for the man who is to specialize in this profession. It is well recognized that the School of Criminology at the University of California at Berkeley has attained increased educational stature through the training of people to enter crime laboratory work. Michigan State offers some courses but their efforts in this area have favored police investigation procedures, police administration, police record systems and all, at the expense of laboratory technician training. This condition, in part, may be so because of the fact there is no law school or medical school at Michigan State College. In training personnel to enter the crime laboratory service as a dedicated lifetime profession, one should begin with a firm background in basic sciences. Exceptional students, then, after completion of basic science offerings in the best schools, should be given the opportunity to serve an apprenticeship in a laboratory selected both because of its excellence in a narrow field of endeavor and its staff of dedicated professional practitioners. This specialized apprenticeship, or internship, is essential and it is supplementary to the basic training that has been mentioned.

This question of specialized training is extremely important. The confusion of the term "ballistics" with the term "firearms identification" illustrates what a lack of fundamental thinking can lead to. Ballistics is actually divided into two areas—interior and exterior. Interior ballistics deals with coefficient of friction, rates of acceleration of the projectile in the barrel, gas pressures, ignition times, instrumental velocities, and the like, from the time the firing pin strikes the timer until the projectile leaves the muzzle of the weapon. From the minute the projectile leaves the muzzle until it comes to rest we are concerned with exterior ballistics which treats of range, energy, impact, velocity, deceleration, rate of fall, and similar matters. There is nothing in either of these ballistics areas related to firearms identification which is the subject intended to be inferred by the use of the other term. One can imagine an unfortunate person going into court, hoping to qualify as an *identification* specialist, and being led by a lawyer down the primrose path of the ballistics expert. If opposing counsel should ask him fifteen questions directly in the field of ballistics, he could not answer a single one of them. This underlines the importance of interprofessional understanding between counsel and expert witnesses, as well as the importance of preparation where expert testimony is to be involved.

It has been observed, all to frequently, that some clinical pathologists and some general practitioners of medicine have not had the benefit of specialized medico-legal training in the area of death by violence. Without such training, some of these people, seemingly afflicted with a professional disease, attempt to make out teeth charts of the deceased, to interpret bullet wounds as to caliber, type of weapon, distance—findings completely foreign to their training as pathologists. Admittedly, a clinical pathologist is better than a general practitioner, if you have to have an autopsy performed involving a gun shot wound situation. But this reflects a need, at the medical school level, of acquainting these people, at the same time they are undertaking their training in the specialty of clinical pathology, with the need for caution, or the necessity of exercising caution, under such conditions. If you approach the medical schools on this situation the response is, "There isn't enough time now to get in all the courses that are required and desired." A possible answer to this is the short, intensified course, to be given to those who are going to be called upon to perform this type of work. The clinical pathologist, though primarily concerned with the cause of death, often has no occasion to see death by violence Once in Madison, a doctor passing through the morgue gave an off-hand opinion related to a gun shot wound victim on one table. He gave a pronouncement on the direction of the shot fired. As it happened the victim was right handed and this doctor had the bullet going in the wrong direction. Reflection of the scalp made it perfectly apparent that the bullet had entered on one side, tumbled as it transversed the skull, and then exited. This doctor should have stuck to his specialty. Such off-handed opinions can be exceedingly dangerous.

The pathologist should not be shackled with the necessity of recovering trace evidence in the clothing, or of handling the photographic recording of matters which interest the firearms specialist or the laboratory technician. A trained crew with adequate facilities available, including photographic equipment, should back up the autopsy surgeon in cases of death by violence. These people should take over the trace evidence recovery problems.

In conclusion, it is submitted that there are economic, administrative and functional relationships pertaining to the establishment and functioning of crime detection laboratories which should be very carefully explored by people outside of the enforcement field. The people who make this exploration should be familiar to some extent with law enforcement problems. This evaluation is long overdue because relatively little progress has been made in these areas in 32 years. This would suggest that administration in the enforcement field is moving too slowly, even though it may be moving slowly in the right direction.

NOTES

(1) *American Journal of Police Science*, vol. 1, pp. 60-78 (1930). This journal was published as a separate journal from 1930 to 1931. It was then incorporated and has since been published as a section of the *Journal of Criminal Law and Criminology*.

(2) *American Journal of Police Science*, vol. 1, pp. 13-37 (1930); vol. 2, pp. 125-155 (1931).

(3) Boolsen, Frank M., Peper, John P., "Law Enforcement Training in California," *California Peace Officers' Training Publication N. 72*, California State Department of Education, Sacramento, (1959).

(4) Mathews, J. Howard, "Firearms Identification," 2 vols. University of Wisconsin Press, Madison (1962).

(5) The reader is referred, for full information on the statutory provisions discussed here, to Wisconsin Statutes. Ch. 165 (State Crime Laboratory) §§ 165.01-165.06 (1961).—Ed.

III.

The Status of Criminalistics in the United States and Abroad

INTRODUCTION

Criminalistics is only one component of the total forensic science field, but in terms of sustained impact on the administration of justice, no other specialty can match its contributions. The number of crime laboratories in the United States has grown to over two hundred which now funtion within police agencies, district attorneys' offices, medical examiners' systems, and as independent units of state or local government. Forensic scientists at these laboratories are prepared to undertake scientific investigations of crime scenes, to examine physical evidence, to interpret the meaning of laboratory tests, and to deliver expert testimony in court. The sophistication of these laboratories has increased tremendously over the last five decades, but the fundamental objectives of the staff scientists have changed little. They serve as neutral and unbiased scientists who, depending upon the results of their examinations, will testify to the innocence of an accused party as well as to the involvement of the guilty.

Crime laboratories provide a wide range of scientific services. Beginning with Paul L. Kirk's article, "Criminalistics," which appeared in *Science* ten years ago, this section presents several status reports by well-known criminalists of laboratory operations in the United States, Great Britain, Northern Ireland, Canada and France. A. S. Curry, the well-known British toxicologist who heads the Home Office Research Establishment at Aldermaston, describes the services offered by his laboratory and those in England's other Regional Forensic Science

Laboratories. He emphasizes the work of his laboratory in improving its system of information collection, storage, and retrieval to efficiently handle the increasing volume and complexity of technical information.

An even more detailed examination of forensic science services available in the United Kingdom is provided in two additional articles, the first by Ray L. Williams of the London Metropolitan Forensic Laboratory. It is understandable why the British have developed such an excellent reputation in forensic science when one learns of the breadth and depth of scientific techniques utilized in the London laboratory. This laboratory is world famous for its pioneering work in the individualization of dried bloodstains, based upon the electrophoretic separation of particular enzymes and proteins. Cecil L. Wilson of Queen's University in Northern Ireland provides a fine survey of existing instrumental techniques for analyzing evidence, as well as a summary of recent document examination and blood alcohol testing procedures. He observes the tremendous challenge the forensic scientist faces in learning the latest laboratory techniques.

In the article, "Crime Labs Expand as Business Flourishes," Arnold E. Levitt comments on the recent growth of forensic science services in this country and describes the development of forensic science programs at major colleges and universities throughout the United States.

The final selection in this section is reprinted from the *FBI Law Enforcement Bulletin*, which commemorated the fortieth anniversary of the FBI Crime Laboratory in 1972. There is perhaps no better known laboratory in the world than the one within the Federal Bureau of Investigation. As this laboratory moves into its new quarters in the J. Edgar Hoover Building in Washington, D.C., it is exhibiting a rededication of purpose and commitment to assist state and local crime laboratories throughout the nation. While this selection does not reflect this new direction, recently implemented programs demonstrate the FBI's dedication to progress in the fields of scientific research and training.

CRIMINALISTICS

Paul L. Kirk

The clothing of a burglary suspect is brought to the laboratory. In the burglary being investigated, glass was broken. Glass fragments removed from the clothing are routinely compared with broken glass from the scene of the crime by means of the density-gradient method. The clothing is found to contain glass from four different sources, none of them from the scene of the crime. The suspect is probably a burglar, but he had no part in this particular crime. An old man is struck and killed by a hit-run automobile driver. Paint chips caught in his clothing identify the vehicle as probably a 1959 Dodge of a particular color. The type of damage to the automobile is deduced from a study of the types of bodily injury, the location of the paint on the victim's clothing, and the known behavior of human bodies struck by vehicles. A 1959 Dodge of the correct color and with corresponding damage is located, and another crime is solved. A dope peddler is identified by tiny fragments of marihuana leaves, or by traces of herion, in his pockets.

Happenings such as these constitute the daily routine of a criminalistics laboratory, which quietly provides factual information to the authorities and assists in determining the guilt or innocence of thousands of suspects every year. Criminalistics is an occupation that is poorly understood by the great majority of people, including the scientific public. It is generally assessed in terms of high-grade detective work rather than in terms of a serious and very demanding type of applied science. Its evolution from the natural sciences and its current trends, its limitations, and its future possibilities are the subject of this discussion.

SHIFT OF ORIENTATION IN THE HISTORY OF SCIENCE

In the realm of the natural sciences, the history of the development of human thinking is a complex and fascinating study. The ancients were concerned with natural philosophy, from which modern science evolved, and they made extensive and accurate observations. However, their thinking was on the intellectual plane; they did not experiment. With the early experimental approach of Archimedes, Copernicus, Galileo, Leuwenhoek, Newton, and Lavoisier, to mention only a few, fundamental disciplines that we now recognize as individual sciences developed. The monumental achievements of these men became the foundations of structures that their originators could not have predicted or even comprehended. Indeed, we still cannot forsee their ultimate evolution.

In more modern times, a different type of discipline emerged, one based on the practical needs of humanity rather than upon mere curiosity about nature, important and productive as that was. From this newer trend developed, among others, the disciplines of medicine, engineering, and law. For such disciplines the term *profession* was more suitable than *science*, for some of them made no direct use of science as currently defined, and others synthesized many scientific principles and facts into a heterogeneous whole of which the central core was a human need. In the latter category, medicine is the best example. It adopted knowledge from every science that bears on the physical nature of man, his abnormalities, and his diseases in order to minister to his health. Similarly, engineering adopted those principles and data that were of use to it in constructing the man-made world. In these and other disciplines the significant alternation in thought was related to human activity rather than to the broader and more objective concerns of pure scientific development. Nevertheless, some of these disciplines did develop specific new sciences within themselves.

As scientific knowledge in any broad category has been extended past the stage of easy comprehension, it has been divided and subdivided into specialties which can be mastered by the individual. The process is now being reversed in many of the more complex enterprises of modern man. Physicists and engineers must not shoot men into space without extensive and thorough consideration of man's physiology under stress, his psychology, and his basic biological needs. Atomic energy was not born without great preoccupation with mineralogy, metallurgy, ceramics, microchemistry, and medical science, as well as with the physics and chemistry that were basic to solution of the primary problems.

Crime is just such a complex problem. It is perhaps the oldest problem that confronts mankind, and the one that has received the least attention from scientists and other thinkers. Quantitatively, the problem of crime is far greater than many of the problems on which untold millions have been spent—for example, spectacular diseases such as cancer of poliomyelitis. According to reliable statistics, one person out of every 67 to 70 will be the victim of a felony each year. Thus, at man's present life expectancy, every citizen is likely to be the victim of a major criminal act in the course of his lifetime. As compared with cancer or any other specific disease, crime gives us very poor odds indeed.

Furthermore, the economic aspects of crime are generally not appreciated, partly because reliable figures are not available. A study made some 20 years ago gave an estimate for the total cost of crime in the United States as $20 billion a year. This figure included a large item for organized crime, but it seems reasonably certain that inflation, increase in population, and a general increase in the crime rate have augmented the cost significantly, whether or not organized crime is included. Reliable or not, the statistics indicate the magnitude of the problem and justify the conclusion that more is needed to deal with it than the almost random and inexpert methods that are the norm.

Criminalistics is one of a very few activities based on natural science that have arisen in response to this need. It is concerned with the study of physical objects and physical facts relevant to the crime, from which a reconstruction and understanding of the crime may be developed. It helps to establish the facts and to determine the guilt or innocence of an accused person, although the latter is not its primary function. Criminalistics has not been extended into areas currently based on sociological and psychological concepts, which also are in an early stage of investigation. That it may intrude into these areas in the future is not unlikely. Because evidence is of every imaginable kind, criminalistics, like medicine, has borrowed from all science that which is applicable to its needs. Also like medicine, it has developed a limited science of its own, made necessary by its special requirements.

THE REALM OF THE UNLIKELY

Criminalistics is concerned with the unlikely and the unusual. Other sciences are concerned primarily with the likely and the usual. The derivation of equations, formulas, and generalizations summarizing the normal behavior of any system in the universe is a major goal of the established sciences. It is not normal to be murdered, and most persons never experience this unlikely event. Yet, when a murder occurs, some combination of circumstances suddenly alters the situation from unlikely to certain. What happens here has never been mathematically analyzed, although the need for such an analysis has long been apparent. Mathematical analysis is even more necessary for interpreting the significance of each fact that is elicited relative to the evidence. However, we do not yet know how to make such an analysis, despite technical success in determining the actual facts of a crime through study of physical evidence. The lack of mathematical exactness in the interpretation of the facts, and its effect upon an accused person, is sometimes tragic. Despite the so-called safeguards of the law, it is not possible to prevent the release of many guilty persons or the conviction of a few innocent men. Until this area of science also is reduced to reasonable mathematical exactness, the administration of justice will be correspondingly hampered.

For example, in one murder case, misuse of statistical reasoning produced the argument that the chances that a particular gun was the murder weapon were several hundred to one, because it was a revolver rather than a pistol, it had six lands and grooves and a right-hand twist, and it was of a particular caliber. The interdependence of several of the variables was disregarded, as was the fact that firearms with these exact class characteristics could be very plentiful. In the absence of actual identification of the weapon as having fired the fatal bullet, such an argument could lead to unjust conviction.

Too much cannot now be expected of criminalistics as an exact science. Too many criminalists are still being trained by working in a crime laboratory under more experienced but sometimes unscientific persons. This is analogous to the early days of medicine and law, when the future doctor was apprenticed to the practitioner and the embryo lawyer "read law" in a law office. All professions have abandoned this hit-or-miss method of training. Although criminalistics is a discipline, it is not yet a mature enough discipline to have emerged from the apprenticeship system. The universities, the public, and even the law-enforcement agencies have been slow to recognize that systematic, thorough, and complete training must be made available to individuals on whose knowledge the liberty and even the lives of other persons may later depend. This is a responsibility second to none. The responsibility is made even heavier by the fact that the criminalist cannot hide his errors by attributing them to acts of God or to unavoidable circumstances. His testimony is a public record under the spotlight of publicity. His performance needs to be perfect, for it cannot be repeated or amended.

PRINCIPLES, TECHNIQUES, INSTRUMENTATION, OBJECTIVITY

What characteristics warrant the recognition of criminalistics as an independent discipline? As with the other disciplines, there is a thread of principles that bind the parts into a coherent whole. These principles center on identification and individualization of persons and of physical objects. Determination of the nature of an object and of its specific origin is basic in interpreting a crime or an accident. In addition, there must be standards of performance, training, and ethics. In California all of these requirements have been met through the efforts of the California Association of Criminalists (1) and of several colleges and universities of the state; in some other jurisdictional areas limited progress has been made.

Along with principles must go techniques. These are applied not at random but rather to the degree to which they lead to reliable identification and reveal the individual origin of the item identified. While the variety of instruments and of techniques is very great, each is useful only in the limited context of its direct contribution to the individualization of the object of evidence. It is in the area of new techniques and instruments that criminalistics is now making its greatest strides, even before there is a reliable basis for exact interpretation of the results.

For instance, it is possible to identify all types of textile fiber with exactness, through a variety of methods that include microscopy, chemical testing, x-ray diffraction, and pyrolysis-gas chromatography, However, the probabilistic value of a fiber transfer between two sets of clothing, as in a crime, is still a matter of controversy, even though such transfers constitute one of the more valuable types of evidence.

Just as the skill of the doctor does not rest on the excellence of his stethoscope or the sharpness of his scalpel, the excellence of the criminalist does not depend on the multiplicity of his instruments. A master of all techniques may remain merely a technician, and the best of all technicians is not necessarily a satisfactory criminalist. The criminalist must analyze the problem and understand the principle in order to arrive at a correct interpretation of the criminal act. In addition, he must be second to none in objectivity, for on his objectivity may depend the lives and liberties of other people. These obvious facts bear repeating only because they are often disregarded.

According to an old axiom, nature never reproduces herself exactly; thus no two objects in the universe are ever totally indistinguishable. However, two pieces of the same original object share many properties and are so much alike that, if one piece is of known origin, the origin of the other can be established.

The properties that may be used for establishing the source of a sample are of three types—morphological, compositional, and spatial. Since two objects cannot occupy exactly the same space at the same time, the spatial property of an object is of ultimate value, but only in those infrequent cases where it is applicable. Thus, for most identification problems, only morphological and compositional properties are useful. Until recently, morphological properties were, by a very large factor, the most valuable, because they are often a means of definitely establishing the origin of a sample. For example, a broken piece of glass may show an exact fit with the fracture surface of another piece of glass. This type of morphological agreement constitutes the most exact means of establishing a common source. Compositional comparisons have not ordinarily been able to provide such clear proof of common origin.

Morphological evidence is generally "pattern" evidence. Evidence of the broken-glass type depends upon pattern, as do fingerprint, bullet striation, and many other common classes of evidence. Compositional factors may also yield a pattern—for example, an absorption curve or the tracings from a recorder attached to an x-ray diffraction apparatus, a gas chromatograph, or any one of a number of other instruments. Pattern evidence has been considered the most reliable indicator of the identity or nonidentity of origin of two samples. Now it appears that evidence of even greater value can be obtained from the detailed evaluation of compositional impurities by means of neutron activation analysis.

It is apparent that, in the criminalistic sense, two samples having exactly the same absolute composition could never be distinguished except through morphological or spatial comparison; nor, theoretically, could two samples of an absolutely pure compound be distinguished. (Actually, no pure compound exists or has ever existed.) Two samples from different sources would never be expected to have the same absolute composition. With respect to any given sample, chemical analysis is concerned with only a few elements, despite the fact that any sample on earth, however small, may be expected to contain some quantity of any, or even all, of the elements on earth.

IDENTIFICATION AND INDIVIDUALIZATION

The development of neutron activation analysis has provided a new and highly significant approach to the solution of the problem of individualization. By chemical methods many elements cannot be detected in dilutions greater than 1 part per million, and few, if any, are detectable chemically in concentrations of less than 1 part per billion. Yet 1 gram of a material could contain an impurity of atomic weight 100 at the level of 1 part per billion to the extent of about 10^{12} atoms. It is evident that there is ample opportunity for chemically nondetectable contamination of any sample by any and every element. This seeming obstacle becomes an advantage under neutron activation analysis, by which some elements can be detected, identified, and (in favorable instances) determined quantitatively in quantities in the picogram range (10^{-12}g). This constitutes a major breakthrough. In this process the sample is subjected to a high flux of thermal neutrons (or sometimes high-speed neutrons) and the radioactive isotopes of both the major and the minor constituents are formed. Neutrons may be generated by more than one method, but the highest flux has been obtained in the nuclear reactor, which is becoming increasingly available for this use. The resulting active mixture can be subjected to direct gamma-ray spectrometry for immediate analysis, or the products can be separated chemically and evaluated quantitatively by means of a simpler counting device for gamma or occasionally beta rays. If it can be used, gamma-ray spectrometry is preferable for two reasons: (i) it is a rapid, non-destructive method of analysis, and (ii), because it *is* rapid, the short-lived isotopes can be measured. In destructive chemical operations, no matter how rapidly they are carried out, some of the short-lived isotopes inevitably decay past the point of evaluation. The major advantages of chemical separation are that mutual interference of isotopes of very similar energies is eliminated and that beta rays as well as gamma rays can be counted.

Already, major advances have been made in individualization studies of a wide variety of evidential materials through neutron activation analysis, and work is progressing rapidly at several sites where facilities are available. Perhaps the most notable advance is apparent in the work on human hair. As early as 1961 a group of Canadian researchers(2) reported the detection in human hair of measurable amounts of gold, cobalt, manganese, molybdenum, selenium, chlorine, bromine, iodine, mercury, germanium, and chromium, in addition to the arsenic, copper, zinc, iron, silicon, sodium, and vanadium which had been recognized earlier(3). Not all of the newly reported elements appear in all hair samples, and the concentrations differ for different people. In a study of hair samples from 30 persons, no two samples from different individuals showed similar patterns of trace-element content, while in replicate determinations for different samples from the same person, the results were reproducible to within the precision of the individual determinations. Thus, with a limited number of samples it was shown that the individuality of human hair is demonstrable through quantitative determination of the components. Study of one individual's hair over a period of a year showed some slight changes in composition, especially with respect to selenium, copper, and gold. However, the general pattern was clearly recognizable over that period. Samples from a single individual taken 14 years apart showed appreciable variation, as would be expected with the changes that occur in environmental factors and diet. General confirmation and considerable extension of this work have been accomplished by a group at Oak Ridge National Laboratory(4).

Similar studies of tissues, blood, dust, soil, cloth fibers, and numerous other materials have been, or are being, made by the Oak Ridge group and by other groups of researchers. An unusual application of neutron activation analysis is its use in determining whether or not a particular person has fired a gun(5). Although the dermal nitrate test has been employed widely for many years, it is known to be unreliable, and recommendations against its use have been made by the California Association of Criminalists and possibly by other organizations. With the neutron activation method, a finding of antimony, barium, and copper (gunshot residues) in swabbings of the hands appears to be a reliable indication that the individual has fired a gun. This would be the first reliable indicator we have had. Furthermore, the data obtained also indicate the type of ammunition used and the number of shots fired. It is safe to predict that activation analysis will soon make it possible to solve a large number of criminalistic problems of types that have hitherto seemed baffling.

Neutron activation analysis, spectacular as it is in the area of criminalistics, is not the only new development in this field. Infrared absorptiometry, very familiar to the chemist, is now being used extensively in the crime laboratory for individualizing organic materials because it furnishes a complex pattern with many points of comparison. Highly sophisticated techniques such as nuclear magnetic resonance and electron spin resonance are being used occasionally on an experimental basis.

Gas-liquid chromatography is another technique now being used to solve some of the more difficult problems of the crime laboratory. A relatively new technique in criminalistics, though for years a tool of the petroleum chemist, this method is now used for identifying and separating many drugs and poisons that were formerly thought to be insufficiently volatile to be separable in the vapor phase. Pyrolysis in combination with gas-liquid chromatography promises to be a simple and very powerful method for identifying samples of organic materials of all types(6). The usefulness of gas-liquid chromatography in the investigation of fires and explosions and of industrial accidents involving volatile organic materials is obvious.

Techniques of the biologist are also being used extensively in criminalistics. For example, it now appears that through immunoelectrophoresis, largely a biochemical and medical tool, we will soon take a long stride toward determining the individuality of blood (7).

The forensic sciences, and especially criminalistics, are the sole point of contact between science and the administration of justice. Although science, in the form of medical, chemical, criminalistic, and engineering service to the courts, has been of enormous value, its full potential in this role is yet to be realized. Not only are scientists unacquainted with the law and its operation but they are often reluctant to be involved in legal matters. Law enforcement personnel and attorneys are less reluctant to utilize the techniques of science, but often they are ignorant of the services that are available to them and of how to engage them. The result is slow progress in establishing the necessary understanding and liason.

PROBABLE FUTURE TRENDS

The recent exceedingly rapid development of science in general has not extended to forensic science. Signs abound that the ultimate role of criminalistics will be far broader and more significant than merely the study and interpretation of evidence. To illustrate, there is now strong evidence that certain mental diseases, notably schizophrenia, are associated with abnormal blood components(8). It also is recognized that alcoholics and drug addicts have metabolic abnormalities. Conditions such as these are certainly related to criminality, and it may well be that detectable physiological or other abnormalities may also be characteristic of certain forms of criminality. Questions of "legal insanity," or of the distinction between illness and crime in the case of addicts and others, should be decided on the basis of improved laboratory methods rather than the inconclusive and controversial methods now available. The vast areas of electronics, of computers, of psycho-pharmacology, and of other active fields of scientific research have had little impact upon the administration of justice. When more widespread understanding and interest are accorded forensic science—criminalistics in particular—a complete revolution in our methods of combatting crime, the oldest problem of society, may be confidently expected.

NOTES

(1) L.W. Bradford, *J. Criminal Law Criminol. Police Sci.* 53, 375 (1962).

(2) R.E. Jervis, A.K. Perkons, W.D. Mackintosh, M.F. Kerr, "Activation Analysis in Forensic Investigation," *Proc. Intern. Conf. Modern Trends in Activation Analysis, College Station, Tex.* (1961), p. 107.

(3) O. Szep, *Z. Physiol. Chem.* 267, 401 (1940); T.F. Dutcher and S. Rothman, *J. Invest. Dermatol.* 17, 65 (1951).

(4) G.W. Leddicotte *et al.*, *Nucl. Sci. Eng.*, in press.

(5) R.R. Ruch, V.P. Guinn, R.H. Pinker, *ibid.*, in press.

(6) J. Janak, *Nature* 185, 684 (1960); D.F. Nelson and P.L. Kirk, *Anal. Chem.* 34, 899 (1962); D.F. Nelson, J.L. Yee, P.L. Kirk, *Microchem. J.* 6, 225 (1962).

(7) A.F. Laudel, B.W. Grunbaum, P.L. Kirk, *Science* 137, 862 (1962); ————, J. *Forensic Med.*, in press.

(8) W.J. Fessel and B.W. Grunbaum, *Ann. Internal Med.* 54, 1134 (1961).

CHEMISTRY AND CRIME

A.S. Curry

The modern policeman is a highly skilled technician whose job is as far from the Victorian picture of a man who supplies the correct time as the horse carriage is from Apollo 11. The police service in 1969 has to be capable of dealing with a diversity of situations from the Great Train Robbery, the Aberfan disaster and multi-car crashes on the M1, to traffic control by helicopter, computer retrieval of crime information and finger-prints and the tracking of criminals, who think in terms of New York yesterday, London today, and Argentina tomorrow, or clandestine laboratories manufacturing drugs of addiction on a massive scale.

The laboratory service for every police officer in England and Wales is provided by the Metropolitan Police Laboratory, eight Home Office Regional Forensic Science Laboratories and the Central Research Establishment at Aldermaston. In these laboratories over 300 scientists provide the chemical and biological expertise that again is as far from Sherlock Holmes as our Gilbertian Police Officer is from his modern counterpart.

The policeman in his panda car patrolling at night noting the travellers has to be a reliable, competent officer capable of making decisions that will later stand scrutiny by several Queen's Counsel, Her Majesty's judges and even perhaps, on appeal, the House of Lords. His decisions at 1 am on a cold winter night when he comes across a blazing car in a country lane in which he can see the body of a man have to be immediate yet finely balanced between conflicting interests. He has to attempt to save life, to call the fire brigade, summon further police assistance, consider the possibility that this may be the disposal of a body by a murderer who may be making his escape and that vital clues may be lost for ever by ill considered or incompletely remembered deeds.

The forensic scientist rarely has to act in a matter of seconds but when he arrives at the scene, perhaps an hour or so later, his decisions are none the less testing. The road has been closed to traffic, the fire brigade have illuminated the burnt-out car and the obviously dead body is still in position in the driving seat. Precise information is minimal—the car is registered over 100 miles away and police enquiries are just beginning. Laboratory aid has been sought for two reasons—the enquiry is obviously going to be technical involving pathological and scientific aspects and, because of the possibility of murder, work has to begin immediately. The experience of the laboratory scientist in this type of case is wide. He serves several police forces covering a population of about five million and consequently acquires an accumulated experience in all types of serious crimes.

In the next 12 hours the car and its surrounds, after detailed photography, are examined in minute detail; the body is searched and burnt papers carefully removed and rushed back to the laboratory where they provide the first concrete clues as to the identity of the individual. Slowly the pattern emerges: the fire has been intense and, although the petrol can in the car is empty, a gas chromatographic examination of unburnt tissue from the body shows the presence of petrol—the moving finger of the recorder trace writes its story of inhaled vapours prior to the fire; the pathologist finds evidence of disease and previous trauma but no violent injuries, bullet or stab wounds; the toxicologist using paper and thin-layer chromatography to purify his extracts identifies, by ultraviolet and infrared spectroscopy, therapeutic quantities of a tranquillizer which the missing owner of the car was known to take. In the deceased's hip pocket is found a substantial sum of money—even the numbers of the burnt notes can be deciphered—and so the possibility of murder recedes into the background and it is left to a coroner's jury to weigh the evidence that is presented to them.

THE FORENSIC SCIENTIST AT WORK

Forensic science is one of the most intellectually demanding and yet rewarding professions; as one of the common services provided by the Home Office for all police forces it seeks to help the police officer ascertain the truth in all the situations that come to their attention in this modern civilization. The scientist has to have a considerable degree of inter-disciplinary expertise. In a hit-and-run motor car accident case, for example, he may have to compare the paint, plastic and glass fragments found on the deceased with those from damaged areas of a suspect car and the hairs caught in the broken windscreen, fibres on the bonnet and blood on the roof have to be compared with those from the deceased. The scientific examination of these materials by the laboratory involves such instrumental techniques as the x-ray diffraction of the paint fillers, arc emission spectroscopy of the paint and glass fragments, pyrolysis-glc of the paint and plastic, neutron activation analysis of the hairs to compare their trace element composition, the determination of a number of blood group factors and genetically related protein and enzyme systems as well as the less esoteric occupations of fitting together jig-saw fashion the glass fragments on the body with those from a broken headlamp and the matching of scrape marks on the bonnet with the damage to the deceased's clothing. Obviously very few can claim to be experimentally competent in all these areas and the laboratory work will most probably be shared between two or three court-going scientific officers, each backed up by an experimental officer.

It is vital for the scientist or policeman who collects the evidence at the scene of the incident to have intimate knowledge of every facet of the work of the laboratory. The responsibility of the scientist who trains police scene-of-crime scientific aids officers is therefore heavy. Inadequate sampling or incorrect preservation can easily cause vital evidence to be lost. For example, although research into the individuality of blood promises a high return it will be only as profitable and as efficient as the police officer or scientist who finds and correctly packs the sample at the murder scene. Interdisciplinary expertise has to be combined with the practical application of science in the detection of crime. It is in this area that experience is a vital factor. The scientist who goes to the scene of a fire or a sudden death for the first time is unlikely to be of much value in the enquiry. His emotions have yet to trained so that he can view with detachment the human problems of a tragedy and get down to the task of putting together a story from the visual picture and minutiae of the scene with perhaps the essential facts such as flash point temperatures, explosive gas limits, fatal doses of poisons, colour sequence of car paints, or the percentage Group 'A' individuals in the community, as the foundations to make or break a theory as to how a crime was committed.

However, the budding forensic scientist will soon discover the satisfaction that comes when a scientific deduction is shown to be justified and a crime is solved that without his expertise might have remained undetected or at best would have involved extra man hours of work by the police. He will also cease to be surprised at the vagaries of human behaviour and come to know a little of the cunning of the criminal mind against whom he has to pit his wits. He will be surprised at the depth of human as well as scientific knowledge demanded of him. His knowledge and judgement will be most tested not by a QC's cross examination but by a Detective Chief Inspector whose interrogation bears none of the former's niceties.

Sometimes the memory of an experiment long since confined to the almost inaccessible regions of his brain will be recalled in the most unlikely environment. This happened to me at 3 am on a very cold winter night in a Yorkshire market town where the police were trying to understand a mysterious death of a young man and the sudden collapse with respiratory oedema of two of his relatives, five hours after a terrible smell had caused the evacuation of a row of houses. The realization that this smell had been phosgene was forced upon me by the recollection of a laboratory accident many years before when, after opening a stored bottle of specially purified chloroform, a colleague had to be sent to hospital. The discovery that there were cylinders of liquid phosgene in a dwelling house involved the local Medical Officer of Health, the Borough Surveyor, ICI, the Chemical Defence Experimental Establishment at Porton and at least two professors of chemistry. The solution of that particular problem only began to be found after analysis (involving incidentally glc and mass spectrometry) of liquid from a drain.

GROWTH OF FORENSIC SCIENCE

Perhaps one of the first forensic scientists was Archimedes who ran from his bath to the court with a solution to the problem of distinguishing base metal from gold. Little was heard of his successors until the 19th century when forensic medicine rather than science came into the university curriculum although chemists were sometimes tempted to enter the field of toxicological analysis. The early 1900s saw science entering the legal arena more and more and by the 1930s the Home Office and Scotland Yard had decided that a national service was required. Scotland Yard laboratory remains to this day a police laboratory in that its staff are responsible to the Commissioner of Police but the Home Office laboratories are part of the Scientific Civil Service.

There are now eight Regional Laboratories, geographically arranged to cover England and Wales, at Nottingham, Harrogate, Newcastle, Preston, Birmingham, Bristol, Cardiff and Aldermaston and with Scotland Yard they handle an annual load of about 50,000 cases. (This should be contrasted with the figure of less than 200 murders that occur each year.) There is hardly a type of crime in which scientific assistance is not required; from simple forgeries to assault, rape or arson. The analysis of blood for alcohol under the new Road Safety Act has significantly raised the case load but so also has the entry into the social scene of cannabis, heroin, the amphetamines and the hallucinogens.

A new phenomenon is becoming apparent in serious crime—the use of scientists by the criminal fraternity. The clandestine laboratory, manufacturing perhaps a few kilogrammes of hallucinogen worth millions of pounds on the black market and offering attractive terms to the organic chemist, is but one example. It is often said that criminals learn much of their trade in prison; let us watch out for the chemistry degree, Grad. Parkhurst in Chemistry (GPIC).

FORENSIC RESEARCH

Research into forensic science problems was envisaged by the Home Office at the beginning of the service but it was not until 1966 that a Central Research Establishment came into being. The CRE aims to find methods that will enable the Regional Laboratories to obtain evidence not previously available, to increase the value of scientific evidence, and to increase productivity.

Six divisions have been set up to cover major areas of work involved in forensic science investigations. Biological research concentrates on the individuality of human blood (especially in the form of blood stains) and is co-operating with the MRC Unit at Mill Hill (Dr. Tristam Freeman) in a study of two-dimensional crossed antigen-antibody serum protein patterns. This division is also studying the chemistry involved in the ageing of blood stains and the morphology of hair. Co-operation with workers at Scotland Yard and the Regional Laboratories who are actively researching in genetically linked cell and serum blood group and enzyme systems is maintained. Regular colloquia on all aspects of forensic science are held at CRE and provide a much needed forum. Speakers are invited from industry and the universities as well as from within the service and a Scientific Advisory Committee is available to provide assistance.

Another division of CRE is concerned with the methods of analysis of paint and glass fragments; these are the Regional Laboratories bread-and-butter being found regularly in crimes against property. These crimes may vary from a simple housebreaking, to a Great Train Robbery, or perhaps a murder committed in furtherance of theft. In one murder case the evidence against the accused consisted of paint on his clothes similar to that from a door that had been forced; wood similar to that from the door; glass with the same physical properties as glass fragments found on the cellar floor and blood on his jacket of the same group as the deceased. The pattern of the blood on the cuff of the jacket was consistent with it having been deposited during a right-handed beating attack.

The silent witnesses of a murder are so often inanimate particles of dust and debris which speak loudly if the right analytical questions are put to them. To interpret the significance of the presence of minute fragments of glass or paint on or in clothing it is necessary to measure the discrimination of the analytical techniques and also the distribution of their natural occurrence in the environment. This type of survey work is being undertaken by both CRE and the Regional Laboratories and in external research contracts. The possibility that the concentrations of trace elements may vary between batches or probably within batches of a mass production product is being investigated using both neutron activation analysis and inorganic spark source mass spectrometry (AEI MS702).

The desire to obtain more, and better, evidence leads to the conclusion that fundamental research into aspects of inorganic and organic chemistry is to be encouraged as a long term project in forensic science and already there have been significant results on the infrared examination of sub-microgram amounts in trapped gc fractions. Now, for the small cost of modifying existing equipment at the Regional Laboratories, the sensitivity of detection and identification of the barbiturates, for example, has been increased over 100 fold.

The use of gas chromatography-mass spectrometry is yielding information on trace compounds present in body tissues in a study of poison extraction systems for use in toxicological analysis. The development of automatic machines for toxicological analysis, to increase manpower productivity, is another area of work in the Toxicology Division which also co-operates with the RAF in investigating aircraft accidents. A recent notable example was the successful detection of carbon monoxide in the tissues of a dead aircrew leading to the discovery of a faulty cabin heater in the wreckage of the crash. It is very doubtful whether this would have been discovered if the RAF/Home Office Unit at CRE had not been researching into the analytical methodology of this type of problem and developed gas chromatographic techniques suitable for use in this most difficult biochemical problem area. The detection of sub-therapeutic quantities of drugs in aircrew, in small samples of blood, tissues or urine will obviously be of interest in the problem area associated with drugs and car driving.

COMPUTERIZED LITERATURE SEARCH

Until 1967 each Regional Laboratory provided its own information service but the system was inefficient and it was not surprising that, in suggesting areas of work for the new Central Research Establishment, the directors of the Regional Laboratories put information services high on their list of priorities. There were four main areas into which the required service would fall: (i) searching of the current world scientific literature and provision to each laboratory, at monthly intervals, of details of papers of interest published or noted in the previous month; (ii) provision of literature searching facilities on subjects that might occur in a particular case; (iii) collection and distribution of specialized collections of data; (iv) provision of training manuals containing the relevant published work on selected general topics.

The Central Research Establishment was fortunate to be included in the first year's trial period of The Chemical Society Information Retrieval Unit and is continuing to use the service. About 200 papers from a survey of over 700 journals are received each two weeks in response to the 42 search terms fed to the computer. Manual searching of the literature is still necessary and any papers of interest noticed in abstracts journals are obtained from external sources. In this way, in each calendar month, about 150 papers of immediate interest to forensic scientists are collected as well as a number of other papers of potential interest, those involving current research topics at CRE and a number of value for background information. Papers of immediate interest are catalogued into five disciplines—pathology, chemistry, biology, toxicology and general criminalistics—copied, and circulated to all the Regional Forensic Science Laboratories. Other papers are filed for future use.

Copying of this material onto microfilm, together with up-to-date indexing, was the next logical development and all the Regional Laboratories now have a Filmac Reader Printer Unit. Print-out facilities are provided because it may be necessary for the scientist to refer later to a particular item on the microfilm not only in the laboratory, but also in the witness box, and the easy and rapid provision of relevant copy for each set of case records is a valuable addition to the straightforward microfilm technique. The index already includes approximately 2500 search terms and further work into the best method of indexing has been started. It is hoped that by the early 1970s, the Regional Laboratories will be on-line with the National Police Computer fed by CRE for an information service.

The provision of literature searching facilities on particular subjects was the second main service facility and the value of having a centralized unit for this has been shown. Contacts made with industry, universities, etc., are more numerous than hitherto and are hence more easily developed. Other specialized laboratories have welcomed having to deal with only one forensic science unit instead of receiving similar queries from all the Regional Laboratories. The problems met in searching the literature for specific topics are being investigated and some measure of international co-operation is being developed, for example, in the toxicological field with the National Library of Medicine in Washington.

SPECIALIZED DATA COLLECTIONS

Three projects on the collection and distribution of specialized collections of data have been completed. First, the infrared spectra of over 2000 compounds of forensic science interest (mainly toxicological in emphasis) were available from the North Eastern Forensic Science Laboratory and these have been provided on microfilm to all the Regional Laboratories. A system for expanding this collection to 10,000 compounds with a simple means of retrieval for an unknown curve has been developed using a film optical coincidence card made by Information Handling Ltd. The use of optical coincidence cards of this type is likely to be of great value in other fields of forensic science: for example, the characteristics on a bullet or cartridge case that enable an identification to be made of the type of weapon involved, the dimensions and shape of motorcar tyre treads for identification of the manufacturer, and the identification of pills and capsules from physical characteristics. Centralized collection of new compounds has been organized, and arrangements made to ensure that it is kept up to date.

Professor E. G. C. Clarke of the Royal Veterinary College kindly supplied CRE with samples from his collection of over 700 alkaloids and the ultraviolet curves have been prepared and microfilmed for circulation to all laboratories. The third completed project of this type concerns shoe and boot impressions. These are sometimes found at scenes of crime and it is of assistance in the police enquiry to know the make, size and type of footwear that made the mark. The Shoe and Allied Trades Association and the Shoe and Heel Manufacturers' Association made available to CRE their collections which are now copied and supplied to each Regional Laboratory.

With these collections, the problems of updating, *i.e.* adding new data as soon as possible after it is published, have to be faced. When roll film is used (the normal length of which is 100 ft. containing about 2000 pages of print) the difficulties of adding, say, half a dozen extra sheets of new information are formidable; the film has to be cut, the extra images inserted and a complete new film produced. Training manuals, the fourth main project, also require routine updating. To overcome this problem, our Treasury and O and M advisers suggested the use of microfiche cards. In this system the main collection is microfilmed and then made into 6 in. x 4 in. film cards each containing 60—70 pages of print or diagrams. Reproduction of such sets by diazo copying is done at CRE for circulation to all Regional Laboratories. When updating is required, only the last card in the series has to be altered so expensive reduplication of previous effort is avoided.

COMMUNICATION WITH THE LAYMAN

The problem of intercommunication between scientists, which Information Division at CRE is attempting to solve in relation to forensic scientists and toxicologists, serves to emphasize that in the end the results have to be communicated to policeman, lawyer and juryman. The value of good scientific evidence can be lost if this channel of communication breaks down, or, worse still, weak scientific evidence can be overemphasized in a manner prejudicial to the defendant. The increase in complexity of analysis has done nothing to ease this problem and in my opinion there is a need for intensive study of the way in which science can best be interpreted to a person who does not know a filter paper from a football pool coupon. Although the responsibility of the scientist is high, there has been up to now, little interest by the interpreters, i.e. solicitors and barristers, in this relatively new area. When only a microscope or an x-ray was needed in court, this was understandable; when a juryman has to take into account results of mass spectrometry and immunoelectrophoresis as well as Archimedes' principle, some effort must be put into this communicative channel.

In conclusion, although emphasis has been placed on the need for communication, there may be many chemists who may realize now that their new research tool, technique or specialized knowledge could play a part in the forensic scientist's work; will they please communicate with the author?

FORENSIC SCIENCE – THE PRESENT

AND THE FUTURE

Ray L. Williams

I should emphasize right at the beginning that any article of this nature is bound to contain a number of unavoidable biases. I am a physical chemist, and I have no doubt that if this paper were written by an organic chemist, a biochemist, a toxicologist, or a biologist, that the emphasis would be quite different (1, 2). Furthermore, I would point out that although the United States and the UK have basically similar legal procedures, there are differences in the acceptance of scientific evidence which necessarily mean that what constitutes "proof" in one court is not so regarded in another.

In the UK, the Criminal Justice Act of 1967 permitted the use of written statements by scientists instead of their giving oral testimony. Counsel or the judge can still ask for the scientist to attend court, but since then, the number of court appearances by expert witnesses has declined dramatically. For the Metropolitan Police Laboratory, for example, in 1967 there were 7973 cases and 2336 court appearances: in 1972 with 36,814 cases, there were only 723 appearances. Written statements have to be quite brief. The experimental details on which the expert opinions are based are therefore kept to a minimum. This reduces the emphasis on which techniques are used in the examination and disguises the fact that there are considerable differences in what is regarded as acceptable as an identification. For example, some experts rely on crystal tests to identify a drug. Others may insist on spot tests plus thin-layer chromatography and gas chromatography data, whereas others insist on infrared, ultraviolet, and perhaps mass spectra in addition.

The methods are not accentuated in the written statement, and it is up to the defence to raise this point in cross-examination if it thinks fit. The trend in English courts at present seems to be to accept the facts, by whatever techniques they may have been obtained, and to dispute the interpretation. The situation therefore places considerable responsibility on the expert witness in his attitude to analytical methods.

I would be very surprised if the situation were exactly the same in all the courts in the U.S. Differences in emphasis are bound to occur, and because of this, there will be differences in the methods used, not only in the two countries but also from laboratory to laboratory. In this article, I am reflecting predominantly current British attitudes, particularly those prevailing in my own laboratory.

FORENSIC SCIENTIST'S ROLE

May I remind you first of all that the forensic scientist's task is to assist the court in deciding whether or not a particular person has been involved in a crime. The scientist has items—"exhibits"—submitted to him by the police for examination, and he has two questions to answer about anything of significance which he may find on the exhibits. Firstly, what is it? For example, is the dark stain on a jacket, blood? Are these tablets amphetamines? Secondly, if it is an item which can be associated indisputably with a suspect, it is identical with that found at the scene of a crime, and what are the chances that this identity might be accidental? For example, is the flake of paint found on the clothing of a person thought to have robbed a house, the same as the paint on the window frame through which entry was made? What are the odds against a similar flake of paint turning up from some other source?

The forensic scientist is conservative in his outlook, partly because over the years he has had to acquire his methods slowly and painfully: I have deliberately used the word painfully because the acquisition has been accomplished against a background of growing work load, shortage of money for equipment, and in the face of some scepticism of the value of scientific evidence from the legal profession. The last factor, of course, is absolutely right; every scientific method and deduction should be closely questioned and scrutinised when a person's innocence or guilt depends thereon. However, the process has not been made easy by the tactics of some lawyers who have relied on emotive rather than rational criticism.

ANALYTICAL METHODS

Fortunately, the situation has improved in all three respects over the last few years but has left a legacy which substantially dictates which forensic methods are practicable. These must use relatively inexpensive equipment, be capable of application to a wide range of problems, be rapid in their operation, and preferably nondestructive! The parameters measured should be those giving good discrimination between two samples which are apparently the same; however, they must not be so discriminating that microheterogeneities within a single sample become significant.

Let us now consider some areas where, in my opinion, there has been rapid development. Because of the factors which I have just mentioned, many of these changes may seem less than new to the analytical chemist working in industrial, university, or big defence laboratories. Nevertheless, they are having a great impact on forensic science.

The most important items which turn up as evidence are materials such as paint, glass, fibres, drugs, and poisons; inflammable substances from arsons; surface marks or striations typified by those made by tools, and those on bullets, and finally the biological fluids blood, semen, saliva, and sweat. In all these areas, considerable improvements have taken place in techniques of examination; these are outlined in Figure 1 which shows their applicability to the materials I have listed above. The techniques fall into two groups—those in the top half of the diagram deal with compounds, those in the lower half with elements. Some of the well-established standard methods are also shown to emphasize that they are still and will continue to be essential weapons in the forensic scientist's armoury.

Before considering these in detail, I must comment on one entirely physical development, viz., the use of the profile recorder (e.g., a Tallysurf) in measuring the scratches or marks made by tools in the forcible entry into houses or coin boxes, telephone boxes, and so on. It is also equally applicable in the comparison of striation marks on bullets. Figure 2 gives profiles from a bullet

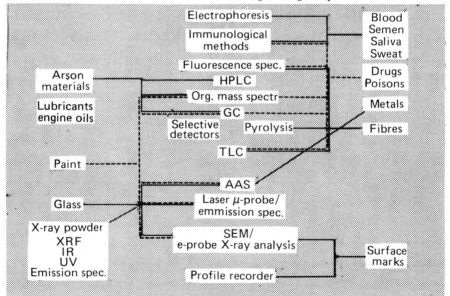

Figure 1. Evidential items and potential methods of examination

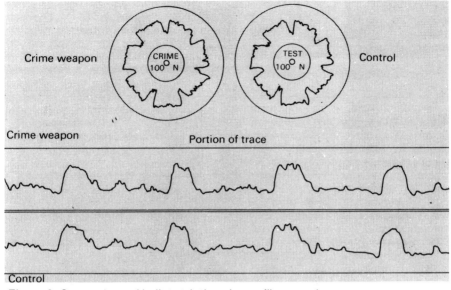

Figure 2. Comparison of bullet striations by profile recorder

recovered from a shooting and one fired from a queried weapon. The match in this example is good, but the instrument does not take into account the severe distortions which often occur in the queried item. The technique is therefore used principally for sorting, the final examination still being made visually with a comparison microscope.

SEM IN POLICE WORK

It is an obvious step in these examinations from an optical microscope to the scanning electron microscope (SEM). This instrument has considerable advantages over the optical microscope, both in magnification and in depth of focus. It can therefore be used for looking at striation marks of the order of microns in size, which could be located in sites which are inaccessible to the optical microscope, for example, the mark made by the firing pin of a gun on the base of a cartridge cap(3). Although the SEM has been relatively costly, particularly when fitted with X-ray microanalysis attachments, its versatility is such that the expenditure is justified in big crime laboratories(4). Moreover, a number of low-price machines are beginning to appear on the market which makes it possible for the smaller laboratories to consider its use.

Quite recently, comparison or split-field SEM has been achieved by van Essen and Morgan at the Metropolitan Police Laboratory(5). Figure 3 shows how it is possible to match two specimens side by side in the SEM in a single examination rather than view them separately, take pictures, and try to produce a montage. The total width of the mark in this example is 0.5 mm, which emphasizes that scratches on a microscale can yield useful information.

The SEM provides extremely valuable information of a different sort. The characteristic X-rays given off by the specimen when the scanning beam of electrons strikes it can be analysed to give both qualitative and quantitative information on the elements present in the specimen. Elements from about atomic number 5 upward can be examined in this way, and usually concentrations down to about the 0.1% level can be detected in a volume of material potentially as small as a 10-μ cube. This corresponds to an absolute sensitivity of about 10^{-12} gram of a particular element. Classical electron probe micro-analysis by comparison has a sensitivity of the order of parts per million, but it is rarely possible for a forensic laboratory to have sufficient funds to have both SEM and the electron microprobe equipment. The SEM with X-ray analysis accessory is thus a good compromise. Moreover, it has the advantage that the area of specimen which is analysed is the same as that seen topographically by its secondary electron emission. The method is in addition virtually nondestructive.

In the Metropolitan Police Laboratory in the first full year of operation, 114 cases were examined by the SEM, the majority of which could not be dealt with by any other method. The samples were 40% paints, each specimen being analysed for up to 10 elements, frequently for each layer when the specimen was multilayered.

Two examples indicate the value of the SEM in case work. In one instance, $119,000 worth of selenium was stolen in an armed robbery. Clothing from a person believed to have been involved in the attack was examined in the Laboratory and a small fragment about 0.2 x 0.2 mm found on one of the shoes. Analysis showed it to be pure selenium. In the second case, some ceremonial regalia were recovered from a car abandoned after a robbery at Arundel Castle; they included an Earl Marshal's baton coated with ruby glass. Two control pieces of the latter were compared with a fragment measuring 0.9 x 0.2 mm found on the instep of a shoe worn by a suspect. Table I gives an analysis of the controls and queried item which are in excellent agreement for all elements present except silicon.

Figure 3. Matching of tool marks by split-field SEM. Total width of scratch is 0.5 mm

Table I. Compositions of Queried and Control Ruby Glasses

	Queried sample	Control 1	Control 2	Emission spectrograph
Silicon	17.63 ± 0.27	19.46 ± 0.17	20.5	w
Lead	9.77 ± 0.28	10.08 ± 0.43	9.8	s
Potassium	2.86 ± 0.23	2.55 ± 0.32	1.4	ft
Antimony	1.25 ± 0.09	1.42 ± 0.05	1.3	vft
Calcium	1.01 ± 0.04	1.01 ± 0.04	1.0	m
Tin	0.25 ± 0.05	0.28 ± 0.03	0.2	ft
Aluminum	0.11 ± 0.01	0.14 ± 0.03	0.1	ft ·
Copper	0.27 ± 0.04	0.09 ± 0.05	0.2	vft
Iron	0.08 ± 0.04	0.07 ± 0.05	0.1	ft
Magnesium	...	...	...	w
Gold	...	...	...	vft

LASER PROBE

The use of the laser microprobe in analysis in many ways parallels that of the SEM(6,7). In this instrument a pulse of energy from a laser is used to vapourise a small amount of material from a preselected part of the specimen. The vapour then triggers an electric discharge between two graphite electrodes, and the resulting uv-visible emission can be analysed by a spectrograph in the usual way. It is possible to adjust the size of the areas of sample analysed from 10 to 250 μm in diameter. Only a small crater is produced; hence, it is possible to obtain analyses within individual layers in a paint-chip. Alternatively, the laser can be defocussed and because of the consequent low penetration, surface films on samples can be analysed. Sensitivities range from 0.1% concentration for small craters to 0.01% for large ones, i.e., 10^{-10} to 10^{-11} gram absolute sensitivity.

Other items, such as alloys, can be analysed by this method, but glass, because of its transparency to the laser pulse, has to be pelleted with graphite powder. The smallest sample of this material that can be handled is thus about a miligram, and the sensitivity is limited to elements present in greater than 150-200 ppm concentrations.

AAS APPLICATIONS

There are indications that problems arising in glass analysis may be overcome by atomic absorption spectrometry (AAS) where the greater sensitivity in terms of concentrations enables many trace elements to be determined. The equipment is also relatively inexpensive and can yield quantitative results readily. Hitherto, trace elements in the lowest concentration ranges have had to be measured either by spark source mass spectrometry or neutron activation analysis. Neither of these, however, has been widely used in forensic casework, partly because the high cost of the equipment restricts it to a few laboratories, partly because the techniques are time consuming, and partly because special training is needed for their operation.

In the UK, the practice has been to use the methods for acquiring reference data. For example, analyses down to trace elements levels have been carried out by the Home Office Central Research Establishment (HOCRE, which was set up in 1966 specifically to carry out research in forensic disciplines for the benefit of the operational laboratories in England and Wales) over 1000 samples of glass, mainly window glass, using mass spectra and NAA(8, 9). An evaluation of these results has shown that maximum discrimination between samples can be obtained by measuring the concentrations of about a dozen elements, including vanadium, titanium, strontium, rubidium, and arsenic. It is therefore possible, in principle, to choose for operational forensic laboratories cheaper and more specific methods of analysis to look for these elements. AAS is one such technique, having high sensitivity particularly when used with a heated graphite furnace (Massman)(10) for vapourizing the sample. There are difficulties in handling small glass samples, particularly because of the large differences in concentrations of the important elements. Dissolution in hydrofluoric acid followed by dilution of aliquots to the right concentration range for the AA spectrometer may prove satisfactory. The major problem is then the determination of those elements such as calcium, which have insoluble fluorides. The other difficulty which arises with the use of the graphite furnace is when an element, e.g., barium, forms a refractory carbide. However, if the concentration is greater than a few parts per million, emission spectrography can be used to overcome this.

Atomic absorption spectrometry, particularly now that multielement lamps are available, can also be used for many other types of sample as in the estimation of the levels of toxic metals in biological specimens, for instance. One such toxicological application has been the detection of thallium at a level of several parts per million in the cremation ashes of a man previously thought to have died from natural causes. No thallium could be found in controls from the container of the ashes or from the ground wherein the ashes were interred(11).

Trace metals in paints could also be measured by AAS if necessary, but an alternative approach to paint comparison is to identify the matrix which carries the pigment. In the past, various methods such as IR spectroscopy, effect of solvent, or methanolysis combined with gas chromatography of the resulting methyl esters have been used.

PYROLYSIS GC

The advent of Curie-point pyrolysers(12), however, has made possible the rapid and reproducible thermal decomposition of polymeric materials. A small quantity of paint (10-20 μg) is attached to a ferromagnetic wire which is inserted in a small induction furnace. Induction heating raises the temperature of the wire to its Curie point in a few microseconds, and the pyrolysis products are swept by carrier gas into a gas chromatograph. The resulting chromatograms are

Figure 4. Pyrograms of two alkyd resins differing in glycerol-pentaerythritol composition. (a) Glycerol - pentaerythritol, 8.4:1 by weight. (b) Glycerol–pentaerythritol, 0.01:1 by weight. Peak 1, acrolein; 2, methylacrolein; 3, benzene; 4, allyl alcohol

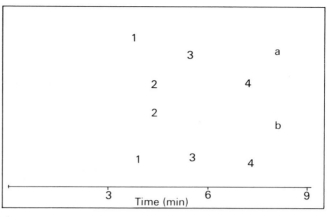

Figure 5. GC analysis of quinal barbitone in acetone by use of (a) flame ionization, (b) thermionic detectors. Each represents two-μl injections at concentration of 0.02 μg/μl; note difference in solvent peak

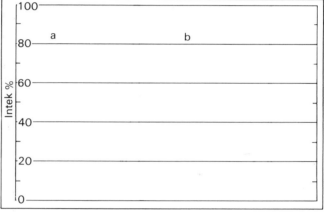

characteristic of particular polymers and can be used in a "fingerprint" fashion for identification of the material by reference to collections of standard pyrograms. If the compounds giving rise to some of the peaks in the chromatogram can be identified, e.g., by using gas chromatography/mass spectrometry, then it is possible to infer the type of polymer without reference to standard pyrograms. Even resins prepared from the same starting materials, but in varying proportions, can be differentiated by this technique (Figure 4).

As an example, the case may be quoted where the pyrogram was obtained of a black speck of material found embedded in the skull of a 38 year old woman who had died from head injuries. It turned out to be that of a styrenated alkyd, a coating used for tools; it matched similar pyrograms from paint on the tool kit of an abandoned car from which the wheel brace was missing. There is no need to point out the significance!

The extension of pyrolysis GC to the characterisation of other organic materials is quite obvious. Pyrograms of top-soil extracts, adhesives from items such as Sellotape, carpet backings, and fibres, to name but a few, can be dealt with quite easily(13). The latter use promises to be of great potential since fibres are of great evidential value, and a lot of effort has already been devoted to trying to improve their characterisation.

For example, the use of beam condensers and micro-KBr discs to obtain the IR spectrum of 2-3 mm length of a single fibre is already well established(14). The extraction of the colouring matter from a fibre by use of a suitable solvent such as di-methylformamide, followed by thin-layer chromatographic separation of the component dyes, is also being used increasingly by forensic chemists. It should, in the latter instance, be a relatively simple matter to develop means of obtaining absorption spectra from these chromatographic spots, since it already is possible to obtain their fluorescence spectra by use of microspectro-fluorimeters.

Pyrolysis GC, because of its ease of operation, is a powerful addition to these methods.

CHROMATOGRAPHIC APPLICATIONS

The importance of GC and mass spectrometry in the identification of drugs and poisons is beyond dispute, as shown by the large number of papers published on this topic (15-18). New sources of ions for mass spectrometry (viz., chemical ionization, field ionization, and field-desorption ionization) are significant, not only for simplifying the spectra but also in extending the range of mass spectrometry to difficult volatile materials(53).

However, it is worth commenting on a strictly GC development, viz., selective detectors. Some of these such as the electron capture detector(19) are well known and can be used in forensic work to enhance the sensitivity of detection of a drug by preparing, for example, its perfluoracyl derivative. Others, such as the thermionic detector(20), are sensitive only to compounds containing nitrogen and phosphorus. This means that the work-up of material before GC analysis can be greatly reduced. The specificity of the detector ensures that only the compounds of interest (e.g., barbiturates with nitrogen or organic pesticides with phosphorus) are "seen" by the gas chromatograph, and coextractants which would previously have interfered with the identification pass through the machine almost unnoticed (Figure 5). It is almost superfluous to add a note of caution at this stage; the technique is applicable only to those circumstances where it is desired to know whether a particular compound is present or not.

The second application of gas chromatography is one of which petroleum chemists are already well aware. It is in the characterisation of hydrocarbons. It is now fairly commonplace with arson cases to extract the debris from the fire and to identify the incendiary material according to its type, whether it is aviation spirit, gasoline, light oil, heavy oil, diesel fuel, and so on. Capillary columns are used for this. Occasionally, if the police are fortunate enough to find the arsonist with fuel in his possession, it is possible to say whether that particular fuel was used to cause the fire.

Not all hydrocarbons are amenable to gas chromatography. Some are too involatile, and the development of high-pressure liquid chromatography (HPLC) has opened up new possibilities for the analysis of these and other difficult substances such as the more polar or thermally unstable drugs. There are many examples in the literature of analyses of the latter types of compound(21-23). In the Metropolitan Police Laboratory, for instance, it has been used for the identification of benzodiazepine metabolites in toxicological samples. A more commonplace example is the estimation of LSD by use of a fluorescence detector. The sensitivity is quite high. For example, by use of a microcell and a spectrofluorimeter as detector, quantities of LSD as low as 10 pg in a 5-μl injection can be detected for aqueous LSD solutions(24).

With hydrocarbons, the analysis of engine lubricating oils by HPLC looks quite promising(25). As the oil in the engine gets progressively older, many degradation products appear, including polynuclear aromatics whose proportions seem to be characteristic of the particular engine. The use of different detectors, such as uv absorption, fluorescence, and refractive index, increases the versatility of the technique in a similar fashion to gas chromatography (Figure 6). It is also possible to use reagents such as dansyl chloride and 7-chloro-4-nitrobenzo oxadiazole to convert many drugs to fluorescing derivatives prior to the HPLC separation.

Lloyd has used a different technique for tackling this problem, viz., synchronous scanning of the fluorescence spectrum(26). In this, the excitation monochromator and the monochromator analysing the fluorescence spectrum are scanned synchronously with a fixed and predetermined wave-length interval

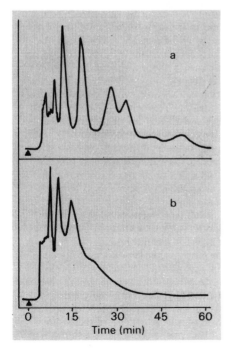

Figure 6. HPLC analysis of an engine oil by use of (a) fluorescence, (b) ultraviolet detectors

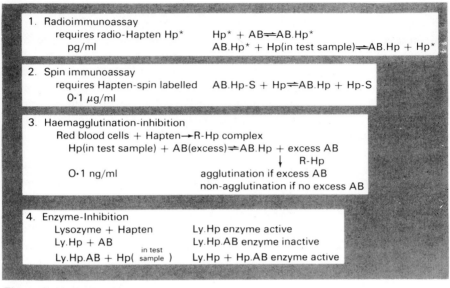

1. Radioimmunoassay
   requires radio-Hapten Hp*   Hp* + AB⇌AB.Hp*
   pg/ml   AB.Hp* + Hp(in test sample)⇌AB.Hp + Hp*

2. Spin immunoassay
   requires Hapten-spin labelled   AB.Hp-S + Hp⇌AB.Hp + Hp-S
   0·1 μg/ml

3. Haemagglutination-inhibition
   Red blood cells + Hapten→R-Hp complex
   Hp(in test sample) + AB(excess)⇌AB.Hp + excess AB
                                          ↓ R-Hp
   0·1 ng/ml   agglutination if excess AB
                                    non-agglutination if no excess AB

4. Enzyme-Inhibition
   Lysozyme + Hapten   Ly.Hp enzyme active
   Ly.Hp + AB   Ly.Hp.AB enzyme inactive
   Ly.Hp.AB + Hp(in test sample) Ly.Hp + Hp.AB enzyme active

Figure 7. Methods of immunoassay

between them. Highly characteristic and reproducible spectra are thereby produced, and a sensitivity comparable to liquid chromatography is achieved. One example of the use of the method is a murder case in which oil on the weapon was matched against oil from the scene of the crime.

FLUORESCENCE SPECTRA

Fluorescence has a high intrinsic sensitivity so that it is well suited to the characterisation of the small objects that occur in forensic work. Fortunately, the development of a number of microspectrofluorimeters has been reported in the literature(27), and one such instrument has been constructed in the M.P. Laboratory. The apparatus is used frequently for fibre identification in which it often happens that two fibres of apparently the same colour have different fluorescence spectra. A more novel application has been the comparison of a fluorescent marker powder used to tag some bank notes with a single small crystal found in the pocket of a suspect.

It is worth noting in connection with fluorescence spectroscopy that it is relatively easy by small additions to the fluorimeter to measure the phosphorescence of a substance(28). When this can be excited, it provides a second identifiable parameter which is often more characteristic than the fluorescence spectrum. For instance, the rodenticide, warfarin, can be distinguished quite readily by this method.

IMMUNOLOGICAL METHODS

I would like to discuss now the application of immunological methods to forensic problems. This, in my opinion, is one of the most important developments which is taking place at present. The basis of the method is the production by living organism (be it human, horse, or rabbit) of antibodies which react specifically with foreign substances, termed antigens, which may be introduced into the body(29,30). Antigens have to be macromolecules or larger for this response to take place, so that if it is desired to produce antibodies specific to a small molecule, such as LSD, cannabis, or heroin, it has to be coupled to a carrier—usually albumen. The small molecule is then termed a hapten. Schematically, the sequence for the production of a specific antiserum is thus:

$$\text{Hapten} \xrightarrow[\text{Albumen}]{\text{Bovine}} \begin{array}{c}\text{Hp–BSA}\\\text{conjugate}\end{array} \xrightarrow{\text{Animal}}$$

$$\begin{array}{c}\text{Anti-Hp–BSA}\\\text{antibodies}\end{array} \xrightarrow{\text{Extraction}} \begin{array}{c}\text{Anti-Hp}\\\text{antiserum}\end{array}$$

I have, of course, grossly oversimplified this procedure, but once a specific antiserum has been made, it can be used to detect the presence of a drug in a complex mixture by at least four ways (Figure 7).

In radioimmunoassay, a quantity of radioactively labelled hapten is needed(31). This is complexed to the antibody. When the test sample is added to this, if it contains the hapten (e.g., heroin), this will displace the radiohapten from the antibody-antigen complex in the usual mass-action fashion. In consequence, the radioactivity of the antibody-hapten complex (which can be precipitated out) falls, and the radioactivity of the supernatant liquid rises. The method is quantitative and sensitive to levels of about pg/ml. One of the most interesting applications of this by Taunton-Rigby and her colleagues has been the detection of LSD in the urine of subjects who had taken 200-μg doses(32). The concentration in the urine was about 1000 pg/ml.

A variation on this process is in spin immunoassay(33). In this method, a quantity of hapten is electron spin labelled by attaching a stable free radial to it. The lines in the ESR spectrum of the antibody-labelled hapten complex are broad; when the labelled hapten is displaced from the complex by unlabelled hapten from the test solution, its ESR spectrum becomes sharp-lined. The sensitivity is about 0.1 μg/ml.

The two other methods are more biochemical in nature. The first relies on absorbing the hapten onto red blood cells; these then can be used as the equivalent of a "spot" reagent. If an excess of antisera is added to the hapten in the unknown solution, unused antisera will remain after the interaction(34). Addition of the mixture to the red-cell-hapten complex will then cause these to agglutinate. If there is no free antiserum, then the cells remain unaffected.

Enzyme inhibition relies on the inactivation of an enzyme previously coupled to the hapten, when this complex is itself bound by the anti-hapten antibody. Addition of more hapten displaces the hapten-enzyme complex from the

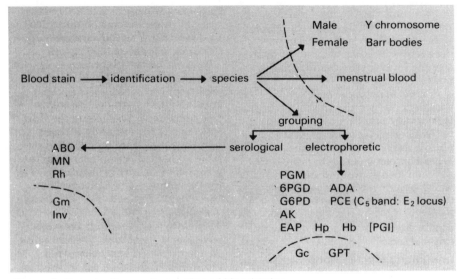

Figure 8. Examination and grouping of bloodstains

antibody. The enzyme is no longer inactive and can be detected by its reactions(35).

None of the antisera is *absolutely* specific. Usually each antiserum will complex with molecules of similar structure to that of the hapten for which it is intended, but the complex is so weak that the concentration of the "foreign" molecule has to be at least 1000 times greater than that of the true hapten to produce the same response. This usually is well within the range of detection of more conventional means of analysis and can therefore be confirmed or not.

BLOOD GROUPINGS

So far, I have been discussing chemical aspects of forensic science; progress in the biological field has also been great. Some of this, one would like to believe, is the result of stimulus from either physics or chemistry. Developments in blood grouping are such that one can now think about the possibility of blood being as unique an identification as a fingerprint. It is also becoming possible to derive additional information from blood; for example, whether it is from a man(36) or woman(37); whether or not it is menstrual blood. Figure 8 summarises the situation in general terms: those areas bounded by dotted lines are still in the research or development stages; the remainder are fully operational methods.

Blood enzymes and proteins are frequently polymorphic and can be examined by electrophoretic methods(38). These are all based on separation of the blood enzymes or proteins by migration through a gel under the influence of an electric field. The gel acts as a molecular sieve, and the rate of migration is also affected by the electrical charge on the protein. It is clearly impossible to separate completely all the different components in the serum by this process.

However, just as with selective detectors in gas chromatography, it is possible to develop colour reactions specific to a particular enzyme. For example, with phosphoglucomutase (PGM) the sequence of reactions is as follows, with the production of a blue-coloured formazan in the presence of PGM. Treating an electrophoretic plate with such a reagent will then only show the presence of that enzyme and ignore the other components. Moreover, the catalytic role of the enzyme ensures very high sensitivity because it can transform many molecules of the reagent. With PGM there are three forms PGM-1, PGM-2, and PGM 2-1, corresponding to 58.4, 5.5, and 36.1%, respectively, of the British population(38).

The most recent enzyme system to be put into case work is erythrocyte acid phosphatase (EAP) which can be detected by its fluorescence under UV light. Figure 9 shows some of the variants possible with EAP. There are three homozygous forms A, B, and C, corresponding to 12.9, 35.4 and 0.2% population and three heterozygous forms BA, CA, and CB, corresponding to 42.7, 3.3, and 5.5% population(39).

Serological grouping systems based on antibody-antigen reactions are complementary to the electrophoretic systems. The ABO and MN systems have been in forensic use for some time, while Rhesus grouping is now equally well established and gives excellent discrimination since it divides the population into at least 15 different phenotypes. The method has been automated, and the results of a grouping can be presented on a recorder chart(38). The Gm and Inv systems based respectively on antigens in the IgG and in the IgG, IgM, and IgA fractions of the blood have also been examined carefully, and it is hoped to put them into routine case work this year(40).

The present situation for grouping is summarised in Figure 10 which gives frequency distributions for the British population. If we take the most

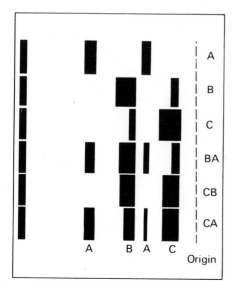

Figure 9. Erythrocyte acid phosphatase phenotypes

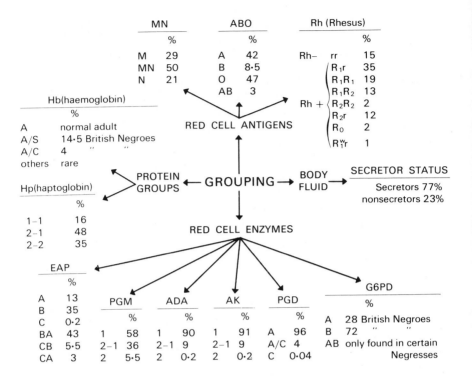

Figure 10. The present situation for grouping

Table II. Probabilities of Occurrence of Most Common and Rare Sub-Groups in Blood Grouping Systems

System	Commonest	%	Rarer	%
ABO	O	47	AB	3
Rh	R_1r	34	Several <1%, e.g., r″r, r′r, R^u	1
MN	MN	50	N	22
PGM	1	58	2	5
AK	1	91	2–1	8
ADA	1	91	2–1	9
PGD	A	95	A/C	4
EAP	BA	43	CA	3
Hp	2–1	48	1–1	16
All systems combined		0.75		4.56×10^{-10}

commonly occurring section of each group (Table II), the overall discrimination is 1 in 100 of the UK population: if we take some of the rarer sections, a discrimination of 1 in 200,000,000,000 is attained, which can cope with the whole world population at present!

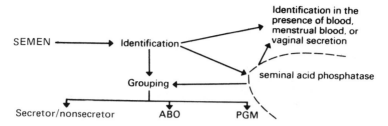

Figure 11. Examination and grouping of seminal stains

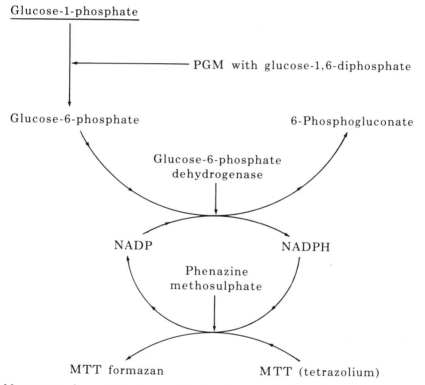

Matters are less satisfactory with the characterisation of other stains, and much research is needed to reach anything approaching the discrimination achieved for the grouping of blood stains. Figure 11 summarises the situation for stains from the next best characterised body fluid, semen. It can be seen that only three grouping systems at present are possible, but recent reports by Japanese workers indicate that the polymorphism of seminal acid phosphatase may soon be added to these(41). Some useful developments have also taken place in the identification of semen in the presence of blood. These have depended on specific antisera, viz., antihuman semen antisera and anti-whole blood antisera. Discrimination is easily obtained by use of these antisera in immunoelectrophoresis (Figure 12). More recently, it has been found possible to

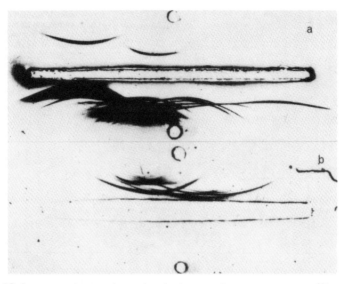

Figure 12. Immunoelectrophoresis of mixture of semen, upper well, and blood, lower well, onto (a) antiblood antiserum (b) antisemen antiserum

identify semen in the presence of blood, menstrual blood, or vaginal secretion by using either electrophoresis or a combination of immunoelectrophoresis with antisemen sera, followed by staining of the plate with a specific reagent for acid phosphatase(43).

Hitherto, we have been concerned with developments in methods. These are much reduced in utility if background data are not available or if the methods are unable to cope with heavy workloads. Figure 13 summarises the relation of these three factors.

GLASSES AND PAINTS

It is clearly of vital importance to have information and statistics on everything which crops up in forensic examinations. We need to know the frequency of occurrence of glasses of different composition, what the range and

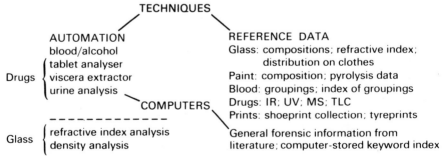

Figure 13. Data retrieval and automation

distribution of their refractive indices are; similarly with paints, oils, adhesives, and so on. In so vast a country as the U.S., with many manufacturers the task of data collection is formidable. Even in the UK, with fewer manufacturers of a particular product and with a much smaller area to cover, the task is daunting. Nevertheless, a start has been made. HOCRE acts as a centre for this work, both by way of literature surveys and also by undertaking the measurement of many basic properties. In addition to this, the nine operational forensic laboratories also carry out data acquisition and send their results to HOCRE to swell the amount.

Some of the investigations of the sort indicated in Figure 13 have already been carried out. The refractive indices of over 3000 window glass samples from houses throughout England and Wales have been measured, and histograms of frequency of occurrence of the refractive index ranges are available(44). The compositions of nearly 1000 of these have been determined by NAA or mass spectrometry(8, 9)(Table II). A survey of 100 suits submitted to dry cleaners has shown that there was only a likelihood of 1 in 3000 of a piece of glass bigger than 1 mm occurring by chance on the clothing(45). A total of 3558 paint fragments was found for the same suits!

Elemental compositions of paints are also recorded in a similar way to glass, while pyrolysis of paints under controlled conditions with a standard gas chromatographic stationary phase has yielded atlases of pyrograms for identification purposes. Other items of forensic interest, blood, drugs, shoe prints, and tyre-prints, for example, all have data collections referring to them. In many instances this is available in microfilm form, especially spectral data and shoe and tyreprints, copies being held in all the forensic laboratories. Abstracts of forensic interest from the scientific literature are circulated monthly from CRE under the headings of Biology, Drugs and Toxicology, Chemistry, and General. These are reissued periodically in microfilm form wherein the abstracts are identified numerically. In conjunction with this, a glossary has been devised, and the abstracts are stored in a computer in terms of the key words of the glossary. It is possible to extract the identification number of an abstract from the computer by feeding in the necessary key words. The output consists of the numbers of the relevant abstracts which can then be consulted on the microfilm in the Laboratory. It is hoped eventually that each Forensic Laboratory will have access to the computer via its own terminal.

AUTOMATIC ANALYSES

With increasing work loads, it is more and more important to consider the use of automated analytical methods. Rhesus grouping has already been cited as an example(38). Analysis of samples from drunken drivers is a second. In the UK, the law concerning drunken driving requires the quantitative analysis of alcohol in either blood or urine samples from the driver. The Metropolitan Police Laboratory handled 24,870 such cases in 1972 involving a minimum of two analyses per case. It was found only just possible to cope with this throughput

Table III. Compositions of Some Window Glasses as Determined by NAA

CONCENTRATION, PPM

Element	St. Helens Mean	SD	Pontypool Mean	SD	Belgian Mean	SD	Chance Mean	SD
Arsenic	ND[a]	...	ND	...	1290	95	1050	200
Aluminium	0.647%	0.008	0.732%	0.025	0.485%	0.009	0.652%	0.014
Barium	146.2	6.5	249.7	8.5	59.6	9.4	322.0	24.2
Calcium	5.98%	0.22	6.46%	0.54	5.69%	0.22	6.78%	0.42
Cobalt	0.71	0.11	0.52	0.12	0.42	0.17	0.43	0.10
Chromium	6.07	0.94	2.71	1.61	4.83	0.38	5.70	1.90
Caesium	0.76	0.07	ND	...	0.16	0.03	0.23	0.04
Europium	0.13	0.04	0.06	0.02	0.11	0.03	0.13	0.03
Iron	890	103	780	136	720	91	730	99
Hafnium	1.26	0.14	0.94	0.08	0.99	0.02	3.59	0.41
Lanthanum	3.77	0.18	2.71	0.13	3.71	0.19	3.67	0.11
Lutecium	0.044	0.005	0.016	0.004	0.038	0.007	0.049	0.004
Magnesium	2.65%	0.21	2.48%	0.11	1.72%	0.27	1.62%	0.27
Manganese	102.3	5.4	101.0	3.7	53.4	6.5	43.4	3.9
Sodium	9.82%	0.05	9.95%	0.07	12.96%	0.13	10.20%	0.07
Rubidium	22.5	1.8	8.04	0.74	3.21	0.74	7.56	1.41
Antimony	0.70	0.29	ND	...	2.75	1.46	21.3	1.5
Scandium	0.50	0.02	0.16	0.01	0.37	0.01	0.45	0.02
Samarium	1.14	0.10	0.59	0.03	1.27	0.11	1.07	0.02
Strontium	ND	...	173	39	ND	...	ND	...
Tantalum	0.21	0.02	0.11	0.03	0.22	0.04	0.12	0.01
Thorium	1.09	0.10	0.29	0.02	0.71	0.08	0.53	0.03
Ytterbium	0.28	0.03	0.12	0.02	0.25	0.06	0.32	0.04
Zirconium	58.5	12.9	48.4	28.5	67.5	27.7	155.5	34.0

[a] ND, not detected.

Figure 14. Prototype tablet analyser. As many as 14 spot reagents can be applied to produce colour reactions for identification of drugs. (Now produced by Bird & Tole Ltd., Bledlow Ridge, Bucks, England)

by using eight manually operated gas chromatographs. Two Perkin-Elmer F-40 analysers coupled to a small computer have therefore been installed and have been used for casework for over three months. The capacity is about 17,000 cases per annum, and a further two F-40's are now being brought into use.

The HOCRE has devoted considerable effort to automate drug analyses and has produced prototype working instruments for urine analysis(46), tablet analysis(47), and for the extraction of poisons from viscera(48). Figure 14 shows the prototype tablet analysis machine.

The particular drugs exemplified in the urine analysis (viz., morphine, barbiturate, and amphetamine) were detected by fluorimetry, ultraviolet absorption, and colorimetry and/or fluorimetry, respectively.

There are many other areas ripe for automation, glass density and refractive index determinations being typical. It would also be highly desirable to devise means of automating fibre searches!

QUALITY CONTROL

A forensic laboratory, even if lavishly equipped, is only as good as the skills of its scientists allow. It is therefore particularly important that quality control of analyses should be undertaken in some way or another. In England and Wales with nine operational laboratories, this is achieved by test samples being sent out from the HOCRE to all the units. Results are returned to HOCRE who then analyse what has gone on, and in light of this, the directors of the laboratories can decide what changes are needed to improve the efficiency of their group. For example, 10 blood-alcohol analytical trials have been carried out to date. Aliquots of the same sample were submitted to all laboratories in such a way that the analysts could not distinguish them from ordinary drunk driving cases. The mean standard deviation for all the trials carried out at the laboratories was 1.78 mg% with a standard deviation of this between trials of 0.48.

Similarly, 11 bloodstains on cotton sheeting were sent to the laboratories for grouping by whatever systems were used in that particular laboratory. Of the

500 results returned, only two were reported incorrectly. Other subjects of trials have included refractive indices of glass, paint fragments, carbon monoxide in blood, barbiturates in blood, and most recently, defective tyres. Clearly, this principle is of the utmost importance in maintaining standards and also in trying to ensure a uniform performance throughout the country.

A LOOK AHEAD

What of the future then? There will be big developments in immunological methods for detecting drugs. The discrimination of body fluids—blood, semen, and saliva—will continue to progress rapidly. For example, the possibility of examining several enzyme systems on the same electrophoretic run is already being realised(49, 50). In analytical methods, liquid chromatography will take its rightful place beside gas chromatography in the forensic laboratory. Atomic absorption spectrometry with multiple lamp systems will be applied increasingly to quantitative analysis of elements, and probably atomic fluorescence will also come into prominence. In the larger and perhaps even the medium-size laboratory, the SEM with X-ray microanalysis has a useful role to fulfill. The ion microprobe and ESCA, with their high sensitivities and elemental discrimination, present themselves as other possibilities if it were not for their expense(51, 52).

We have now reached a stage where the technical limitation on forensic science is the ability to pick out the vital item of evidence in the initial search. The importance of this cannot be overemphasized. Once that item has been found, there is a wealth of methods for dealing with it. However, for each of these to realise its full potential, there must be considerably more background data about both the material and the method. Hence, the increasing development of data banks and quality control methods is essential for the future.

The change which has taken place in forensic work over the last two decades has been dramatic. I feel confident that this will continue and accelerate so that we will be able to look back in a few years time and perhaps wonder how we all managed in "those days."

NOTES

(1) P.L. Kirk, *J. Forensic Sci. Soc.*, 10, 97 (1970).

(2) A.S. Curry, *Nature*, 235, 369 (1972).

(3) C.A. Grove, G. Judd, and R. Horn, *J. Forensic Sci.*, 17, 645 (1972).

(4) R.L. Williams, Proc. IV Annual SEM Symposium, p. 537, 1971.

(5) C. van Essen and J.E. Morgan, Proc. VI Annual SEM Symposium, p. 159, 1973.

(6) H. Moenke and L. Moenke-Blankenburg, "Introduction to Laser Microemission Spectral Analysis," Akad, Verlag, Leipzig, Germany, 1968.

(7) H. Neuninger, *Jena Rev.*, 4, 235 (1970).

(8) B. German and A. W. Scaplehorn, *J. Forensic Sci Soc.*, 12, 367 (1972).

(9) G.C. Goode, G.A. Wood, N.M. Brooke, and R.F. Coleman, AWRE Report O 24/71, Her Majesty's Stationery Office, London, England, 1971.

(10) H. Massman, *Spectrochem. Acta,* 23B, 215 (1968).

(11) J.R. Cavanagh, N. Fuller, and H.R.M. Johnson, to be published.

(12) D.A. Leathard and B.C. Shurlock, "Identification Techniques in Gas Chromatography," p. 114, Wiley-Interscience, London, England, 1970.

(13) B.B. Wheals and W. Noble, *Chromatographia,* 5, 553 (1973).

(14) R.H. Fox and H. Schuetzman, *J. Forensic Sci.,* 13, 397 (1968).

(15) G.A. Junk, *Int. J. Mass. Spectrom. Ion Phys.,* 8, 71 (1972).

(16) R. Bonnichsen, A.C. Maehly, Y. Mardi, R. Ryhage, and B. Schubert, *J. Legal Med.,* 67, 19 (1970).

(17) J.N.T. Gilbert, B.J. Millard, and J.W. Powell, *J. Pharm. Pharmacol.,* 22, 897 (1970).

(18) B.S. Finkle and D.M. Taylor, *J. Chromatogr. Sci.,* 10, 312 (1972).

(19) D.A. Leathard and B.C. Shurlock, "Identification Techniques in Gas Chromatography," p. 165, Wiley-Interscience, London, England, 1970.

(20) L. Guiffrida, *J. Ass. Off. Anal. Chem.,* 47, 293 (1964).

(21) J.A. Schmit, "Modern Practice of Liquid Chromatography," J.J. Kirkland, Ed., p. 386 et seq, Wiley-Interscience, London, England, 1971.

(22) P.J. Cashman and J.I. Thornton, *J. Forensic Sci. Soc.,* 11, 115 (1971).

(23) P.J. Cashman and J.I. Thornton, *ibid.,* 12, 417 (1972).

(24) I. Jane and B.B. Wheals, *J. Chromatogr.,* in press, 1973.

(25) C.G. Vaughan, B.B. Wheals, and M.J. Whitehouse, *ibid.,* 78, 203 (1973).

(26) J.B.F. Lloyd, *J. Forensic Sci. Soc.,* 11, 83, 153, 235 (1971).

(27) C.A. Parker and W.T. Rees, *Analyst,* 87, 83 (1962).

(28) C.A. Parker and C.G. Hatchard, *ibid.,* 664 (1962).

(29) I. Roitt "Essential Immunology," Blackwell, Oxford, England, 1971.

(30) E.A. Kabat, "Structural Concepts in Immunology and Immunochemistry," Holt, Rinehart and Winston, London, England, 1968.

(31) D.S. Skelley, L.P. Brown, and P.K. Besch, *Clin. Chem.,* 19, 146 (1973).

(32) A. Taunton-Rigby, S.E. Sher, and P.R. Kelley, VIth International Meeting of Forensic Sciences, Edinburgh, Scotland, 1972.

(33) R. Leute, E.F. Ullman, A. Goldstein, and L.A. Herzenberg, *Nature New Biol.,* 236, 93 (1972).

(34) F.L. Adler and C.T. Liu, *J. Immunol.,* 106, 1684 (1971).

(35) K.E. Rubenstein, R.S. Schneider, and E.F. Ullman, *Biochem. Biophys. Res. Commun.,* 47, 846 (1972).

(36) P.L. Pearson and M. Bobrow, *Nature,* 226, 78 (1970); A.P. Phillips, VIth International Meeting of Forensic Sciences, Edinburgh, Scotland, 1972.

(37) S. Renard, *J. Forensic Sci. Soc.,* 11, 15 (1971).

(38) B.J. Culliford and (in part) M. Pereira, The Examination and Typing of Bloodstains in the Crime Laboratory, U.S. Dept. of Justice, Law Enforcement Assistance Administration, Washington, D.C., 1971.

(39) D.A. Hopkinson, N. Spencer, and H. Harris, *Nature,* 199, 969 (1969); B.G.D. Wraxall, IVth International Meeting of Forensic Sciences, Edinburgh, Scotland, 1972.

(40) M. Pereira, private communication.

(41) S. Ueno and H. Yoshida, *J. Legal Med.,* 72, 169 (1973).

(42) B.G.D. Wraxall and E.G. Adams, IVth International Meeting of Forensic Sciences, Edinburgh, Scotland, 1972.

(43) G.B. Divall and P.H. Whitehead, IVth International Meeting of Forensic Sciences, Edinburgh, Scotland, 1972.

(44) M.D.G. Dabbs and E.F. Pearson, *J. Forensic Sci.* 17, 70 (1972): HOCRE Reports 47 and 63.

(45) E.F. Pearson, R.W. May, and M.G.D. Dabbs, *ibid.,* 16, 283 (1971).

(46) D.J. Blackmore, A.S. Curry, T.S. Hayes, and E.R. Rutter, *Clin. Chem.*, 17, 896 (1971).
(47) A.S. Curry, private communication.
(48) A.S. Curry, private communication.
(49) B. Brinkmann and G. Thoma, *Vox Sang.*, 21, 90 (1971).
(50) H.W. Goedde and H.G. Benkmann, *Humangenetik*, 15, 277 (1972).
(51) C.A. Evans, *Anal. Chem.*, 44, (13), 67A (1972).
(52) C. Nordling, *Angew. Chem., Int. Ed.*, 11, 83 (1972).
(53) E.M. Chait, *Anal. Chem.*, 44 (3), 77A (1972).

FORENSIC SCIENCE AND THE ANALYST

Cecil L. Wilson

It is a far cry from the occasion on which Mr. Sherlock Holmes(1), holding in his right hand a slip of litmus paper, said to Dr. Watson, "You come at a crisis, Watson. If this paper remains blue, all is well. If it turns red, it means a man's life." It was even longer ago(2) that Dr. Watson *first* met Mr. Holmes and found him to spring to his feet with a cry of pleasure. " 'I've found it! I've found it!' he shouted to my companion, running towards us with a test-tube in his hand. 'I have found a reagent which is precipitated by haemoglobin and by nothing else!' " Naive, perhaps; but the budding forensic scientist can gain much from a careful perusal of Arthur Conan Doyle—a man much before his time—and of that equally prescient writer, R. Austin Freeman (3, 4).

There are no, or few, 'black boxes' in the writings of either of these authors—they did their *thinking* long before the days of *'black boxes'*. They present, however, object lessons in thought processes that are essential for the forensic scientist; and particularly for the forensic scientist who has been brought up with 'black boxes' in his cradle.

In the space available, this account of the various techniques available nowadays to the forensic scientist cannot be comprehensive. The references given will also be selective, being only a preliminary guide to the literature. Various recent and comprehensive reviews(5-11) are available for more detailed information.

THE APPLICATION OF INSTRUMENTAL METHODS

The view that the man in the street has of the present-day forensic scientist is undoubtedly one of a man surrounded by 'black boxes'. It is, of course, not so long ago that the traditional picture of the forensic scientist was that of a man with a lens and bloodhound.

That extension of the human eye, *the lens,* and its further extension, *the microscope,* were first made available to scientists through Hooke and van Leeuwenhoek in the 17th century. The microscope, as a tool of the chemist, probably reached its peak in the late 19th and early 20th century. Gradually, the chemist became much intrigued with the 'black boxes' which began to proliferate from the 1930s, and the microscope took a back seat—possibly because it required rather more effort than just pressing a button in order to use it properly!

Yet it is probably true to say that no forensic laboratory should consider its equipment complete without a considerable range of the low-power and high-power microscopes available—or its staff complete without someone capable of using them.

Since I have always believed that the properly trained analytical chemist should have reasonable acquaintance with the use of the microscope, I am very pleased to see that recent publications (5, 12) give some account of the wide range of uses to which the microscope can be put.

Indeed, Holden(12) says: "The only reason that I can think of to explain the lack of use of [the microscope] by chemists is that very few of them have been taught microscopy. This is not, however, peculiar to chemists; very few science graduates, even in biology, have been given a proper course in the use of the microscope."

The microscope can take us from the limit of resolution of the eye of about 0.1 mm, down to particles, almost at the limit of detection (10^{-12} g) of emission spectrography. It is therefore possible(12) to compare with controls, *optically,* samples which would possibly not be capable of identification by emission spectrography. With a proper training in the use of the petrographic microscope, a surprising range of properties can be determined on small specimens.

Many would regard colorimetry—in its strictest sense of the measurement or comparison of colours—as akin to mediaeval torture! It was, of course, used early in foresnic work, as in general analytical chemistry, for the determination of elements by colour reactions. It has survived in forensic work in a somewhat different application: in the identification of paint flakes, particularly from motor vehicles. The paint on a motor car consists of a number of layers, of different colours and often with different plastic constituents. In recent years, in the United Kingdom(13), in the United States(5) and in Canada(7), 'banks' of standard colour plates, supplied by car manufacturers, have been built up. (Some European manufacturers also co-operate with the British 'bank'). These permit the scientist to determine, in many cases, the probable make and model of a car involved in a hit-and-run case. It is true that frequently the actual colour measurements may be combined with a number of the other techniques that will be mentioned later. But this is a common procedure in forensic work.

Tristimulus colorimetry has also been investigated(7) as a possible method of determining, for example, that two samples of soil have come from the same area, and seems promising, at least as a sorting technique.

It is hardly necessary to mention that *ultraviolet spectrophotometry* became established a long time ago in forensic work, first and foremost for toxicological purposes; naturally it became extensively applied in other fields(7,11,14). Indeed Curry(14) has claimed that when asked whether the forensic scientist should equip himself first with a gas chromatograph, an infrared spectrophotometer or an ultraviolet spectrophotometer (although all three ought to be available and will extend the capabilities of the forensic scientist enormously), he would still put the ultraviolet spectrophotometer as his first choice. In the future, of course, it may not continue to be the main tool of the three.

Infrared spectrophotometry is again a technique, well-tried in general analysis, whose applications become increasingly extensive in forensic work every year(15-20). Lubricating greases (even contraceptive sheath lubricant in the case of rape), drugs and poisons, paints and plastics, explosives, and petrols are only some of the fields to which straightforward infrared spectrophotometry has been applied.

Two newer uses of the infrared region of the spectrum are of some interest. One is the application of *attenuated total reflectance*(10,21), particularly for layers of paints films; the other is the utilisation of *infrared luminescence.* Instead of the well-established technique of stimulating visible fluorescence by ultraviolet light, visible light is used to stimulate fluorescence in the infrared(5,7). This is then either photographed, or examined by one of the now quite sophisticated image converters. The principal application, so far, of this latter technique seems to have been in the inspection of documents for alterations—this is an application which in a sense follows on from the quite early photography of documents by infrared light(22).

Both *emission spectrography* and *x-ray diffraction* have for long been used in forensic work, both separately and, more recently, in conjunction. My first venture into the forensic field, more than 30 years ago, was in spectrography; on that occasion the aim was to try to establish the identity of paints in a case of breaking and entering. Minerals and paint pigments comprise perhaps the most extensive group of substances to which these two techniques have been applied. An intriguing use has been the identification of a titanium pigment as anastase, not rutile(10). This was a constituent of a make-up cream used by a girl who had been kicked in the face; the same crystal form was found on the shoe of the suspect. There have been other interesting applications of these techniques in aircraft crashes—both to prove sabotage, and to disprove it(5).

An interesting possible development of emission spectrography is mentioned by Walls(10,11) in which a laser beam is employed to volatillise the sample. In this way, it may be possible to achieve better sensitivity with a smaller sample than that consumed in the conventional arc or spark methods, and even, by means of spark excitation of the vapour, to render the method quantitative. Indeed, with a little imagination one can see an increasing use of lasers by the forensic scientist, rather than by the criminal!

X-ray photography has, of course, obvious applications in certain aspects of forensic work, involving such things as suspicious parcels or shot wounds. A much more sophisticated use of this technique has a number of interesting overtones(23). In the early fifties a man died in Scotland, leaving to his widow a large estate, unfortunately entirely in whisky, which was all in bond; the Excise authorities said it could not be released until the duty was paid; and the duty could not be paid till some of the whisky was sold. However, there are large fluctuations in the price of whisky in a bonded store; over four years it went from £150,000, to £100,000 to £170,000. Naturally, when the price (and duty) was high, the excise authorities offered to find ways of releasing the whisky; when it was low, somehow they were unwilling to collaborate with the solicitors to the estate. Stalemate lasted for four years. In the meantime, the various solicitors involved with the estate were, from time to time, advancing sums to the widow. One of the later solicitors became suspicious about a considerable batch of receipts which had been passed on to him—so much so that he asked the police to investigate. Their handwriting experts divided the receipts into two fairly definite groups, one of which they classified as genuine, the other as forgeries (with a few doubtfuls). The widow was of no help, being very vague, with little idea of when she had signed for money, how much she had, or if the signatures were really hers. The Procurator Fiscal was not prepared to proceed on handwriting evidence alone.

One night, one of the investigating officers noticed his daughter sticking stamps in her stamp album, and observed that she had stuck in two twopenny Queen Elizabeth stamps. He asked why. She explained that the stamp's colour had been changed from dark brown to light brown. This was right in the middle of the period of the questioned receipts. The officer thought that this might be worth following up, and found that in addition to the change in colour there had been two changes in watermark. This, in fact, gave three earliest possible dates for the twopenny stamps using the colour and—of one could determine it—the watermark. But how to determine the watermark of a stamp that was stuck on paper and could not be removed (otherwise, legally, of course, the document was destroyed)?

Ultimately the police found two workers in a hospital x-ray laboratory who were prepared to carry out some experiments. By means of soft x-rays, photography of the watermarks was eminently successful(24). It was, in fact, possible to show that the police division of the receipts into genuine and false had been quite correct.

An investigation of whether the ^{14}C-impregnated paper now available from Amersham(25) might be used for the same purpose, could be profitable.

Because of certain advantages which are characteristic of *neutron-activation analysis* (e.g. the irrelevance of contamination after irradiation, and the high sensitivity for a wide range of elements), this technique has been an obvious one for forensic investigations. However, the high sensitivity and the novelty of the technique emphasise one important aspect of the work of the forensic scientist. He must always lag behind the pure scientist since he must always be certain that his methods are valid and above reproach. Always, in his work he must remember the life or liberty of the subject.

This is undoubtedly why the first presentation of results by this method in a British Court(26) did not, apparently, take place until 1967.

The case was one of breaking and entering, where £15,000 work of silver was stolen. A piece of glass in the sole of the shoe of the suspect was compared with the glass in a broken window at the scene of the crime. Five points of comparison weighed heavily to suggest that the two types of glass were rather unusual in composition and were of common origin. When this (and other) evidence was presented for the prosecution, the suspect pleaded guilty.

With a thermal neutron flux of 1.8×10^{12} n. cm^{-2}. sec^{-1}, the sensitivity for 69 elements examined lies between $0.000\,\mu$g (for some rare earth elements) and $0.01\,\mu$g for 38 elements; and between 0.01 and $0.1\,\mu$g for another 17 elements(27). This makes it the most sensitive method so far devised for more than half of the elements in the periodic system.

The technique is being increasingly applied to the examination of poisons, firearm residues, hair, glass, rubber, plastics, greases, soils and metals(5,7,11,27,28). One of its more curious applications is cited by Lucas(7); it was possible to show, 20 years after a suspected murder had been committed, that a hole in a skull was probably a bullet hole, because of the high antimony content.

Probably the greatest publicity for the technique came from the examination of Napoleon's hair for evidence of arsenic poisoning. The method is certainly capable of the precision required, but it seems clear from more recent work(29,30) that there was insufficient appreciation of external contamination. Thus it would be necessary to establish that cosmetics and other preparations for hair treatment in Napoleon's time did not contain a high arsenic content. Morgan(29) cites the high iodine content in many specimens of hair nowadays because of the use of iodinated detergent shampoos. He warns us, very aptly, that we should 'stress the importance of not being impressed by the elegance of technique. Just as in general, we are not interested in the tool which a carpenter uses to drill a hole, but only in the result, so here. It is not particularly important to catalogue methods; the relevance of the result is the important factor'. How appropriately that applies to all forensic investigations.

Some investigations of the arsenic content of hair(31) indicate how the pattern of arsenic uptake can be determined much more precisely by neutron activation than by chemical methods, where 1-cm lengths are examined. Neutron-activation analysis permits the determination of arsenic by 1-mm stages along a single hair. Since the daily growth of hair is approximately 0.5 mm per day, it is possible to plot arsenic uptake over intervals of 1-2 days.

Over-enthusiastic claims have been made, in their first days, for many techniques, and neutron-activation analysis is no exception. The premature claims that a hair could probably be tied as closely to a head as a finger-print to a finger are now discounted. Like the reports of Mark Twain's death(32), they were somewhat exaggerated. But it is now clear that there *are* significant differences between hairs, and that after further work, the results, when properly assessed statistically, will be of considerable value(9).

The method is, in fact a valuable 'future' method, still on trial, and is likely for sometime to continue to be applied, with proper discrimination, only non-routinely.(10).

All the varieties of *chromatographic techniques* were applied early in forensic work, and increasing use has been made of them(10,33-35): paper and thin-layer chromatography for inks, fats, oils, greases, and waxes, drugs and poisons, insecticides, tars, dyes, explosives, and metals (as the organic derivatives): vapour-phase chromatography, with its rapidly extending applications(10,35,36) for petrols, volatile drugs, paint and other resins (after pyrolysis); and of course, the determination of blood-alcohol (see p. 158) Walls, indeed, claims(10) that vapour-phase chromatography may be perhaps the most versatile technique in forensic science.

Scanning electron-probe analysis is likely to be increasingly important as apparatus becomes more readily available(10,11,37). By this technique, characteristic x-rays of the elements down to boron can be excited in particles as small as a few microns in diameter, and the method is capable of quantitative and qualitative applications. As Walls(10) says, it is another of the 'future' techniques.

Carbon-14 dating has had preliminary trials for determining the age of natural fibres (wool, cotton) and for investigating time of death from tissues or from bones(38); it is pointed out that in the present era strontium-90 may be another significant radioactive element.

Differential thermal analysis and *mass spectrometry*(10) are both techniques likely to be of future significance. Curiously, *atomic absorption spectroscopy* appears up to the moment to have given little other than 'hypothetical' uses(39).

After all this catalogue of highly sophisticated techniques, it is almost a relief to turn to an account of a straightforward *chemical* reaction for restoring erased serial numbers on aluminium, using a variant of the old 'whisker' production by a mercury salt(40); and to learn that 'real' chemistry is still useful. Even the *plastic arts* may be useful, for example in an identification from a bitemark in cheese(41)! The use of *combined techniques* rather than a single technique to produce an answer has already been mentioned. This will, of course, be an increasing trend. A typical instance, quite common at present, is the identification of drugs(42) by a combination of extraction, vapour-phase chromatography, thin-layer chromatography and ultraviolet spectrophotometry (probably also infrared spectrophotometry). Again, for paints a combination of chromatography, infrared spectroscopy, nuclear magnetic resonance and mass spectrography has been proposed(43).

This sort of thing brings in its train many complications, and Walls has adverted to it at some length in his Presidential Address to the British Academy of Forensic Sciences(9). He explains that earlier forensic workers were probably talented scientists, or doctors with a scientific bent, who as a sideline, liked to get mixed up with the police, and who enjoyed the sort of problems this association brought them. 'They could still, in those days, without being geniuses, cope with all the science the job demanded. Now, most people realize that this is not true.'

No one, he points out, can nowadays either be expert in all the necessary fields, or indeed (partly because of the well-known desire of the expert to advance his own expertise, regardless of its relevance) can have a broad enough view to make a proper use of the skills available. He admits that he may perhaps be exaggerating slightly when he continues 'It may not be too fantastic to look forward one day to computerised laboratory programming, with which the man in charge feeds into the computer, suitably coded, both all the questions asked, and details such as sensitivity and specificity of the possible techniques, and the times needed to get an answer by them; the computer would then tell the optimum procedure to yield the greatest amount of information with the minimum consumption of time and material.'

However, there, are still many areas of forensic work, where on the whole, the sophisticated techniques mentioned above are not always necessary and indeed, in many cases, are inapplicable.

The first of these is the examination of *glass*. It is clear from publications on the subject(5,44-47) that the principal scientific techniques employed are basically observation, deduction, and physical measurements of properties such as specific gravity, refractive index and dispersion.

Out of eight points which Nelson(45) suggests as offering useful evidence from glass, four are in the nature of a very complex jig-saw puzzle and one is essentially inspection to determine, if possible, the type of object from which the glass came. The remainder largely consist of simple physical measurements; actual determination of the chemical constitution cannot be expected to be of much help, except in unusual cases such as that mentioned earlier(26) (p. 153). Variations are only likely in the trace elements; one would find little help from the normal silicate analysis. And even the spectrograph may not be sensitive enough to show the type of variation to be expected.

THE EXAMINATION OF DOCUMENTS

It is probably in the field of *document examining* that procedures entirely different from those discussed above are most often essential. It is true that the document examiner, as has been mentioned in a number of cases already in passing, makes use of instrumental techniques and sophisticated separation processes for the examination of inks and of documents on which they are applied.

The extent to which the examination of documents may form part of the work of the forensic laboratory is perhaps not generally realised. According to

Conrad(5) documentary evidence accounts for more than half of all the items received in the F.B.I. Laboratories for examination. And this is by no means the whole story since it is stated(48) that 'most of the work of a document examiner . . . consists of the examination and comparison of handwritings'; indeed, this is my own experience.

The identification of handwriting is probably the most controversial part of a document examiner's work. The ability to recognise the important characteristics in a sample of handwriting appears to be partly innate. This view is supported by a well-known test piece(49) consisting of a random arrangement of 64 specimens of a single work written by 32 writers. The speed with which inexperienced test individuals sort the specimens into the appropriate pairs varies very widely. Some people can do this quite rapidly; others appear to suffer from what is often called 'form-blindness' and are either very slow in the test or are unable to complete it.

However, given that the innate ability is there, the person who would then become a 'handwriting expert' must collect and study as extensive a range of specimens of handwriting as possible. The general nature of the writing is, of course, important; but the study must extend to the details of the writing—some authorities list well over a hundred so-called 'minor characteristics' which may be of evidential value and which should therefore be studied. Examples of this type of characteristic are the way in which the letter 'o' is closed—whether it is closed directly on top, or to the right or left of the top, or left open, or looped, and the size and shape of the loop; the method of forming and placing the stroke of the 't'—short or long, curved or tilted up or down, before, through or after the vertical stroke; the relation of the arches of the letter 'm' to each other—and if the letter falls at the end of a word, the direction and nature of the final stroke; and many more points of this kind.

By long study it is possible to learn to recognise the relative importance of various characteristics, based on their relative frequency in the writings of a large number of people. In this way it is possible to decide that some types of formation are relatively frequent and have low evidential value whereas others are relatively rare and carry more weight as indications of identity. Since an increase in the number of identical formations in two pieces of writing involves a multiplication of probabilities, the existence of, say twenty similarities, even of common occurrence will give a remarkably high probability that the writings are by the same person; and if even a few of the similarities are uncommon formations the probabilities can very easily run into ratios of millions to one. If these values are not offset by any significant differences then a sound case can be made for identity.

It must, of course always be borne in mind that there are always minor variations in handwriting. Indeed, if one found two signatures which were absolutely identical one would immediately suspect forgery by some copying process. Yet these minor variations produce the strongest argument used against the handwriting expert. It is always argued that the writing of most people varies markedly from day to day, even sometimes from hour to hour. In spite of this, it is indubitable that the basic characteristics are still there, permitting identification; just as an individual can be recognised by basic facial or other characteristics, although the general appearance may change markedly through such causes as age or illness.

Many tests have been carried out, particularly in the United States, which show conclusively that specialised training produces people capable or reaching the right conclusions about the identity or non-identity of handwriting in tests where untrained people, or even people with a different sort of training in handwriting, e.g. bank clerks, cannot achieve this.

Possibly the most spectacular example of the identification of handwriting that has ever occurred is quoted by Conrad(5) in the case of the Weinberger kidnapping of 1956. A ransom note was used as the basis of comparison. It was stated to be a 'non-normal' type of handwriting (though even experts with over 20 years of experience, might hesitate to try to define 'normal' and 'abnormal' handwriting). A team of 90 specially trained special agents was then briefed by the experts in the F.B.I. Laboratories, and an examination was begun of all handwriting specimens in the various local public records. Any records that looked promising were pulled out and examined further by the experts. Approximately 2,000,000 handwriting samples were examined over a period of about 6 weeks, and a single file was then turned in to the experts; this they were able to identify as being in the same handwriting as the ransom note. It is interesting to note that this file, a probation office file, was actually out of the office when the specimens were first examined. But the team went back specifically for the purpose of examining any files not available on their first examination. La Marca, the person to whom the file pertained, admitted the kidnapping.

In a rather similar case, by no means so spectacular but nevertheless, in its way difficult, since it involved some 300 schoolboys, who usually have much more 'unformed' handwriting than adults, the writer of a malicious letter was identified and confessed.

In the United Kingdom, expert evidence on handwriting was first allowed in Court in a civil action in 1856 and in a criminal action in 1865, but it is only relatively lately that it has been generally accepted that handwriting experts are not necessarily witch doctors. A jury is relatively easy to convince about the expert evidence of a chemist or physicist, since he is talking of things which they hardly comprehend. But because they can (usually) write they are very ready to assume that they know as much about writing as the expert.

In many cases writing which is otherwise undistinguished may have very characteristic capital letters. Although this may have use in identification, such unusual formations must be examined with considerable care. The very nature of the capitals lend itslef to attempted simulation and many instances are on record where the capitals have been carefully copied or traced, and little or no attention has been paid to the apparently less revealing small letters. Such copying is often quite apparent when the writing is examined under an appreciable magnification. The care with which the 'drawing' has been done produces in the line a character readily distinguishable from a freely written line. Indeed, on occasion it is possible to observe under magnification the remains of a pencilled or carbon line, insufficiently erased (or even an identation made by a dry point) and to see clearly that the inked line subsequently added has not been able to follow the guide line exactly, although no irregularity can be seen with the naked eye.

Finally, any document requires a careful and complete examination for any anomalies whatsoever, apart from the actual content as outlined above. This might be termed the application of scientific observation and logical deduction (or commonsense). In this region every case is different from every other.

As an example, one case concerned a document brought forward to show claim to a right of way. This document dated 15th December, 1952, turned up after both the alleged writer and the alleged witness were dead. The official Examiner was suspicious of the handwriting, and in particular of the similarity between the alleged writing of the witness and that in the remainder of the document; after a time he turned his attention to the Queen Elizabeth one-shilling stamp. Queen Elizabeth came to the throne in February 1952, and New Reign Stamps, particularly the less used values, tend to be delayed in their date of issue. A quick check with a stamp catalogue showed that in fact, the shilling stamp was issued on 6th July 1953. In a sense, that finished the case, but since a stamp catalogue might not be regarded as the best evidence by the Courts, an enquiry was made to the G.P.O. in London. Some six weeks later (possibly the time taken to consult a stamp catalogue), their Philately Department wrote to confirm that the first date of issue was, in fact, 6th July 1953!

It should be emphasised that no document examiner can give a positive answer in every case submitted to him. Indeed, he is lucky if he can do this in 30 per cent of his cases. Many forgeries may (indeed, undoubtedly do) go undetected because no question has been raised about them. If, however, a document is queried it soon becomes clear that the forger requires a great deal of intelligence, knowledge, and luck, if his handiwork is to go undetected.

THE DETERMINATION OF BLOOD-ALCOHOL

The *determination of blood-alcohol* has been the subject of much controversy. It is perhaps worth noting the slightly disturbing fact(50) that apparently the action of bacteria frequently present at a post-mortem, can convert compounds such as glucose, sucrose and lactose into ethyl alcohol in significant amounts.

It has been shown, in a sample of more than 200 drunk-in-charge cases, that it is undesirable to calculate blood-alcohol from the figure for a random specimen of urine, and indeed if this is done it may be prejudicial to the defendant(51). Indeed, why a urine test should ever have been considered as an alternative to a blood test is something of a mystery, since apparently the taking of a blood sample by the police costs one-third less than that of a urine sample!

The permissible maximum content of alcohol in the blood in Great Britain is 80mg/100 ml. (In the North of Ireland, since the 1968 Act, 80 mg/100 ml constitutes a minor limit with, if no other complications exist, a minor penalty.

There is then a major limit at 125 mg/100 ml, at which point one is considered to be completely incapable of driving). The Alcotest, or 'Breathalyser' is, of course, merely a screening test, and is not really evidence. The blood-alcohol *analysis,* on the other hand, is above suspicion. In the United Kingdom, spit samples (or two simultaneous samples) are run on two separate gas-chromatographs with different packings and with independent operators. One cannot attempt to quarrel with the figure.

But in fact, the major controversies in this connection have been in respect of what these figures mean in terms of human behavior—over a range of age, sex, drinking habits, etc. A number of laboratories have tried to relate blood-alcohol with such matters as coherence and muscular and mental control. In this connection it is of interest to quote a series of experiments designed to go some way into this question(52).

The objects of the study were (a) to establish what blood level might be expected from consumption of different alcoholic beverages when consumed with or without food; (b) to attempt to correlate the amount of alcohol in the blood with the reading of the Alcotest using the breath, and (c) to attempt to correlate the amount of alcohol in the blood with the behavioural pattern of the individual at the same time. Two experiments were carried out, the first being a preliminary 'screening' one.

In the preliminary experiment six subjects were used in order to establish what happened at an 'ordinary business lunch.' One hour was allowed for pre-lunch drinking, there was then a four-course lunch which, if requested, could be accompanied by a half-bottle of wine, and this was followed by brandy or liqueurs. The total drinking time was 2½–3 hours; the participants were, of course, asked to restrict themselves to so-called 'normal' drinking. The consumption and the results are shown in *Table 1.*

Table 1. Correlation of Alcotest and blood-alcohol test(52)

No.	Sex	Total consumption	Alcotest	Blood-alcohol (mg/100 ml)
1	M	5 double whiskies	–	24
2	F	2 double whiskies ½ bott. claret 1 brandy	±	40
3	F	3 sherries ½ bott. champagne 1 Benedictine 1 brandy	+	53
4	M	3 double whiskies ½ bott. burgundy 2 brandies	+	64
5	M	1 double sherry 2 double whiskies ½ bott. burgundy	+	122
6	M	5 double whiskies	+	69

They were then asked to write 100 words on 'Drinking and Driving.' No. 5, who was over the limit, in *his* '100 words' wrote a coherent account asking for this type of test to be carried over to a major test; he used an ingenious device 'to complete the required 100 words' which then came to a total of 45! No. 6 said that after two more double whiskies he would probably have called a taxi! But it would appear that *he* was not *quite* sober.

The second experiment was designed to test 'week-end luncheon drinking'—interpreted as being, in Great Britain, drinks and *perhaps* snacks, simulating a pub or a club and starting about 11:30 a.m. Drink was unlimited but restricted to the legal drinking hours, and the amount was noted by bar chits. Sixty-two males and seventeen females, a total of seventy-nine, with drinking habits reported as ranging from occasional drinkers to heavy regular drinkers 'competed.' The results are summarised in *Table 2*. A remarkable figure of 220 was achieved by a 'spirits drinker only, who did not eat.'

Table 2.

Number of individuals	Alcotest	Blood-alcohol
21	−	<70
21	±	<80
1	±	>80
16	+	<80
20	+	>80

The conclusions drawn by Camps and Robinson(52) are that 'for those participating in this trial, the blood alcohol level did not exceed 80 mg/100 ml after consuming either five measures (5/6 fluid oz; 1/6 gill, i.e. the English measure) of spirit *or* six half pints of bitter beer *or* seven drinks (one drink = 1 measure of whisky or half a pint of bitter), some of spirits and some of beer. This confirms that although half a pint of beer contains the same amount of alcohol as one measure of spirits, the blood alcohol figure resulting from consumption of each is not necessarily the same.

CONCLUSION

Over the past 30 years or so, analytical chemistry and forensic science have developed very extensively, but in the application of new techniques, the forensic scientist must lag behind, since, where the life or liberty of the individual may be at stake, the methods used must be of proven reliability in the general field. In much of the work of the forensic scientist, a proper knowledge and appreciation of analytical techniques is essential, but these must be supported, always, by precise observation, logical deduction, and the ability to use 'every branch of knowledge that could prove useful,' even including, as two of the above examples have shown, pastimes such as philately and the plastic arts. The intricacies of the analytical techniques involved and the breadth of knowledge required over many disciplines are indeed formidable.

The forensic scientist, faced by a battery of lawyers, is presented with another formidable task. There is a well-known legal story(52) which has some bearing on this. Lord Birkenhead, then Mr. F. E. Smith, was dealing with a 'difficult' judge, and offered an explanation in a longish speech.

"Mr. Smith, I have listened to you patiently, but I am no wiser."

"No, my Lord, merely better informed."

Few expert witnesses would have the temerity to make that reply to the learned Judge; but the truth inherent in it is very obvious. In conjunction with that story I would like to refer to Nicholls(45) who says, "I must . . . express my strong disapproval of the use of the word 'evidence' associated with the work of the forensic scientist. It is the job of the scientist to produce information—specialised information—and to give this information, together with an assessment of the scientific value of the information, to the appropriate authorities."

For years, because of what, to the mild fury of my legal friends, I call the intriguing difference between 'scientific' and 'legal' truth, I have maintained that the expert, or a board of experts, should act as assessor to the Court. Nothing can be more harmful to the reputation of the expert witness than to have two of them disagree because, as is so often the case, neither has the whole story. Each is then presented in Court with the other half of the evidence, and is regarded as something of a charlatan if he cannot do a week's—or a month's—work in five minutes.

This problem has been referred to by others than myself(54), and it would appear that there is some hope(55) that what is now at least suggested by the 1966 Winn Committee for medical experts, where 'the true facts can be determined impartially,' might be extended to the evidence of the expert forensic scientist.

Until this happens, we can only hope that no one will revive(56) Trail by Ordeal, Trial by Combat, or Compurgation.

NOTES

(1) A.C. Doyle. *The Naval Treaty: Short Stories*, Murray, London, 1952, p. 500.

(2) A.C. Doyle. *A Study in Scarlet, Long Stories*, Murray, London, 1946, p. 10.

(3) R. A. Freeman. *Mr. Polton Explains*, Hodder & Stoughton, London, 1940.

(4) R. A. Freeman. *Dr. Thorndyke Omnibus*, Hodder & Stoughton, London, 1929.

(5) I. W. Conrad, *Applied Optics* 8, 1 (1969).

(6) O. Hilton *Med. Sci. and the Law* 3, 107 (1963).

(7) D. M. Lucas. *Applied Optics* 8, 15 (1969).

(8) F. Lundqvist and A. S. Curry, eds. *Methods of Forensic Science*,

Interscience—J. Wiley, New York & London, Vols. I—IV, 1962—1965.

(9) H. J. Walls. *Med. Sci. and the Law* 6, 183 (1966).

(10) H. J. Walls. *Criminologist* 4, 7 (1969).

(11) H. J. Walls. *Applied Optics* 8, 21 (1969).

(12) I. G. Holden. *J. Forensic Sci. Soc.* 6, 7 (1966).

(13) C. F. Tippett. *Med. Sci and the Law* 4, 22 (1964).

(14) A. S. Curry. *Med. Sci. and the Law* 7, 138 (1967).

(15) A. Alha and V. Tamminen. *Methods of Forensic Science*, Ed. A. S. Curry, Interscience—J. Wiley, New York, Vol. IV, 1965, p. 265.

(16) B. Cleverley. *Med. Sci. and the Law* 7, 148 (1967).

(17) B. Cleverley. *J. Forensic Sci. Soc.* 8, 69 (1968).

(18) K. Jones and C. F. Tippet. *Med. Sci and the Law* 2, 184 (1962).

(19) S. S. Kind and C. G. Broster. *J. Forensic Sci. Soc.* 5, 115 (1965).

(20) C. F. Tippett. *Med. Sci. and the Law* 3, 282 (1963).

(21) S. Denton. *J. Forensic Sci. Soc.* 5, 112 (1965).

(22) C. A. Mitchell. *The Analyst* 60, 454 (1935).

(23) J. Ferrie, Private Communication.

(24) D. Graham and H. C. Gray. *X-Ray Focus* (Ilford), 5, No. 3, 12 (1964).

(25) U.K. Atomic Energy Authority. *Scientific and Technical News Service.* STN/11/68. May 6, 1968.

(26) R. F. Coleman and N. J. Weston. *J. Forensic Sci. Soc.* 8, 32 (1968).

(27) V. P. Guinn. In *Methods of Forensic Science* Ed. A. S. Curry, Interscience-J. Wiley, New York, Vol. III, 1964, p. 47.

(28) R. F. Coleman. *Forensic Sci. Soc.* 6, 19 (1966).

(29) F. Morgan. *Med, Sci and the Law* 6, 155 (1966).

(30) H. Smith. *J. Forensic Sci. Soc.* 7, 97 (1967).

(31) H. A. Shapiro. *Criminologist* 4, 43, (1969).

(32) S. L. Clemens, Sources various and unreliable.

(33) B. B. Coldwell. *The Analyst* 80, 946 (1955).

(34) G. Machata. In *Methods of Forensic Science.* Ed. A. S. Curry, Interscience— J. Wiley, New York, Vol. IV, 1965, p. 229

(35) K. D. Parker, J. A. Wright, and C. H. Hine. *J. Forensic Sci. Soc.*, 7, 162 (1967).

(36) N. C. Jain, C. R. Fontan and P. L. Kirk. *J. Forensic Sci. Soc.* 5, 102 (1965).

(37) P. W. Wright. *J. Forensic Sci. Soc.* 6, 13 (1966).

(38) A. Walton. *J. Forensic Sci. Soc.* 6, 2 (1966).

(39) J. Ramirez-Munoz. *J. Forensic Sci. Soc.* 7, 151 (1967).

(40) W. J. Chisum. *J. Forensic Sci. Soc.* 6, 89 (1966).

(41) J. J. Layton. *J. Forensic Sci. Soc.* 6, 76 (1966).

(42) J. Bogan and H. Smith. *J. Forensic Sci. Soc.* 7, 37 (1967).

(43) L. A. O'Neill. *Med., Sci. and the Law* 7, 145 (1967).

(44) P. G. W. Cobb. *J. Forensic Sci. Soc.* 8, 29 (1968).

(45) D. F. Nelson. In *Methods of Forensic Science*, Ed. A. S. Curry, Interscience—J. Wiley, New York, Vol. IV. 1965, p. 99.

(46) L. C. Nicholls. *J. Forensic Sci. Soc.* 6, 180 (1966).

(47) P. O. Rees. *J. Forensic Sci. Soc.* 8, 15 (1968).

(48) R. M. Mitchell. *J. Forensic Sci. Soc.* 8, 99, (1968).

(49) A. S. Osborn. *Questioned Documents*, Boyd Printing Co., Toronto, 2nd edn., 1929, p. 248.

(50) D. J. Blackmore. *J. Forensic Sci. Soc.* 8, 73 (1968).

(51) W. H. D. Morgan. *J. Forensic Sci. Soc.* 5, 15 (1965).

(52) F. E. Camps and A. E. Robinson. *Med. Sci. and the Law* 8, 153 (1968).

(53) K. Simpson. *Criminologist* 4, 51 (1969).

(54) C. J. Maletskos. *Proceedings of the First International Conference on*

Activation Analysis, Ed. V. P. Guinn, Gulf General Atomic, San Diego, California, 1967, p.3.

(55) J. Grant. *Med. Sci. and the Law* 6, 206 (1966).

(56) B. Hargrove. *J. Forensic Sci. Soc.* 6, 171 (1966).

CRIME LABS EXPAND AS BUSINESS FLOURISHES

Arnold E. Levitt

Recently, two Wisconsin banks were burglarized, the attempted safe drilling on one proving unsuccessful but the vault of the other yielded to a terrific blast. Shortly afterward, two persons were arrested in San Diego, Calif., for disturbing the peace. After a possible connection with the Wisconsin safe jobs had been established, the clothing, car debris, and tools from the car owned by one of the suspects were sent to the Federal Bureau of Investigation laboratory in Washington, D.C.

Examination disclosed that green paint on the two safe dials in question was similar to paint on a sledge hammer found in the car and could have come from that source. Various deposits of safe insulation, brick, mortar, and brown coat and white coat plaster from the two banks in question were found to match specimens obtained from the clothing, debris from the car, and the sledge hammer from the car trunk. Laboratory experts later testified to their findings, and both defendants were found guilty as charged. Each received five years on each count, the sentences to run concurrently.

The nation's crime rate continues to rise. Serious crime in the U.S. increased 11% in 1970 over 1969, according to the FBI's Uniform Crime Reports for 1970. Narcotics and drug abuse has become a serious national problem. All of this is piling an increased case load on federal, state, and local crime laboratories.

Some existing crime laboratories have been forced to increase their staffs, and new crime laboratories have been formed. Others have expanded their facilities and have moved into new quarters or added additional branches or buildings. In the past few years many new jobs in forensic science have been created.

The Omnibus Crime Control and Safe Streets Act of 1968 created the Law Enforcement Assistance Administration (LEAA) as the Federal Government's major effort in the fight against crime. LEAA's goal is to improve the nation's criminal justice system. LEAA does this primarily by giving states and local communities the resources to improve all facets of law enforcement. With the aid of grants from LEAA many state and local crime laboratories have been able to upgrade their facilities and add more workers.

For instance, one state that has benefited greatly from LEAA assistance is New Jersey. The New Jersey State Police Crime Laboratory in West Trenton has increased its professional staff from 12 to 44 in just the past two years, according to Dr. Richard Saferstein, the laboratory's chief chemist. Of the 44, 35 are chemists and four hold Ph.D.'s. To aid the West Trenton laboratory, the state is planning to establish three additional "satellite" laboratories, each of which will have 12 employees.

Taking advantage of the large supply of science graduates competing in the job market, the New Jersey State Police Crime Laboratory has hired 27 scientists (mostly new graduates or Vietnam veterans) in the past year. The majority have had no previous experience in forensic science. The plan is to give them at least one year of training at the West Trenton laboratory and then send them to work at one of the satellite laboratories.

The New Jersey State Police Crime Laboratory is maintained in the police division's Forensic Science Bureau, which serves 600 law enforcement agencies throughout the state. The Forensic Science Bureau comprises six units: chemistry-biology laboratory, document-voiceprint, photo-composite drawing, ballistics, latent print, and laundry-jeweler's marks. By far the unit with the largest number of personnel is the chemistry-biology laboratory. Largely because of a huge increase in drug arrests, the workload volume of the chemistry-biology laboratory in fiscal 1970 doubled over the previous year.

SERVICE

In Virginia, with the aid of LEAA funds the Northern Virginia Police Laboratory in Fairfax began operation last July to provide better service for law enforcement agencies in the northern part of the state. The laboratory has a professional staff of five, including three Ph.D.'s, and deals mainly with drugs and narcotics. In the first four months of its operation, the laboratory handled 700 cases, including more than 150 cases a month concerning drugs and narcotics, according to Dr. J. William Magee, the lab's director.

One of the important functions of the Northern Virginia Police Laboratory is police education. The laboratory has a classroom in which 1000 northern Virginia police officers are being instructed in forensic methods. In addition, the U.S. Bureau of Narcotics and Dangerous Drugs has given a three-day school there for police officers concerning legal aspects of drugs and narcotics.

Dr. Magee believes that a solid background in chemistry is essential for a person entering forensic science. College training in criminalistics or forensic science is not necessary, he believes, as this can be obtained more efficiently on the job.

Another small-crime laboratory that has been started with the aid of LEAA funds is the Law Enforcement Assistance Council Laboratory on the campus of Southeast Missouri State College in Cape Girardeau. The laboratory has the use of all the instrumentation of the college's chemistry, physics, and biology departments, and the college faculty is available for consultation.

Two chemistry-major seniors working closely with the laboratory have testified successfully in court cases, says Dr. Robert C. Briner, director of the laboratory. He points out that other interested chemistry seniors conduct independent research under the lab's direction in areas of forensic chemistry, such as drug analysis and blood grouping techniques. "This research is quite useful to the laboratory as it enables us to investigate potentially useful areas which we would not have time to look at without the interested students," Dr. Briner says.

At present the laboratory is handling about 10 to 20 cases per month—about 90% of the work load is drug cases. Besides drug cases, the laboratory is working on blood stain typing, sewer analysis, alcohol analysis, and microscopic analyses of paint, soil, and fibers.

NARCOTICS

Spurred by the drugs and narcotics problem, the U.S. Justice Department's Bureau of Narcotics and Dangerous Drugs has greatly expanded and updated its laboratories in the past few years. The bureau now has regional laboratories in Washington, D.C., New York City, Chicago, Dallas, San Francisco, and a new laboratory to open early in 1972 in Miami. In addition, the bureau operates a special testing and research laboratory in Washington, D.C.

In 1969, BNDD laboratories employed 56 professionals (mostly chemists) and 12 supporting workers. At present the laboratories employ 116 professionals and 36 supporting workers. The bureau hopes to add nine chemists and six supporting workers to its laboratory staff in fiscal 1972, says John W. Gunn, Jr., chief of the laboratory division of the bureau's office of scientific support.

The case load of BNDD laboratories has increased markedly, Mr. Gunn says. The laboratories handled 19,731 exhibits or samples (three to five examinations per exhibit) in fiscal 1970 and 29,000 exhibits in fiscal 1971, he points out.

BNDD hires few Ph.D.'s, preferring to hire most of its laboratory scientists at the bachelor's level right out of school. Most of them start at the GS-5 or GS-7 level. Mr. Gunn believes that the best place to train a forensic chemist is on the job in the laboratory. New people all take part in a formal on-the-job training program which includes instruction in general drug analysis, the opium alkaloids and cocaine, LSD and the tryptamines, amphetamines, barbiturates, other controlled drugs and frequently encountered noncontrolled drugs, marijuana and tetrahydrocannabinol, clandestine laboratories and drug synthesis, and legal aspects and court testimony.

BNDD laboratories do considerable work for state and local law enforcement agencies (and have worked with many foreign law enforcement agencies). The bureau has helped the states in setting up state crime laboratories. BNDD also sponsors an active program of week-long seminars for forensic chemists, which aids employees of state, municipal, and federal laboratories that conduct analysis of drug evidence in criminal cases.

The U.S. Treasury Department's Bureau of Customs is another federal bureau that handles a considerable amount of forensic work. The bureau has laboratories in New York City, Boston, Los Angeles, San Francisco, Chicago, Baltimore, New Orleans, and Savannah. In addition, the bureau operates a special research laboratory in Washington, D.C., and two small narcotics laboratories that were established during the past year in San Antonio and San Diego.

Customs Bureau laboratories employ a total of 168 persons, including 105 professionals, points out Melvin Lerner, director of technical services. The New York laboratory is the largest, with a total of 53, including 35 professionals.

One of the important functions of the Customs laboratories is furnishing technical and scientific information to assist Customs officers in detecting fraud, smuggling, and sabotage. A large proportion of samples analyzed by Customs laboratory chemists represent seizures of narcotic drugs and other articles prohibited from entering the country.

EDUCATION

Perhaps because rapid growth of forensic science laboratories has been recent, colleges and universities in the U.S. that offer special degrees in criminalistics or forensic science are few. Probably most scientists enter the forensic field after majoring in a broad scientific discipline such as chemistry, biology, or physics.

A pioneering school in forensic science education is the University of California, Berkeley. The late Dr. Paul L. Kirk set up the department of criminalistics in the university's School of Criminology in 1937. The department now offers bachelor's, master's, and Ph.D. degrees. At present, 12 undergraduates and six graduate students are majoring in criminalistics. Most of Berkeley's advanced degree holders in criminalistics have gone into academic work, teaching at such places as the John Jay College of Criminal Justice and the University of Southern California toxicology department. A majority of the bachelor's degree holders have joined one of the 17 public-funded crime laboratories in California which together employ about 150 people.

John Jay College of Criminal Justice in New York City is another school offering degrees in forensic science. At present more than 100 students at the college are studying for a bachelor's degree in criminalistics and about 20 are candidates for the master's degree in forensic science. Dr. Alexander Joseph is director of the college's forensic science program.

The University of Illinois at Chicago Circle has given about 120 bachelor's degrees in criminal justice in the past two years. Of these, 15 to 20 students have specialized in the physical sciences. At present there are about 340 majors in criminal justice at the university with 20 to 40 students specializing in the physical sciences. The university is awaiting approval of a special B.S. program in criminalistics and also has plans for an M.S. degree in the discipline.

George Washington University and Georgetown University, both in Washington, D.C., also offer a master's degree in forensic science. Since it started its program four years ago, George Washington has awarded 41 master's degrees. Currently the university has more than 60 people enrolled in forensic science. In addition to its master's degree program, Georgetown is offering nine short courses this summer in specialized forensic science topics to workers in the field.

According to faculty members at the various schools, there is no shortage of jobs in forensic science for qualified graduates. None of the schools has experienced any difficulty in placement.

In addition to the few schools that offer degrees in forensic science, 326 junior and community colleges offer a two-year associate of arts degree program in law enforcement technology to police officers, law enforcement administrators, and security officers, according to the American Association of Junior Colleges. Many of these programs include a course in criminalistics and a science survey course.

FORTY YEARS OF DISTINGUISHED

SCIENTIFIC ASSISTANCE TO

LAW ENFORCEMENT

Law Enforcement Bulletin

A scheduled airliner crashed near the southeastern tip of North Carolina, taking the lives of all aboard. Experts from the Federal Bureau of Investigation's Laboratory, experienced in many areas of scientific examination, rushed to the scene to assist in determining the cause of the disaster.

Some of the first pieces of evidence to be examined were various articles of clothing from the body of one of the passengers found some 16 miles from the crash scene. These were soon followed by hundreds of other pieces of evidence which quickly set into motion the . scientific personnel and equipment representing virtually every segment of an elaborate crime detection facility—the FBI Laboratory. Slowly the test tubes, microscopes, and spectrographs yielded from the debris found at the crash site the grim evidence that a bomb had been responsible for the fatal disaster to the aircraft, its crew, and passengers.

The final report compiled by the FBI Laboratory indicated that a dynamite explosion had taken place aboard the ill-fated flight. Triggered by means of a dry cell battery, the bomb had vented its carnage in the passenger compartment near the seat occupied by the victim whose body was found a considerable distance from the main crash scene.

Each day, in similar manner, the resources of the FBI Laboratory, which celebrates its 40th Anniversary November 24, 1972, are mobilized in the mounting struggle against crime.

The 40-year history of the FBI Laboratory is one of growth and accomplishment. During the fall of 1932, a few file cabinets were removed from one room in the old Southern Railway Building, 13th and Pennsylvania Avenue, NW., Washington, D.C., in order to find available space for the crime laboratory of the FBI, then known as the Bureau of Investigation. One microscope was moved into the room, along with ultraviolet light equipment, a large drawing board, a helixometer, and some surplus bookshelves. A few tables were added to the equipment, and plans were made to bring in photographic instruments. A crime lab was in the making.

During the formation of its Laboratory, the FBI launched a program to locate businessmen, manufacturers, and scientists whose knowledge and experience might be useful in guiding the new facility through its infancy. With the future in mind, an FBI Special Agent was enrolled in a course of study offered by the scientific crime detection laboratory of a large midwestern university.

The mere collecting and grouping together of scientific equipment, however, certainly did not constitute a complete laboratory for service to law enforcement. It needed qualified personnel. Training and selection of the Laboratory's staff were among the most important initial efforts. Then followed the slow but necessary task of educating law enforcement agencies throughout the country to the potential value of scientific examinations in criminal investigations.

Following the acquisition of some basic scientific instruments, the selection of properly trained personnel to operate them, and the notification of interested law enforcement agencies of its purpose and availability, the FBI Laboratory was officially established on November 24, 1932.

The FBI Laboratory facilities and experts are available without charge to all duly constituted Federal, State, county, and municipal law enforcement agencies of the United States and its territorial possessions. Examinations are made with the understanding that evidence is connected with an official criminal investigation.

During the first month of service, FBI Laboratory examiners handled 20 cases. In its first full year of operation, the volume increased to a total of 963 examinations. By the next year that figure was more than doubled. But this was only a thin shadow of the potential that loomed ahead for the FBI Laboratory. By the end of fiscal year 1972, total examinations had reached 495,000 for the preceding 12 months.

While the new Laboratory gave assistance to law enforcement agencies of all sizes and from all regions of the Nation, the FBI received commensurate cooperation from them in return. In addition, manufacturers from throughout the country provided assistance in the form of reference collections or standard files. Typical are the Typewriter Standards File, the Automotive Paint File, and numerous other files for comparing known manufactured items with suspect samples. Just as the fingerprint examiner depends heavily on the comparison of a known print and a questioned print, so too does the Laboratory scientist, in many instances, depend on a comparison examination. The standard files are invaluable for this purpose.

The FBI Laboratory is staffed with specialists experienced in many scientific and technical fields. Specialization enhances the examination capability of the Laboratory, in that each unit limits its examinations to a relatively narrow field, thus making it possible for that specific department to research intensively in its discipline. This enables each unit to apply the most up-to-date equipment and knowledge to every aspect of its examinations.

A continuous program of adaptation and innovation is underway in the FBI Laboratory utilizing new developments in the examination of evidentiary materials. Many of the crimes investigated by local law enforcement agencies result in submissions of objects and samples found at the crime scenes to the FBI Laboratory for analysis and possible information of investigative value. Cases involving homicides and assaults on very young children place particularly heavy emphasis on the work of the crime laboratory because of the victim's frequent inability to offer effective testimony to the crime or make a positive identification of the assailant.

Almost the entire spectrum of criminal violations is represented by evidence received in the Document Section. Examinations of handwriting, hand printing, typewriting, indented writing, obliterated writing, charred papers, shoe prints, and tire treads result in the appearances of document experts of the FBI Laboratory in all jurisdictional levels of courts throughout the United States and territories with ever-increasing frequency.

Recent testimony by a document examiner aided in conviction of a burglar and attempted rapist who, during the night of September 27, 1971, broke into the home of a Charles County, Md., woman who was alone and asleep in an upstairs bedroom. The intruder used matches from several paper matchbooks to light his way through the home, discarding the matches as they burned near the end.

The intruder proceeded to the upstairs bedroom where he attempted to rape the victim. He fled after the woman was successful in resisting the attack.

A short time later the suspect was arrested by local police. In his pockets were found several matchbooks which were submitted to the FBI Laboratory along with the match stems found at the crime scene. A Document Section expert identified two of the match stems found at the crime scene as having been torn from two of the books of matches found in the suspect's pockets.

The National Fraudulent Check File, Bank Robbery Note File, and Anonymous Letter File of the Document Section are familiar names to law enforcement agencies. These reference files serve as invaluable tools in associating unidentified evidence from throughout the country with particular suspects or crimes.

For example, during the period from 1965 to early January 1971, 168 questioned documents were submitted to the FBI Laboratory for examination in a case involving scurrilous, racist, and threatening letters which had been mailed to many prominent persons including a former Vice-President and three U.S. Senators. These letters, although anonymous and submitted from various parts of the country, were associated with each other, based on handwriting and hand printing, as a result of the Document Section's Anonymous Letter File.

Examination by the FBI Laboratory of one of the letters revealed a distinctive watermark. Another letter was found to contain the name "Morris" (fictitious) in indented writing.

Using information furnished by the FBI Laboratory concerning the watermark, the paper was traced by FBI Agents to a midwestern city siding and roofing contractor. A review of company records revealed the firm had an employee named Melvin James Morris (fictitious) who subsequently was identified by an FBI document examiner as the writer of the letters.

Morris was arrested, tried, and found guilty of violating the Federal Extortion Statute, thus ending a steady flow of threats which had spanned more than a 5-year period.

Because of the wide range of analytical techniques employed in the Physics and Chemistry Section, a correspondingly wide variety of evidence, much of it from crimes of violence, is handled in this Section.

Hair and fiber analysis is of special value where bodily contact is made with an object or another individual. While the examination of a human hair sample normally does not permit a certain person to be identified as the only possible source of the hair, a great number of comparable characteristics permits a strong probability to be established. It is also possible to eliminate a person as the source of a hair. Observation of hair characteristics will normally permit a determination to be made of the race of the person from whom the hair originated, as well as the part of the body from which it came. Hair studies may also reveal if the hair was forcibly removed or naturally fell from the body; if it was cut, crushed, or burned; if it was bleached or dyed; or if it was artificially waved. The nature and composition of clothing fibers exchanged during body contact in violent crimes against a person may be determined and compared with those of the clothing of a victim and suspect. Examinations are also made in this unit for invisible laundry marks and identifying characteristics of rope, string, tape, fabric patterns, and features related to woven material.

The body fluid most commonly associated with violent crimes is blood. The presence of blood on clothing, weapons, automobiles, home furnishings, in scrapings from fingernails, from surfaces at crime scenes, and on every conceivable object relating to a bodily injury may be relevant both in establishing a criminal act and in associating a suspect with the crime. In other instances, small stains of blood on objects may be determined to have come from nonhuman sources through analytical methods. These findings may thereafter be associated with another animal source, verifying a suspect's story and helping to clear the innocent. In still other situations, semen, saliva, and other body fluids are identified and sometimes classified as having originated from a person possessing a particular blood group if the person from which the body fluid originated is a secretor. Recent developments in dried blood grouping techniques in the Serology Unit have enabled stains to be more specifically classified into additional blood grouping systems, thus narrowing down the possible sources from which they originated.

The examination of soils and combinations of mineral substances requires utilization of instruments specially designed for petrographic work. Various particles of physical evidence found on the property of a suspect or on his person may be used to associate him with the scene of a crime based on the results of the Mineralogy Unit's analyses. These substances include soils, safe insulation, concrete, plaster, mortar, ceramics, glass, ore, and abrasives.

A number of different types of chemical examinations are conducted in the Chemistry—Toxicology Unit utilizing gas chromatography, infrared, and ultraviolet spectroscopy as well as chemical analyses to identify poisons, drugs, and other toxic materials as possible causes of a victim's death. Other materials, such as probable accelerants found at a scene of a fire or sabotage incident, are analyzed to determine if the act was in fact a criminal effort and to determine if the materials contain any unusual substance that could provide a lead for investigators.

Probably best known of the examinations conducted in these areas is that of determining whether or not a questioned bullet was fired from a specific weapon. The firearms examiner may also be called upon to determine if firearms are operating properly or to conduct gunpowder and shot pattern tests. In other instances, examinations of a questioned bullet or cartridge case may assist in ascertaining the type of weapon used in a crime. Also possible, utilizing the basic principles of firearms examinations, is the identification of telltale marks left at crime scenes by punches, hammers, axes, pliers, screwdrivers, chisels, wrenches, and other objects. The explosives specialist is called upon to examine evidence recovered at the scene of explosions—a problem rendered the more difficult because of the inherently destructive nature of the crime.

The popularity of motorcycles and the ease with which they may be illegally obtained and transported have resulted in a substantial increase in the number of altered serial numbers submitted for restoration to the FBI Laboratory. Obliterated numbers can also be restored on firearms, sewing machines, watches, outboard motors, slot machines, automobiles, tools, and other metallic items. Tests may show whether two or more pieces of metal are in any way related, the possible cause of metal separation, and if production specifications for the metals have been met.

Examiners in the Instrumental Analysis Unit conduct microscopic, microchemical, and instrumental analyses of a wide variety of physical evidence such as paints, plastics, metal, glass, rubber, and other minute specimens of materials too small for examination by other means. Spectrographs, spectrophotometers, chromatographs, and X-ray diffraction apparatus provide the Laboratory experts with the data necessary for the identification and quantitative analysis of trace evidence.

In neutron activation analysis a sample of unknown material is irradiated with neutrons (nuclear particles). Some of the irradiated atoms in the unknown material are thereby made radioactive and begin to disintegrate (radioactively) with the emission of gamma rays. The energy of these gamma rays is measured with a gamma ray spectrometer. These energy values are then used to identify the element in the original material. Quantitative measurement of the elements present can be made by comparing the radioactivity of the elements in the evidentiary material with the radioactivity of known amounts of these elements.

The President's declared war against the gambling interests of organized crime and the increased emphasis on antigambling enforcement by State and local authorities have dramatically increased the examinations conducted in the FBI Laboratory's Gambling Unit. Its personnel have a rich depth of experience in identifying, defining, and demonstrating the meaning and significance of wagering records and related materials used by bookmakers and numbers writers in the conduct of their illicit profession. Similar examinations are performed on recorded material obtained through court authorized interception of telephone communications.

Attempts to thwart recognition of gamblers' records through the use of codes and ciphers are unmasked by FBI Laboratory cryptanalysts using electronic data-processing equipment. Through the joint efforts of gambling examiners, chemists, and document examiners, specialized papers used by bookmakers and number writers are identified or their sources established. The existence of gambling records also is frequently proved through the development of indented-writing impressions made on an underlying piece of paper and, in other instances, by the restoration of burned or multilated papers.

In casino and carnival games, the Laboratory cryptanalysis staff possesses the capacity and experience to mathematically define the odds favoring the game's operator. This includes detailed examinations of pinball machines, various types of slot machines, roulette wheels, and other gambling devices. Rigged equipment such as altered dice, marked cards, and electrically controlled dice tables can be exposed and their effects demonstrated.

The Organized Crime Control Act of 1970 caused some sports bookmakers in South Carolina to hire legal counsel in their search for loopholes in the new laws prohibiting certain gambling operations. The bookmakers were advised by their counsel to decentralize, thus—they thought—avoiding the prohibition of an enterprise involving five or more persons. Through a tangled web, layoff wagers were handled telephonically with seemingly fewer persons involved.

Into this gambling operation drifted a compulsive bettor with connections enabling him to place wagers with top New York bookmakers. The bettor was permitted by his New York sources to manipulate the handicap by one-half point, provided he furnished a minimum of $500 in wagers on each of the 13 professional football games each week. Lacking such resources, he began handling layoff wagers for local bookmakers. Soon he accepted these wagers at the established handicap and took advantage of the one-half point manipulation when forwarding the wagers to New York. This last tactic moved him from the ranks of a mere bettor to those of a layoff bookmaker using an interstate facility in violation of the law. His connections and those of others were traced, resulting in convictions against him and the bookmakers furnishing him layoff wagers.

It was an FBI Laboratory expert on gambling who explained the complexities of this bookmaking operation to the court and clearly refuted the defendant's denials of bookmaking activity.

The trial also established a precedent by holding that decentralized bookmakers, even though acting as independent businesses when dealing with the public, constituted a single enterprise when they exchanged layoff wagers with one another in violation of the law.

In addition to the assistance given gambling investigators in the breaking of bookmakers' codes and ciphers, the cryptanalytic staff can frequently recover the true meaning of encrypted messages in criminal matters. Many examinations of this type have very materially contributed to successful prosecutions in local investigations involving, for example, murders and narcotics.

In recent years, one of the fastest developing phases of law enforcement has been in the field of radio communications. Cities have grown to megalopolises, towns have become cities, and the need for larger radio systems and more sophisticated communications equipment has grown proportionately. The Radio Engineering Section of the FBI Laboratory is equipped with the most modern and up-to-date instruments, tools, and equipment and is staffed with specialists in this field. These specialists are primarily responsible for insuring that all of the field divisions are equipped with efficient, modern FM automobile two-way radio communications systems. This responsibility includes systems engineering, installation, evaluation of equipment, and maintenance procedures to be effected in each field division system.

Continual contact is maintained with the various commercial firms which manufacture radio communications equipment, as well as with military services and other civilian Government agencies. In this way, Laboratory engineers are kept abreast of the latest developments so that agents in the field may at all times be provided with the finest radio communications facilities in carrying out the Bureau's investigative responsibilities.

The expertise in radio and electronics required of the technical personnel assigned to the Radio Engineering Section is also used to advantage in responding to requests of other law enforcement agencies for examinations and testimony in matters involving electronic or mechanical devices. For instance, a recent marked increase in submissions by State and Federal officials of illegal electromechanical gambling devices has resulted in related testimony in State and Federal courts. Pinball machine gambling has often formed a financial base for organized crime-associated activities in States where the machines are in operation. Expert testimony has been found to be an essential element in establishing the nature of such machines in court.

Recent testimony was important in gambling cases in several Southern States involving over 4,000 machines valued at approximately $8 million. The successful conclusions of these cases to date have been in large part the result of long hours of preparation and excellent presentation in court by Laboratory experts assigned to the Radio Engineering Section.

Impressive as they are, the hundreds of technical reports, the thousands of exhibits presented from the witness stands, the tens of thousands of words of expert testimony given and the hundreds of thousands of scientific examinations conducted annually fall far short of measuring the full influence of the FBI Laboratory's contribution in the nationwide solution of crime. Of much greater importance is the growing realization that scientific crime detection is an essential tool in effective law enforcement performance. It is this impact on modern investigative procedures which is revitalizing present-day law enforcement efforts. It is a welcome and timely trend—in this 40th Anniversary Year of the FBI Laboratory—to be enjoyed not only by the entire law enforcement profession, but also by the people of our Nation who demand and deserve to have the best in crime detection.

IV.

The Statistical Individualization of Physical Evidence

INTRODUCTION

One question that the forensic scientist is frequently asked is whether a questioned item of physical evidence originated from a particular person or matches some physical object. Did the dried blood found at the scene of the crime come from the defendant and no one else? Was the broken headlight glass originally from the suspect's automobile? Is the latent fingerprint in question the offender's? Forensic scientists have to be particularly careful in responding to such inquiries and should not form a conclusion of individuality (the two substances in question have a common origin) unless it is based on adequate data. Determining a bloodstain sample is Type A and a suspect has Type A blood by no means constitutes an individuality, although it may ·be helpful in narrowing the number of suspects. The student of forensic science must be completely familiar with the concepts of individuality as they relate to the interpretation of physical evidence.

The natural sciences have developed a strong tradition for imposing rules to guide the collection, analysis, and interpretation of information. The collection of data in a controlled manner is the scientist's way of ensuring that conclusions made following a series of examinations are based upon observations truly representative of the evidence or event in question. An expert will sometimes testify about the individuality of certain physical evidence, based upon years of experience with hundreds of examinations, rather than upon hard statistical data. Although experience is absolutely essential in determining the relative significance of evidence, it must be supported by quantitative data which are less biased and subject to error.

In this section are five selections which explore a number of important issues in the use of statistical techniques in the interpretation of physical evidence. The initial article by P.L. Kirk and Charles R. Kingston outlines several fundamental considerations in determining the applicability of statistical techniques to problems of evaluating evidence. In criminalistics, probability is primarily a guide to decision-making and an "estimate of the situation." The utilization of statistics can reduce the chance for error in interpreting single or repeated events. If one scientist's experiences and findings can be expressed quantitatively, they can be more broadly utilized by the entire profession. The authors present an example of applying a statistical approach to a typical problem of evaluating evidence.

In another article Charles R. Kingston discusses the concept of "subjective probabilities," based upon intuitive, personal judgments of the significance of available information. He selects those criminalistics cases in which the shape or pattern of evidence (the jigsaw fit) forms a basis of comparison yet are extremely difficult to analyze quantitatively. In other situations in which a physical matching is impossible, e.g., in the comparison of blood or fibers, a compositional analysis can generate data that may be used to indicate common origin of evidence. The author calls for the collection of statistical data on all important forms of physical evidence and for meaningful strategies designed to interpret such data.

The concluding selections are reprinted from law journals and address two additional issues of mathematical probabilities and evidence: the statistical meaning or equivalent of "reasonable doubt," and the possibility that law may become too mathematically oriented. H.J. Walls notes that in 1827 Jeremy Bentham recognized the possibility of statistics aiding the courts in decision-making. Attempting to construct a quantitative model for determining "reasonable doubt," H.J. Walls suggests at least one way for making such a determination. Laurence H. Tribe, challenging the use of mathematics in court, cites several cases, including the Dreyfus trial and more recently, *People vs. Collins*, in which the California Supreme Court rejected the calculations of a college mathematics instructor. Unless probabilities are used correctly and judiciously, they can result in miscarriages of justice, suspicion, and possible rejection by the courts.

THE USE OF STATISTICS IN CRIMINALISTICS

Charles R. Kingston
Paul L. Kirk

There are many philosophically oriented fundamental ideas of probability. Perhaps the most practical basic approach to the subject lies in the concept of frequency, in which statements of probability express the relative frequencies of repeated events. Such generalizations are usually derived from prior observation of frequencies exhibited in a series of trials, plus the assumption that these same frequencies will recur in the future.

For practical use in criminalistics, it is of little interest what might happen in a long series of trials; the crime is committed only once. Of what use, then, is the above frequency concept? The answer to this lies in another way of looking at probability, which is to consider it as a degree of belief. For instance, in throwing a normal die, we would wish to decide just how much we believe that a given number, say six, will occur in the next toss. It is accepted today that the rational man will base the degree of belief upon the frequency concept. This means that the degree of belief that the number six will come up on the next toss would be about .17, which is about the probability that six will occur in an unbiased die. The exact interpretation of this can cause a bit of puzzlement. What the figure actually means is that out of many tosses of the die, six would be expected to occur in roughly 17% of the total number of tosses. But only the *next* toss is of interest, not a series of tosses, and six cannot occur in 17% of the next toss.

Under these circumstances the figure of .17 can only represent a guide to a decision. We wish to decide either that six will occur or will not, and the degree of belief in its occurrence, .17, will be a guide to this decision. In this case, if a decision were made solely on the basis of this figure, it would be that six will not occur.

Now consider a problem of evaluating the significance of the coincidence of several properties in two pieces of glass. Suppose that the probability of two fragments from different sources having this coincidence of properties is .005, and that the probability of such coincidence when they are from the same source is .999. What do these figures mean? They are simply guides for making a decision about the origin of the fragments, either in the form of an opinion by the expert or as a question of fact by the jury. Since the consequences of a decision will enter into the evaluation, no set figures can be given to establish the dividing point between the two possible decisions. The contrast between the requirement of "proof beyond reasonable doubt" that is demanded in criminal cases and the preponderance of evidence" acceptable in civil cases illustrates the bearing of the consequences upon the making of a decision.

Now that some insight into the meaning of probability as applied to a single event has been gained, it is necessary to see whether or not such a probability is applicable in criminalistics, and whether it offers any advantages for making decisions. Only the more general aspects of this question will be considered here.

As shown above, a probability figure is related to past experience, and its accuracy will depend on the amount and applicability of this experience as well as upon the analytical processes applied to evaluate it. A decision is made by utilizing this probability, in conjunction with considerations as to the consequences of the decision, as a guide. If the term "estimate of the situation" is substituted for "probability" or "probability figure" in the above, the statements apply to decision-making processes used at present in criminalistics. Thus the difference between the generally-used approach and the statistical approach lies in the terms "estimate of the situation" and "probability figure."

In the majority of cases, the "estimate of the situation" is obtained through an intuitive evaluation based upon past experience—not only one's own experience, but often also that obtained indirectly from the study of others' combined experiences. This is unavoidable, since no one person could hope to have personal experience with the multitude of situations encountered in the practice of criminalistics. In the intuitive approach, therefore, there are two places where error can occur: one, in the communication of experiences from different sources; and two, in the intuitive evaluation of these experiences, whether others' or one's own. The communication can suffer from semantic difficulties, while the evaluation is likely to be biased by the experimenter's own prejudices.

A probability figure can suffer from the same sources of error. That is, statistical information can be presented in such a way that the true meaning is obscured, and an experimenter can inject his own biases into the data being processed. The difference between the two approaches, then, lies in the fact that the means of minimizing the errors introduced are incorporated into a proper statistical approach and can be spelled out for the experimenter, whereas such definite controls are not easily applied to the intuitive approach. We believe that this is sufficient justification for advocating the use of statistics in criminalistics, for then the emphasis is upon a formal system rather than on a person.

In order to derive the maximum benefit from a statistical approach, the conditions and limitations imposed must be known and understood. Unfortunately, many opponents of the use of statistical methods in criminalistics have pronounced dogmatically that these conditions are so limiting as to invalidate completely any results. However, we know of no rational argument ever presented purporting to uphold this view. The difficulties inherent in the conditions should be judged only after they have been intelligently analysed, and not from general impressions which may stem from misunderstandings about the subject. Some of the limiting conditions will be discussed in this section.

Planning. A statistical analysis is not a remedy for poorly or inappropriately gathered data. If the data are to be applied to any particular problem or type of problem, it is essential to define exactly what is going to be demanded of the analysis. A method of analysis must be chosen with respect to the type of data which it is possible to gather. Then, and only then, are the data collected and the projected analysis applied. It is rare that data collected by one not versed in statistical techniques will allow the extraction of even fifty percent of the information that could be obtained from proper data with the same, or even less, effort and expense. When presented with inappropriate data, that statistician feels much the same as does the criminalist when the inexperienced investigator brings to the laboratory a paper bag into which he has stuffed the evidence from the scene of the crime along with the clothing of the suspect.

This does not imply that even inappropriate data cannot be analysed for mean values, variance, independence of variables, and so on, but these values will have meaning in the original problem only if the data have been properly collected with respect to the problem.

Randomness. The majority of cases in which the criminalist might employ statistical methods present two related aspects: 1: A problem arises which would require data on each member of a very large population for a 100%-accurate analysis. 2. The only practical way to approach the problem is to gather data on a limited selection of members from the population and then apply the results of this limited study to the problem.

In such a study, randomness enters into two different selection processes. One, unless a specific, partially non-randomized sampling scheme is planned, the sample taken from the population for study must reflect a random distribution of the objects with respect to the properties of interest; and two, the particular item of evidence that is being examined must show a similar randomness with respect to these properties. The obvious way of achieving this in selecting a sample for study is to make a random selection from the population; that is, to select the items in such a way that any one item has the same probability of being chosen as any other item. In many cases it will not be possible to do this.

For instance, in selecting a sample from headlight glass, it is not possible to go about smashing up people's headlights to obtain fragments thereof. Then the sampler must be content to take what is available if it can be reasonably inferred that this will reflect a random distribution with respect to the properties of interest. This was done in reference 2 which is discussed later.

The choice of the sample is more or less under the control of the experimenter, whereas the choice of evidence received is not. Therefore, it will inevitably be necessary to make a careful study of the type of evidence that is likely to appear in any one type of activity so that the population selected will be one from which the evidence will be equivalent to a random sample. Only under these conditions will the information obtained from a statistical analysis have meaning.

Independence. The idea of independence is often bandied about in discussions of statistical applications. It should be common knowledge to criminalists that properties must be statistically independent before the probability of a conjunction of these properties can be derived from the multiplication rule, that is by multiplying together their separate probabilities. Note that the term "statistically" is used here. Independence is defined by specific mathematical relationships and should always be tested by reference to these relationships.(1) To judge independence from our general concepts or information about the physical world can lead to error.(2)

It should be emphasized that independence is not necessary before a statistical analysis can be utilized. It is certainly a desirable property which greatly simplifies the work involved in most instances, but the problem is far from hopeless when there is a lack of statistical independence among some of the properties.

Uncertainty. A statistical analysis is used when uncertainty must exist. If there were a way of arriving at a *certain* answer to a problem, statistical methods would not be used. But when uncertainty does exist, and a statistical approach is possible then this approach is the best one available since it offers an index of the uncertainty based upon a precise and logical line of reasoning. It is almost incredible that this very reason for the development of statistical methods is seized upon by its opponents and used as an argument against the use of statistics. They will show that an occurrence which was deemed extremely improbable did actually happen and contend that therefore the methods by which its improbability was calculated cannot be trusted.

Although the uncertainty involved in a situation to which a statistical analysis is applicable constitutes a limitation on the appropriateness of *any* decisions made, the fact of uncertainty validates the contention that the statistical approach offers the *best possible* solution to the problem. This is not meant to condone the misuse of statistics just because such an approach is indicated. It is undoubtedly true that serious errors have been made in applying incorrect statistical methods to the evaluation of physical evidence, but such misuse does not support the generalization that statistics cannot be properly used in criminalistics at all.

Some of the questions raised in the above discussion will be illustrated by the problem of comparing glass fragments. The problem will be limited to the determination of whether or not the fragments were at one time part of a particular larger glass object. Only two properties, density or specific gravity, and refractive index, will be considered. Two publications have been chosen for reference since they present some of the actual pertinent data. The publications will be called reference 1 (ref.1) and reference 2 (ref.2) respectively. Ref. 1(3) presents the results of determinations of the specific gravity and refractive index of 100 glass samples collected from miscellaneous glass objects. Ref. 2(4) presents the results of determinations of the density $(20^{\circ}C, g/ml)$, refractive index $(20^{\circ}C)$, hardness and color of 50 samples from different Lucas 700 headlamps obtained from motor-repair depots in one city.

Planning. In ref. 1 there was no initial planning, relative to a subsequent statistical analysis, before collecting the samples, although planning is shown relative to the overall aim of the study, which was to examine the significance of the measured properties in glass origin determinations. Since no statistical handling was attempted, the lack of prior considerations in this respect is understandable. Several considerations would have to be taken into account if useful and reasonably accurate information were to be obtained. These include the type of crime and its location, and the bearing of these two factors upon the choice of population or populations to be studied. The sampling should then be planned so as to reflect any significant effects of these variables.

In ref. 2 it is stated that the data therein are sufficient to describe a particular population. Here a definite statistical problem is stated: describing a particular population. Two factors led the experimenter to choose a limited population consisting only of Lucas 700 headlamp glass, the factors being, 1. the evidence received was from a Lucas 700 headlamp, and 2. the majority of British cars in New Zealand were equipped with this same type of headlamp. The variables involved here are quite limited; the main concern would be the effects of different batches of glass on the distribution of the properies. The bimodal distribution of the densities might be attributable to some chance difference in different batches of glass or, as suggested in the article, to some change in manufacturing processes. This would be a difficult thing to foresee, and would be difficult to prepare for in a planning stage. However, such occurrences should be considered and incorporated into the overall planning wherever possible. Complete records, including detailed information about the samples, might make it possible to explain any unexpected behavior of the data.

It is suggested that a general discussion of the variables considered and taken into account, as well as the bearing of the choice of population upon the type of evidence being considered, be made a part of every report involving statistical evaluations. Such inclusions would serve the double purpose of helping the criminalist to assess the applicability of the data to his particular problem and of awakening a general awareness of the problems to be considered in using statistical methods in criminalistics.

Randomness. In ref. 1 it is stated that the glass samples were "collected at random." The persons undertaking the study collected any stray pieces of glass that might be observed in the course of their daily routines. (This explains the "unknown" category listed in the publication.) This manner of collection may have indeed resulted in a random sample, but experience has shown that true randomness is difficult to achieve on an intuitive basis. The human mind seems to have channels that work against randomness, and that tend to introduce an unconscious bias into any selection process. This is one reason for the considerable expenditure of time in the construction of tables of random numbers, which can be used truly to randomize a selection process. Another mental process that works against randomness is the tendency to wish to cover a given area evenly. For instance, if different colored beads are scattered about a checker board, there is a tendency in sampling the beads to take one bead from each square and call this a random sample. Obviously it is not, since the beads remaining on a square after a selection there have a zero probability (no chance) of future selection. For random sampling, each bead must always have the same probability of selection as any other bead left on the board. However, the above sampling method on the checker board might be appropriate for a stratified sampling scheme; but then the data would be analyzed differently.

One way of checking the randomness of the sampling would be to investigate the possible presence of bias for or against any portions of the population. One such bias might favor objects that are found in the street, though these are not necessarily typical of the population in general. An obvious example of such a class of objects is bottle fragments. Indeed, the original data sheets for ref. 1 show that 40% of the samples consisted of bottle glass. This percentage may have resulted from bias, or it may actually reflect the distribution of the population chosen.

The appropriateness of the population to be sampled would of course be determined from a study of the evidence likely to be received. Since the concern in ref. 1 was with criminal acts in general, an extensive population is clearly indicated. Still, if certain types of crime were known to produce the bulk of evidence where glass was involved, and therefore limited the majority of evidential glass to a few types of objects, to be valid a general sampling would have to reflect this limitation. For instance, if burglary and automobile accidents comprised a large percentage of activities where glass appeared as evidence, there might be a significantly larger percentage of building window glass, automobile window glass, and automobile headlight glass as evidence than glass from all other sources combined. The chosen population should then reflect this distribution of sources.

In ref. 2, the evidence is indicated to be glass from Lucas 700 headlamps that is in evidence from automobile accidents. The applicability of the entire population of Lucas 700 headlamps would intuitively seem reasonable. If, however, one particular make of automobile happened to be designed so that it was more disposed to headlamp breakage than other makes, and if the manufacturer had purchased a large order of Lucas 700 headlamps, which just happened to have been molded from one deviant batch of glass, the result might be a significant bias in the population resulting from accidents.(5)

Some other considerations in connection with the sampling from various motor-repair depots might be made. The sources of the headlamps sampled in the depots should be questioned; whether they are from lamps broken in accidents or from burnout replacements might be important. The makes of automobiles that the depots handle could be considered; the samples from depots that handle only one make of automobile could be significantly different from samples obtained in depots that handle a large variety of makes.(6)

It should be obvious that most of the points mentioned in the above discussion of randomness must be considered in the planning stage, and settled before the data are obtained.

Independence. Suppose that previous experiments had been conducted with glass fragments, and that any one experiment considered only density or refractive index, but not both, and that these experiments showed that the probability of the occurrence of density X was $P(X)$ and of refractive index Y as $P(Y)$. Would the probability of both X and Y occurring simultaneously in one fragment of glass, say $P(X,Y)$, be equal to the product of the separate probabilities; i.e., would $P(X,Y) = P(X) \times P(Y)$? This would be true only if the two properties were independent. Now consider Figure 1. The scatter diagram is reproduced from the original data for ref. 1. There is a very definite visual indication of a correlation between the two properties under consideration. If this is in fact the case, these two properties are not independent, and the multiplication rule would not be applicable. If it were concluded that the data gave a reasonable fit to a bivariate normal distribution, it would be possible to utilize existing tables to find the probability $P(X,Y)$.

There is a tendency in references to the evidential value of various properties to pick some probability figure as representative of each property and, with proper warning about the independence requirement, to show that the properties considered have a probability of occurrence equal to the product of the separate probabilities. This is an extremely dangerous and misleading practice. First of all, it fosters a general concept that this is the proper way to analyze statistical data, and thus leads to the incorrect application of the multiplication rule when the independence of the properties is not easily checked. Next, the use of a single probability is not correct unless the properties all show a uniform distribution, which is extremely rare in practice. Mollification is sometimes offered with such statements to the effect that the estimate is conservative or that it sets some sort of maximum bound to the probability figure. If the calculation does indeed show the maximum bound on the probability for any property combination within the distribution, there can be no quarrel as to its technical correctness, but it still tends to mislead persons not sufficiently versed in statistical methods. Further, if this conservative estimate shows too large a probability, the properties involved may be deemed inappropriate for evidential use. But combinations that define an area remote from the central portion of the overall distribution may show a sufficiently low probability to be of value. The general and uncritical use of the multiplication rule has caused more criticism about the application of statistics in criminal investigation than any other factor.

Figure 2 is a scatter diagram derived from the tabulated data in ref. 2, and shows an interesting distribution of points. It is stated that there does not seem

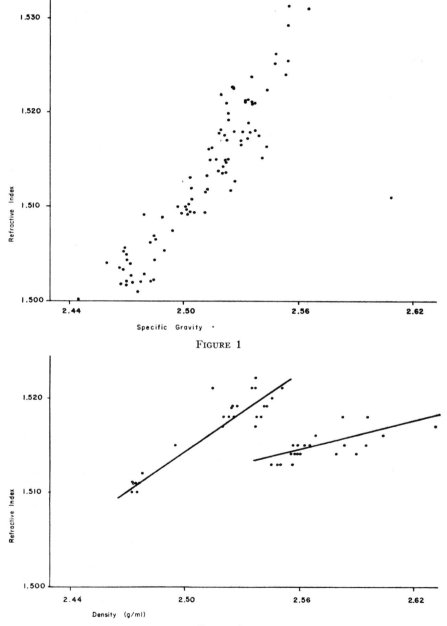

FIGURE 1

FIGURE 2

to be any correlation between the two properties except for some samples in the lower density group. In this case, with the exception of values in the lower density group, we would have $P(X,Y) = P(X) \times P(Y)$. Note that variables are used in the expression to indicate that the probabilities are not fixed, but assume a value dependent on the value of the property. The multiplication rule is used only as a simple way of arriving at the combined probability, and should not exclude the consideration of the distribution relative to density and refractive index as a bivariate distribution over the plane.

But now look at the diagram from a slightly different viewpoint. There is one group of points that lies roughly along a $45°$ line from the lower left corner, and then another group that lies on a line at about $30°$ and which is to the right of the first group. The first group is close to what might be expected from an inspection of the grouping in Figure 1, whereas the second group would be a bit surprising if the data in ref. 1 were considered as typical of glass in general. If instead of looking at the distribution as a single bivariate one, it is viewed as two bivariate distributions, as represented by the two indicated groupings, then the visual indication is that a correlation within each group exists which approximates that seen in Figure 1.

If now, as an exercise, the second group in Figure 2 is shifted to the left, it will fill up a "hole" that appears in the first group, thus bringing the data more into line with that in ref. 1. At times, such grouped deviation of values may be indicative of a consistent bias occurring in the measuring process. This would be especially suspect if the group of objects showing this shift were examined at a separate time or even consecutively. Another cause of such a shift could lie in a bias that occurred in the sampling. Suspicion would be enhanced here if the shifted group of glass came from one particular repair depot. The difference in distribution between the two sets of data in these two studies is interesting, and poses a problem to be considered in future research.(7)

CONCLUSION

In conclusion we will discuss some of the more immediate implications of the foregoing discussion in the field of criminalistics. First of all, there is no need for all criminalists to become statisticians in order to utilize statistics in their profession, but there is a need for them to become aware of some of the more general aspects of statistics.

Next, the determination of a suitable population for study should preferably be based upon the collected experiences of many criminalists. Perhaps the organization of a national evidence report might be desirable. Summary information could be submitted by interested laboratories at specified intervals. This data could then be used to choose appropriate populations for study, as well as to compile other useful statistics about the occurrence and examination of physical evidence. An analysis of this information could then be disseminated for general use, followed later by the results of a study on a sample from the chosen population.

The use of statistical evaluations of physical evidence cannot be rushed. It will take time to determine appropriate areas of applicability, to decide upon the proper methods of analysis, to gather the necessary data, and to establish a confidence in the results both among the criminalists and in the courts. At first, the responsibility will fall upon a few with the necessary time and interest to study the problems involved and to work out the fundamental concepts and methods. But even here, the aggregate considerations, both favorable and unfavorable, of criminalists in general will be of significant value.

One way to develop some further insight into the problems involved and some methods of approaching these problems from a general statistical point of view is for the criminalist to reflect for a while on the logic used in forming interpretative opinions. As an example, consider the opinion that a particular suspect left the partial fingerprint in evidence, the basis being a coincidence of 12 elements with no observable differences in the patterns of the evidential print and an area of the print taken from the suspect. What logic leads from the basis to the opinion? Even though the opinion is considered by the courts as an acceptable one from the given basis, there is some disagreement on the connecting logic. Some will say that the connection depends alone on experience, others will argue that the connection is essentially a statistical one. A satisfying discussion of this would be too long to include in this paper; perhaps the following two points will help to indicate that the problem is a bit more complex than might be evident at first.

1) The bulk of verifiable experience relates either to an entire set of prints as taken on a fingerprint card or a complete fingerprint, not to partial prints.

2) No statistical analysis appropriate to partial prints has, to our knowledge, ever been published.

It is hoped that this paper has stimulated the reader to more serious thought about the role of statistics in criminalistics as well as pointing the way to a clearer view of the subject. In discussing the illustrative investigations it has not been the purpose here to pass judgment upon the methods used by the authors of the articles, or to make precise analyses of the data, but only to indicate the kind of considerations which must be taken into account.

NOTES

(1) The simplest relationship is that the probabilities do combine by the multiplication rule; e.g. that $P(AB) = P(A) \times P(B)$.

(2) For an example of this see: Feller, William, An Introduction To Probability Theory and Its Applications, Vol. 1; John Wiley and Sons, Inc., N.Y.: 1st ed., p. 86, example (d).

(3) Gamble, Lucy, Burd, David Q., Kirk, Paul L., *J. Crim. Law & Criminol.*, *33*: 416 (1943).

(4) Nelson, D.F.: *The Analyst, 84*: 388 (1959).

(5) There is no implication here that the more remote possibilities mentioned might actually obtain; the important factor is that they are recognized as possibilities and then rejected, rather than rejected by virtue of not being considered. Such possibilities might rapidly be ruled out by a criminalist who has

had practical contact with the physical situation, but could be considered as serious possibilities by those who have not had such contact.

(6) Dr. Nelson was kind enough to examine this paper and offer some comments. It seems appropriate to mention some of these which demonstrate the criminalist's point of view.

> . . . it (manufacturer purchasing a large batch of headlamps) is *unlikely* because the purchase of headlamps by car manufacturers is *probably* a continuing process rather than a series of "batch processes" repeated once or twice per year.
>
> If cars are in accidents severe enough to break headlamps, one would not *expect* great differences in disposition to headlamp breakage. The headlamps studied were broken, not burnt-out. (The italics are the authors'.)

(7) We consider the possibility of an actual bias in this particular example to be remote, and are only suggesting that such questions be considered when planning, executing or reading statistically oriented studies.

THE LAW OF PROBABILITIES AND THE CREDIBILITY

OF WITNESSES AND EVIDENCE

Charles R. Kingston

Witnesses and evidence play a critical role in every criminal trial. It is through witnesses and evidence that the jury seeks to find the unknowns of what happened and who caused it to happen. The information provided by the witnesses and the evidence must be sufficient to prove that the correct conclusions have been reached. Yet the legal process does not require that the jury be *certain* of their conclusions, only that they believe in their correctness "beyond a reasonable doubt." And indeed we rarely, if ever, do know for certain what happened, and who caused it to happen after hearing all of the witnesses and examining all of the evidence in a criminal trial.

Whenever we are dealing with a situation involving uncertainty, even when that uncertainty is so small that it does not create a reasonable doubt, we are dealing with probabilities. It follows therefore, that since the interpretation of the unknowns in a criminal trial almost always involves some uncertainty, we are concerned with probabilities in almost every criminal trial, if not in every one. The men or history who laid the foundations for our legal processes recognized this and created a probabilistic guideline that could be followed by the average juror. I am of course referring to the "reasonable doubt" guideline.

Sometimes we become so accustomed to certain conclusions that are accepted without question that we tend to give these conclusions that status of certainty. For instance, one author has commented:

> It is internationally recognized by specialists that probabilities are
> excluded in the field of indentifying a crime print. Either the proof of

identity is possible with absolute certainty, or the print is insufficient and considered as unusable.(1)

If someone here touches an object and leaves a latent fingerprint impression, how could any of us know for certain that no one else also could have left a fingerprint impression with the same characteristics? An expert might well make a statement that in his opinion nobody else could have left a print with the same pattern, and he might act as though that were a true statement. Statements such as this have been called "posits" by Reichenbach. He says:

A posit is a statement which we treat as true although we do not know whether it is so. We try to select our posits in such a way that they will be true as often as possible . . . The degree of probability supplies a *rating* of the posit; it tells us how good the posit is.(2)

A verdict of guilty in a criminal trial is like a posit, and the court acts as though this were a true conclusion, even though the jury may only believe it to be true beyond a reasonable doubt. Thus the criterion "beyond a reasonable doubt" is a rating, or a degree of probability, that must be attained before the belief that a person is guilty is pronounced as a verdict. Such a verdict is the ultimate posit in a criminal trial.

The probability assigned to the final belief in a person's guilt or innocence is built up from the bits and pieces of information provided by the witnesses and evidence. Each bit of information has its own rating. All of the individual ratings, or probabilities, are combined to provide a probability which guides the jury to the ultimate posit. This fact was noted by Francis Wellman in his book on cross-examination. He said:

It requires but little experience in court to arrive at the conclusion that the great majority of cases are composed of a few principal facts surrounded by a host of minor ones; and that the strength of either side of a case depends not so much upon the direct testimony relating to these principal facts alone, but, as one writer very tersely puts it, 'upon the *support* given them by the probabilities created by establishing and developing the relation of the *minor* facts in the case.(3)

The reader is probably asking who assigns the individual probabilities and how are they assigned? The answer is that everyone who evaluates the evidence in a trial assigns these probabilities in one way or another. The problem in understanding this sometimes rests on the fact that most people are acquainted with probability through introductory courses in school or through general reading. These sources usually discuss probabilities in terms of precise mathematical calculations. But we generally do not know how to apply such calculations to testimony and evidence, so how can we talk in terms of probabilities?

The answer to this lies in the concepts of subjective probability. It has been recognized for some time that there are many situations where the basic rules of probability calculations are followed even though precise figures are not available. Instead of numbers derived from counts or measurements, subjective estimates of probability are based upon personal assessments of the significance of available information. In an article on subjective probability which appeared a few years ago, Cohen said:

> Our actions are based upon our private assessment of our chances, which in turn depends upon our experiences and maturity in reasoning. We develop subjective concepts of probability, which permeate and guide our thoughts and actions.(4)

Jurors intuitively apply such concepts when they make a decision at the end of a trial. Forensic scientists also apply the concepts of subjective probability in their interpretation of physical evidence. In his book on the scientific examination of documents, Hilton said:

> In most document problems it would be impossible, or at least extremely impractical, to measure mathematically the degree of probability of accidental coincidence ... Despite our present inability, however, to measure mathematically the improbability of chance duplication in a document problem, the document examiner depends upon the principles of probability in reaching his conclusion.(5)

In view of this subjective nature of evaluations of testimony and evidence, we should ask how good such evaluations are. The direct way of determining this is to conduct a series of controlled experiments in which different persons, or experts, are asked separately to examine the same sets of evidence and to offer their conclusions. One such experiment was conducted by Inbau and reported in 1939.(6) In the study, three experts were asked to examine 28 signatures and to determine which of the signatures were written by a given person.

Another way of approaching the question is by examining how well subjective estimates of probability correspond to objective ones. Cohen (supra) made some experimental studies on this question. In general, he found that most of the subjects used were guided mainly by psychological rather than mathematical considerations. Another study was made by Osterburg. In his own words:

> An effort was made by the writer to determine the reliability of fingerprint experts' evaluations of how common or uncommon or unusual were the various fingerprint characteristics.(7)

The general conclusion of the study was summed up in the following sentence: "Clearly subjective evaluation of the significance to be attached to a fingerprint characteristic is suspect." To keep the record straight, his further clarification is also quoted: "So that no attorney can misinterpret what has been stated above let it be clearly understood that 12 such characteristics are sufficient to identify a fingerprint."

Meehl's book on Clinical vs. Statistical Prediction(8) offers further information on our question. The entire book is directed to the question: Shall we make use of explicit, mathematical manipulations of data or shall we rely upon the subjective interpretation of our data through skilled judgment? The book is written around the judgments of the clinical psychologist, but the general concepts are applicable to this discussion. Although the studies analyzed in that book do not allow any definite conclusions to be made, they do suggest that decisions made objectively can be correct more often than those made subjectively. Meehl states:

> In spite of the defects and ambiguities present, let me emphasize the brute fact that we have here, depending upon one's standards for admission as relevant, from 16 to 20 studies involving a comparison of clinical and actuarial methods, *in all but one of which the predictions made actuarially were either approximately equal or superior to those made by a clinician.*(9)

I might add that the type of psychological situations represented by the studies would appear to be far more difficult to measure objectively than would most types of physical evidence.

In relatively simple situations, it is reasonable that objective estimates of probability are more reliable than subjective ones. This is because we can substitute experimental data for subjectivity. However, when influencing factors become numerous and complex, the experiments become more difficult to perform. This is due to the difficulty in either knowing exactly what should be measured, or in actually making the measurements. Thus it is difficult to say whether objective or subjective estimates will be more reliable in the sense that they will result in fewer errors in the more complex situations. It depends upon how the estimates are made and the insights into the situations possessed by the persons making the estimates. Most forensic scientists have apparently developed a high degree of reliability even though their conclusions are based to a large extent upon subjective evaluations. It is hoped that the same thing may be said for juries.

We thus come to three basic conclusions: 1. Trials inevitably involve probabilities; 2. objectivity in probability situations is generally better than subjectivity; but 3. true objectivity is not easily obtained in complex situations.

Whenever we are confronted with complex situations where we either do not know exactly what should be measured or do not have means for making the measurements (which often leads to "conservative estimates"), there is little to be gained by making pseudo-objective estimates. In fact, there is much to be lost since such estimates generally create more confusion than clarity. This has been apparent in some trials where amateurish attempts have been made to support a conclusion with improper probability calculations.

There are, however, many situations where the compilation and analysis of statistical data can be of great value, even though we may not yet attempt to assign a specific probability to support an opinion in court. Cases in which we have physical materials or traces and wish to estimate how well the measurable properties of those materials will allow us to determine and prove their general or specific origin are notable examples of this. There are basically two categories of these materials or traces. One category consists of those types of materials that allow us to posit that a suspected origin is the true origin. Examples of this category are fingerprints, fired bullets, handwriting, and numerous items for which jig-saw fits are possibly the correct origin. Obviously there are cases in which materials that are usually in the first category may belong in the second, and vice-versa.

If we think about the kinds of materials for which origin determinations are possible, it will become apparent that we are dealing with shapes and patterns in the majority of cases. The quantification of shapes and patterns is quite difficult, although it may be possible to measure certain key features such as the number of matching minutiae in fingerprint comparisons. Generally it is difficult to do even that. This is a situation that does not lend itself well to the collection and analysis of statistical data. We can only hope that the problems of quantifying morphological features can be solved by using modern technology and the computer.

Perhaps more important is the question of why we would want to solve them. One reason is the desirability of establishing objective thresholds which can be used to decide whether or not the evidence clearly points to a specific origin. Such a threshold would provide a valuable guide to the court and jury in evaluating the credibility of the evidence. We have this situation with fingerprints, for which there is a threshold based upon the number of matching minutiae. This threshold (generally 12 in the United States) is not of course an absolute cut-off point. If there are 12 or more minutiae that match, and no unexplainable differences, there should be little question about properly prepared evidence. If there are fewer than 12, the expert has the flexibility to form and express his opinion as to its significance. Whether or not the jury accepts his opinion is up to them; but at least it has an independent criterion to refer to. A second reason is that a threshold would be valuable in training student forensic scientists in properly evaluating evidence in category one.

In the second category we find that many different properties are used to examine evidence materials and make comparisons. In some cases shapes and patterns play an important role in the examination, but their complexity is not sufficient to place the material in the first category. In the majority of cases there are properties that we can measure. For example, we can measure the density, refractive index, and other properties of glass, and we can determine the specific group substances in blood. The compilation of statistical data on such measurements for properly chosen samples can give us a picture of the significance of the properties as indicators of a possible origin. For example, knowing that type AB blood occurs in approximately three to five percent of the population is far more illuminating and useful than just knowing that it does not occur very frequently.

This kind of data can provide a solid basis for evaluating evidence. The expert must of course use his own experience and knowledge to determine if the conditions of the particular case permit the proper use of the data, and whether or not the results indicated by the data seem reasonable. This will bring about a constant interplay between experience and objective data. Experience may suggest that the data are not being properly collected; the data may suggest that subjective evaluations are missing the mark. The most useful data will be those which are collected for new techniques. It might take many years for sufficient experience to be built up for a proper evaluation of new techniques. Even with adequate experience, the evaluations will remain subjective and essentially closed to critical review by the court and jury. On the other hand, a well planned program for collecting objective data will offer a much better evaluation that is open to critical review in far less time.

As an example of the last statement, consider the dermal nitrate, or "paraffin" test. This test was introduced into the United States around 1933, and has been controversial ever since. It was never really accepted (although the results have been used in court), and it was never really rejected. The general tone of statements about the test was that great care must be taken but that the test was probably useful in an expert's hands (10, 11, 12). This puts the court and jury in a position of having to judge the expert but of not being able to judge the technique. The issue of credibility is more realistically met when there exists independent grounds for judging both the expert and the techniques he uses. This is only possible when we have collected objective data relevant to the techniques and have made these data available.

It has only been within the last few years that the accumulated experience with the dermal nitrate test has prompted forensic scientists to make a definite stand on its use. At the first I.C.P.O.—Interpol Seminar on Scientific Aspects of Police Work, which was reported in 1964, the following conclusion was arrived at:

> The seminar did not consider the traditional paraffin test to be of any value, neither as evidence to put before the courts, nor even as a sure indication for the police officer. The participants were of the opinion that this test should no longer be used.(13)

An extensive evaluation of the test reported on by Cowan and Purdon pointed to the same conclusion.(14)

The point that is important here is that the paraffin test was in a nebulous position for thirty years or so. Maybe it still is. Now we are tackling the problem of gunshot residues armed with the most modern of scientific methods—neutron activation analysis. The seeds are there for that same kind of nebulousness to occur all over again and grow for years. Fortunately, the need to gather objective data and properly analyze them has at last been recognized by those groups who have been instrumental in developing the technique. At least one group is currently gathering data and a report on this is scheduled during this meeting.(15) Perhaps the analysis will not settle everything about the technique, but it will provide a sound independent means for the lawyer, the court and the jury to evaluate it. The period from the time when the need for the statistical analysis of objective data was recognized and acted upon to the time of a generally acceptable status of the method will probably be only a few years.

Although the example of the paraffin test does not exactly fit into the category of origin determinations. it does illustrate the point. It also illustrates the kind of situation which may be simple enough for the statistical data to be used at the present time in court. Care must be taken that no probabilities are used for pseudo-objective calculations in court. In other words, in this or similar situations, we should not say that since x is the probability that the suspect fired a gun, and y is the probability of some other condition, then x times y is the probability of some conclusion. We are not prepared to properly handle this kind of calculation now.

There are stages that we must go through before we will be able to relate probabilities to the facts in a case, and bring these probabilities to bear on the credibility of witnesses and evidence. The first stage will be to collect statistical data for selected types of evidence according to valid experimental plans. These data will be useful to the expert in evaluating the evidence, and, in the simpler situations, might be used in court for the edification of the jury and others. With actual data available, we can then proceed with the second stage of exploring the various ways in which probability figures can be derived from the data and their significance within the legal system. This will conclude a study of the ways of combining probabilities to relate the minor facts of a case together. The third stage will be to find out how we can clearly convey the proper handling and significance of objective probabilities to lawyers, the court and the jury.

Until we have passed the third stage, we can help avoid a credibility gap by allowing the subjective processes within the court to proceed unhampered by the injection of pseudo-objective calculations. But we must also continue to develop objective data and methods of analysis. As long as probability plays a dominant role in reconstructing what happened during a crime and in determining who did it, we should make every effort to see that the handling of probabilities best serves the interests of justice.

NOTES

(1) Steinwender, E. Dactyloscopic Identification. *Finger Print and Ident. Mag.,* 41, 4 (1960).

(2) Reichenbach, H. The Rise of Scientific Philosophy. University of California Press, Berkeley, Calif. (1957) p 240.

(3) Wellman, F. L. The Art of Cross-Examination. Collier Books, New York, N.Y. (1962) p 182.

(4) Cohen, J. Subjective Probability. *Scientific American,* 197, 128 (1957).

(5) Hilton, O. Scientific Examination of Questioned Documents. Callaghan and Co., Chicago, Ill. (1955) pp 8-9.

(6) Inbau, F. E. Lay Witness Identification of Handwriting. *Ill. L. Rev.* 34, 433 (1939).

(7) Osterburg, J.,W. An Inquiry into the Nature of Proof— The Identity of Fingerprints. *J. of Forensic Sci.* 9, 413 (1964).

(8) Meehl, P. E. Clinical vs. Statistical Prediction, University of Minnesota Press, Minneapolis, Minn. (1960).

(9) *Ibid.,* p 119.

(10) Hatcher. J. S., Jury, F. J. and J. Weller. Firearms Investigation, Identification and Evidence. The Stackpole Co., Harrisburg, Penn. (1957) pp 435-438.

(11) Kirk, P. L. Crime Investigation. Interscience Publishers, Inc., New York, N.Y. (1953) p 358.

(12) Turner, R. Forensic Science and Laboratory Techniques. Charles C. Thomas, Springfield, Ill. (1949) pp 98-101.

(13) First I.C.P.O.—Interpol Seminar on the Scientific Aspects of Police

Work. *Internat. Crim. Police Rev.* 174 (1964) p 28.

(14) Cowan, M. E. and P. L. Purdon. A Study of the "Paraffin Test." *J. of Forensic Sci.*, 12, 19-36 (1967).

(15) Twenty-First Annual Meeting, Am Acad. Forensic Sci., Chicago, Illinois (1969).

WHAT IS "REASONABLE DOUBT"?

A FORENSIC SCIENTIST LOOKS AT THE LAW

H. J. Walls

Forensic science may be looked on as a symbiotic relationship between the disciplines of science and the law. But it is a rather odd and not always happy one. The late L. C. Nickolls used to illustrate this by a piece of anthropology which he had picked up somewhere. According to the creation legend of a certain primitive Eastern tribe, God first made man and turned him loose on the earth. Before very long man felt lonely and asked God to give him a companion. So God did: He created woman. Some time later, man came back to God again. "Please, God," he said, "I can't live with woman. Take her away again." So God took her away again. Not very long afterwards, man returned yet again to God. "Please, God," he said, "I know I said I couldn't live with woman. But it's even worse without her. Give her back to me again." God did so, and she has been with us ever since.

That story sums up neatly the peculiar relationship inherent in forensic science. The law, it has often seemed to me,(1) does not really understand science, but cannot now do without her. One fundamental difference between them is the part played by deductive reasoning in their operations. The law defines, and it is then a matter of deduction whether an action is a crime as so defined; deduction therefore comes first in the operations of the law. In modern science, on the other hand, deduction comes second. There the first, creative, act (science *is* a creative activity) is one of induction.

The ultimate business of science is to answer the questions: how is the universe constructed, and what makes it tick? In trying to do so, it proceeds as follows. 1. Something stimulates the scientist's curiosity, or a practical problem does not seem to have a solution within the existing framework of science. (Why does the moon go round the earth? Did King Hiero's goldsmith cheat him? [Archimedes' problem.] Why do bluebottles' eggs not turn into jellyfish? Why does a bicycle pump get hot?) 2. The scientist chews and worries over the problem. 3. A solution occurs to him. 1-3 constitute the inductive part: what is the general principle of which the puzzling facts are an illustration? 4. The principle suggested at 3 will have, logically, certain consequences. (This is the deductive part.) The scientist chooses that consequence most easily tested by experiment. 5. He designs and makes the experiment. 6. If its results are as the induced principle predicts, that is provisionally accepted as being correct, subject to further verification. If a different result is obtained, the principle is wrong and a different one must be sought.

The crucial step in that process is the third. It is not a deductive one. The seminal explanatory idea just happens; it is a brain-wave, an act of pure creation. It almost invariably occurs to the scientist when he is *not* thinking about the problem. The history of science is packed with examples of correct solutions coming to the scientist's mind when he has relaxed and has stopped worrying over his problem. (Newton in his orchard is a classic example; the incident is historically well authenticated.)

This picture of the advance of science is admittedly somewhat simplified and idealised. Both the formulation of the hypothesis and its experimental testing may be continuous processes rather than isolated events: the first experimental results may cause the hypothesis to be modified, which will necessitate a change in the design of subsequent experiments, and so on. Nevertheless the general principle remains valid.

At this point two parenthetical observations are in order.

The first is relevant to the comparison—to which I shall return—between scientific and legal proof. According to many (though not all) philosophers of science, of whom the prominent is Professor K.R. Popper,(2) the mode of scientific discovery which I have just outlined makes it logically impossible ever to *prove* an hypothesis (that is, a scientific law) with finality. It can at best be established with a very high degree of probability, if there is a large and well-attested body of experimental evidence supporting it. However, it requires only one incontrovertible datum inconsistent with the hypothesis to make this untenable—that is, to make a different scientific law necessary. Hence an hypothesis or law can be *disproved* with logical finality.

Secondly, it is unfortunate and semantically confusing that the same word "law" is used for both the principles of science and the rules imposed by society on its members. An inductively derived scientific law is provisional; it exists as a law only until it is broken, and if it is once irreparably broken it ceases to be a law. A social law, on the other hand, is laid down *a priori* and remains a law however often it is broken. (It may indeed be more frequently broken than observed—the 30 m.p.h. speed limit for example!)

To return to the scientific method, Bertrand Russell sums it up by saying somewhere that the true function of science is the verification or disproof of hypotheses. Therefore the scientist is interested in *facts* only in so far as they are relevant to this task. This (or so it seems to the scientist) is where the primary misunderstanding of science by the law creeps in. The law often appears to look on science as being concerned with the collection of accurate data as an end in itself. Nothing could be more mistaken. Mere data are only raw material, and as such useless unless they are suitable for the purpose in hand.

Where the relevant data are numerically quantifiable ones, the most important thing about them is normally their magnitude. Hence the scientist makes it his business to measure them as accurately as he can. It is presumably this fact which has caused the second mistaken impression which the law has of science: that the scientist is busy measuring with absolute accuracy the data which he collects. I used to find this faith rather touching. It is unjustified for two reasons. In the first place, there is no such thing as absolute accuracy. All measurement is subject to error. The scientist accepts this fact and is content, having made his measurement as accurately as he can, to know how large the residual irreducible error is likely to be. Secondly, the refined and sophisticated techniques used in scientific measurement are not developed because of a gratuitous delight in refinement and sophistication; they are developed because they are necessary for the measurement of the very small quantities in which science is often interested. To take a very simple example, if the scientist needs in the course of his investigations to weigh a barely visible speck of dirt he cannot do so with the kind of balance the housewife uses in making a cake; he must use a micro-balance capable of registering differences of not more than say, a microgram.(3) (Incidentally, to return to our first reason, the possible error in his measurement, expressed as a proportion of the total weight he is measuring, may well be as great as that tolerated by the housewife in weighing out her flour.)

As I have already pointed out, scientific "proof" merely means showing that the probability of an hypothesis being true is very high indeed. In some fields of investigation this is admittedly implicit rather than obvious, and the experiments may seem to give a clear yes/no answer. There are other fields, however, in which the element of probability is inescapably prominent throughout. This applies particularly to experiments with living organisms (including human beings), where the inherent variability is bound to affect the results. Valid results from investigations of this kind are normally to be obtained only in a statistical form which tells us what the mathematical probability is that they really were due to their apparent cause and not to chance variation. I doubt whether the average non-scientist realises how many accepted scientific conclusions are reached in this way. The connection between lung cancer and cigarette smoking is one example. Another, perhaps more apposite in our present context, comes from the Road Safety Act 1967. This relies heavily for its scientific justification on the drink-and-driving statistics collected in Grand Rapids (Michigan) in the early 1960s. These rested on data collected over a period of a year from 5,895 drivers included in accidents and 7,590 drivers not so involved but exposed, as far as could be determined, to identical traffic risks. To separate the effects of alcohol from those of other factors affecting the liability to accident—age, driving experience and so forth—the data had to be statistically "processed" before any valid conclusions could be drawn. Only then did they show with reasonable certainty that drink was more important than any other factor as a cause of accidents. Moreover, "reasonable certainty" could be given a numerically precise meaning: it meant that a connection between drink (or any other factor) and the incidence of accidents was taken as established only after, and if, statistical calculations showed that the probability of the connection being due to chance was less than 0.05—i.e., that the odds in favour of the connection being a truly causal one were at least 19 to 1.

We may now, after digressing so far, get back to our theme: what is "reasonable doubt"? In the first place, it should by now be apparent that the courses of a scientific investigation and of a criminal trial are much more alike than (it has always seemed to me) lawyers have realised. Both start with an hypothesis: in the one case, that of the scientist that his theory is correct; in the other, that of the prosecution that the accused is guilty. The theory is "proved" (that is, provisionally accepted as being true) if it is supported by sufficient reliably established experimental data; guilt is proved "beyond reasonable doubt" by a sufficiency of credible evidence. Moreover, if we accept Professor Popper's views, the parallel goes even further: just as one reliable result inconsistent with the scientific hypothesis can cause it to be abandoned, so can one incontrovertible piece of evidence (e.g. an unbreakable alibi) demolish the legal one, and prove thereby with logical finality the innocence of the accused.

It would, however, be over-optimistic to assume from that parallelism that guilt can be established with the same sort of clarity as can the truth of a scientific hypothesis. The logical frameworks may be the same, but the problems arising within them are different. In both science and the law there are *penumbrae* of uncertainty in the data, but the origins and natures of these are totally dissimilar in the two disciplines. In science, the unavoidable uncertainty arises from the inherent irreducible errors of the measurements or observations, but there are ways of coping with these, as I have already shown. Mistakes, lies or delusions need not, logically, be considered. It is true that scientists, like the rest of mankind, may be vain, fallible or deluded, and may honestly think that they are seeing what they expected to see. It is, however, one of the fundamental rules of science that no observation or experimental result is finally accepted unless it can be repeated independently by someone else. The law has, unfortunately, to deny itself that rigorous proviso. It is true that it seeks corroboration where possible, but this is not always or even often to be found, and the law has frequently to do the best it can with what science would consider very dubious and inferior data. In short, it has to take the facts as it finds them; it cannot, like science, design its experiments to produce the best possible information.

One may perhaps distinguish three causes for the poor quality of the law's data: 1. The witness may be lying; how does one arrive at a "coefficient of credibility"? 2. The witness may be honest and truthful, but less than certain: how can the degree of uncertainty be assessed, and how does one assign relative "weights" to conflicting pieces of apparently honest testimony? and, 3. The evidence—even the best evidence—is rarely, or at least not always, quantifiable; it may therefore be impossible to assign to it a numerical probability that it is true.(4)

We are therefore a long way from being able to gratify the wish sometimes expressed by naive scientists that "beyond reasonable doubt" could be given a numerically precise meaning expressible as a mathematical probability or in some similar manner. It might be gratifying(5) to be able to do so, but it is normally quite impossible to say that it means with a probability of 0.9 or 0.99 or 0.99999 or any other figure we care to specify.(6) The calculation of a probability is a mathematical operation and cannot therefore be applied to non-numerical data.

Nevertheless, the idea that a calculus of probabilities might sometimes take the place of, or at least be brought in to assist, a court's decision-making process is an attractive one. It was mooted as long ago as 1827 by Jeremy Bentham, and again in 1837 by the famous French mathematician Poisson, but as far as I know no one pursued their suggestions. However, within the last few years several people have begun to concern themselves seriously with the application of probability theory to the problems of judicial proof.(7-12) It would not be unfair to say that some of these papers are too theoretical and academic to be of much help to the lawyer who is not already versed in methematical statistics, but the paper by Kingston and Kirk(8) is practical and down-to-earth, and would I imagine be of interest to any practising criminal lawyer. Neither of the two most recent papers is easy reading. That by Parker(11) is an outcome of the work at Aldermaston on the analysis of hair specimens, and embodies the development of a new statistical method for the evaluation of the results. I shall return to the other recent paper by Finkelstein and Fairley.(12)

At the same time as this new thinking about the problem was being published, another development has been taking place: courts have been getting accustomed to the mention of probabilities in connection with certain kinds of scientific evidence, particularly that based on blood grouping. When only ABO grouping was used in criminal investigation, evidence about it was in effect confined to corroboration that the blood of a stain could have been shed by a particular person, or proof that it could not. However, the civil law has long been used to considering probabilities of exclusion in paternity cases, where much more extensive tests using fresh blood were possible, and the criminal law is now catching up in this respect. Now that dried blood can be grouped under several (at least six) different independent systems, of which the ABO is only one, it is meaningful and valuable—and the courts appear to find it helpful—to give in evidence a figure indicating the proportion of the population from which blood showing a particular combination of groups might have come. If a sufficient number of systems can be used, this figure is not a large one (of the order of 5 percent of the population) even if the blood belongs to the commonest group in each system, and if it exhibits one or more rare groups the figure may be quite minute, corresponding to one person in many thousands or even millions. The use of this kind of numerical evidence is tantamount to using probability figures. To state that a particular combination of blood groups occurs in, say, 1 person in 10,000 is merely another way of stating that the probability that a person taken at random will *not* have this combination is 0.9999.

We might also consider in this connection the use of fingerprint evidence. One should note in the first place that, although fingerprints like faces are infinitely variable, their comparison has become valuable to the criminal courts because and only because it can be *quantified* by the enumeration of characteristics; it could therefore be treated mathematically. Fingerprint evidence is universally admitted to be the best possible evidence, and is generally assumed to be based on a certainty—namely, that no two fingers can leave identical prints. However, there is no scientific law of nature which says that no two fingerprints can be identical. The "certainty" that all fingerprints are different exists merely because the number of possible patterns is enormously greater than the number of fingerprints that have ever been taken or are likely to be taken, so that the probability of finding two identical ones is too small to be worth considering. But that is not certainty; it is merely an extremely large probability. (This has been estimated, but I cannot remember the figure; in any case it would need so many nines to write it down as a probability that it would be meaningless here.) The criminal courts would, no doubt, be rocked to their foundations if two persons *were* ever found to have the same fingerprint. Nevertheless, scientifically speaking, this should not affect the value of fingerprint evidence if it did happen. The improbable *can* happen, but it is no less improbable if it does. If four bridge players found themselves dealt one complete suit in each hand, which is a possible event, that would not invalidate the normal and reasonable assumption that this will not happen in a lifetime of playing bridge.

If we are going to mention probabilities in evidence, there are several fundamental points failure to consider which will lead, and has led, to confusion.

1. It is generally appreciated as a matter of common sense that the conjunction of two or more individually imporbable events provides very cogent evidence indeed. Mathematically, this is expressed as the *Principle of Conjunctive Probability*. If the probability of X happening is, say, 0.1, and that of Y happening is, say, 0.2, then the probability of Y happening *when X has happened*—that is, of both events happening—is 0.1 x 0.2, or 0.02. This is a much smaller probability than those of either X or Y alone.

However, this principle applies *only if the events are causally independent*. This proviso is vital; calculations in the making of which it has been forgotten, although they have all too often been made, are worthless and can be dangerous because of their specious appearance of precision. For example, if we assume for the sake of argument that 5 percent of the men in London are 6 feet tall, and that 3 percent have red hair, the probability that any given male Londoner will have both characteristics is 0.05 x 0.03, or 0.0015, as long as we are safe in assuming that there is no correlation between height and hair colour. On the other hand, if we further assume that 5 percent of the men in London take size 11 in shoes, we *cannot* say that the probability of a male Londoner being 6 feet tall and taking 11s in shoes is only 0.0025 (i.e. 0.05 x 0.05). That would be a totally unjustifiable conclusion, because height and shoe size are not independent characteristics; they are strongly correlated, taller men tending to have bigger feet.

2. We must be clear whether we are calculating the probability of an isolated event, or that of a certain event when another intrinsically improbable event has already occurred. Much evidence, especially that about the distribution of blood-group types, is based on the first type of calculation. However, the second type, if it can be used, is likely to be more valuable. Unfortunately the numerical data on which to base it are rarely available. Suppose, for example, that a victim's blood is of a rare type found in only a small proportion of the population. If a stain of this blood is found on the accused's clothing, a probability figure for occurrence of this type of blood is obviously useful evidence. What would be even more useful, however, and what the court really wants to know, is: given that the inherently improbable event of the spillage of this type of blood has occurred, what proportion of people are likely to have it as stains on their clothing? To calculate that, however, we would need to know, *inter alia*, how many people have bloodstains on their clothing in any case—a figure certainly unknown and for all practical purposes unknowable.

3. It is important that in considering the probability of an event we use for our calculation data drawn from a similar *population* of events. "Population in this technical sense means the totality of events of which the one we are concerned with is an instance. No one, for example, would be likely to make the mistake of citing blood-type distribution figures relating to some other country where the distribution of types might be quite different. However, less obvious mistakes of this general type are easily made. For example, suppose that a broken piece of some article turns up in connection with a crime, and this article is recognised as being Messrs. A. B.'s product. If we know that only 1 percent of such articles in use are made by Messrs. A. B., the occurrence of this broken piece would seem prima facie to constitute valuable evidence; if such an article is broken, we might say, the probability that it is one of A. B.'s is only 0.01. It may be, however, that Messrs. A. B.'s articles are much more liable to breakage than those of rival manufacturere (which would be why A. B. have only 1 percent of the market), so that far more than 1 percent of the broken articles of this kind are A. B.'s; the probability of the broken one connected with the crime being *in any case* one of this manufacturer's products is therefore much greater than 0.01, and the evidence of its occurrence is correspondingly much less valuable.

By way of illustration of some of the points I have raised, imagine the following hypothetical but not impossible case. Suppose that in the town of Exchester a blue Vauxhall being driven by A is hit and damaged by another car which does not stop and which A thinks was a grey Ford. Suppose that the police discover a grey Ford which B admitted driving in the area at about the same time, and which bears recent damage and some flakes of "foreign" blue paint. Suppose that laboratory examination shows that grey paint flakes from the Vauxhall are identical with Ford paint, and that the blue flakes from the Ford are identical with Vauxhall paint. Many people might, I imagine, consider this sufficient for proof "beyond reasonable doubt" that B was the driver responsible. However, although I have called this case hypothetical, I have known a bench of magistrates find evidence of just this kind to be insufficient to prove a charge against B (which I must say I thought rather perverse of them!). Could then one arrive at some sort of probability figure which even the most perverse bench would consider sufficient?

It seems to me in principle not impossible to do so. We would admittedly have to use statistical averages rather than precisely ascertainable data, but the scientist at least would think a figure obtained in this way more reliable than one based on a quasi-intuitive decision, which is the only alternative. The problem in a nutshell is: given that a collision occurred, and accepting the laboratory results as proof that the offending car was a grey Ford, what is the probability of there being more than one grey Ford in Exchester which has recently been in collision with a blue Vauxhall? To calculate that, we would have to know or be able to estimate: the total number of cars in Exchester; how many of these are likely to have been on the road at the time of the accident; what proportions of these are blue Vauxhalls and grey Fords; the proportion of all cars on the road which show recent collision damage. All of these figures should be available from local authorities' or manufacturers' records, from statistics compiled by the Ministry of Transport or the Road Research Laboratory, or from simple observation and counting. I have no idea what the actual figures would be in my hypothetical case, but guessing at what seem reasonable ones for the purposes of the calculation, and omitting some of its steps, suppose that there were 100 grey Fords which might have been in motion in Exchester at the time of the collision, that 1 car in 40 (i.e., 2½ percent of all cars) shows recent collision damage, and that 1 car in 50 (i.e. 2 percent of all cars) is a blue Vauxhall. We will also assume that all makes and colours of cars are equally likely to be involved in a collision—that is, that we have chosen to correct "population" for our calculation. On these assumptions, the proportion of the 100 grey Fords which have recently been in collision with a blue Vauxhall is 2 percent of 2½ percent—that is, in this case 1/20 of a car. We would therefore be justified in concluding that the occurrence of even one Ford car with the specified characteristics is an improbable event, and the occurrence of more than one *ipso facto* very improbable. It seems also legitimate to say that this figure of 1/20 of a car means that the odds against there being even one such car are 20 to 1, against there being two 400 (i.e. 20^2) to 1, against there being three 8,000 (i.e. 20^3) to 1, and so on. That is, the probability that 2 or 3 or 4 or . . . (i.e. more than 1) of the 100 grey Fords shall have the specified characteristic is given by the sum of the first 99 terms of the convergent series $1/400 + 1/8,000 + 1/16,000$ . . . , which is approximately 0.0026. The probability that there is *not* more than one such car is then $1-0.0026$, or 0.9974, which means odds of about 380 to 1 against there being another such car. Would that be sufficient to establish beyond reasonable doubt that the car driven by B is the one responsible?

I will admit to a doubt whether statisticians would approve my identification of a statistical $1/20$ of a car with odds of 20 to 1 against there being even one car, but I cannot see any rational objection to the procedure when the statistical figure is, as in this case, a small fraction of a car. The procedure would admittedly be quite invalid if our initial estimate gave us a figure approaching, or even more than, 1 car. Suppose that Exchester was such a large city that we must consider not 100, but 10,000 grey Fords. Our $1/20$ of a car would then become 5 cars; the rest of the calculation would then be both impossible and meaningless. Obviously, if the figure were 5 cars, although that only predicts a statistically probable number and does not guarantee the actual existence of even one car, it is most likely that there would be more than one; that is, there are likely to be other such cars besides the one which, *ex hypothesi*, we know exists. The court would then have to look for some other evidence against driver B.

There will in fact in most cases be a limit beyond which, the data being unquantifiable or unsuitable for calculation, we can no longer use a statistical approach. Suppose for example that Exchester was the large city, but that B freely admitted driving his grey Ford along the street where the collision occurred and about the same time, and that the police could trace no other grey Ford of which this was true. These facts would greatly increase the probability of B's guilt, but how could one give them numerical expression? Or, to use our original figures again, suppose that A thought, but was not certain, that he was hit by the front wing of the Ford, and that B's Ford was damaged on the back wing. The court must then decide which is the more probable: that A is mistaken, because of the high probability that B's is the correct Ford; or that A is right and some other Ford was involved. No calculation could help with that decision unless we could somehow put numerical values on the subjective strength of A's belief and on the objective likelihood of his being correct in his recollection.

Most attempts to substitute probability calculations for the usual weighing of evidence will in fact run into just such a difficulty: there will nearly always be pieces of evidence which are self-evidently relevant but which cannot be fitted into a calculation. To take a different sort of example, suppose that a woman is murdered, that a man with whom she has been associating is suspected, that both her blood and a bloodstain on the suspect's clothing are of the same ABO group, and that the blood grouping cannot in this case be taken any further. Suppose also that he had been heard to threaten her during a violent quarrel. A numerical presentation of the blood-group evidence would be simple, but it would be quite unrealistic not to take the other more cogent evidence into account merely because it could not be fitted into the calculation.

Finkelstein and Fairley, in the paper I have mentioned,(12) have attempted boldly to deal with just this sort of situation by going back to the work of the 17th century mathematician Bayes, who concerned himself with the problem of calculating the probability that, an event having happened, it happened *in consequence* of a specified earlier event with its own prior probability. These authors, one of whom is a lawyer and the other a statistician, suggest that in cases such as those I have been discussing it may sometimes at least be possible to assign by a sort of intelligent guesswork or informed intuition a meaningful "prior probability" to the unquantifiable part of the evidence, whereby a probability calculation based on the *whole* of the evidence becomes feasible.

It is a noble attempt, and the topic undoubtedly deserves the further attention of those qualified to develop it—of whom I cannot unfortunately claim to be one. It appears to me that at present the most useful next step would be to decide what sort of probability figure represents "beyond reasonable doubt." This seems to be not an impossible task. Assume that a number of cases could be found in which the evidence admits of a realistic and meaningful calculation of probabilities. The first step would then be "try" these cases in parallel—on the one hand by a statistician calculating probabilities, on the other by a court (if the case actually came to trial) or a panel of lawyers (if it did not). A comparison of the results might then enable us to decide what sort of probability figure is equivalent to proof "beyond reasonable doubt." If anything approaching consistency emerged from these comparisons, something very useful would have been discovered.

That is perhaps as far as we can go. There is however one last question which persists in coming up in my non-legal mind: does "beyond reasonable doubt" mean with the same rigour of proof whatever the crime? Does a serious crime require a more rigorous standard than a trivial offence? If a probability of, say, 0.99 was sufficient to "prove" a minor traffic offence, would a murder require a figure of, say, 0.999? I throw the question out; I offer no opinion.

NOTES

(1) Any statements which I make about the law in this article are purely subjective; hence no one need waste ammunition shooting them down.

(2) Karl R. Popper (1962): "The Logic of Scientific Discovery" (Hutchinson, London).

(3) An aspirin tablet weighs approximately 350,000 micrograms.

(4) For the benefit of the mathematically uninformed reader, the probability of an event is defined as:

$$\frac{\text{The number of possibilities favourable to the event}}{\text{The total number of possibilities}}$$

where all possibilities are equally likely. If the event is impossible—that is, is certain not to happen—that fraction will be 0; if the event is certain to happen, the numerator and denominator of the fraction are equal, and it will be 1. The probability of an event is therefore expressible by a figure between 0 (impossibility) and 1 (certainty). Sometimes a percentage figure between 0 and 100 is used. For example, the probability of drawing an ace from a pack of cards is 4/52, i.e. 1/13, which is approximately 0.0769, or 7.69 percent.

(5) To the scientifically-minded, that is. It has been pointed out to me by a successful writer of psychologically slanted crime thrillers that this kind of precision has its disadvantages. If "beyond reasonable doubt" meant with a probability of, say, 0.99, that would imply that, although the verdict was correct in 99 percent of the cases, 1 person in 100 was wrongly convicted. The realisation of this would be much more disquieting, and much more damaging to the reputation of the law, than a vague general idea that with proof "beyond reasonable doubt" someone sometimes might be wrongly convicted, even though the actual number of wrong convictions was in fact no smaller.

(6) I used to find that courts, or at least the advocates practising in them, did not like to hear an expert witness talk of probability. "You are a scientific witness," they would protest, "we want facts, not probabilities." However, the same evidence was often acceptable if one talked of "odds" rather than of "probabilities." Has this any connection with our reputation as a sporting nation?

(7) E. B. Mode (1963): Probability and Criminalistics," *Journal of the American Statistical Association*, vol. 58, p. 628.

(8) C. R. Kingston and P. L. Kirk (1964): "The Use of Statistics in Criminalistics," *Journal of Criminal Law, Criminology and Police Science*, vol. 55, p. 514.

(9) C. R. Kingston (1965): *Journal of the American Statistical Association*, vol. 60, pp. 70, 1028.

(10) C. R. Kingston (1966): "Probability and Legal Proceedings," *Journal of Criminal Law, Criminology and Police Science*, vol. 57, p. 93.

(11) J. B. Parker (1967): "The Mathematical Evaluation of Numerical Evidence," *Journal of the Forensic Science Society*, vol. 7, p. 134.

(12) M. O. Finkelstein and W. B. Fairley (1970): "A Bayesian Approach to Identification Evidence," *Harvard Law Review*, vol. 83, p. 489.

TRIAL BY MATHEMATICS: PRECISION AND

RITUAL IN THE LEGAL PROCESS

Laurence H. Tribe

The system of legal proof that replaced trial by battle in Continental Europe during the Middle Ages reflected a starkly numerical jurisprudence. The law typically specified how many uncontradicted witnesses were required to establish various categories of propositions, and defined precisely how many witnesses of a particular class or gender were needed to cancel the testimony of a single witness of a more elevated order.(1) So it was that medieval law, nurtured by the abstractions of scholasticism, sought in mathematical precision an escape from the perils of irrational and subjective judgment.

In a more pragmatic era, it should come as no surprise that the search for objectivity in adjudication has taken another tack. Yesterday's practice of numerology has given way to today's theory of probability, currently the *sine qua non* of rational analysis. Without indulging in the dubious speculation that contemporary probabilistic methods will one day seem as quaint as their more mystical predecessors, one can at least observe that the resort to mathematical techniques as alternatives to more intuitive tools in the trial process has ancient roots. Nor is it entirely accidental that those roots seem oddly twisted when examined outside their native soil. For, although the mathematical or pseudo-mathematical devices which a society embraces to rationalize its systems for adjudication may be quite comprehensible to a student of that society's customs and culture, those devices may nonetheless operate to distort—and, in some instances, to destroy—important values which that society means to express or to pursue through the conduct of legal trials. This article discusses the respects in which this is the case—and, in so doing, suggests a framework of analysis for the assessment of the potentialities and dangers of current and proposed uses of mathematical methods in the trial process.

In speaking of mathematical methods "in the trial process," I am referring to two related but nonetheless separable topics: not only to the use of mathematical tools in the actual conduct of a particular trial, but also to the use of such tools in the design of the trial system as a whole. The first topic encompasses such questions as the propriety of allowing the parties in a lawsuit to employ explicitly statistical evidence or overtly probabilistic arguments for various purposes,(2) and the wisdom of permitting or encouraging the trier to resolve the conflicting claims of a lawsuit with the assistance of mathematical methods.(3) The second topic, in contrast, centers on the desirability of employing such methods in establishing the procedural and evidentiary rules according to which lawsuits generally should be conducted. Both topics, of course, share a common core: both involve the wisdom of using mathematical tools to facilitate the making of choices among available courses of action with respect to the trial process. In this sense, both topics form part of the larger subject of when and how mathematical methods ought to be employed in decisionmaking. And this subject, in turn, is part of the still more inclusive topic of when it is desirable to make decisions in a calculating, deliberate way, with the aid of precise and rigorous techniques of analysis. To the extent that this article sheds any light on those larger matters, I will of course be gratified. I will not, however, attempt to deal directly with them here, and will instead confine myself to the narrower inquiries outlined above.

Two further introductory remarks are in order. First, my subject is the use of mathematics as a tool for decisionmaking rather than simply as a mode of thought, as an instrument rather than as a language. Conceivably, the very enterprise of describing some phenomena in precise mathematical terms, and particularly the enterprise of quantifying them, might be shown to entail some significant costs in addition to its obvious benefits. Perhaps it is in some sense "dehumanizing" to talk in highly abstract or quantitative terms about some subjects,(4) but this is another issue not to be treated here.

Second, although my central concern is the wisdom of using mathematical methods for certain decisionmaking purposes even when those methods are rationally employed, I will also examine what must be regarded as clearly irrational uses of those methods. Thus, some might charge that, by relying on such misuses in any overall assessment, I have confused the avoidable costs of using a tool badly with the inherent costs of using it well. It is rather like the claim that statistics can lie. One may always respond that this claim is false while conceding that the devil can quote Scripture to his own purposes. In a sense, this is obviously the case. But in another sense, it is only a half-truth, for the costs of abusing a technique must be reckoned among the costs of using it at all to the extent that the latter creates risks of the former. To be more precise, in at least some contexts, permitting *any* use of certain mathematical methods entails a sufficiently high risk of misuse, or a risk of misuse sufficiently costly to avoid, that it would be irrational not to take such misuse into account when deciding whether to permit the methods to be employed at all.

Finally, a word about objectives. This analysis has been undertaken partly because I suspect that the lure of objectivity and precision may prove increasingly hard to resist for lawyers concerned with reliable, or simply successful adjudication; partly because a critique of mathematical efforts to enhance the reliability and impartiality of legal trials may yield helpful insights into what such trials are and ought to be; and partly because such a critique may ultimately contribute to an appreciation of how rigor and quantification, once their real costs and limits are better understood, might actually prove useful in processes of decisionmaking. Most fundamentally, though, I write in reaction to a growing and bewildering literature of praise for mathematical precision in the trial process,(5) a literature that has tended to catalogue or to assume the virtues of mathematical approaches quite as uncritically as earlier writers(6) tended to deny their relevance.

FACTFINDING WITH MATHEMATICAL PROBABILITIES

The infamous trial in 1899 of Alfred Dreyfus, Captain in the French General Staff, furnishes one of the earliest reported instances of proof by mathematical probabilities. In attempting to establish that the author of a certain document that allegedly fell into German hands was none other than Captain Dreyfus, the prosecution called several witnesses who theorized that Dreyfus must have written the document in question by tracing the word *intérêt* from a letter written by his brother, constructing a chain of several of these traced words in a row, and then writing over this chain as a model when preparing the document—in order to give it the appearance of a forgery and thereby to protect himself should the document later be traced to him.(7) To identify the writing in the document as that of Dreyfus, the prosecution's witnesses reported a number of close matches between the lengths of certain words and letters in the document and the lengths of certain words and letters in correspondence taken from Dreyfus' home. Obscure lexicographical and graphological "coincidences" within the document itself were said by the witness to indicate the high probability of its disguised character and of its use to convey coded information.(8) To establish the validity of the hypothesis that the document had been traced over the handwriting of Dreyfus' brother, the prosecution's witnesses computed the "amazing" frequency with which certain letters in the document appeared over the the same letters of the word chain constructed by repeating *intérêt* a number of times, once a variety of complex adjustments had been made.(9)

The very opacity of these demonstrations protected them to some degree from effective spontaneous criticism, but the "mathematics" on which they were based was in fact utter nonsense. As the panel of experts appointed several years later to review the evidence in the Dreyfus case easily showed,(10) there was nothing statistically remarkable about the existence of close matches in some word lengths between the disputed document and Dreyfus' correspondence, given the many word pairs from which the prosecution was free to choose those that displayed such similarities.(11) Moreover, the supposed coincidences within the document itself reflected no significant deviation from what one would expect in normal French prose. Finally, the frequency with which various letters in the document could be "localized" over the letters of *intérêt* was likewise statistically insignificant.

Armand Charpentier, a prominent student of the Dreyfus affair, reports that counsel for Dreyfus and the Government Commissioner alike declared that they had understood not a word of the witness' mathematical demonstrations.(12) Charpentier adds that, although the judges who convicted Dreyfus were in all likelihood equally mystified, they nonetheless "allowed themselves to be impressed by the scientific phraseology of the system."(13) It would be difficult to verify that proposition in the particular case, but the general point it makes is a crucial one: the very mystery that surrounds mathematical arguments—the relative obscurity that makes them at once impenetrable by the layman and impressive to him—creates a continuing risk that he will give such arguments credence they may not deserve and a weight they cannot logically claim.

The California Supreme Court recently perceived this danger when it warned that "[m]athematics, a veritable sorcerer in our computerized society, while assisting the trier of fact in the search for truth, must not [be allowed to] cast a spell over him."(14) The court ruled improper a prosecutor's misconceived attempt to link an accused interracial couple with a robbery by using probability theory. The victim of the robbery, an elderly woman, had testified that she saw her assailant, a young woman with blonde hair, run from the scene. One of the victim's neighbors had testified that he saw a Caucasian woman, with her hair in a dark blonde ponytail, run from the scene of the crime and enter a yellow automobile driven by a male Negro wearing a mustache and beard. Several days later, officers arrested a couple that seemed to match these descriptions.(15) At the week-long trial of this couple, the victim was unable to identify either defendant, and her neighbor's trial identification of the male defendant was effectively impeached.(16) Moreover, the defense introduced evidence that the female defendant had worn light-colored clothing on the day of the robbery, although both witnesses testified that the girl they observed had worn dark clothing. Finally, both defendants took the stand to deny any participation in the crime, providing an alibi that was at least consistent with the testimony of another defense witness.

In an effort to bolster the identification of the defendants as the perpetrators of the crime, the prosecutor called a college mathematics instructor to establish that, if the robbery was indeed committed by a Caucasian woman with a blonde ponytail accompanied by a Negro with a beard and mustache and driving a yellow car, there was an overwhelming probability that the accused couple were guilty because they matched this detailed description.

The witness first testified to the "product rule" of probability theory, according to which the probability of the joint occurrence of a number of mutually independent events equals the product of the individual probabilities of each of the events.(17) Without presenting any supporting statistical evidence, the prosecutor had the witness assume specific probability factors for each of the six characteristics allegedly shared by the defendants and the guilty couple.(18) Applying the product rule to the assumed factors, the prosecutor concluded that there was but one chance in twelve million that any couple chosen at random would possess the characteristics in question, and asked the jury to infer that there was therefore but one chance in twelve million of the defendants' innocence.

The jury convicted but the California Supreme Court reversed, holding the mathematical testimony and the prosecutor's associated argument inadmissible on four separate grounds. First, the record was devoid of any empirical evidence to support the individual probabilities assumed by the prosecutor.(19)

Second, even if the assumed probabilities were themselves correct, their multiplication under the product rule presupposed the independence of the factors they measured—a presupposition for which no proof was presented, and which was plainly false.(20) If two or more events tend to occur together, the chances of their separate occurrence obviously cannot be multiplied to yield the chance of their joint occurrence.(21) For example, if every tenth man is black and bearded, and if every fourth man wears a mustache, it may nonetheless be true that most bearded black men wear mustaches, so that nearly one man in ten—not one in forty—will be a black man with a beard *and* a mustache.

Third, even if the product rule could properly be applied to conclude that there was but one chance in twelve million that a randomly chosen couple would possess the six features in question, there would remain a substantial possibility that the guilty couple did not in fact possess all of those characteristics—either because the prosecution's witnesses were mistaken or lying, or because the guilty couple was somehow disguised. "Traditionally," the court reasoned, "the jury weighs such risks in evaluating the credibility and probative value of trial testimony,"(22) but—finding itself unable to quantify these possibilities of error or falsification—the jury would be forced to exclude such risks from any effort to assign a number to the probability of guilt or innocence and would be tempted to accord disproportionate weight to the prosecution's computations.

Fourth, and entirely apart from the first three objections, the prosecutor erroneously equated the probability that a randomly chosen couple would possess the incriminating characteristics, with the probability that any given couple possessing those characteristics would be innocent. After all, if the suspect population contained, for example, twenty-four million couples, and if there were a probability of one in twelve million that a couple chosen at random from the suspect population would possess the six characteristics in question, then one could well expect to find two such couples in the suspect population, and there would be a probability of approximately one in two—not one in twelve million—that any given couple possessing the six characteristics would be innocent.(23) The court quite reasonably thought that few defense attorneys, and fewer jurors, could be expected to comprehend these basic flaws in the prosecution's analysis.(24) Under the circumstances, the court concluded, this "trial by mathematics" so distorted the jury's role and so disadvantaged defense counsel as to constitute a miscarriage of justice.(25)

But the California Supreme Court discerned "no inherent incompatability between the disciplines of law and mathematics and intend[ed] no general disapproval . . . of the latter as an auxiliary in the fact-finding processes of the former."(26) Thus expressed, the court's position seems reasonable enough. Any highly specialized category of knowledge or technique of analysis is likely to share in some degree the divergence between impressiveness and understandability that characterizes mathematical proof; surely, adjudication should not for that reason be deprived of the benefits of all expertise. On the contrary, the drawing of unwarranted inferences from expert testimony has long been viewed as rectifiable by cross-examination, coupled with the opportunity to rebut. Particularly if these devices are linked to judicial power to give cautionary jury instructions and to exclude evidence altogether on a case-by-case basis if prejudicial impact is found to outweigh probative force, and if these techniques are then supplemented by a requirement of advance notice of intent to use a particular item of technical proof, and by some provision for publicly financed expert assistance to the indigent accused confronted with an expert adversary,(27) there might seem to be no valid remaining objection to probabilistic proof.

But can such proof simply be equated with expert evidence generally, or does it in fact pose problems of a more pervasive and fundamental character? A consideration of that question requires the more careful development of just what "mathematical proof" should be taken to mean, and what major forms it can assume.

In an examination of the role of mathematical methods in the trial itself, whether used by one or more of the parties in the presentation of proof or employed by the trier in reaching a decision, we may set aside at the outset those situations in which the very issues at stake in a litigation are in some sense mathematical and hence require the explicit trial use of mathematical techniques—when, for example, the governing substantive law makes a controversy turn on such questions as percentage of market control,(28) expected lifetime earnings,(29) likelihood of widespread public confusion,(30) or the randomness of a jury selection process.(31) My concern is with cases in which mathematical methods are turned to the task of deciding what occurred on a particular, unique occasion, as opposed to cases in which the very task defined by the applicable law is that of measuring the statistical characteristics or likely effects of some process or the statistical features of some population of people or events.

With this initial qualification in mind, it is possible—and will occasionally prove helpful—to separate mathematical proof into three distinct but partially overlapping categories: 1. those in which such proof is directed to the *occurrence* or nonoccurrence of the event, act, or type of conduct on which the litigation is premised; 2. those in which such proof is directed to the *identity* of the individual responsible for a certain act or set of acts; and 3. those in which such proof is directed to *intention* or to some other mental element of responsibility, such as knowledge or provocation. In dealing with the utility of mathematical proof in the trial process. I will later show how such a tripartite division can be useful. It is sufficient to say at this stage that the significance, appropriateness, and dangers of mathematical proof may depend dramatically on whether such proof is meant to bear upon occurrence, identity, or frame of mind.(32) Several examples should suffice to illustrate the contents of each of these categories.

Occurrence.—Consider first the cases in which the existence of the legally significant occurrence or act is itself in question. A barrel falls from the defendant's window onto the plaintiff's head. The question is whether some negligent act or omission by defendant caused the fall. Proof is available to support a finding that, in over sixty percent of all such barrel-falling incidents, a negligent act or omission was the cause. Should such proof be allowed and, if so, to what effect?(33)

A man is found in possession of heroin. The question is whether he is guilty of concealing an illegally imported narcotic drug. Evidence exists to support the finding that ninety-eight percent of all heroin in the United States is illegally imported. What role, if any, may that fact play at the defendant's trial?

A man is charged with overtime parking in a one-hour zone. The question is whether his car had remained in the parking space beyond the time limit. To prove that it had not been moved, the government calls an officer to testify that he recorded the positions of the tire air-valves on one side of the car. Both before and after a period in excess of one hour, the front-wheel valve was pointing at one o'clock; the rear-wheel valve, at eight o'clock. The driver's defense is that he had driven away during the period in question and just happened to return to the same parking place with his tires in approximately the same position. The probability of such a fortunate accident is somewhere between one in twelve and one in one hundred forty-four.(35) Should proof of that fact be allowed and, if so, to what end?(36)

Identity.—Consider next the cases in which the identity of the responsible agent is in doubt. Plaintiff is negligently run down by a blue bus. The question is whether the bus belonged to the defendant. Plaintiff is prepared to prove that defendant operates four-fifths of all the blue buses in town. What effect, if any, should such proof be given?(37)

A policeman is seen assaulting someone at an undetermined time between 7 p.m. and midnight. The question is whether the defendant, whose beat includes the place of the assault, was the particular policeman who committed the crime. It can be shown that the defendant's beat brings him to the place of the assault four times during the relevant five-hour period each night, and that other policemen are there only once during the same period. In what way, if at all, may this evidence be used?(38)

A man is found shot to death in the apartment occupied by his mistress. The question is whether she shot him. Evidence is available to the effect that, in ninety-five percent of all known cases in which a man was killed in his mistress' apartment, the mistress was the killer. How, if at all, may such evidence be used?(39)

A civil rights worker is beaten savagely by a completely bald man with a wooden left leg, wearing a black patch over his right eye and bearing a six-inch scar under his left, who flees from the scene of the crime in a chartreuse Thunderbird with two dented fenders. A man having these six characteristics is charged with criminal battery. The question is whether the defendant is in fact the assailant. Evidence is available to show that less than one person in twenty has any of these six characteristics, and that the six are statistically independent, so that less than one person in sixty-four million shares all six of them. In what ways, if at all, may that calculation be employed?(40)

Intention.—Consider finally the cases in which the issue is one of intent, knowledge, or some other "mental" element of responsibility. A recently insured building burns down. The insured admits causing the fire but insists that it was an accident. On the question of intent to commit arson, what use, if any, may be made of evidence tending to show that less than one such fire out of twenty is in fact accidentally caused?(41)

As in an earlier example,(42) a man is found possessing heroin. This time the heroin is stipulated at trial to have been illegally imported. In his prosecution for concealing the heroin with knowledge that it had been illegally imported, what effect may be given to proof that ninety-eight percent of all heroin in the United States is in fact illegally imported?(43)

A doctor sued for malpractice is accused of having dispensed a drug without adequate warning, knowing of its tendency to cause blindness in pregnant women. Should he be allowed to introduce evidence that ninety-eight percent of all doctors are unaware of the side-effect in question?

An Overview.—The reader will surely note that this collection of cases might have been subdivided along a variety of different axes. Some of the cases are civil, others criminal. Some involve imputations of moral fault; others do not. Some rest upon statistical calculations that might readily be made; others, on figures that are at best difficult to obtain and at worst entirely inaccessible. Some entail the use of probabilistic evidence to establish liability; others, to negate it. In some, the probabilities refer to a party's own involvement in a category of events; in others, they refer to the proportion of similar events in which a certain critical feature is present, or in which the responsible party has a certain important characteristic. In some of these cases, the mathematics seems best suited to assisting the judge in his allocation of burdens of production or persuasion; in others, its most natural role seems to be as evidence for the finder of fact.

My aim in classifying the cases in terms of occurrence, identity, and intention is not to imply that these other ways of carving up the topic have less significance, but merely to sketch one possible map of the territory I mean to cover—using a set of boundaries that are intuitively suggestive and that will prove helpful from time to time as the discussion unfolds.(44)

Courts confronted with problems of the several sorts enumerated in the three preceding sub-sections have reacted to them on an almost totally ad hoc basis, occasionally upholding an attempt at probabilistic proof,(45) but more commonly ruling the particular attempt improper.(46) A perhaps understandable pre-occupation with the novelties and factual nuances of the particular cases has marked the opinions in this field, to the virtual exclusion of any broader analysis of what mathematics can or cannot achieve at trial—and at what price. As the number and variety of cases continue to mount, the difficulty of dealing intelligently with them in the absence of any coherent theory is becoming increasingly apparent.

NOTES

References in the notes refer to the original publication of this article in the *Harvard Law Review*, April, 1971 Volume 84, No. 6.

(1) *See* M. Cappelletti & J. Perillo, Civil Procedure in Italy 35-36 (1965); A. Engelmann, A History of Continental Civil Procedure 41-47 (1927); R. Ginsburg & A. Bruzelius, Civil Procedure in Sweden 33 & n.131, 295 & n.471 (1965); J. Glaser, Lehre Vom Beweis im Strafprozess 132-35 (1883); Kunert, *Some Observations on the Origin and Structure of Evidence Rules Under the Common Law System and the Civil Law System of "Free Proof" in the German Code of Criminal Procedure*, 16 Buff. L. Rev. 122, 141-42 & nn.99-100, 144-45 (1966). *See also* A. Esmein, A History of Continental Criminal Procedure 264-71 (J. Simpson, transl. 1913); I F. Hélie, Traité De l'Instruction Criminelle 650-53, 656-57 (1845); F. Voltaire, A Commentary On Beccaria's Essay on Crimes and Punishments 227-28 (1872).

(2) I am, of course, aware that *all* factual evidence is ultimately "statistical," and all legal proof ultimately "probabilistic," in the epistemological sense that no conclusion can ever be drawn from empirical data without some step of inductive inference—even if only an inference that things are usually what they are perceived to be. *See, e.g.*, D. Hume, *A Treatise Of Human Nature*, bk. I, pt. III, § 6, at 87 (L.A. Selby-Bigge ed. 1958). My concern, however, is only with types of evidence and modes of proof that bring this probalistic element of inference to explicit attention in a quantified way. As I hope to show, much turns on whether such explicit quantification is attempted.

(3) By "mathematical methods," I mean the entire family of formal techniques of analysis that build on explicit axiomatic foundations, employ rigorous principles of deduction to construct chains of argument, and rely on symbolic modes of expression calculated to reduce ambiguity to a minimum.

(4) One senses that much of the contemporary opposition to the technological emphasis upon rationality and technique rests on some such premise.

(5) *See, e.g.*, Cullison, *Probability Analysis of Judicial Fact-Finding: A Preliminary Outline of The Subjective Approach*, 1969 U. Tol. L. Rev. 538 (1969) [hereinafter cited as Cullison]; Finkelstein & Fairley, *A Bayesian Approach to Identification Evidence*, 83 Harv. L. Rev. 489 (1970) [hereinafter cited as Finkelstein & Fairley]. *See also*, Becker, *Crime and Punishment: An Economic Approach*, 76 J. Pol. Econ. 169 (1968) [hereinafter cited as Becker]; Birmingham, *A Model of Criminal Process: Game Theory and Law*, 56 Cornell L.

Rev. 57 (1970) [hereinafter cited as Birmingham] ; Kaplan, *Decision Theory and Factfinding Process*, 20 Stan. L. Rev. 1065 (1968) [hereinafter cited as Kaplan]; *cf.* Broun & Kelly, *Playing the Percentages and the Law of Evidence*, 1970 Ill. L. F. 23 [hereinafter cited as Broun & Kelly].

(6) *See, e.g.*, W. Wills, An Essay on the Principles of Circumstantial Evidence 6-10, 15, 282 (4th ed. 1862); M. Houts. from Evidence to Proof 132 (1956).

(7) *See* the trial testimony of Jan. 18, 1899, and Feb. 4, 1899, reported in a special supplement to Le Petit Temps (Paris), April 22, 1899.

(8) For example, one witness stressed the presence of four coincidences out of the 26 initial and final letters of the 13 repeated polysyllabic words in the document. He evaluated at .2 the probability of an isolated coincidence and calculated a probability of $(0.2)^4 = .0016$ that four such coincidences would occur in normal writing. But $(0.2)^4$ is the probability of four coincidences out of four; that of four or more out of 13 is some 400 times greater or approximately .7. *See Rappord de Mm. Les Experts Darboux, Appell, et Poincaré, in Les Documents Judiciares de l'Affaire Dreyfus, in La Révision du Procés de Rennes (1909) [hereinafter cited as Rappord].* Cf. note 40 *infra.*

(9) Two witnesses observed that, when the word chain "*intérêt/intérêt/intérêt/intérêt · · ·* " was compared with the document itself, allowing one letter of slipping-back for each space between words and aligning the word chain with the actual or the ideal left-hand margin as convenient, the letter *l* appeared with particular frequency over the word-chain letter *i*; the letters *n* and *p* appeared frequently over the word-chain letter *n*; and so on. Far from being in any way remarkable, however, the probability that *some* such pattern can be discerned in any document is nearly certainty. *See Rappord* 534.

(10) *See id.*

(11) *See* the discussion of the "selection effect," note 40 *infra.*

(12) A. Charpentier, The Dreyfus Case 52-53 (J. May transl. 1935).

(13) *Id.* at 53. *See also id.* at 265.

(14) People v. Collins, 68 Cal. 2d 319, 320, 438 P. 2d 33, 66 Cal. Rptr. 497 (1968).

(15) There was testimony that the female defendant's hair color at the time of the robbery was light blond rather than dark blond, as it appeared at trial. The male defendant had no beard at trial or when arrested and told the arresting officers that he had not worn one on the day of the robbery. There was testimony corroborating his claim that he had shaved his beard approximately two weeks before the robbery, but other testimony that he was bearded the day after the robbery.

(16) The neighbor admitted at trial "that at the preliminary hearing he [had] testified to an uncertain identification at the police lineup shortly after the attack . . . " 68 Cal. 2d at 321, 438 P. 2d at 34, 66 Cal. Rptr. at 498.

(17) *See* explanation in note 63 *infra.*

(18)

Characteristic	Assumed Probability of its Occurrence
1. Partly yellow automobile	1/10
2. Man with mustache	1/4
3. Girl with ponytail	1/10
4. Girl with blond hair	1/3
5. Negro man with beard	1/10
6. Interracial couple in car	1/1000

(19) *See* State v. Sneed, 76 N.M. 349, 414 P. 2d 858 (1966); People v. Risley, 214 N.Y. 75, 108 N.E. 200 (1915), *discussed at* pp. 1344-45 & notes 47-49 *infra*. *See also* Campbell v. Board of Educ., 310 F. Supp. 94, 105 (E.D.N.Y. 1970).

(20) The sixth factor, for example, essentially restates parts of the first five. *See* note 18 *supra*.

(21) Precisely this mistake is made in C. McCormick, Handbook of the Law of Evidence § 171 (1954) and in J. Wigmore, The Science of Judicial Proof § 154, at 270-71 (erd. 1937). One court has treated such dependence, I think mistakenly, as going only to the "weight" of the product and not to its admissibility. State v. Coolidge, 109 N.H. 403, 419, 260 A.2d 547, 559 (1969), *cert. granted on other issues*, 399 U.S. 926 (1970) (No. 1318 Misc. 1969 Term; renumbered No. 323, 1970 Term), *discussed at* note 40 *infra*.

(22) 68 Cal. 2d at 330, 438 P .2d at 40, 66 Cal. Rptr. at 504.

(23) In a separate mathematical appendix, the court demonstrated that, even if the number of suspect couples approaches only twelve million, the probability that *at least one other couple* (in addition to the actually guilty couple) will possess the six characteristics rises to somewhat over *forty-one-percent*, even on the assumption that the prosecutor was correct in concluding that the probability that a radomly chosen couple would possess all six characteristics is but one in twelve million. More generally, the court showed that the probability of such duplication equals

$$\frac{I - (I - Pr)^N - NPr(I - Pr)^{N-1}}{I - (I-Pr)^N}$$

where Pr equals the probability that a random couple will possess the characteristics in question and N is the number of couples in the suspect population. 68 Cal. 2d at 333-35, 438 P .2d at 42-43, 66 Cal. Rptr. at 506-07. If $\lambda \ \iota^\tau \ ]\epsilon\pi\xi\chi \ ]\theta \ [\xi\rho[\xi \ \xi\chi] \ ]\kappa\xi \ oe \ \eta\xi \ \theta^\tau$ X • Pr, then the Poisson approximation for the above quotient is $I - \frac{sA}{\xi e\lambda - I}$, where e is the transcendental number 2.71828. . . . that is used as the base for natural logarithms. *See* I W. Feller, An Introduction to Probability Theory and Its Applications 153-64 (3rd ed. 1968); Kingston, *Applications of Probability Theory in Criminalistics*, 60 J. Am. Statist. Ass'n. 70, 74 (1965). On the assumption that Pr = 1/N (so that λ = 1), which is approximately .42, as the court correctly concluded. *See* Cullison, *Identification by Probabilities and Trial by Arithmetic (A Lesson For Beginners in How to be Wrong With Greater Precision)*, 6 Houst. L. Rev. 471, 4 84- 502 (1969).

Finkelstein and Fairley suggest that the court's argument was mathematically incorrect because "the court's assumption that one in twelve million is a fair estimate of the probability of selecting such a couple at random necessarily implies that it is a fair estimate of the number of such couples in the population." Finkelstein & Fairley 493; *accord*, Broun & Kelly, *supra* note 5, at 43. But this completely misconceives the argument. Of course, if the figure of one in twelve million had represented an estimate, based upon random sampling, of *the actual frequency of Collins-like couples in a known population*, the criticism of the court's opinion would be well taken. But in fact the "one-in-twelve-million" figure represented nothing of the sort. Since nothing was known about exactly who was and who was not a member of the population of "suspect" couples, that figure represented only an estimate of the probability that any given couple, chosen at random from an unknown population of "suspect" couples, would turn out to have the six "Collins" characteristics—with that estimate itself based only on a multiplication of component factors, each representing the frequency of one of the six characteristics in a much larger population.

(24) *See also* note 40 *infra.*

(25) The court stressed the fact that the prosecutor had criticized the traditional notion of proof beyond a reasonable doubt as "hackneyed" and "trite"; that he "sought to reconcile the jury to the risk that, under his 'new math' approach to criminal jurisprudence, 'on some rare occasion . . . an innocent person may be convicted' "; and that he thereby sought "to persuade the jury to convict [the] defendants whether or not they were convinced of their guilt to a moral certainty and beyond a reasonable doubt." 68 Cal. 2d at 331-32, 438 P .2d at 41, 66 Cal. Rptr. at 505. The interaction between mathematical proof and reasonable doubt is discussed at pp. 1372-75 *infra.*

(26) 68 Cal. 2d at 320, 43 8 P .2d at 33, Cal. Rptr. at 497.

(27) *See, e.g.,* 1967 Duke L.J. 665, 681-83, *discussing* State v. Sneed, 76 N.M. 349, 414 P .2d 858 (1966).

(28) *E.g.,* United States v. United Shoe Machinery Corp., 110 F. Supp. 295, 304-05 (D. Mass. 1953) (Wyzanski, J.), *aff'd per curiam,* 347 U.S. 521 (1954).

(29) *See, e.g.,* Louisville & N.R.R. v. Steel, 257 Ala. 474, 59 So. 2d 664 (1952); Von Tersch v. Ahrendsen, 251 Iowa 115, 99, N.W. 2d 287 (1959).

(30) *See, e.g.,* United States v. 88 Cases, More or Less, Containing Bireley's Orange Beverage, 187 F .2d 967, 974 (3d Cir. 1951).

(31) *See generally,* Finkelstein, *The Application of Statistical Decision Theory to the Jury Discrimination Cases,* 80 Harv. L. Rev. 338 (1966); Zeisel, *Dr. Spock and the Case of the Vanishing Women Jurors,* 37 U. Chi. L. Rev. 1 (1969) [hereinafter cited as Zeisel] . *But see* State v. Smith, 102 N.J. Super. 325, 341, 246 A.2d 35, 50 (1968), *aff'd,* 55 N.J. 476, 262 A.2d 868 (1970), *cert. denied,* 400 U.S. 949 (1970).

(32) *See* pp. 1365-67, p. 1381 & notes 33, 37 & 41 *infra.*

(33) A sensible, and now quite conventional, approach to this question is "to treat the probability as the fact if the defendant has the power to rebut the inference." Jaffe, *Res Ipsa Loquitur Vindicated,* I Buff. L. Rev. 1, 6 (1951). On this theory, if the defendant produces a reasonably satisfactory explanation consistent with a conclusion of no negligence, and if the plaintiff produces no further evidence, the plaintiff should lose on a directed verdict despite his mathematical proof—unless 1. he can adequately explain his inability to make a more particularized showing (a possibility not adverted to in *id.*), or 2. no specific explanation is given, but there is some policy reason to ground liability in the area in question on a substantial probability of negligence in the *type* of case rather than to require a reasoned probability in the *particular* case, *cf.* note 100 *infra,* thereby moving toward a broader basis of liability. It will be noticed that no such policy is likely to operate when the mathematical evidence goes to the question of the defendant's *identity* and the plaintiff does not explain his failure to produce any more particularized evidence, for it will almost always be important to impose liability on the correct party, *whatever* the basis of such liability might be. *See* p. 1349 *infra. See also* notes 37 & 102 *infra.*

(34) It has now been settled as a federal constitutional matter, *see* Turner v. United States, 396 U.S. 398 (1970), that this statistical fact permits a legislature to authorize a jury to find illegal importation once it finds possession "unless the defendant explains the possession to the satisfaction of the jury." 21 U.S.C. § 174 (1964); *cf.* Leary v. United States, 395 U.S. 6 (1969). At least one commentator has urged the alternative position that the jury should not in such

cases be instructed that proof of possession is sufficient to find illegal importation (for that shifts to the accused the practical burden of persuasion, with its accompanying pressure to testify, notwithstanding any contrary jury charge) but should instead be told that ninety-eight percent of all heroin in the United States is illegally imported (for that leaves the jury more likely to give even the non-testifying accused the benefit of the doubt created by the remaining two percent). Comment, *Statutory Criminal Presumptions: Reconciling the Practical With the Sacrosanct*, 18 U.C.L.A. L. Rev. 157 (1970). But it is by no means clear, despite the commentator's assertion, that "the jury is more likely to consider other relevant circumstances unique to the particular case on a more equal footing with the 98 percent statistic than it would with a presumption." *Id.* at 183 n.102. *See generally* the discussion at pp. 1359-65 *infra*.

(35) If tires rotated in complete synchrony with one another, the probability would be 1/12; if independently, 1/12 x 1/12, or 1/144.

(36) A Swedish court, computing the probability at 1/12 x 1/12 = 1/144 on the dubious assumption that car wheels rotate independently, ruled that fraction large enough to establish reasonable doubt. Parkeringsfragor, II. Tilforlitligheten av det S.K. locksystemet for parkernigskontroll. *Svensk juristidining*, 47 (1962) 17-32, cited in Zeisel, *supra* note 31, at 12. The court's mathematical knife cut both ways, however, for it added that had all four tire-valves been recorded and found in the same position, the probability of 1/12 x 1/12 x 1/12 x 1/12 = 1/20, 736 would have constituted proof beyond a reasonable doubt. *Id.* For a discussion of why no such translation of the "reasonable doubt" concept into mathematical terms should be attempted, see pp. 1372-75 *infra*.

(37) In Smith v. Rapid Transit, Inc., 317 Mass. 469, 58 N.E. 2d 754 (1945), the actual case on which this famous chestnut is based, no statistical data were in fact presented, but the plaintiff did introduce evidence sufficient to show that the defendant's bus line was the only one chartered to operate on the street where the accident occurred. Affirming the direction of a verdict for the defendant, the court observed: "The most that can be said of the evidence in the instant case is that perhaps the mathematical chances somewhat favor the proposition that a bus of the defendant caused the accident. This was not enough." 317 Mass. at 470, 58 N.E. 2d at 755. *See also* Sawyer v. United States, 148 F. Supp. 877 (M.D. Ga. 1956); Reid v. San Pedro, L.A.&S.L.R.R., 39 Utah 617, 118 P. 1009 (1911). If understood as insisting on a numerically higher showing—an "extra margin" of probability above, say, .55— then the decision in *Smith* would make no sense, at least if the court's objective were the minimization of the total number of judicial errors in situations of this kind, an objective essentially implicit in the adoption of a "preponderance of the evidence" standard. *See* Ball, *The Moment of Truth: Probability Theory and Standards of Proof*, 14 Vand. L Rev. 807, 822-23 (1961) [hereinafter cited as Ball]. But cases like *Smith* are entirely sensible if understood instead as insisting on the presentation of *some* non-statistical and "individualized" proof of identity before compelling a party to pay damages, and even before compelling him to come forward with defensive evidence, absent an adequate explanation of the failure to present such individualized proof. *Compare* p. 1349 *infra with* note 33 *supra*.

(38) Note that in this criminal case, as in the preceding civil one, *a fact known about the particular defendant* provides reason to believe that the defendant is involved in a certain percentage of all cases (here, cases of being at the crucial place between 7 p.m. and midnight) possessing a characteristic shared by the litigated case.

(39) In this case, unlike the preceding two, it is *a fact known about the particular event that underlies the litigation,* not any fact known about the defendant, that triggers the probabilistic showing: a certain percentage of all events in which the crucial fact (here, the killing of a man in his mistress' apartment) is true are supposedly caused by a person with a characteristic (here, being the mistress) shared by the defendant in this case.

(40) This is, of course, People v. Collins, 68 Cal. 2d 319, 438 P. 2d 33, 66 Cal. Rptr. 497 (1968), minus the specific mathematical errors of *Collins* and without the inter-racial couple. One special factor that can lead to major mathematical distortions in this type of case is the "selection effect" that may arise from either party's power to choose matching features for quantification while ignoring non-matching features, thereby producing a grossly exaggerated estimate of the improbability that the observed matching would have occurred by chance. *See* Finkelstein & Fairley 495 n.14. This difficulty may well have been present in People v. Trujillo, 32 (Cal. 2d 105, 194 P .2d 681, *cert. denied,* 335 U.S. 887 (1948), in which an expert examined a large number of fibers taken from clothing worn by the accused and concluded; upon finding eleven matches with fibers taken from the scene of the crime, that there was only one-in-a-billion probability of such matching occurring by chance. A particularly egregious case of this sort is State v. Coolidge, 109 N.H. 403, 260 A.2d 547 (1969), *cert. granted on other issues,* 399 U.S. 926 (1970) (No. 1318) Misc., 1969 Term; renumbered No. 323, 1970 Term), where particles taken from the victim's clothing were found to match particles taken from the defendant's car and clothing in twenty-seven out of forty cases.

> In expressing his conclusion based upon statistical probabilities, the [consultant in micro-analysis and director of a university laboratory for scientific investigation] relied upon previous studies made by him, indicating that the probability of finding similar particles in sweepings from a series of automobiles was one in ten. Applying this as a standard, he determined the probability of finding 27 similar particles in sweepings from independent sources would be only one in ten to the 27th power.

109 N.H. at 418-19, 260 A.2d at 559. The court upheld the admissibility of that testimony, 109 N.H. at 422, 260 A.2d at 561, notwithstanding the weakness of the underlying figure of 1/10 and the expert's own concession that the particle sweepings "may not have been wholly independent," 109 N.H. at 419, 260 A.2d at 559. *See* note 21 *supra.* Most significantly, the court was evidently unaware that the relevant probability, that of finding 27 or more matches *out of 40 attempts,* was very much larger than $1/10^{27}$—larger, in fact, by a factor of approximately 10^{10}. Indeed, even the 40 particles chosen for comparison were visually selected for similarity from a still larger set of particle candidates, 109 N.H. at 421, 260 A.2d at 560—so large a set, conceivably, that the probability of finding 27 or more matches in sweeping over such a large sample, even from two entirely different sources, could well have been as high as 1/2 or more. *Cf.* note 8 *supra.* Oddly, the expert testimony in *Coolidge* has recently been described as "not misleading." Broun & Kelly, *supra* note 5, at 48.

(41) It is, of course, a fair question how such evidence could ever be compiled; the difficulty, and perhaps the impossibility, of compiling it no doubt reflects the "nonobjective" nature of the intent inquiry. *See* pp. 1365-66 *infra.*

(42) *See* p. 1339 *supra.*

(43) Turner v. United States 396 U.S. 398 (1970), sustained an authorized jury inference of knowledge in these circumstances. *See* note 34 *supra.*

(44) *See* note 32 *supra.*

(45) *See, e.g.,* People v. Trujillo, 32 Cal. 2d 105, 194 P .2d 681, *cert. denied,*

335 U.S. 887 (1948); State v. Coolidge, 109 N.H. 403, 260 A.2d 547 (1969), *cert. granted on other issues*, 399 U.S. 926 (1970) (No. 1318 Misc., 1969 Term; Renumbered No. 323, 1970 Term), *discussed in note* 40 *supra*. *See also* Note, *The Howland Will Case*, 4 Am. L. Rev. 625 (1870), *discussing* Robinson v. Mandell, 20 F. Cas. 1027 (No. 11,959) (C.C.D. Mass. 1868), *discussed in* note 47 *infra;* People v. Jordan, 45 Cal. 2d 484, 490 (1955), *discussed in* note 155 *infra*.

(46) *See, e.g.*, People v. Collins, 68 Cal. 2d 319, 438 P.2d 33, 66 Cal. Rptr. 497 (1968), *discussed at* pp. 1334-37 *supra*; State v. Sneed, 76 N.M. 349, 414, P.2d 858 (1966); People v. Risley, 214 N.Y. 75, 108 N.E. 200 (1915). *See also* Smith v. Rapid Transit, Inc., 317 Mass. 469, 58 N.E. 2d 754 (1945), *discussed in* note 37 *supra*; Miller v. State, 240 Ark. 340, 399 S.W.2d 268 (1966), *discussed in* note 155 *infra*.

V.

Issues in Crime Laboratory Management and Administration

INTRODUCTION

Traditionally, research in forensic science has focused on the development of new or improved laboratory techniques to identify or individualize physical evidence. Scientists in the laboratory were preoccupied with the problems of applying techniques to the examination of micro-quantities of often contaminated physical materials. As laboratories and the rest of the criminal justice system became more complex, other serious problems surfaced. Why were the police not using laboratories more? What services should a crime laboratory be able to provide and where should it be positioned in the general law enforcement organization to achieve greatest effectiveness? What managerial qualifications should a laboratory director possess to head a large scientific operation? Concern was also expressed over the different techniques used by laboratories examining the same evidence and over the unacceptable quality of much laboratory work. Evidently, systematic studies of crime laboratory operations were needed.

The first article is excerpted from the book, *Municipal Police Administration*, by Joseph Nicol, Professor of Criminalistics at the University of Illinois, Chicago Circle Campus. Although directed primarily at the police administrator, the selection first outlines the scope and limitations of criminalistics services. The author stresses the importance of maintaining a good relationship between the laboratory and the police investigator, especially during the initial investigation of a crime scene. Robert Borkenstein's paper originally appeared in the four-volume, *Methods of Forensic Science*. The position of the crime laboratory in the general law enforcement organization and the benefits of centralizing laboratory services are two subjects discussed in detail. Important is a section, "What is Management?" outlining a number of fundamental requirements for the director of a successful laboratory.

The selection by Walter Benson of the Midwest Research Institute is a condensed version of a report of a year-long study conducted with funds from the National Institute of Law Enforcement and Criminal Justice. The team of systems analysts who undertook this study quickly discovered that very few laboratories compiled data that could be assessed nationally. The inquiry did yield some significant findings that had never been previously quantified, including the inverse relationship that existed between the physical distance separating the police agency and the laboratory and its utilization. Also documented was the crisis of drug examinations within laboratories which were consuming a disproportionate ratio of available resources.

John W. Gunn and Richard S. Frank of the Drug Enforcement Administration in the next selection suggest a plan for a forensic laboratory. Several practical recommendations are made, including building specifications, necessary equipment, operating budget needs, and staffing the laboratory with qualified personnel.

CRIMINALISTICS

Joseph D. Nicol

Under present requirements of the criminal justice system, the criminal investigator must prove his case through the wise utilization of all available evidence. Since many crimes are not witnessed, the only information accessible to the investigator will be that obtained from inanimate, physical evidence. Although the evidence is silent, through skillful analysis, evaluation and "interrogation" the investigator may derive information that is far more significant than anything that might be obtained from living witnesses. By an understanding of the scope and limitations of criminalistics,(1) an investigator can use police laboratory services to provide him with answers to questions associated with the investigation of a criminal activity.

SCOPE AND LIMITATIONS OF CRIMINALISTICS

All problems presented to the police investigator, however suspicious, are not necessarily the outgrowth of criminal activity. The first mission of criminalistics, therefore, is to assist the criminal investigator in establishing that a crime actually has taken place. For example, through a determination of shooting distance, the crime laboratory may provide the basis for differentiating accidental, homicidal, or suicidal shootings. Or in the case of a suspicious fire, it may be possible to show that the origin was accidental and not incendiary.

In order to establish exactly what has occurred, one of the most important parts of a criminal investigation is the reconstruction of the activity that has taken place. This involves determining what happened, when it happened, and why it happened—in brief, gathering those facts which will provide a clear picture for later presentation in court. In this respect, criminalistics can often provide valuable assistance to the criminal investigator when he couples his imagination with the objective output of the crime laboratory.

Assuming that a crime has been committed, the chief objective of criminal investigation is to establish the identity of the perpetrator to the degree that a court will readily recognize the responsibility of this individual for the crime. It is unlikely that a good investigation will be conducted without the utilization of some aspect of criminalistics. It is equally unlikely that criminalistics will ever serve as a substitute for a good investigation nor can criminalistics make up for the difficulties created by slipshod effort on the part of the criminal investigator. Together they provide the necessary team for the solution of crimes in a complex society. How well the ultimate goal is reached will depend on enlightened administration and use of all available facets of technology.

Generally, criminalistics is concerned with the identification of persons, the identification of material, and the identity of things. As a corollary to the identity of evidence, criminalistics may shed some light on the dynamics of a criminal activity by identifying motives or establishing the gravity of the offense.

Standard Identification Tests. Perhaps the most common means of personal identification is through the development of fingerprints or other skin impressions at the crime scene. With lesser frequency, personal identification of found bodies through fingerprints may provide important starting points for a criminal investigation. As a rule, the field of criminalistics is not concerned with the development of latent fingerprints except as a part of the general evidence collection problem. In special cases, however, the crime laboratory may be able to provide techniques by which fingerprints can be developed on unusual materials. This might involve the utilization of relatively simple chemical processes, such as the development of prints on similar surfaces by ninhydrin.

Whether or not the criminalistics laboratory is directly involved in the development of latent fingerprints, the criminalist must be aware of the value of fingerprints on evidence and must always consider the possibility of the development of latent impressions prior to other examinations. A close working relationship between the laboratory and the fingerprint identification section is highly desirable.

Much has been said about the importance of blood and other physiological material as an aid to the identification of criminals. It is important to recognize, however, that physiological fluids, hair, and other evidence originating in or on the body of the criminal or his victim may not be as valuable as fingerprints in positively identifying the donor. Rather, the importance of this evidence may be more negative through its ability to refute an alibi.

For example, the blood on the suspect's clothing which he alleges is his own may not be a type that properly matches his blood. The importance of blood in this case stems, therefore, from the ability to refute an alibi rather than from its identification of a certain individual. This is not to say, however, that blood should not be examined carefully and extensively in order to show its likeness to the blood of the particular person. In the same respect, hair will not indicate identifiable individual characteristics to the exclusion of all others, but it may serve as a link between the suspect and the crime, and be used to refute an alibi.

At the present time, techniques are available for the positive identification of blood and other body fluids and to a lesser degree of certainty, for the determination of categories into which they belong. In the case of hair, the criminalist may classify the hair according to observable microscopic characteristics and demonstrate that specimen characteristics conform to those of the suspect. Research in the area of neutron activation analysis, electrophoresis and other advanced techniques suggest that at some future date, criminalists will have tools available for individualizing blood, hair, and other body material with the same degree of certainty that is now enjoyed by fingerprints.

The identification of a substance recovered in the course of a criminal investigation may provide the necessary elements for a criminal charge. Where the criminalist can identify contraband such as narcotics or a certain amount of alcohol in the blood, the investigator may have sufficient information to support a charge. As a rule these offenses are clearly delineated in the law, methods are readily available for analyses, and the only problem involved is to determine the level of material present. Standard laboratory equipment is normally adequate for treating such problems.(2)

The Problem of Probability. Whereas the identification of heroin is frequently enough to support a narcotics arrest, the mere identification of a substance in other situations may not provide sufficient information for the basis of a criminal charge. For example, the identification of a paint may not provide the specifications necessary for linking the suspect to a crime. The criminalist must demonstrate that the material contaminating the suspect or his possessions has characteristics that could be derived only from the criminal act. This factor distinguishes the forensic from the industrial chemist because the latter is not usually concerned with the source of containments if they do not affect quality control of the product.

When an investigator finds materials common to a general area in the clothing of a suspect, he may not be able to develop a strong argument that this suspect has had contact with a particular crime. Occasionally a substance will belong to a broad class but will have unique properties that make it important to the investigation. For example, some plant material may be limited in its distribution and be confined largely to the locality of the crime scene. The presence of fragments of such plant material on the clothing or possessions of the suspect might indicate that this person had been present at the crime scene area. Likewise, an item in the suspect's possession may be extremely rare or unusual, such as a tool modified to pull locks, and thus may provide strong evidence of the commission of a crime.

The goal of the criminalist is the discovery of unique characteristics which establish the identity of an item to the exclusion of all others, characteristics which are a "fingerprint" of the item. The infrared spectra of a substance may be so peculiar as to provide the basis for identity. One would expect that the craftwork of an individual would possess unique characteristics where the object has been deliberately identified by some mark of the individual through whose hands this has passed. For example, the mark on the label of a child's garment placed there by his mother or the mark on the inside of a watch case inscribed by the jeweler who has inspected and repaired the piece. Even the presence of marks on an object arising out of its use, and identifiable by by an owner, may provide a means of identity.

Perhaps the most difficult means of establishing identity is through the combination of randomly oriented characteristics. For example, the Galton characteristics on a latent fingerprint when found in a matching relationship with the imprint of the suspect, provide a basis for identity. No one point on the fingerprint by itself is adequate; only through the combination of points can the fingerprint expert state that this print was made by a particular individual. In the same way, a questioned document examiner renders his opinion of the identity of the writer based upon a combination of peculiar points on the document. The adequacy of the number of points and the evaluation of each characteristic upon which an opinion is based rests largely on the individual examiner's experience and understanding of the requirements of the field. A lack of proper background often leads the criminal investigator to accept a similarity without sound foundation. Additionally, it is often necessary as a condition for identity to find an absence of gross dissimilarities. Certainly, there should be no mismatch of class characteristics.

Considerable effort still must be made by criminalists to provide a basis for evaluation of characteristics observed in laboratory analyses. It would be helpful, for example, to have available distribution statistics on the chemical components in many of the common mass-produced materials readily found in criminal investigations. The trace contaminants that might distinguish one lot of paint or glass from another would provide the criminalist with the means for determining how important this particular piece of evidence may be in linking the suspect to the crime. Although this brings the criminalist into the nebulous area of probability, it would provide a more sound foundation for evaluation of analytical results than now exists.

At the present time, the criminalist must rely on his particular experience and degree of exposure to the analysis of this type of material. Since the development of adequate probability statistics is time consuming, few if any crime laboratories have sufficient time to devote to statistical research necessary to improve probability theory methods. It is unwise to continue the practice of assuming probability factors, however conservative, in the development of a total probability case. Since probability or circumstantial cases cannot be avoided, it is imperative that police administrators and criminal investigators alike support research efforts which will lead to a solution to these statistical problems.

Often in a criminal investigation important decisions will revolve around the dynamics of the evidence. How did certain contaminants get on the bullet? What does the geometry of blood patterns suggest as to the number of blows struck and the direction of origin? What was the sequence of contacts between the vehicles and other objects? By working together in the initial collection and preservation of the physical evidence and collaborating in its interpretation, the criminalist and the criminal investigator may be able to demonstrate sequences and thereby enable the prosecutor to convince the court and jury not only that the case contains the necessary elements of a crime but also that the manner in which the crime was executed is important.

No magic formula exists by which the crime laboratory can re-establish the original condition of a crime scene once it has been substantially altered by the investigative team. Very often the ability to interpret the action that has taken place will depend largely on the way in which a criminal investigator has made observations and records of the location of items of evidence as found.

Criminalistics is concerned with all physical material and states of matter, from all origins. Evidence might be solid, liquid or gaseous, organic, inorganic, natural or synthetic. It is not possible, nor would it serve any useful purpose, to catalog all types of physical evidence which have been important in past criminal cases. It is the responsibility of the police administrator to guide the thinking of criminal investigators based upon his review of investigation reports. The police chief should develop the ability of his technical services to provide answers to more than the obvious questions. Criminalistics should not serve only as corroboration of the major hypothesis or known facts associated with a case, it should also provide answers to questions not readily apparent.

CRIMINALISTICS SERVICES

It is important for the ciminal investigator and the police administrator to recognize the limitations of criminalistic services as well as the value—to the ongoing criminal investigation effort. Science cannot provide a substitute for a good investigation nor can it be regarded as a panacea for all of the crime problems besetting a community.

All police agencies do not need or could not make adequate use of a crime laboratory. There is no department, regardless of size, however, that does not have to concern itself with proper preservation and collection of evidence. This is a basic and first step in the total criminalistics process. Because of the necessity for a concentrated effort, it is important that a department so organize its investigative efforts that certain personnel be specifically responsible for the collection and preservation of evidence. A department too small to justify specialization costs in both personnel and equipment should consider utilizing the services of an agency having such a staff to collect evidence.

No general formula exists by which the police administrator can determine at what point evidence collection facilities should be established. This decision can only rest on the individual administrator's good judgment. As a general rule, evidence can be important in any criminal investigation. Collection of evidence should not take place only in major crimes such as a homicide, but should occur in all types of crimes. From a technical standpoint, there is no intrinsic difference between paint collected at a homicide and this same material collected from a burglary. Therefore, where there is a high density of crime, the agency should establish a group of officers responsible for the processing of crime scenes. In moderate sized departments, this function might be the responsibility of three or four men capable of covering each shift throughout the week and especially trained and equipped for this duty. Smaller departments should call upon other police agencies for such technical assistance. Where possible, the collection and preservation of evidence should be the main concern of these technicians, and they should be the main concern of these technicians, and they should not be expected to handle other facets of a criminal investigation. Concern for collection of evidence should also be independent of the existence of local criminalistics facilities. It is always possible to transport evidence to other crime laboratories once the material has been properly collected at the local level.

Departments with technical laboratory facilities should be able to provide crime scene processing through mobile crime scene units. In order to provide laboratory service for less technical problems some large departments, such as Chicago, use evidence technicians. These technicians are widely distributed throughout the city and are trained to handle physical evidence problems in uncomplicated cases, as well as to process traffic accidents and chemical tests for intoxicants. Usually the system relies on the judgment of the criminal investigators and the evidence technicians to determine at what point support services from the crime laboratory units may be required.

The larger technical staff created by the evidence technician system ensures that more cases will receive consideration for physical evidence. For greater effectiveness, it is important that the evidence technicians have a close working relationship with the laboratory. The crime laboratory supervisor should have direct avenues of communication with evidence technicians to insure that the day-to-day operation is maintained at the highest level of quality. It would also be advisable to structure the system in such a way that the experience gained by the evidence collection unit on a day-to-day basis can be preserved in each staff member and yet permit the individual technicians to advance in the organizational structure. It would be difficult to over-emphasize the value to a criminal investigation of an individual with proven ability, dedication, and the kind of alert imagination necessary to search successfully for obscure clues to the crime and its perpetrator. To have successful technical operations requires that the crime scene technician be equally as important as the forensic chemist who evaluates and interprets the raw material submitted to the laboratory.

No matter how knowledgeable an investigator or other police officer may be, he cannot function without proper tools. This applies equally to the tools needed for collection and to those for preservation of evidence. Without an adequate supply of appropriate containers, tools, and other crime scene processing equipment, the evidence technician cannot expect to perform his responsibility adequately. The basic equipment for crime scene work does not require a large capital investment. Excluding photography, an excellent collection of evidence tools and supplies may be assembled for less than $100.

Since the identification of a criminal through his fingerprints is one of the most potent means of crime solution, a fingerprint kit will probably become the most used item in the whole armory of the crime scene technician. It is not necessary, however, that the crime scene kit contain a wide variety of exotic powders. As a rule, the technician will find a dark and light powder quite adequate for the vast majority of problems. Nor does the kit have to contain a wide array of application equipment; usually two brushes are sufficient for the two commonly used powders. Some means should be provided for the photographic recording of developed latent prints and although there are special cameras designed for this purpose, a normal crime scene camera with double extension bellows will take fine fingerprint photographs.

Occasionally a crime scene technician will find that the surface on which fingerprints may be developed is totally unsuited for development by powder. If this material can be brought into the office, it can be processed with greater certainty of successful results. If, however, this is not possible, it is conceivable that the crime scene technician can develop fingerprints at the scene using such media as iodine fumes and silver nitrate. A moderate amount of skill is required for successful work with these latter two techniques.

The crime scene technician should have facilities for making reasonably accurate measurements and sketches of the crime scene and of the position of evidence as discovered. Whether the rough sketch made at the crime scene is to be reproduced by departmental personnel as a scale drawing or whether this will be farmed out to some other skilled draftsman, will be a matter of decision by the department. Where properly made and skillfully used by the prosecutor, a crime scene scale drawing can be a very important exhibit in a criminal trial. Usually all of the tools and supplies needed for crime scene sketching can be obtained from a local stationery store.

Frequently evidence will be found in the form of a three dimensional imprint of some object such as a foot, tire, tool, finger, weapon, and so forth. While these impressions should be photographed using an appropriate scale and good photographic technique, it is advisable to preserve them for futher examination by some appropriate casting technique. Large impressions such as footprints and tire prints should be cast in high quality plaster. Neither the technique nor the equipment for this step is complicated and with a little practice, any police technician should be able to make an excellent reproduction under most conditions.

When fine detail must be recorded, plaster is not adequate for suitable impressions. Several dental reproduction substances may be used, the most popular of which is a silicone rubber product which sets up rapidly under a wide range of temperature. Silicone rubber has the further advantage over some other media in that it is easily transported and has excellent dimensional stability. As an added feature, silicone rubber may be used to lift fingerprint powder from irregular objects where tape and other flat lifting media would be totally unsuited. Although somewhat expensive, it is not prohibitively so and is not outside of the reach of even a modest departmental budget. Like plaster casting procedures, casting using silicone rubber is relatively simple and can be mastered by police personnel in a relatively short period of time. Silicone rubber may be used to preserve tool marks, anatomical peculiarities such as scars and warts, and for the preservation of wounds.

Photography is a useful and important means by which crime scenes can be recorded for later presentation in court. The technician should be able to take both black-and-white and color photographs with some form of artificial light, such as single or multiple flash, as well as close-up photographs of tool marks, fingerprints, and other subjects of fine detail. Although one seldom sees a tripod in use at a crime scene, it is difficult to visualize accurate top quality photographs of footprints, fingerprints, and the like without the aid of a good sturdy tripod. Unfortunately, in the field of photography most police administrators are rank amateurs and, therefore, are ready to accept any photograph that shows, in the most elementary way, some aspect of the crime scene. Seldom is the administrator able to look at the product of the work of his department and exercise any real judgment as to its acceptable quality. It is for this reason that one sees so many very inadequate representations of crime scenes and criminal evidence presented in the courtroom.

Some attention should be given to the development of a container kit. Brown paper bags are suitable for clothing, plastic bags are useful for preservation of dry evidence, and small objects can be preserved in leak-proof salve cans, plastic boxes and so forth. The normal mailing envelope is totally unsuited to the preservation of any finely divided material. Envelopes have leaky corners and the character of any contents will be altered or lost by transportation in such a container. Usually a little bit of thought and imagination will develop an adequate container kit using locally available materials. Some means should be provided in this kit for closing and sealing any container of evidence. Labels, scotch tape, sealing wax and so forth, might be employed in this respect. Although tags may be provided for certain objects, it should be remembered that tags can be moved and, therefore, such identification is no absolute guarantee that the evidence has not been substituted. Along with adequate containers, the kit should be provided with tools for handling a variety of evidence. Good tweezers, sharp scalpels, medicine droppers, tongue depressors, spoons and so forth, should be available and arranged so that they are conveniently accessible to the crime scene technician.

To round out the evidence preservation equipment, the unit might find use for such things as a shovel, magnet, vacuum cleaner, portable floodlights, sieves, an assortment of hand tools and so on. How much is brought to the crime scene will depend upon the distance from a source of supply and the type of transportation available. The above equipment cannot be packaged into a single container nor would this be wise since the weight would preclude easy transportation at the crime scene. Since all techniques are not necessary at each crime scene, it is advisable to separate the kits into the general categories enumerated above and to provide adequate and convenient containers for each individual kit. These can be easily formulated around an inexpensive tool or fishing tackle box.

Whatever form the crime scene kit may take is of relatively minor importance. What is important, however, is that the department recognize that this is one of the primary tools that must be accessible to the criminal investigator and to the crime scene technician. Without these aids, the police administrator cannot hope to have his staff perform its necessary evidence collection duties in a suitable fashion. It is important to recognize that what has been discussed is designed solely for the collection of evidence at the crime scene and not for on-the-spot analyses. It would be sheer fantasy to assume that the vast number of instruments available in a well equipped crime laboratory could or should be brought directly to a crime scene. Under the normal conditions that prevail, it would be virtually impossible to expect a quality of results which would be acceptable by most courts. This is not to say that certain preliminary tests might not be considered. These might be preliminary tests for blood or perhaps some preliminary tests for common narcotics; however, it should be recognized that these are just what they are, "curbstone" tests, which must be verified later in the laboratory.

OPERATION OF A CRIME LABORATORY

Several factors should be considered in the operation of a crime laboratory including a determination of the laboratory service needed, the method of organization and staff need, financial support, and administrative controls.

Before an agency embarks on the development of a crime laboratory, a careful analysis of need should be made. Obviously there must be sufficient work for one or more technicians. However serious a single case might be, it does not justify the creation of a local crime laboratory. The administrator should examine his department's investigation caseload for the past two or three years and determine how many cases are in the evidence producing categories (homicide, assault, sex offenses, burglary, hit and run narcotics, and so on). If these cases total more than 500, there may be sufficient potential for a minimum crime laboratory.

Departmental Laboratory. Some police administrators are of the opinion that a crime laboratory can be established simply through the acquisition of a microscope and a few pieces of glassware. Because of the broad scope of physical evidence analysis, such a laboratory would quickly find itself inadequate and would need to seek other help. Because of the professional risks associated with analyzing evidence already examined by another laboratory, many crime laboratories refuse to conduct a second examination. A second problem arises when a single analyst attempts to qualify in several unrelated fields. The courts may be reluctant to accept a witness in the morning as a specialist in one field and in the afternoon as a specialist in another.

Although there is a certain amount of public relations value in having a room designated as a crime laboratory or technical service department, the administrator and the criminal investigator should not be deluded into thinking that any space devoted to searching for latent fingerprints, developing photographs, and wrapping evidence constitutes a crime laboratory. However important these operations may be, they are not sufficient to warrant the title of a crime laboratory. Furthermore, a police administrator should understand that the establishment of a crime laboratory may involve an initial capital investment of $50,000 to $150,000 and that it is not unusual for a large city or state laboratory to have as much as a half million dollars invested in laboratory facilities.

At what point an administrator may venture into the crime laboratory field will depend upon the outcome of surveys in the following areas: 1. criminal activity requiring laboratory services, 2. the geographic distribution of crime laboratories in the region, and 3. the general interest in physical evidence in the criminal justice system in the area. Using as a rough bench mark the figure of 1,000 Index crimes per 100,000 people (considering that of this total approximately 500 crimes likely are amenable to physical evidence studies), the administrator may be able to visualize an adequate caseload to keep an analyst busy. Considering the amount of case work generated by 500 or more cases, the department will have to allocate funds for salaries for two analysts in order to provide court appearances and vacation periods.

Other Choices. The speed with which an investigation must be conducted may not permit the easy utilization of laboratory facilities where long distance or mail facilities must be used to transport evidence to the laboratory. Studies have demonstrated that little use is made of a crime laboratory when located more than two hours driving distance away. Where sufficient justification for a single departmental laboratory is not apparent, several police agencies may jointly establish one sharing the costs and setting priority schedules. As an alternative to the multiagency unit, consideration might be given to the establishment of satellite laboratories associated with a larger facility such as a state laboratory.

A satellite laboratory need not have all of the facilities normally comprising an independent laboratory. Through the establishment of minimal general facilities, many of the simpler problems can be resolved. More sophisticated instrumentation of a main laboratory could be used for backup when problems become too complex. From each satellite unit, crime scene collection facilities and other regionally required services could function with the highest possible efficiency. Naturally, the development of satellite laboratories will require some consideration for caseload as well as travel distance to the main unit. One advantage of a satellite system would be closer supervision over the quality of analyses conducted at the outlying laboratory by the central unit. One problem would be the transfer of evidence from one laboratory to another, particularly when some aspect of the investigation had already taken place in the satellite unit.

An analysis of crime laboratory needs in a metropolitan area may demonstrate that the problem is regional rather than local, and that needs extend across state boundaries. A regional need likely suggests the development of common service facilities which might include a crime laboratory as well as criminal identification and intelligence information. In the case of a state service facility, the financing may not be difficult but where interstate laboratories are created, special consideration must be given to the financial support and to the establishment of authority for staff to function in both states. At the present time, most laboratories serving on an interstate basis (other than federal facilities) do so out of generosity. This provides a very tenuous solution to the problem since the nonpaying recipient feels reluctant to press too hard for service and, where overload of case work exists, the laboratory's administrator may have to make unpopular decisions in favor of the parent organization.

The precedent for interstate agencies has been established in areas of transportation, flood control, water, and others. There is no reason, therefore, why similar arrangements could not be developed for establishment of crime laboratory facilities serving more than one state. Whether such an interstate agency should be closely allied with larger supporting facilities would depend upon the availability of a large laboratory within access. It would be expected, however, that through the greater caseload generated by a metropolitan area, justification for major investments would exist and that a high degree of independence could be achieved by such a regional laboratory.

Where a region is clearly confined to state boundaries, the creation of a state laboratory is a simple and natural solution to the provision of available services because the financial base would be significantly broad and legal problems easily rectified. The form which the state crime laboratory might take is not clearly established by any existing precedent. Such laboratories may be associated with the state criminal identification system or with the state police, or it may be a separate and independent entity such as that established by the State of Wisconsin.

Such an agency would need to be careful not to intrude into local prerogatives, especially in the area of criminal investigations. Since the use of state facilities is likely to be voluntary, considerable effort should be expended by the state agency to "sell services to local departments. Close lines of communications must be established in order to convince all local agencies that the state agency is prepared to render service in any problem where proper solutions can be developed through laboratory analyses. The state agency must use tact and persuasion in stressing the value of laboratory service in order to be given an opportunity to provide service.

States with large areas to be served might establish satellite units: crime scene service, polygraph service, or laboratory facilities, for example. Through careful administrative control such a system can provide high quality service.

Federal Role. Because of the interstate nature of crime and the high degree of interstate mobility of criminals, many crime laboratory problems need a national reference. In an integrated criminalistic system, consideration should be given to the involvement of federal facilities such as the Federal Bureau of Investigation laboratory, the Food and Drug Administration laboratories, the Postal Inspector's laboratories, and others.

Three important contributions can be made by the federal agencies: 1. the development of procedures and methods in analyzing problems and in testing of newly developed equipment, 2. the development of standards by which evidence can be compared or evaluated, and 3. providing laboratory services to agencies which otherwise could not obtain sophisticated services. Research output, the training of new staff, and the upgrading of present criminalists would be an invaluable contribution to the use of science in criminal investigations. It is difficult for all but the largest crime laboratories to devote any attention to new methods or to the extension of the interpretation of presently available analytical techniques. A federal research institute touching on criminalistics must not, however, be independent of the working laboratory but allied in such a way that the research staff is acutely aware of day-to-day problems besetting the criminalist.

Early in the planning of a crime laboratory, a decision must be made as to how the unit will be staffed. Excellent laboratories have been developed with either civilian or sworn personnel. In fact, both types of individuals are needed. Some police departments may find officers within the department who have had college or university training in physical or biological sciences. Through a combination of academic training and police experience, such laboratory personnel are in a position to assist a criminal investigator more fully than just a trained scientist. Any attempt to establish a laboratory without an adequate mix of strong basic training in science, as well as a clear and sympathetic understanding of the investigator's needs, is likely not to be effective.

Managing a crime laboratory is not a simple/administrative problem. The laboratory administrator must be capable of evaluating the performance of the unit, individually and as a whole, and he must actively oversee the technical operation of the unit as well. The police administrator must decide whether the crime laboratory's supervisory staff will be developed by orienting a civilian to police problems or by acquainting a police person with the broad areas of science. Where deficiencies of knowledge exist in either quarter, a police administrator must set up an active program for the development of a well-rounded crime laboratory supervisor. At no time can the laboratory function as a haven for the department's "discards," at any level of rank.

Although some laboratories have been established and still function as part of the criminal investigation unit, many departments have recognized that a laboratory is a general service function and have combined it with communications, criminal records, and other like services into a technical or auxiliary element. This combination tends to provide excellent cross-fertilization as well as to minimize duplication of equipment and staff. The director of auxiliary services, as a part of the administrator's "cabinet," is better able to keep abreast of long-range plans for the development of the department than would be possible with a separate independent unit. Separation of the crime laboratory from the investigative group recognizes the difficulty that a laboratory staff has in maintaining objective and independent judgment as part of an investigative unit. Additionally, separating the laboratory unit from the investigative unit could serve to stimulate other units of the police department to request assistance more frequently.

The crime laboratory staff should be selected with two objectives in mind. First to be considered is the type of individual who is most certain to make a sizeable contribution to the solution of criminal investigation problems, and second, the kind of individual who will best represent the laboratory results in court. An individual who cannot function in both areas may be of little use to the department. There are certain basic considerations by which an administrator can select personnel. These requirements may vary somewhat according to the local requirements; generally, however, they represent basic bench marks for successful laboratory staffing. Crime laboratory staff may be divided into two categories: 1. those involved in "opinion" areas such as the identification of document material or the identification of firearms, and 2. those involved in the scientific analysis and identity of materials submitted for examination.

Since opinion fields draw only slightly from the science areas, the staff must have a lengthy practical exposure to a particular specialty. Such training and experience can only come from long association with laboratories having specialists and a fairly heavy caseload. It is difficult and risky to attempt to develop an opinion expert entirely independent of tutelage from experienced practitioners. Academic training would, of course, not be without value; however, it should not be an overriding basis for selecting a suitable candidate. More important is the particular skill needed by the laboratory.

If a department must select an untrained candidate for an opinion specialization, arrangements should be made with a large laboratory or with an independent expert for specialized training to assist in developing qualified witnesses. This often requires a commitment of a year or more.

The sophistication of available analytical instruments will determine the type of person best suited by academic training to handle the analysis and evaluation of evidence. Proper utilization of a spectrograph, X-ray, and other such instruments will require some degree of understanding of physics, electronics, and chemistry—knowledge best obtained at the college level. Analyses involving wet chemistry will require that the individual have a strong background in analytical chemistry of soil or crystallographic problems may wish to recruit staff having background in geology with emphasis on petrography. Evidence with a biological origin such as blood and other physiological fluids, hairs, fibers and so forth would be best handled by staff which has emphasized biology and microscopic techniques in its academic training. These are decisions which the police administrator must consider in seeking qualified personnel.

Although a few universities offer coursework in criminalistics, it is unlikely that the graduates of such programs have such a level of training that they can be considered court qualified at the outset of their careers. All new staff will have to undergo a period of training and indoctrination. This should include exposure to crime scene techniques, observation experience with investigative units, visited to established crime laboratories, attendance at seminars, and a study of available research reports. A new staff member should learn a particular specialty well before turning to new ones until all of the major phases are mastered. In the development of a broad gauge criminalist, it is conceivable that some aspects of training may extend over five to ten years. For this reason, staff should be selected from candidates who are interested in developing their skills through intensive study, training, and experience. A scientist who is neither aware of nor concerned for the needs of the criminal investigator may devote time to unimportant matters while ignoring the salient parts of the criminal investigation.

Recent national studies have indicated that the total expenditure for state and local crime laboratories over the past 20 years has been less than $10 million. This is a rather small amount when compared with total police service costs for all law enforcement activities. This is particularly apparent when one considers that most of this money spent on laboratory service represents capital investments prorated over a period of years.

The major responsibility for these inadequate investments must be shared by the criminalist, who has not sought adequate funds, and the police administrator who, through neglect or lack of knowledge and understanding, has failed to support the suggestions of the crime laboratory staff for the acquisition of new facilities. A crime laboratory is not a luxury but an important aspect of the investigative process and to this end should be allocated a proportionate share of the departmental budget.

If a department has serious reservations about its ability to make a continuous financial contribution to the growth and development of the crime laboratory, perhaps it would be wiser to seek other alternatives for the analysis of evidence. As an illustration, whereas the majority of police department employees may be immobilized by strong local ties, the criminalist is a professional who is prepared to move to the area of greatest professional and personal opportunity. If a department cannot expect to keep pace with salary expectations in the criminalist field, it would be unwise to make a significant capital investment and not have qualified staff to operate it.

The foregoing statements do not suggest that a laboratory functions without a sense of fiscal responsibility. After a reasonable period of operation, the laboratory supervisor should be able to provide the police administrator with estimates of month-by-month costs for expendable supplies and an outline of future needs for the growth and development of service. Because of the broad scope of physical evidence, it is difficult for laboratory staff to anticipate all possible supplies needed to analyze every conceivable type of evidence. Sound budget procedure provides for emergency purchases as the need arises.

In order to conserve limited funds, a careful survey should be made of recurring expendables in order to purchase these in the largest convenient quantity and to take advantage of minimum costs. Where there is a large number of reappearing problems that might overtax a single instrument or work area, the laboratory supervisor might want to consider the possibility of establishing a second shift, thereby making the maximum use of capital equipment. This procedure is often followed in large laboratories handling a heavy caseload in the area of firearms identification and drug and narcotic analysis, for example.

Generally speaking, the equipment and supply needs of a crime laboratory are susceptible to careful analysis and documentation, and as a result any police administrator has a right to expect adequate justification for the needs of the criminalist. There is little excuse for the submission of budget requests unsupported by adequate data. Too often the criminalist is guilty of a lack of understanding of the department administrator's needs for supporting arguments when budget matters are considered.

A crime laboratory should be established on the principle that, in addition to handling current problems, it should have as a part of its mission the improvement of existing methods, the adaption of new instrumentation, and the development of unique and novel solutions to developing problems. This cannot be accomplished unless both the staff and the administrator clearly understand that research is necessary for sound scientific analysis.

As each new budget is formulated, consideration should be given to the allocation of sufficient funds to provide for this aspect of work. As previously mentioned, the police administrator should also take steps to insure that all laboratory staff are given proper encouragement to advance their knowledge and improve techniques. Unfortunately, the vast majority of law enforcement personnel, including too many criminalists, regard research as an area beyond the realm of possibility in a working unit. Meaningful research must be coupled with day-to-day application to become effective.

From time to time, the responsible police administrator should visit the crime laboratory to ascertain that the overall operation is satisfactory. Evidence of improper housekeeping, poor custody of evidence, and general indications of slipshod work should give rise to immediate remedial action. The daily output of the laboratory should be examined carefully to establish the degree of helpfulness to the criminal investigator. A crime laboratory that serves as nothing more than a rubber stamp of the criminal investigator's preconceived hypothesis is likely not to be functioning properly. If the laboratory reports indicate a lack of assistance in the criminal investigations, the administrator should determine whether this is the result of a weakness in the evidence submitted or the inability of the laboratory analyst to find characteristics useful in an investigation. From time to time the administrator should prepare simulated unknowns and send these through the laboratory as case evidence in order to check the work of the laboratory staff. Only through constant check and review can any operation be kept at a high level of quality.

Although it is difficult to establish the quantity of examinations which should be conducted in any given time span, through discussion with other police and laboratory administrators, the police administrator can establish some norms by which to judge the work of laboratory analysts. Not only should the work of the laboratory itself be reviewed, but also the effectiveness of the courtroom presentation should be stressed by the administrator. In order to evaluate this aspect of work, checks should be made with the prosecutor's office and through occasional visits to the courtroom when testimony is given.

Technical services do not replace good investigations; the criminalist only augments the investigator's efforts. On the other hand, the investigator can project his senses, wit, and intuition only so far. Through the astute and knowledgeable combination of good investigative and evidence evaluation, crimes that might go undetected and criminals unidentified can be successfully processed through the criminal justice system.

NOTES

(1) The application of the physical and biological sciences to the solution of crime has been called police science, criminalistics, criminology, or forensic sciences depending upon the region or era in which the topic is discussed. For the purpose of this chapter, the technology utilized in criminal investigation will be called criminalistics.

(2) This includes suitable chemicals and glassware, supported by a moderate amount of laboratory instruments such as polarizing microscopes, infrared spectometers and some form of chromatographic separation equipment. Additionally, the laboratory should have proper reference standards, both in the form of suitable literature as well as control standards.

THE ADMINISTRATION OF A

FORENSIC SCIENCE LABORATORY

Robert F. Borkenstein

Today's enlightened and informed investigator hardly considers the forensic science laboratory a luxury. The value of the development and interpretation of obscure evidence as the most important source of objective proof has become progressively more accepted. The subjective and capricious nature of testimony of eye-witnesses is well known to psychologists theoretically and to police officers and prosecuting attorneys practically. Legally admissible confessions are becoming more and more difficult to obtain because of limitations imposed on interrogators. These restrictions have caused the laboratory to become an integral part of almost every major case. Physical evidence with either obvious or latent information competently interpreted promises to become the principal product of investigation. There is no indication that without a concerted diplomatic, educational programme this will be a spontaneous changeover.

The function of the forensic science laboratory is to extend and supplement the fact-finding ability of investigative organizations. In countries where courtroom procedure is adversary in nature, forensic science laboratories tend to be appended to police agencies. In those countries where the adversary system is not prevalent, they are more likely to be independent of either prosecution or defence and to serve through some other administrative channel.

Law enforcement, including the investigation of crimes, was a simple function of government in the nineteenth century. In a day of snail-like transportation and surface-letter communication and of low-density urban population, there was hardly a need for complex special services.

The forensic science laboratory is one of the service organizations, relatively new in the governmental complex, that emerged as the product of intensified urbanization and the increased crime rate associated with it. It is one of the tools that has found its place among the most important special services of an efficient investigative agency, either as a part of it or available to it. Nevertheless, it has problems in common with other recently created governmental agencies.

The city manager of a middle-size, average American city recently mentioned that during the last 100 years functions of city government have increased from fourteen to well over 200. Each of these functions is struggling for its share of tax money. The public service forensic science laboratory is no exception, and it has a particularly heavy budgetary problem in that academic qualifications for professional laboratory personnel necessarily imply high salaries. Scientific apparatus is expensive, especially the newer probative tools required for modern examination of trace materials. In a field that is constantly advancing the threshold of recognition, the solution to a problem is often presented by the laboratory to the investigator before he appreciates its need. Budgeting for an expensive analytical device that offers possibilities not yet generally recognized or anticipated places a heavy burden on laboratory administration.

ADMINISTRATION OF THE FORENSIC SCIENCE LABORATORY

Operation of a forensic science laboratory involves five levels of personnel. First is the administrator, the head of the agency within which the laboratory is positioned. Next comes the executive director of the laboratory. For lack of a better term, the professional, scientifically trained laboratory workers will be called examiners. Serving the examiners are technicians. Service employees comprise secretaries, stenographers, shop men and maintenance persons.

The administrators of organizations in which such laboratories are located must co-ordinate the efforts of the laboratories in their charge with others concerned with the administration of justice. The administrator may be the head of a police department, an attorney general, a minister of the interior, a minister of justice, a minister of health, or the Home Office Secretary. Usually within these organisations a subordinate is given responsibility for a group of related activities in which the forensic science laboratory falls. Within a police agency this may fall under the direction of the officer-in-charge of special services or the administrator of the investigative section. In the case of the minister of justice or the attorney general, this administrative responsibility may be delegated to an assistant. Within the ministry of the interior or the Home Office, this position is that of an Undersecretary. Nevertheless, wherever it falls, the responsibility is administrative in nature, and decision-making may be implemented by consultants and advisors—for example, the 'forensic science advisor' to an Undersecretary of the British Home Office.

INFLUENCE OF GOVERNMENT ON LABORATORY ADMINISTRATION

The position of the forensic science laboratory in the political structure influences the type of administration. When attached intimately to a police organisation, the quasi-military form often extends into the laboratory. Administration in such cases is fixed by departmental rules and regulations. When the forensic science laboratory is relatively free of a police agency, its management and operation are more flexible and they are knit into the governmental fabric through various channels. These include ministries of the interior (Germany, Austria or Great Britain, where the Home Office is a counterpart), departments of justice (France and Holland), departments of health (Paris) and attorneys general (Ontario, Canada). Another location of forensic science laboratories is within universities with support by some governmental agency (Australia).

The need for a complex of special services to support law enforcement in small or limited jurisdictions scatters available funds, resulting in mediocrity because of the small sums of money available for each special service. Because of the extremely heterogeneous nature of communities, there is no single solution to this problem. New York City has a police force of about 25,000 men, but many towns requiring equally effective policing have forces of 25 or less. The services of a forensic science laboratory are equally important to all these communities, and each citizen has the right to the same protection.

In the United States there are about 50 departments with police forces numbering in excess of 500 officers, and approximately 850 departments range from 25 to 500. The larger departments are reasonably self-contained. A force of 500 men or more can well support a special service function such as a forensic science laboratory. The only solution for smaller departments is a pooling of resources to create a forensic science laboratory that will serve a sufficient number of departments to make its existence feasible.

However, a large national or state police laboratory does not necessarily mean that this problem is automatically solved, because of a geographical remoteness factor. Intimate availability of the services of the forensic scientist during an investigation can often contribute substantially to a successful solution. Unless there are some alleviating factors such as a mobile crime laboratory, regional laboratory or air transportation, this intimacy may be lost. Easy accessibility makes possible the use of the laboratory by the investigator as a part of the fact-finding investigation as well as a means of submitting a more effective case in court.

THE NEW ADMINISTRATOR

Half a century ago Frederick W. Taylor wrote 'Let me say that we are now but on the threshold of the coming era of direct cooperation. The time is fast going by for great personal or individual achievement by any one man who stands alone without having made use of the help of those around him. The time is coming when all great things will be done by the cooperation of many men, each man performing that function for which he is best suited and each man preserving his own individuality. He will be supreme in his particular function and suffer no loss of his originality and proper personal initiative, and yet he will be controlled by and will have to work harmoniously with other men.'

During the years that have followed, this prophecy has been fulfilled in industry. The small shops of the nineteenth century have been replaced by medium-size, large and giant industries. Mass production has inspired great specialization. Minimum operating overhead has increased enormously because of tax and insurance problems. This has tended to encourage larger organizations and to promote more efficient and effective tools of management.

The tendency towards bigness has not been restricted to industry. Since the advent of the present century, functions of government have increased astronomically. Previously unheard-of public services have become indispensable. As governments have increased in size, complexity and scope of public responsibility, economy of operation has demanded more efficient processes of administration. Theories of management have passed through many phases, ranging from rule of an organization by managers with nothing more than operational skill in the processes of the organization to the pure public administrator who has little if any operational skill.

Oscillation between these two extremes has gradually evolved the concept that a modern public administrator is one skilled in policy formation, decision-making, innovation, research and organizational administration. His operational understanding comes through technical consultants, either internal or external. Organizational administration includes delegating responsibility for execution of a specialized service to a director of that particular service and co-ordinating the work of related agencies. The interdependence achieved by the administrator between these related activities is a measure of his success.

When the related activities are all under the jurisdiction of an administrator, this is relatively simple. However, separation of the elements involved in the administration of justice is one of the safeguards against tyranny. For this reason, achieving co-ordination of police agencies, forensic science laboratories, prosecutors and others becomes a complex task achieved only through patience and understanding.

CENTRALIZATION—GOOD OR BAD?

The great dilemma in the application of the forensic sciences to the administration of justice and law enforcement is: to centralize or not to centralize. Centralization tends to promote scientific specialization, perfection of equipment and efficiency in operation. However, there are many very real and practical pressures in the opposite direction. The centralized laboratory must necessarily serve a number of agencies. It has a tendency to be somewhat independent. This often offends local pride, and is not compatible with the jealousies that may exist between departments that are served in common by the same laboratory. Law-enforcement agencies so served may not have control over relations between the mass media and the laboratory. This creates the possibility of interference with the investigation by capricious press releases that would have a negative effect on the investigation or that would usurp credit for the laboratory. A centralized laboratory, remotely located, is not easily accessible to large geographical areas and will not be used to the extent it should be during the process of an investigation.

In many cases the centralized forensic science laboratory charges fees for examinations and cost of transportation, and also fees for appearances in court. This is particularly true when the services are performed for outside agencies. While this does not necessarily preclude the use of forensic sciences, it certainly is a limiting factor. It means that they become last resorts in investigation rather than integral parts of the thinking of the investigator.

Decentralization also involves extensive participation of the forensic science laboratory staff in training investigators in the application of the forensic sciences to fact-finding and in the anticipation, recognition and collection of evidence suitable for laboratory examination. This often makes unnecessary the presence of a laboratory representative at the scene of a crime. Thus every investigator becomes an on-the-spot representative of the forensic science laboratory. The burning question is: at what point should the investigator decide that the problem should be assumed by the examiner?

The principle of decentralized law enforcement is jealously nurtured in some countries. The price that must be paid for retaining this principle is duplication of administration and special services, among which is included the forensic science laboratory. Before specialized modernizations were added, decentralization offered no serious problems. Today, however, regardless of size, every police department must have an administrator, a staff of officers, a records system, identification files, specialized units, motor pool, communications officer, and possibly some type of laboratory.

Decentralization of laboratory services necessarily limits size and therefore specialization. A one- or two-man laboratory can hardly afford a specialized manager. Obviously, management of such a laboratory will differ considerably from one employing possibly hundreds of examiners.

The scope and size of the laboratory and its personnel are further influenced by the number of investigators to be served and by the diversity of their specialized functions. Forensic science laboratories attached to limited-service agencies such as the United States Secret Service tend to limit their functions to satisfy their specialized type of investigations.

THE LABORATORY DIRECTOR

The actual execution of the forensic science laboratory programme is the responsibility of a laboratory director or his equivalent. It is his duty to see that administrative policies and decisions are adhered to and that an effective, scientifically competent programme is carried out. He becomes the liaison between governmental administration and operational performance. He is charged with organizing, planning, staffing, executing and appraising. In a service organization, in addition to being responsible for his own programme, he is charged with supporting others in the execution of theirs.

There seems to be some difference of opinion among forensic scientists as to who should assume the direction of forensic science laboratories. This is only natural, since the forensic sciences do not comprise an integrated discipline but rather span physical, biological and medical sciences and, in the medico-legal sense, law. The name of the journal of the British Academy of Forensic Sciences, *Medicine, Science and the Law*, is an indication of the marriage of these disciplines.

The laboratory manager or director must have a combination of executive ability and philosophical understanding of science. While he may practise a scientific specialty on the examiner level and become highly proficient because of specialized training, it is most important that he relinquish this specialty during the time he acts in a managerial capacity. Only too often, forensic science laboratories tend to be biased in the direction of the specialty of their directors. Such interference with balance can seriously lessen the effectiveness with which the laboratory can serve the practical field.

Prowess in administrative techniques, particularly communication, is very important to laboratory leadership. Effective techniques based on scientific principles for the development of latent possibilities in evidence are useless unless their existence is effectively communicated to prospective users.

The very reason for the existence of the forensic science laboratory is the service it can offer through interrelationship with its associated organizations. These comprise police departments, offices of prosecution and courts. Interdependence is only positive when the related organizations achieve some increase in successful operation as a result of use of the services of the forensic science laboratory.

The laboratory director must make constant use of feed-back to measure how effectively his organization is contributing. It is his duty to return information to directors of the associated organizations to help them assess how effectively their personnel have used services offered by the forensic science laboratories. For instance, in a typical police organization with a comprehensive internal laboratory system, a survey by the laboratory director of the utilization of his laboratory's services over a one-year period revealed that 75% of the laboratory's services were performed for 25% of the personnel performing tasks that should regularly call for this type of aid. This was done without the knowledge of the supervisors of the investigators.

Making use of this information, a further study revealed that the 75% who had not submitted evidence were, in general, deficient in many other aspects of their police service. In some instances failure to submit evidence correlated with unsatisfactory experience with the laboratory in the past.

This information was fed back to the supervisors of the investigative units, resulting in more careful attention by the supervisors to reports submitted by the negligent investigators. A survey the next year showed a decided improvement in distribution of submission of evidence. It also resulted in a reappraisal of his personnel by the laboratory director.

WHAT IS MANAGEMENT?

Management of an organization is the means of assigning responsibilities among the various segments of an enterprise, placing each activity in proper relationship with every other activity. It is concerned with bilateral communication, in which information passes in two directions: from superior to subordinate, or vice versa, and back again in a continuous cycle. In public service it is concerned with the effective relationship between an organization and its superior agency in the government.

Management is also charged with seeing that the services of its organization are understood, accepted and used effectively by the related organizations that are the acceptors and beneficiaries of the service. Internally, the management of a forensic science laboratory must deal with ethics, internal control, personnel selection, training, promotion practices, time allocation, administrative communications, research and budget preparation.

The systematic examination of evidence to expose and interpret latent and obscure possibilities requires sensitive and meticulous planning. The more esoteric these examinations and the larger their scope, the more important careful planning must become if lost motion and expended time are to be kept at a minimum. Planning and control must be effective not only for useful results but also for efficient utilization of resources, facilities and personnel.

Management must recognize the talents of personnel, then make use of this knowledge by specific assignment of specialists to tasks in which they can make greatest contribution to the total effort. This requires separation of functions and allocation of work according to training, experience. degree of skill and demonstrated performance. This is group action and planned action.

This group and planned action is not restricted to internal planning and control. Neither is a 'group' restricted to individual workers as components; it may also be a group of organizations. This is the case in the relationship of the forensic science laboratory to the rest of the groups in the constellation of activities in the administration of justice. Group action can also involve the discrete functions within the laboratory in relationship to the scientific fields within which they work. The dynamics of such relationships produce conferences. Training conferences which bring together many of the related fields involved in law enforcement, including forensic sciences, are well established. The various 'academies of forensic science' with their sub-divisions bring scientific specialists together to discuss and exchange ideas.

The planning of the service of a forensic science laboratory involves identifiable elements. First, the objective must be defined as clearly and as explicitly as possible.

Secondly, once the objectives become sufficiently desirable to accomplish, a review of available resources must be made. This may mean studying the usefulness of already available facilities to which cases may be referred and also the availability of funds to establish new ones.

Quick and effective accomplishment of the objectives depends upon thorough knowledge of the required resources. In the case of a forensic science laboratory, this certainly is not restricted to physical facilities and equipment but must include man-power resources. Collaborative resources must also be included. These involve university and industrial facilities that may temporarily or permanently preclude the need for purchasing expensive and sophisticated instrumentation and hiring of their accompanying personnel.

On the one hand, physical plant, equipment, supplies and personnel requirements in most governmental functions are highly predictable. On the other hand, the very nature of the forensic science laboratory suggests unpredictability, because of the extremely diverse nature of evidence presented to it. Investigations within the forensic laboratory very often make necessary the improvising of both techniques and equipment. The pace at which instrumental techniques are being adapted to forensic sciences makes space requirements difficult to project. Thus planning must remain flexible if the laboratory is to be progressive. When a new laboratory is to be built, the use of an architect who specializes in this field can prevent oversight and can help provide necessary flexibility.

The third step is the formalization of the plan of how use will be made of the resources available in order to achieve the objectives set out in the first step. This is work planning and includes two elements. 1. The forensic science laboratory manager must break down over-all objectives into functional programmes. Each programme must be subdivided according to projects. Each project must be analysed as to the operations involved, and each operation must be studied to determine the specific steps required. 2. The forensic science laboratory manager, from past experience, from a survey of the field to be served and from consultation with advisors, must reasonably estimate the time that will be required for each of these steps, operations, projects and programmes so that the schedule of work will effectively use personnel and other resources and help form a solid basis for recruitment of personnel, procurement of materials and appropriation of funds.

In each case the excellence of the examination must be preserved whether a confession has been obtained, a plea of guilty is anticipated, or a court trial is a virtual certainty. The purpose of the forensic science laboratory is not conviction but exposition of the facts. Although quality is not a matter for administrative decision, quantity of work can be determined by administrative and executive action.

Administra.ive decision can define geographical areas and types of organizations to be serviced and also the type and seriousness of the offences from which laboratory evidence will be accepted. The laboratory director or his agent can screen out cases in which the exhibits have been so poorly collected and presented that they could not possibly provide useful results.

Recommendation for the purchase of equipment, apparatus and instruments to implement the work of an examiner's specialty usually originates with the examiner. This may be the result of original research, information from the literature, or professional meetings. Whether this request is to be fulfilled is subject to decision by the director with eventual approval by the administrator. This decision must be based on apparent answers to such questions as: Will the purchase enable the examiner to increase his service to the field significantly? Will the projected frequency of use justify the expenditure? Can the same work be done by other means, possibly a bit less efficiently regarding time but still within satisfactory limits? Is such equipment or instrumentation otherwise available for those infrequent cases in which it is necessary?

Centralization of expensive and infrequently used instruments can be compared with electronic data-processing equipment in computing centres. These facilities frequently are used by many organizations pooling their interests. Each prepares its data for presentation to the computers and makes use of the processed data. The internal operation of the equipment is so formalized that this is standard for everyone using the machines. Advanced instrumental techniques involve apparatus so expensive that it would be hardly justifiable for every laboratory to have such equipment. Industrial and commercial laboratories often have such facilities available. Co-operation with universities conveniently located is usually easy to obtain.

The preparation of evidence to be presented to the instrument and the interpretation of the results of the instrumental analysis comprise the real skill and knowledge in the operation of the instrument itself. Thus, the decision to purchase an expensive piece of instrumentation must involve the weighing of such considerations. However, should frequency be great enough, qualified operating personnel available and the end-results sufficiently significant, the decision to purchase should be forthcoming.

Two factors influence the tendency towards specialization of overspecialization. One is the frequency with which a given type of evidence is submitted. Sheer volume compels specialization and increase of staff in depth. The other factor is the inherent tendency of the examiner to intensify his interests in a specific vein. The first is desirable only to a point. Intensive specialization can only be afforded when the volume of work justifies it or will tend to justify it. When a given type of evidence is submitted only infrequently, it is possible for the laboratory manager to classify a group of such specialties into an area with very common factors and consider this degree of specialization economically feasible at the moment.

This does not mean that the forensic science laboratory should simply equip itself to cope with the work load that is spontaneously submitted to it. A constant survey of the scientific literature in forensic and allied sciences should suggest techniques that will be of great help to the agency served by the laboratory. If it is the decision of the laboratory administrator that a certain type of service should be offered, the technique may be adopted, staffed, validated and offered to the investigators through in-service communication.

This service can be temporarily attached to a specialty requiring similar qualifications in personnel.

There is always the possibility that evidence material which spans diverse specialties will be presented. This problem can be solved easily by the temporary setting up of 'project groups' of the examiners concerned.

Administrative control must counter the tendency to overspecialization. This does not mean that specialization in itself is undesirable. However, overspecialization implies that the intensity of interest is not compatible with the current or projected work load.

To many people the word 'control' has had an unpleasant, restrictive connotation. Management is a flexible art intended to create a productive environment using controls for the benefit of both organization and employees. Managerial control within an organization is its government. Without government there is anarchy and chaos.

Many scientifically trained people with imaginative and adaptive minds feel that control by management is stifling to their activity. This calls for a clarification of managerial control. If it means time-clocks and measuring effectiveness by number of cases, it is not correct. If it means constant evaluation and measurement of results to see if they match standards, then it is correct. The competent examiner should welcome monitoring by means of internal controls.

Even with the most careful personnel selection based on factors including education, training, experience, character, and apparent day-by-day competence, operational validation of performance is important. An examiner after years of working in the field tends to evolve a 'reputation'. This entity is elusive and ethereal, often based on personality rather than on scientific competence. Letters of commendation indicating popularity in the field lull the supervisor into a false sense of security. This suggests a need for internal controls—the submitting of control cases to the examiner, with or without his knowledge, to validate his technical precision and accuracy of interpretation. This type of control affords the administrator objective knowledge of the efficiency of his organization.

The laboratory director must recognize two types of control over his staff, one which he can use freely and the other which he must delegate to the science of the individual examiner. The statement, 'My only master is my science', should be respected in highly trained employees. This does not preclude the imposing of certain organizational rules, regulations and controls on the examiner, as long as they do not intrude on the examiner's scientific prerogative. This high respect for scientific freedom in the execution of specialized examinations does not necessarily extend to the technician level, which must be under the rigorous control of the examiner for whom the technician does routine, standardized work.

THE ESTABLISHMENT OF STANDARDS

The task of the laboratory manager is to provide an efficient service of high quality. The terms 'efficiency' and 'quality' are not absolutes, and therefore are subject to standards. It is the principal task of the manager to set these standards. The purpose of staffing, equipping and organizing the working body that comprises the forensic science laboratory is to achieve efficiency and service measuring up to the standards. Whatever action the manager takes to adjust all operations to the set standards is justifiable control.

Evaluation of the conformity of operation with the set standards requires feed-back to the manager of the quality of day-to-day operations. Unless this feed-back is available, the manager must blindly accept the competence of operations. This feed-back should never return via the administrative channel through which it passed from the manager; rather should it return directly from the actual work level to him. In industry this is quality control and inspection. In the forensic science laboratory it can take the form of submitting 'unknowns' to the examiners to test effectiveness.

The establishing of standards for the forensic science laboratory is very difficult. Reliability of a given procedure is often dependent on the quality of the evidence submitted. Various techniques have differing degrees of specificity. Thus some techniques do not readily lend themselves to the establishment of standards. These methods, in general, are relegated to the class of tests that might be termed 'investigative aids' not intended for courtroom use. On the other hand, high standards can be set for such methods as firearms identification; examination of poisons, narcotics analyses, etc.; analysis of blood for alcohol; and many others. The laboratory director has the right to expect standard results from every examination, provided the evidence is originally acceptable. For instance, no tolerance can be allowed in opinions involving bullet comparisons in firearms identification. These rarely involve degree but are 'do compare' or 'do not compare' opinions.

In techniques resulting in quantitative figures such as blood alcohol or toxicological analyses, numerical tolerances can be stated. Only by constant feed-back can the manager be certain that these standards are being maintained. Although the examiner may have high integrity and great personal skill, this is no assurance that the technicians working under him will maintain the degree of excellence prescribed by the stated standards.

A second circuit of communication originating with the director involves aiming and planning. This is measuring the adequacy of the service of the laboratory vis-à-vis the investigation field. The manager, by receiving feed-back information from the field being served, must constantly take a critical look at the operational standards to determine their adequacy. Adequacy of standards is not a matter for administrative decision. Standards are actually set by the demands of the courts and the capacity of the forensic science service to meet them. Adequacy of a technique as used by an examiner is determined by its ability to withstand successfully the ordeal of examination and cross-examination.

A technique of post-mortem blood alcohol determination might well conform with the standards set up by the laboratory manager but at the same time be insufficiently specific for ethyl alcohol to satisfy a court. Thus the laboratory standards are not sufficiently high to accomplish the end that is sought and an adjustment of the standards is in order. A laboratory manager who constantly is receiving feed-back informing him of operational efficiency in achieving his standards and who is also regularly receiving information as to the effectiveness of his service in case-solving can exercise corrective control, knowing that his actions are based on operational facts.

This type of control is certainly not oppressive. When the purpose is to adjust operations to predetermined standards, its spirit is clear to every person who is subjected to it. It makes possible the evaluation of employees for promotion purposes. In institutions whose product is not a tangible, standard, repeatable commodity but rather an intangible, original, unique knowledge and service, it is probably the only means of such evaluation. It becomes a means of the manager's safeguarding his own accountability and at the same time transferring authority and responsibility to the examiner, freeing him to use his knowledge and skill to their greatest extent. Thus freedom of operation for the individual examiner is achieved and at the same time management has complete control of the situation. Mandated instructions can thus be kept at a minimum and discretion on the part of the examiner can be maximized.

THE EXAMINER

Since forensic evidence is so highly varied and improvisation is one of the great tools of the forensic examiner, it is most important that he have a high degree of freedom to exercise discretion. This is evaluated by feed-back to the laboratory manager.

The academic and practical qualifications of the examiner, his courtroom demeanour and the relevance of the evidence, all affect the weight placed on his opinion. This weight is the measure of the adequacy of the laboratory service. The examiner must be able to qualify to the satisfaction of the court; he must have made a thorough examination; he must know his general field; and he must properly impress the court and jury as to the validity of his findings. Technical skill is important to the forensic science examiner but is always secondary to his interpretive faculty. The formation of opinion is dependent on long association with his specialized field. Educational background and experience for opinion-forming in one area does not readily transfer to other specialties. There can be some transfer of experience from bullet comparison to tool-marks because these are similar areas that could fall into one category, but opinion-forming should not extend beyond the boundaries of a discipline.

The examiner in the forensic science laboratory is an individual who has been trained academically in some scientific discipline; who has applied his discipline to some forensic problem; who has learned to form critical opinions regarding his examinations; who is skilled in communicating the results of his examinations by report to investigators and by testimony to courts; and who over the years has developed an image of integrity and ability through properly defending these opinions. This complex of qualifications is difficult to develop. Anyone having achieved them successfully should enjoy high status and adequate remuneration. The forensic science laboratory in a police organization is faced with justifying examiners' salaries which, because of the high level of formal education and technical competence required, are often higher than those of some top-ranking police officials. In laboratories administered through other than police channels the same problem arises when comparing examiners' salaries with those of high-ranking subordinates in the controlling agency. Moreover, forensic science laboratories are in direct competition with research organizations and private industry for technically excellent employees.

Unless creativity of the examiner is expressed through research, the forensic science laboratory will remain static. Evidence not infrequently requires improvising apparatus and methods. From these needs emerge new techniques and tools that expand the service repertoire of the laboratory. When such innovations and breakthroughs occur, it is the responsibility of the examiner to share this information with his field through publications and professional meetings. Time should be allocated for such research and writing activity.

The administrative responsibility of the examiner should be kept at an absolute minimum to free him to use the maximum of his time in the perfection of his *expertise*. Does not the delegation of his work to technicians defeat this very purpose?

TECHNICIANS

Technicians perform completely standardized 'cookbook' procedures under the complete supervision of the examiner. Technicians should never have responsibility for interpretation. Here arises a question: Under criminal law the accused has the right to be faced by his accuser. In a sense the examiner constitutes an accuser. His testimony in this light must be based on what he knows personally, never on hearsay, except when citing scientific literature. Can an examiner conscientiously rely on the work of technicians under his supervision in this type of situation?

LEVEL OF SUPPORT

Budget requests are traditionally made by the laboratory director to the administrator. The evidence supporting this budget should be a description and thorough record of laboratory accomplishments as reported by the director. Whether the recommendations and conclusions contained in the report are valid or not can be determined by the administrator. This can be accomplished by setting up his own independent feed-back from the agencies served by the forensic science laboratory. This will confirm the level of support necessary.

A smoothly functioning forensic science laboratory that is making substantial contributions to the success of those using its facilities will find its services in demand in a progressively higher percentages of cases. At the present time this is only about 1%—ranging from 90% in homicides to 0.25% in thefts—according to one study. The potential is obvious.

Where will this spontaneous growth stop? This is unpredictable and matters little. There must be a constant appraisal of the need for expansion of the forensic science laboratory. This must come through good management and administrative communications—those tools that alone can insure adequate service and the eliciting of the support commensurate with the fulfilment of the forensic science laboratory's role in the administration of justice.

BIBLIOGRAPHY

Anderson, Richard C., 'Today's Thinking on Tomorrow's Managing', *Business Horizons* (Indiana University School of Business, Bloomington, Indiana) (1958).

Borkenstein, R.F., 'The Principle of Decentralization in Law Enforcement', *Mayor and Manager* (Thomas Publishing Co., Springfield, Illinois) (October, 1962).

Caldwell, Lynton K., *Research Methods in Public Administration, An Outline of Topics and Readings*, Graduate Program in Public Administration, Albany, New York (undated).

National Physical Laboratory, Teddington, England, 'The Direction of Research Establishments', (Proceedings of a Symposium), London, H.M. Stationery Office, 1957.

Redfield, Charles E., *Communications in Management*, 2nd Ed., University of Chicago Press, 1958.

Smith, H. Ward, 'A Survey of Forensic Science Laboratories—Quo Vadimus', Laboratory of the Attorney General of Ontario, Toronto, 1962.

Smith, Karl U., *Work Theory and Economic Behavior*, Indiana University Foundation for Economic and Business Studies, Bloomington, Indiana, 1962.

Steelman, John R., 'Administration for Research', Vol. 3 of *Science and Public Policy, A Report to the President*, The President's Scientific Research Board, Washington, D.C. Government Printing Office, 1947.

SYSTEMS ANALYSTS LOOK AT THE CRIME LABORATORY

W.R. Benson
J.E. Stacy, Jr.
J.D. Nicol

Systems analysis has emerged as a scientific discipline only in recent times; nonetheless, the study of systems is by no means a new pursuit of the human mind. The development of a set of standards and procedures or a concept of society or even a theory of the universe is as old as history itself. Man has always sought to find relationships that could provide satisfactory explanations for what he sees, hears, or imagines. Indeed, the history of both the physical and social sciences has been a continuing enlargement upon this theme. The scientific method of inquiry, which demands relevant and dependable relationships for its results, is systems analysis in its broadest sense.

The application of systems analysis to the role of the crime laboratory in the entire law enforcement and criminal justice scheme requires a different approach than has heretofore been taken. The scientific crime laboratory has been a part of the criminal justice system for the greater part of this century, and the degree of the exchange of technical information between the practitioners of forensic science is significant. Despite this maturity in the practice of forensic science, a year-long study of crime laboratory operations which we undertook, coupled with an extensive literature search and conferences with outstanding men in the field, revealed a paucity of management information concerning what crime laboratories do or, more properly, what crime laboratories should do(1).

There are few or in some cases no data on which to base an evaluation of the performance of a crime laboratory. The answer to the questions What is the crime laboratory's contribution to law enforcement? and Has it had any affect on the crime index? must remain speculative and subjective for the present. The contribution crime laboratories have made toward protecting the innocent, apprehending the accused, and convicting the guilty in specific cases has been significant; these notable accomplishments alone justify their existence. Yet, the involvement of the crime laboratory with the total body of crime has been so minuscule as to preclude any judgment of the impact of criminalistics on the criminal justice system.

If nothing else, the study revealed and documented the fact that a network of crime laboratories does not exist. While many criminalists exchange technical information concerning laboratory procedures, either through professional societies or by personal contact, the relationship of each laboratory to the jurisdiction it serves is unique, that is, a common basis for the exchange of management-type information does not exist. Some crime laboratories operating in a favorable environment of strong support by law enforcement agencies and ready acceptance of expert testimony by the judiciary have elevated their laboratories to a place of prominence and importance within that particular segment of the law enforcement system. Others have changed little since their inception decades ago, perhaps owing to a lack of recognition of their capability or a lack of support on the part of the jurisdiction served or perhaps because the criminalist employed there has concentrated on perfecting laboratory techniques rather than promoting the application of his available skills.

If a single finding could be said to have pervaded the study, it is the anomaly that for each hypothesis or concept proposed one could find both support and contradiction from the meager data available. It is this lack of data, collected and compiled on a uniform basis, which has established substantial barriers to a systematic analysis of crime laboratory operations. Wide variations in examiner caseload, distribution of type cases reaching the laboratory, laboratory services offered, cases per sworn officer served, and expert witness testimony lead one to the conclusion that despite complaints of overwork and lack of equipment a vast potential exists in the crime laboratories currently in existence to provide significantly increased aid to law enforcement.

The study was funded by the U.S. Department of Justice, Law Enforcement Assistance Administration, National Institute of Law Enforcement and Criminal Justice, under Grant NI-044. (The fact that the National Institute of Law Enforcement and Criminal Justice furnished financial support for the activity described in this publication does not necessarily indicate the concurrence of the Institute in the statements or conclusions contained herein.) Emphasis was placed on quantifying the knowledge of present experts in criminalistics to allow a structured approach that would both enhance and multiply this expertise to the benefit of all areas of the country. The paper describes the results and significant findings of an analysis of crime laboratory operations by a multidisciplinary team consisting of systems analysts, mathematicians, and research scientists, tempered by the advice and counsel of practicing criminalists. It is not our intent to comment on the scientific techniques used in the various the available budget the community is willing to spend for police services. While there are differences in organizations of police departments (sworn officers/civilian ratios, use of evidence technicians, etc.), we considered that the number of sworn officers available has more significance as a gross planning factor than possible differences in organizational structure.

It should be noted at this point, however, that the reason for using the CPO concept is to provide a basis for crime laboratory planning. It should not be construed as being a measure of the effectiveness of a crime laboratory or, for that matter, of the whole criminalistics operation, which would include not only the crime laboratory but also the law enforcement departments served and the prosecutors and courts making use of its expert testimony. The concept of a relationship between laboratory caseload and the number of sworn officers in the jurisdiction which the laboratory serves evolved after extensive review of the literature, analysis of crime laboratory records, and interaction with the criminalist working group.

Table 1 gives the number of laboratory cases per officer for several American cities determined from caseload data reported in the John Jay Study for laboratories in these cities(2). Figure 1 shows a distribution of type cases

TABLE 1—*Laboratory cases per officer, selected cities.*[a]

City	Sworn Police Officers	Cases to Laboratory	CPO
1. New Orleans[b]	1 460	3 516	2.4
2. Oakland	651	3 976	6.1
3. Dayton	427	2 314	5.4
4. San Francisco	1 745	6 372	3.6
5. Fort Worth	580	1 877	3.2
6. Chicago	12 000	34 400	2.86
7. Houston	1 577	4 414	2.8
8. Columbus	807	2 067	2.56
9. Cleveland	2 161	5 006	2.3
10. Kansas City	970	1 458	1.5
11. Buffalo[b]	1 400	1 600	1.1
12. St. Louis[b]	2 170	4 500	2.1
13. Newark	1 379	1 300	0.95
14. Philadelphia	7 319	5 223	0.71
15. New York	29 900	20 978	0.7

[a] Source: Ref *25*, except as updated in this study.
[b] Updated.

involving referrals to the laboratory for selected cities. These cities were selected because of the availability of caseload data and the variations in size and caseload distribution represented. The proportion of drug cases referred to the laboratory varies from 16 to 92 percent, with the average being 54 percent. Drugs have been singled out of the total caseload primarily because of the faster turnaround time normally associated with this type of case. Even though the chemical complexity of certain of the synthetic drugs has increased in recent years, with the result that more extensive laboratory procedures are now employed to analyze and identify drug samples, by and large the crime

crime laboratories or developed by individual criminalists but, instead, to view the crime laboratory in the context of functional organizations which operate in and serve our society.

THE BUSINESS OF THE CRIME LABORATORY

In one sense, the crime laboratory can be considered and compared with a business operation which has three basic operating elements: production, distribution, and marketing. The crime laboratory's production capacity is more analogous to that of a business which provides services rather than one manufacturing a specific product. If the business is to prosper, it must advertise or market the availability of its services, it must have a location that is convenient to its users (or provide a pickup and delivery service), and it must do quality work on a timely basis if it is to enjoy the confidence and repeat business of its customers.

Nonetheless, one would hardly expect a business intended to serve the entire needs of a state to flourish, even with the most elegant plant and modern scientific equipment, if it were remote from the population centers of that state. Yet many state crime laboratories are located in their states' capitols, far from the population centers of those states. The question of the location of a crime laboratory will be examined in some detail below.

USE OF THE CRIME LABORATORY BY LAW ENFORCEMENT OFFICERS

Any analysis of the criminalistic system would be incomplete without due consideration of the use that law enforcement officers make of the crime laboratory. The crime laboratory is not autonomous—it is a tool organised to serve the law enforcement officer. The number of cases that actually reach the laboratory should be in direct proportion to the number of patrolmen and special investigators available for crime scene search and related investigations. Thus, an essential element of any criminalistic system must be the collectors of physical evidence who make requests to the crime laboratory and use its services. The crime lab should be considered a part of the technical support that is available to all sworn police officers.

Since the organization of individual law enforcement departments varies considerably among cities, counties, and states, accurate comparisons of the number of officers actually in contact with the solution of crime would be difficult if not impossible. Still, all sworn officers are empowered to arrest and have the potential to submit evidence to the crime laboratory; thus, gross comparisons of crime laboratory use may be made by measuring the number of cases submitted to the laboratory expressed as annual cases per officer (CPO concept) in the area served. The number of sworn officers in a jurisdiction or community also provides an implied measure of the total amount of crime in the community, since it represents in a very practical sense what the community views as its needs for law enforcement. At the least, it represents how much of laboratory can still process drugs faster than many other kinds of clue materials.

The average number of cases that an examiner can handle varies with the type of analysis that he is performing. The 1967 survey of crime laboratories(2) indicated typical examiner caseloads for a number of city laboratories ranging from 150 to 1000 per year. Based on this information and from a survey of caseload data from laboratories around the country, it was concluded that caseload per examiner values should be assigned to reflect the particular distribution of expected cases in a given jurisdiction. Applying this philosophy,

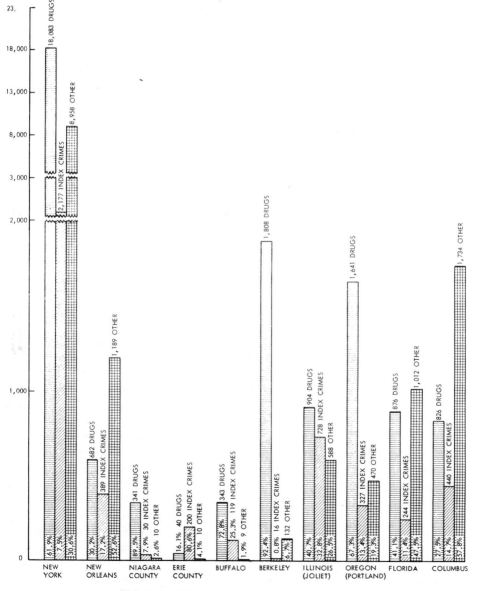

FIG. 1—*Distribution of case types to crime laboratories.*

numerical values of 125 (one-half case per day), 250 (one case per day), and 500 (two cases per day) were chosen to represent low, medium (normal), and high percentages, respectively, of drugs in the caseload distributions. Consider an area with a total of 3000 cases a year. If this includes the normal percentage of drug cases in the jurisdiction, the planner would select 250 cases per examiner as the expected annual workload of any one examiner in his laboratory and should plan on staffing approximately twelve examiners. Note that, if he anticipated a high percentage of drug cases, he would select the assignment of 500 cases per examiner and plan on staffing only six examiners in his laboratory. More definitive staffing and equipment priorities were given in Ref.(1).

The CPO concept provides a simple, consistent means for determining the approximate demand for criminalistics. It recognizes that the crime laboratory is not an entity unto itself, but that it exists solely to serve the needs of law enforcement and criminal justice and that it must be considered as an integral part of the entire system. Moreover, for planning purposes, data on the police population to be served are more readily available than details on crime itself.

CRIME LABORATORY LOCATION

The crime laboratories that exist today are where they are for a variety of reasons. The attitudes of law enforcement officials in the area, budgetary considerations, and the availability of qualified criminalists and examiners, all have had bearing on the decision to establish a crime laboratory. The policies and service attitudes of state crime laboratories, where they exist, also influence the decision on local laboratories. With the possible exception of one or two state crime laboratory systems, crime laboratories have not been established as parts of an overall system designed to provide services in accordance with the demand for laboratory support; that is, laboratories have not been established based on a quantitative analysis of need.

Theoretically, it would be possible to serve the needs of the nation from one single crime laboratory, centrally located, and at the same time achieve significant economies in professional manpower, equipment, and processing efficiency. At the other end of the spectrum, using the 50-mile-radius criterion, more than 400 crime laboratories would be required to serve all local areas within the United States. The total cost of these laboratories would be high, but so would the service level achieved. It is easy to visualize the reluctance of an investigator to wrap up a car bumper and mail it to the central laboratory for analysis when the convenience of taking that same item to the local laboratory in a patrol car is available.

Considering the crime laboratory as a technical support for the sworn police officer, the influence or availability of that support appears to vary as a function of the distance of the laboratory from the jurisdiction or police officer served. The relationship is not clearly defined, nor are data available from which to develop a model to analyze quantitatively all of the factors involved in this phenomenon. There is sufficient evidence, however, to support the hypothesis of convenience, which suggests that law enforcement officers are more apt to request technical support from a nearby local crime laboratory where they have frequent contact with the personnel than to prepare physical clue material for transmission to a distant laboratory which may or may not have a charter to serve their particular jurisdiction.

The factors influencing this diminution or decay of the influence of the laboratory as a function of remoteness or distance are probably complex. The laws of the state, and the attitude of the courts and prosecutors toward the use of physical evidence or expert testimony in court, can have a significant effect on whether or not evidence is sent to the laboratory. Political boundaries can also serve as barriers to sending physical clue material to the laboratory. Jurisdictions outside the city proper are often served by the city laboratory on a second-priority basis, if at all, when the workload is high. While crime laboratories are generally cooperative in providing services to other agencies, their first loyalty is to the jurisdiction which provides their funds and support.

The law enforcement department exercises great influence on the amount of physical clue material that is sent to a laboratory, regardless of the proximity or jurisdiction of the laboratory. Command emphasis on the collection of physical evidence certainly plays a role, as do the level of training of investigators in the collection of physical evidence, the equipment available, the existence of crime scene search teams or evidence technicians, and the amount of time an investigator can spend on each case, among others.

The crime laboratory itself influences its own volume of work. If the laboratory is able to satisfy an investigator's requests for laboratory examinations, then that investigator and others will continue to make similar requests. Conversely, if requests for service are denied, response time is inordinately long, or consistently inconclusive results are provided, the tendency will be to reduce the number of requests for service that the investigators make to the laboratory.

The distance phenomenon does appear to have a characteristic decay curve when cases per officer submitted to the laboratory are plotted against distance from the laboratory. Available data from Florida are shown in Fig. 2. The multitudinous factors which affect decay notwithstanding, it appears that those law enforcement jurisdictions within a 50-mile radius of a laboratory will use the laboratory more frequently than will those beyond the approximate 50-mile radius. The frequency of use drops off sharply as this distance is exceeded.

THE REGIONAL LABORATORY APPROACH

Using data for the average number of cases per officer for city laboratories and several state laboratories, one can construct a hypothetical decay curve from which to approximate a CPO value for a regional laboratory concept (see Fig. 3). From this decay curve, hypothetical or planning CPO values can then be determined which can be used for the analysis of several candidate structures for meeting the criminalistics demand. For the purpose of this analysis, a relatively

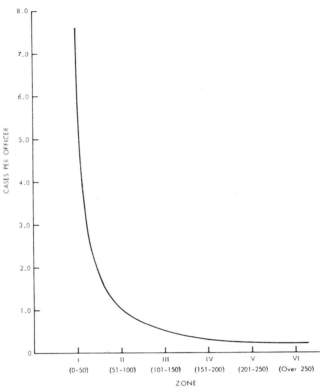

FIG. 2—*Evidence submission decay as a function of distance.*

conservative value for city laboratories of three cases per officer per year was selected. Since the counties which comprise a standard metropolitan statistical area (SMSA) are largely within a 50-mile radius of the principal city, the CPO value for the SMSA should be nearly the same as that for the city(3). A CPO value of 1.0 is used as a planning value for state laboratories, whereas a regional laboratory could be expected to draw on the basis of 0.5 cases per officer per year for the regions served. A CPO value of 0.1 is used for the national laboratory.

In the regional crime laboratory concept, the nine law enforcement regions of the Uniform Crime Report(4) were used: New England States, South Atlantic States, East South Central States, West South Central States, Mountain States, and Pacific States. Seven candidate structures or systems of crime laboratories were examined in the analysis, as follows:

1. A single national crime laboratory (CPO 0.1).

2. Nine regional crime laboratories (CPO 0.5) plus one national laboratory (CPO 0.1).

3. Fifty state laboratories CPO 1.0) plus one national laboratory (CPO 0.1).

4. Sixty city laboratories (CPO 3.0) plus nine regional laboratories CPO 0.5) plus one national laboratory (CPO 0.1).

5. Sixty city laboratories (CPO 3.0) plus 50 state laboratories (CPO 1.0) plus

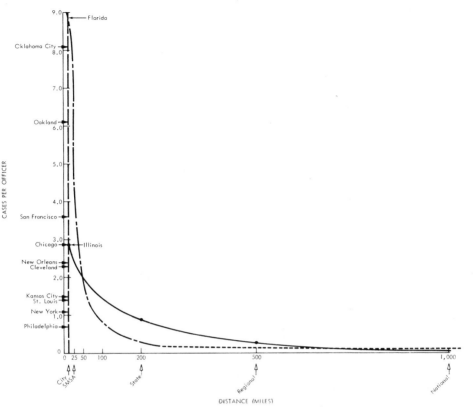

FIG. 3—*Evidence submission decay as a function of laboratory type.*

one national laboratory (CPO 0.1).

6. One-hundred and four SMSA laboratories (CPO 3.0) plus nine regional laboratories (CPO 0.5) plus one national laboratory (CPO 0.1)

7. One hundred and four SMSA laboratories (CPO 3.0) plus 50 state laboratories (CPO 1.0) plus one national laboratory (CPO 0.1).

The difference in those concepts embodying city crime laboratories versus the SMSA crime laboratory is one of including the specific charter of the crime laboratory beyond the city limits of the jurisdiction in which it is established. It is difficult, if not impossible, to separate the city from its surrounding suburbs and dependent counties. The criminal does not recognize these political boundaries and works at his trade freely crossing from one to another. Most communities have cooperative arrangements to meet this problem, but the provision of crime laboratory services is on a convenience rather than authorized basis. The SMSA crime laboratory visualized in this analysis is one which has a specific charter to serve the entire SMSA, is supported financially from all local agencies, and is perhaps supplemented by federal support for this purpose. The advantage of a single open bullet file for the entire SMSA is obvious. The SMSA laboratory would utilize personnel drawn from the many participating departments. Similarly, a regional laboratory would be established to provide

TABLE 2—Demand for crime laboratory examiners in standard metropolitan statistical areas based on a yield of three cases per officer.

SMSA	Estimated Number of Police	Estimated Laboratory Cases	Number of Examiners by Caseload			Cumulative Number of Police	Cumulative Laboratory Cases	Cumulative Examiners by Caseload			Cumulative Percent Index			Rank
			Low	Medium	High			Low	Medium	High	Population	Crimes	Police	
New York, N.Y.	34 119	102 357	819	409	205	34 119	102 357	819	409	205	5.8	12.3	11.1	1
Chicago, Ill.	15 666	46 998	376	188	94	49 785	149 355	1 195	597	299	9.2	16.1	16.2	2
Philadelphia, Pa.-N.J.	10 541	31 623	253	126	63	60 326	180 978	1 448	724	362	11.7	17.8	19.7	3
Los Angeles-Long Beach, Calif.	9 971	29 913	239	120	60	70 297	210 891	1 687	844	422	15.1	25.0	22.9	4
Detroit, Mich.	7 580	22 740	182	91	45	77 877	233 631	1 869	935	467	17.2	28.4	25.4	5
Boston-Lowell-Lawrence, Mass.	6 089	18 267	146	73	37	83 966	251 898	2 015	1 008	504	18.9	30.3	27.4	6
Washington, D.C.-Md.-Va.	4 958	14 874	119	59	30	88 924	266 772	2 134	1 067	534	20.2	32.4	29.0	7
San Francisco-Oakland, Calif.	4 278	12 834	103	51	26	93 202	279 606	2 237	1 118	559	21.7	35.6	30.4	8
Baltimore, Md.	4 183	12 549	100	50	25	97 385	292 155	2 337	1 169	584	22.8	37.6	31.7	9
St. Louis, Mo.-Ill.	3 739	11 217	90	45	22	101 124	303 372	2 427	1 213	607	24.0	39.1	32.9	10
Cleveland, Ohio	3 378	10 134	81	41	20	104 502	313 506	2 508	1 254	627	25.0	40.2	34.0	11
Newark, N.J.	2 939	8 817	71	35	18	107 441	322 323	2 579	1 289	645	25.9	41.7	35.0	12
Pittsburgh, Pa.	2 864	8 592	69	34	17	110 305	330 915	2 647	1 324	662	27.1	42.8	35.9	13
Milwaukee, Wis.	2 593	7 779	62	31	16	112 898	338 694	2 710	1 355	677	27.8	43.3	36.8	14
Buffalo, N.Y.	2 427	7 281	58	29	15	115 325	345 975	2 768	1 384	692	28.5	43.9	37.6	15
Houston, Tex.	2 141	6 423	51	26	13	117 466	352 398	2 819	1 410	705	29.4	45.2	38.3	16
Minneapolis-St. Paul, Minn.	2 079	6 237	50	25	12	119 545	358 635	2 869	1 435	717	30.3	46.3	38.9	17
Dallas, Tex.	2 076	6 228	50	25	12	121 621	364 863	2 919	1 459	730	31.0	47.1	39.6	18

Paterson-Clifton-Passaic, N.J.	1 858	5 574	45	22	11	123 479	370 437	2 963	1 482	741	31.7	47.6	40.2	19
Kansas City, Mo.-Kans.	1 829	5 487	44	22	11	125 308	375 924	3 007	1 504	752	32.3	48.5	40.8	20
New Orleans, La.	1 741	5 223	42	21	10	127 049	381 147	3 049	1 525	762	32.8	49.3	41.4	21
Miami, Fla.	1 698	5 094	41	20	10	128 747	386 241	3 090	1 545	772	33.4	50.4	41.9	22
Seattle-Everett, Wash.	1 675	5 025	40	20	10	130 422	391 266	3 130	1 565	783	34.1	51.3	42.5	23
Cincinnati, Ohio-Ky.-Ind.	1 586	4 758	38	19	10	132 008	396 024	3 168	1 584	792	34.8	51.8	43.0	24
Jersey City, N.J.	1 583	4 749	38	19	9	133 591	400 773	3 206	1 603	802	35.1	52.1	43.5	25
Atlanta, Ga.	1 536	4 608	37	18	9	135 127	405 381	3 243	1 622	811	35.8	52.9	44.0	26
Indianapolis, Ind.	1 532	4 596	37	18	9	136 659	409 977	3 280	1 640	820	36.3	53.5	44.5	27
Denver, Colo.	1 524	4 572	37	18	9	138 183	414 549	3 316	1 658	829	36.9	54.3	45.0	28
San Diego, Calif.	1 496	4 488	36	18	9	139 679	419 037	3 352	1 676	838	37.5	54.9	45.5	29
Prov.-Pawt.-Warwick, R.I.	1 441	4 323	35	17	9	141 120	423 360	3 387	1 693	847	37.9	55.4	46.0	30
Ana.-St. Ana-Gard. Gr., Calif.	1 271	3 813	31	15	8	142 391	427 173	3 417	1 709	854	38.5	56.2	46.4	31
Memphis, Tenn.-Ark.	1 237	3 711	30	15	7	143 628	430 884	3 447	1 724	862	38.9	56.7	46.8	32
Tampa-St. Petersburg, Fla.	1 237	3 711	30	15	7	144 865	434 595	3 477	1 738	869	39.4	57.4	47.2	33
Portland, Ore.-Wash.	1 218	3 654	29	15	7	146 083	438 249	3 506	1 753	876	39.8	58.0	47.6	34
Columbus, Ohio	1 170	3 510	28	14	7	147 253	441 759	3 534	1 767	884	40.3	58.6	48.0	35
Toledo, Ohio-Mich.	1 115	3 345	27	13	7	148 368	445 104	3 561	1 780	890	40.6	58.8	48.3	36
San Bern.-Riv.-Ont., Calif.	1 097	3 291	26	13	7	149 465	448 395	3 587	1 794	897	41.2	59.6	48.7	37
Phoenix, Ariz.	1 079	3 237	26	13	6	150 544	451 632	3 613	1 807	903	41.6	60.3	49.0	38
San Jose, Calif.	1 065	3 195	26	13	6	151 609	454 827	3 639	1 819	910	42.1	60.8	49.4	39
Honolulu, Hawaii	1 054	3 162	25	13	6	152 663	457 989	3 664	1 832	916	42.4	61.3	49.7	40
Huntsville, Ala.	1 051	3 153	25	13	6	153 714	461 142	3 689	1 845	922	42.6	61.4	50.1	41
Louisville, Ky.-Ind.	1 032	3 096	25	12	6	154 746	464 238	3 714	1 857	928	43.0	62.0	50.4	42

services to all of the law enforcement agencies within the states of its region.

For SMSAs, a rank order analysis shows a priority for establishing or augmenting existing crime laboratories by the SMSA under the assumptions contained in the analysis (Table 2). A tabular summary sheet (Table 3) shows the comparison of the seven selected locational strategies. Each strategy is examined under three conditions:

1. In the first case, the cost per examiner is held constant for all size laboratories regardless of location.

2. In the second, the cost per examiner per year is varied with the size of the laboratory, assuming efficiencies resulting from larger laboratory operations.

3. A third analysis is shown using the variable cost per examiner. It includes, in addition, the assumption that city and SMSA laboratories receive a high proportion of routine examination requests such that the caseload per examiner could be considered to be 500 cases per year, whereas examiners in state laboratories average 250 cases per year and regional and federal laboratory examiners only receive 125 cases per year. The reduced figure for state, regional, and federal laboratories reflects the assumption that these laboratories receive the more serious or more complex cases and thus the time demands are greater for each case.

Throughout this analysis, it is assumed that the number of cases per officer sent to the laboratory is characteristic of the CPO decay curve and that law enforcement departments outside of the city or SMSA would average 1 case per year to the appropriate state laboratory, 0.5 case per year to the appropriate regional laboratory, and 0.1 case per year to a national crime laboratory.

Another approach also used was a cost/effectiveness analysis. Each location strategy was measured against a consistent goal to the laboratory of 3 cases per officer for the entire nation's police force. Thus, if a given group of laboratories constituting a location strategy could produce an average of 1.5 cases per officer for the nation's police, it could be said that the performance index of that strategy would be 0.5. Similarly, if the total cost to establish a sufficient number of crime laboratories, each serving a 50-mile radius, to cover the entire United States is assumed, then this cost could be taken as an upper bound of the costs which would be required to provide the 3.0 CPO performance level. Therefore, the total cost for a given set of laboratories constituting a strategy could be measured as that fraction of the maximum cost. A location strategy which provided laboratories at one third of the assumed maximum cost would have a cost index of 0.33.

The effect of varying the number of laboratories within a given strategy, that is, examining the entire range of 10 to 82 city laboratories when considered in terms of performance index and cost index, can produce a curve which is characteristic of that strategy. The results of such an analysis are shown in Figure 4. Strategies X, Y, and Z(I, II, and III of Table 3) are considered static and are shown as single points. Others are varied throughout a feasible range to develop characteristic curves. In establishing cost indices, both annual operating costs and initial startup costs are considered for each laboratory.

Figure 4 demonstrates the application of the location model using certain assumed values. The results should be useful for gross planning purposes and with more refined data could eventually become a more precise planning tool. The purpose of this analysis was to develop the structure for an analysis model and to exercise the model on available data. Refinement of the model and more comprehensive analysis of structures must await the availability of more precise data from which to develop the decay coefficients and laboratory workload capabilities.

LABORATORY PLANNING

From the outset, it was apparent that the planning of a crime laboratory could not be accomplished by a cookbook-type procedure. Characteristics of the area to be served; training and background of available staff; attitudes of law enforcement, prosecutors, and courts; existing capabilities; different priorities; and limitations in budget, all combine to make each laboratory unique.

In recognition of this uniqueness, a planning model designated Laboratory

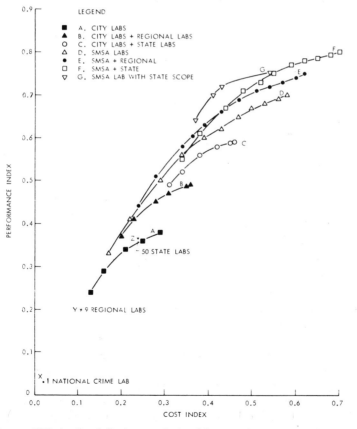

FIG. 4—*Cost/effectiveness of crime laboratory location strategies.*

TABLE 3—*Summary, cost/effectiveness analysis.*

			Cases to Lab-oratory	Number of Ex-aminers	Analysis 1 Fixed Examiner Cost	Analysis 2 Variable Examiner Cost	Analysis 3 Number of Ex-aminers	Analysis 3 Variable Caseload
		Strategy	CPO					
I.	1	national lab	0.1	30 700	123	2.46×10^6	2.09×10^6	246	4.18×10^6
II.	1	national lab	0.1	30 700	123	2.46	2.09	123	2.09
	9	regional labs	0.5	153 500	614	12.28	11.05	1 228	20.88
				184 200	737	14.74	13.14	1 351	22.97
III.	1	national lab	0.1	30 700	123	2.46	2.09	246	4.18
	50	state labs	1.0	307 000	1 228	24.56	23.33	1 228	23.33
				337 700	1 351	27.02	25.42	1 474	27.51
IV.	1	national lab	0.1	30 700	123	2.46	2.09	246	4.18
	9	regional labs	0.5	97 655	390	7.80	7.41	780	14.82
	60	city labs	3.0	335 073	1 340	26.80	25.46	670	13.40
				463 428	1 853	37.06	34.96	1 696	32.40
V.	1	national lab	0.1	30 700	123	2.46	2.09	246	4.18
	50	state labs	1.0	195 309	781	15.62	14.84	781	14.84
	60	city labs	3.0	335 073	1 340	26.80	25.46	670	13.40
				561 082	2 244	44.88	42.39	1 697	32.42
VI.	1	national lab	0.1	30 700	123	2.46	2.09	246	4.18
	9	regional labs	0.5	56 991	228	4.56	4.56	456	8.21
	104	SMSA labs	3.0	579 057	2 316	46.32	44.00	1 158	23.16
				666 748	2 667	53.34	50.65	1 860	35.55
VII.	1	national lab	0.1	30 700	123	2.46	2.09	246	4.18
	50	state labs	1.0	113 981	456	9.12	9.12	456	9.12
	104	SMSA labs	3.0	579 057	2 316	46.32	44.00	1 158	23.16
				723 738	2 895	57.90	55.21	1 860	36.46

Analysis and Budgeting System (LABS) was developed that would accommodate all of the diverse factors needed to plan for a laboratory. The model uses a planning compiler previously developed by the Midwest Research Institute and consists of a series of input lines that itemize equipment, staff, and cost elements for a laboratory. Ten time increments in the model (months, quarters, or years) allow phasing the acquisition of staff and equipment and permit use of incremental cost increase factors. Relationships between input lines, as established by the planner, and the arithmetic capability of the compiler allow sums, differences, and ratios to be calculated. Users of the model may exercise complete control over the content and sequence of the resultant reports.

In an actual laboratory planning operation, the planner would start to determine the criminalistics need of his jurisdiction for region by a study of the environment to be served and a review of sources of planning guidelines. Previous paragraphs of this paper have described methods for determining the relative merit of the several alternatives for the location and service area of a criminalistics operation. The CPO concept, when applied to the area to be served and properly accounting for the decay factors, yields a figure for the total expected caseload to the laboratory. Use of the caseload per examiner averages, properly weighted for factors such as amount of travel and relative degree of the

STAFF PLAN	REPORT	REGIONAL CRIME LAB				L.A.R. MODEL				MAY 1970	
PLANNING ITEM	0	1	2	3	4	5	6	7	8	9	10
			MANNING SCHEDULE								
26 TOTAL NUMBER PROFESSIONALS	-0.0	10.0	15.0	18.0	18.0	18.0	20.0	20.0	20.0	20.0	20.0
27 DIRECTOR	-0.0	0.0	1.0	1.0	1.0	1.0	1.0	1.0	1.0	1.0	1.0
28 ASSISTANT DIRECTOR-FIELD OP.	-0.0	1.0	1.0	1.0	1.0	1.0	1.0	1.0	1.0	1.0	1.0
29 ASSISTANT DIRECTOR-LAB. OP.	.0	.0	.0	.0	.0	.0	.0	.0	.0	.0	.0
30 LABORATORY ANALYST I	1.0	1.0	1.0	1.0	1.0	1.0	1.0	1.0	1.0	1.0	1.0
31 LABORATORY ANALYST II	1.0	1.0	1.0	1.0	1.0	1.0	1.0	1.0	1.0	1.0	1.0
32 LABORATORY ANALYST III	-0.0	0.0	0.0	1.0	1.0	1.0	1.0	1.0	1.0	1.0	1.0
33 LABORATORY TECHNICIAN	-0.0	0.0	1.0	1.0	1.0	1.0	2.0	2.0	2.0	2.0	2.0
34 PHYSICAL EXAMINER I	-0.0	1.0	1.0	0.0	0.0	0.0	0.0	0.0	0.0	0.0	0.0
35 PHYSICAL EXAMINER II	1.0	1.0	1.0	1.0	1.0	1.0	1.0	1.0	1.0	1.0	1.0
36 PHYSICAL EXAMINER III	-0.0	0.0	0.0	1.0	1.0	1.0	1.0	1.0	1.0	1.0	1.0
41 PHYSICAL EXAMINER TECH	2.0	2.0	2.0	2.0	2.0	2.0	2.0	2.0	2.0	2.0	2.0
37 LATENT PRINTS COORDINATOR	1.0	1.0	1.0	1.0	1.0	1.0	1.0	1.0	1.0	1.0	1.0
38 DOCUMENTS III	-0.0	0.0	1.0	1.0	1.0	1.0	1.0	1.0	1.0	1.0	1.0
45 DOCUMENTS I	-0.0	0.0	0.0	0.0	0.0	0.0	1.0	1.0	1.0	1.0	1.0
39 SECURE EVID TRANSIT OFFICERS	-0.0	1.0	1.0	2.0	2.0	2.0	2.0	2.0	2.0	2.0	2.0
40 CRIME SCENE EXAMINER II	-0.0	1.0	2.0	3.0	3.0	3.0	3.0	3.0	3.0	3.0	3.0
41 SATELLITE ANALYST I	-0.0	0.0	1.0	1.0	1.0	1.0	1.0	1.0	1.0	1.0	1.0
46 SATELLITE SUPPORT OFFICER	-0.0	0.0	1.0	1.0	1.0	1.0	1.0	1.0	1.0	1.0	1.0
42 TOTAL NUMBER SUPPORT	-0.0	2.0	4.0	7.0	7.0	7.0	7.0	7.0	7.0	7.0	7.0
44 PHOTOGRAPHIC TECHNICIAN	-0.0	0.0	1.0	1.0	1.0	1.0	1.0	1.0	1.0	1.0	1.0
47 ADMINISTRATIVE ASSISTANT	-0.0	0.0	0.0	1.0	1.0	1.0	1.0	1.0	1.0	1.0	1.0
48 STENOGRAPHER	1.0	1.0	1.0	1.0	1.0	1.0	1.0	1.0	1.0	1.0	1.0
49 CLERK/TYPIST	-0.0	1.0	1.0	2.0	2.0	2.0	2.0	2.0	2.0	2.0	2.0
23 CLERK/TYPIST SATELLITE	-0.0	0.0	0.0	1.0	1.0	1.0	1.0	1.0	1.0	1.0	1.0

FIG. 5 *Manning schedule generated during planning of a regional crime laboratory.*

drug problem, will yield a target level of examiners for the laboratory. The skills of the laboratory staff and the equipment required to maintain the proposed laboratory can then be determined using the factors described herein as a guide.

Forms were developed to be used by the planner as input to LABS. One form provides a line for each item of equipment and requires data on the quantity required, the unit cost, the priority, and the time period in which each should be acquired. The summary section allows the planner to specify cost summaries that are desired, such as Total Equipment Cost—Microanalysis Laboratory. The sum of the cost of each equipment item coded with that summary code would yield that total. Forms that deal with staff, overhead and cost, funds source, and cost share were also developed. These are prepared by the planner in a similar manner to the equipment form above.

These forms, after coding and conversion to machine readable data, are processed on the planning compiler. The resultant computer program edits the input data and performs all calculations that are required. Reports are then generated in accordance with a standard or user specified sequence of lines. Sample reports for one item, , the Manning Schedule, generated during the planning of a regional crime laboratory for greater Kansas City are presented in Fig. 5.

The LABS model is intended to be a dynamic planning tool. A plan that does not meet the expectations of the planner or the needs of the agency can be easily regenerated by making only those changes desired in the input. "What if" questions can also be asked and the effect of alternatives can be simulated. LABS can be used by laboratory planners at several levels of sophistication. The forms can serve as a checklist and the reports can serve as a format to guide a manual planning operation.

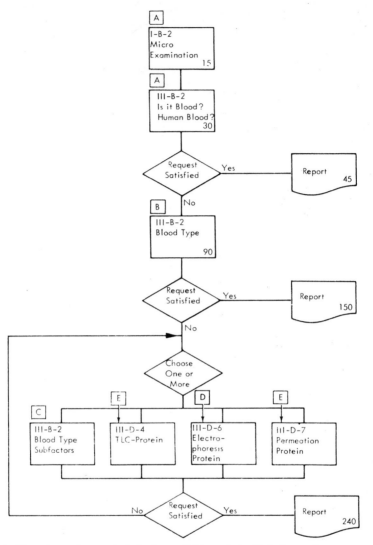

FIG. 6—*Flow chart of an analytical scheme. Evidence item: Stain from crime scene, probably* **blood.** *Request: Is the stain human blood; if so, what type?*

LABORATORY PROCEDURES

Each evidence item is normally subjected to a specific test or series of tests depending on the information desired from the item; for example, on a blood sample, questions can range from Is it human blood? to What is its alcohol content? The question can normally be answered by a known number of specific tests, although under certain circumstances, additional tests are required to ensure a result.

We completed flow charts to represent analytical schemes for typical examples of evidence categories. The flow charts were not limited to what was considered to be the one best way for examination but, rather, reflect many optional routes of methods that might be reasonable for the analysis of the particular evidence item. Several representative flow charts representing schemes for the information required (in blocks) are given in Figs. 6, 7, and 8. A system that establishes a code for spatial (dimensional), physical, molecular, or atomic properties of evidence was developed for use in flow charting laboratory methods. A sample page from this coding system is presented in Fig. 9.

The multiplicity of branches within many of the evidence examination flow schemes generally represented some duplication in the acquisition of essentially

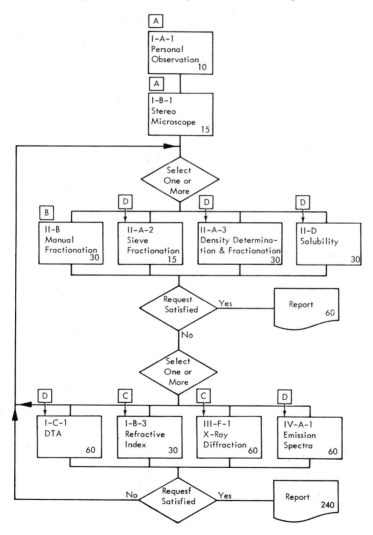

FIG. 7—*Flow chart of an analytical scheme. Evidence item: Building material, fragments and dust. Request: Is material from crime scene; comparison?*

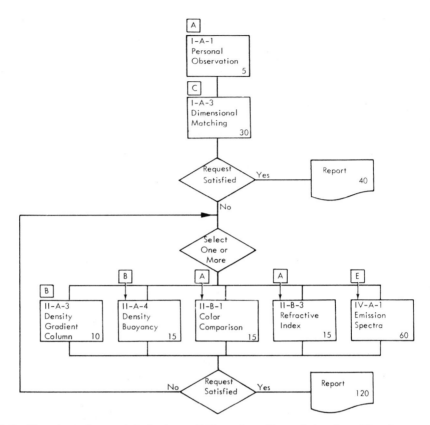

FIG. 8—*Flow chart of an analytical scheme. Evidence item: Piece of glass from hit and run scene. Request: Did fragment come from suspect car?*

identical information by different means. The small letter-containing square above the operation block indicates the probability the operation would be used in the given examination. The key is as follows:

A. Used for all samples in all laboratories (based on our working group survey)

B. Used for most samples in most laboratories

C. Used for some samples or in some of the laboratories

D. Occasionally used

E. Seldom or never used (but possibly will be in the future)

The first entry in an operational block, such as 1-B-2, is a reference key to the property coding system previously discussed. Also included in the operational block is an abbreviated description of the operation, for example, Microscopic Examination. The number in the lower right is an estimate of the average time, in minutes, required for the operation. The time in the report blocks indicates the total average time for completion of the examination and may or may not be equal to the total of the times for individual operations. It represents an estimate of the average total time necessary for completion of the optional operations of the scheme.

The above concept of optional examination methods aids in the evaluation of priorities for the acquisition of laboratory equipment. In a large laboratory any concern that an instrument is of value primarily for the examination of only one type of evidence can usually be disregarded, since the frequent utilization of that instrument may make the initial cost of the instrument insignificant. The presence of the same instrument in a small laboratory might be completely unjustified owing to its infrequent use, especially if the examination could be made using a more versatile instrument capable of use in other examinations.

WORKLOAD ANALYSIS

A generalized computer program developed originally for the analysis of answers to questionnaires was adapted to analyze the existing records of two state crime laboratories. The value of this program was its ability to take existing data in the format of each laboratory and place it in the categories desired by the researcher. The program counts a given code in any card column and compares it to the sum of all entries in that column. For example, it would count all cases coded Murder and calculate the percentage that that crime represents of all cases submitted to the laboratory.

Table 4 presents the results of the application of this technique to the 1969 caseload of the Illinois State Laboratory in Joliet. Of the 2220 cases recorded in 1969, 40.7 percent dealt with violations of narcotic and dangerous drug laws, 16.4 with burglary, 6.9 with auto theft, 3.5 with murder, etc. The table also illustrates three other analyses performed on the data: type of examination, total caseload by month, and caseload by service type. The types of examination performed on each category of offense are detailed. Examples of the application of this technique to the data of the Oregon State Police Crime Laboratory in Portland include a distribution of cases by offense in Table 5 and the evidence categories received in each offense in Table 6.

A UNIFORM CRIMINALISTICS MANAGEMENT REPORTING SYSTEM

Most laboratories keep records in terms of measurement of total activity which are intended to justify the existence of the laboratory. Frequently, the total number of examinations performed is reported; however, in one laboratory the examination of six samples of handwriting from a suspect may be counted as six examinations, while in another it may be reported as only one. One crime laboratory has even included the urinalyses required for annual physical examinations of department personnel in the total number of examinations conducted. In many instances, only the law enforcement department case record contains the information necessary to relate the crime, clue material, laboratory procedure used, and examination results. The case records of those cases with crime laboratory involvement are filed with all other cases, of course, and to extract such information would require laborious file-by-file retrieval. Some

TABLE 4—*Complete Illinois data analysis.*

Category	Number	Percent
Caseload by Type of Offense	2 220	100.0
Murder	77	3.5
Rape	61	2.7
Robbery	64	2.9
Agg assault	9	0.4
Neg manslaughter	7	0.3
Other assaults	24	1.1
Other sex	21	0.9
Family	1	0.0
Kidnapping	2	0.1
Hit and run	35	1.6
Death investigation	7	0.3
Other persons	1	0.0
Burglary	363	16.4
Larceny 50+	153	6.9
Auto theft	1	0.0
Larceny 50−	0	0.0
Arson	75	3.4
Forgery and counterfeit	10	0.5
Fraud	5	0.2
Embezzlement	0	0.0
Stolen property	1	0.0
Vandalism	37	1.7
Bombing	11	0.5
Pets and livestock	0	0.0
Food and drug	0	0.0
Other property	5	0.2
Weapons	56	2.5
Comm vice	1	0.0
Narcotic and D.D.	904	40.7
Gambling	1	0.0
D.W.I.	18	0.8
Liquor	21	0.9
Drunkenness	0	0.0
Suicide	19	0.9
Abortion	0	0.0
Obscene literature	2	0.1
Conservation	0	0.0
Other acts	4	0.2
Persons Index	211	9.5
Persons I and II	53	2.4
Persons other	45	2.0
Property and com index	517	23.3
Property and com I and II	128	5.8
Property and com other	16	0.7
Illegal acts I and II	1 001	45.1
Illegal acts other	25	1.1
Type of Examination		
Firearms	232	10.5
Blood alcohol	31	1.4
Narcotics	692	31.3
Paint	111	5.0
Glass	21	0.9
Latent prints	425	19.2
Dangerous drugs	350	15.8
Toolmark	148	6.7
Document	2	0.1
Serology	156	7.0
Hair and fiber	49	2.2
Bomb (explosives)	18	0.8
Footwear I.D. (prints)	20	0.9

(Continued)

TABLE 4—*Continued.*

Category	Number	Percent
Soil	11	0.5
Arson debris	21	0.9
Alcohol content (liq)	23	1.0
Intoxicating cmpd	5	0.2
Blood exam	1	0.0
Other exam	90	4.1
Total Caseload by Month	2 213	100.0
January	150	6.8
February	232	10.5
March	128	5.8
April	190	8.6
May	149	6.7
June	181	8.2
July	187	8.5
August	250	11.3
September	248	11.2
October	228	10.3
November	158	7.1
December	111	5.0
Caseload by Service Type	2 214	100.0
Laboratory	1 488	67.2
Crime scene	10	0.5
Fingerprint	273	12.3
Polygraph	242	10.9
Phot	1	0.0
Lab and fingerprint	76	3.4
Lab and crime scene	43	1.9
Lab scene finger photo	6	0.3
Lab scene finger	38	1.7
Crime scene finger	27	1.2
Crime scene photo	1	0.0
Lab scene photo	3	0.1
Finger photo	1	0.0
Lab photo	1	0.0
Lab polygraph	1	0.0
Examination by Type of Offense		
Murder	77	
Firearms	47	61.0
Blood alcohol	8	10.4
Narcotics	1	1.3
Paint	2	2.6
Glass	0	0.0
Latent print	17	22.1
Dangerous drug	1	1.3
Tool mark	0	0.0
Document	0	0.0
Serology	31	40.3
Hair and fiber	8	10.4
Bomb (explosive)	0	0.0
Footwear I.D.	1	1.3
Soil	1	1.3
Arson debris	1	1.3
Alcohol content	0	0.0
Intoxicatine cmpd.	0	0.0
Blood	1	1.3
Other	4	5.2
Rape	61	
Firearms	1	1.6
Blood alcohol	0	0.0
Narcotics	0	0.0

(*Continued*)

TABLE 4—*Continued.*

Category	Number	Percent
Paint	0	0.0
Glass	0	0.0
Latent print	6	9.8
Dangerous drug	0	0.0
Tool mark	0	0.0
Document	0	0.0
Serology	30	49.2
Hair and fiber	14	23.0
Bomb (explosive)	0	0.0
Footwear I.D.	1	1.6
Soil	0	0.0
Arson debris	0	0.0
Alcohol content	0	0.0
Intoxicating cmpd.	0	0.0
Blood	0	0.0
Other	1	1.6
Robbery	64	
Firearms	15	23.4
Blood alcohol	1	1.6
Narcotics	0	0.0
Paint	0	0.0
Glass	1	1.6
Latent print	28	43.8
Dangerous drug	1	1.6
Tool mark	2	3.1

laboratories record and emphasize the number of cases handled rather than the number of examinations performed. Data for longitudinal studies of the effectiveness of crime laboratories, or the impact that the laboratory examination had on law enforcement, are nonexistent. In short, crime laboratories usually keep only those records which are necessary to assure continued existence or desired expansion, with management of the laboratory function being something less than formalized.

A coarse estimate of the magnitude of crime laboratory involvement in the fight against crime indicates that only 2 to 3 percent of all reported cases reach the laboratory. Considering index crimes alone, Parker's(5) data show that in only 4 cases out of 3303 was physical clue material received by the laboratory, indicating approximately 0.1 percent laboratory involvement in index crimes. Clearly, if criminalistics is to have any significant effect on crime, the level of its involvement must increase dramatically. A first step toward this end could be the establishment of a system for collecting information on crime laboratory operations and effectiveness, performing management analyses on these data, and furnishing the results to all other laboratories.

The impact of this program on criminalistics would be both immediate and far reaching. Participating laboratories will receive early benefit from the project in the collection of more complete data. This improved data base will permit greater insight into each laboratory's own operations and, also, a comparison on a uniform basis with the operations of other laboratories. The results from these analyses would serve as the first step in developing industry standards for laboratory performance. By establishing a mechanism for recording and

Property	Equipment
C. MOLECULAR SPECTRA	

1. Colorimeter-Spectrophotometer
   a. Determination of specific materials
   b. Quantification of chromogenic
      reaction
	1. Nonrecording Spectrophotometer

2. Visible and UV Spectra
   a. Quantification of chromogenic
      reaction
   b. Determination of inorganics
	2. Recording Vis.-UV Spectrophotometer

3. IR Spectra
   a. Determination of organic and
      inorganic functional groups
   b. Comparative, with standard
      spectra or evidence item
   c. Can be identifying characteristic
	3. Recording IR Spectrophotometer

4. Nuclear Magnetic Resonance
   a. Determined certain, specific bonds
   b. Comparative
   c. Can be identifying characteristic
	4. N.M.R. Apparatus

5. Fluorescence Spectra a. Identifying characteristic	5. Spectrophotofluorometer
D. FRACTIONATION OF MOLECULES	

1. Distillation
   a. Crude separation of large samples
   b. Approximate boiling points and
      amounts of components
	1. Distillation Glassware

2,3. Gas Chromatography
   a. Provides number and approximate
      amount of components
   b. Provides one component charac-
      teristic (rentention time)
      (May be coupled to devices
      for other characteristics of
      components)
   c. For some evidence may be nearly
      specific identification
	2. Versatile G.C.
	3. Dedicated G.C.

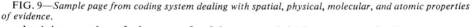

FIG. 9—*Sample page from coding system dealing with spatial, physical, molecular, and atomic properties of evidence.*

obtaining results of the use of a laboratory, initial measures of effectiveness could be established. The program would be of further significance in providing planning assistance and operational guidelines for the establishment of new crime laboratories. References 6-19 offer additional informative and useful literature bearing on this and related matters.

CONCLUSIONS

While the problems of the lack of uniform data have precluded the establishment of quantitative bases on which to make recommendations, several conclusions have emerged as broad principles. Used separately or together, they can be applied to criminalistics operations to increase the involvement of the crime laboratory in the total body of crime and, thus, guarantee a greater significant impact on the law enforcement and criminal justice system.

1. *Improved crime scene search needed.* Clearly, if the crime laboratory is to assume its proper role of increasing technical support capability for the law

TABLE 5—*Distribution of cases to State Police
Crime Laboratory, Portland, Ore.*

Category	Number
Caseload by Type of Offense—	
Total Cases Reported	797
Murder	44
Rape	72
Robbery	6
Agg assault	44
Neg manslaughter	2
Other assault	13
Other sex	7
Family offenses	5
Kidnapping	0
Hit and run	90
Death investigation	146
Burglary	133
Larceny 50 +	26
Auto theft	2
Larceny 50 −	10
Arson	8
Forg and counterfeit	0
Fraud	0
Embezzlement	0
Stolen property	4
Vandalism	37
Bombing	4
Pets, livestock	19
Food and drug	0
Other property	51
Weapons	14
Comm. vice	0
Narcotics and D.D.	0
Gambling	0
D.W.I.	0
Liquor	23
Drunkenness	0
Suicide	2
Abortion	1
Obscene literature	0
Conservation	17
Other illegal acts	14

enforcement officer, there must be a concomitant increase in physical clue material input from the scenes of crimes. While all law enforcement officers should receive training in the preservation of the crime scene and the identification and collection of significant physical clue material, skilled and supervised personnel attached to a laboratory with a primary responsibility for the collection and preservation of evidence appear to offer the greatest potential.

2. *Laboratory response must match demand.* The laboratory has a part in influencing the amount of material that it receives. A negative attitude on the part of an examiner, frequent inconclusive results, or slow response to need will reduce or halt input to the laboratory. Since the laboratory does not normally control its size or budget, the managing agency must share responsibility for the level of service that can be offered.

3. *More trained criminalists are needed.* Even the modest goal of three laboratory cases per year per sworn officer would only represent the crime

TABLE 6—*Evidence yield by type of offense, State Police Crime Laboratory, Portland, Ore.*

Category	Number	Percent
Murder	44	
Physiological Evid	29	65.9
Narcotics	6	13.6
Firearms	25	56.8
Documents	0	0.0
Clothing and fabrics	13	29.5
Fragments	1	2.3
Trace evidence	4	9.1
Marks and impressions	0	0.0
Explosives	0	0.0
Chemical products	5	11.4
Miscellaneous	1	2.3
Crime scene	23	52.3
Rape	72	
Physiological evid	70	97.2
Narcotics	2	2.8
Firearms	0	0.0
Documents	0	0.0
Clothing and fabrics	16	22.2
Fragments	0	0.0
Trace evidence	2	2.8
Marks and impressions	0	0.0
Explosives	0	0.0
Chemical products	1	1.4
Miscellaneous	1	1.4
Crime scene	28	38.9
Aggravated Assault	44	
Physiological evid	21	47.7
Narcotics	1	2.3
Firearms	26	59.1
Documents	0	0.0
Clothing and fabrics	3	6.8
Fragments	3	6.8
Trace evidence	3	6.8
Marks and impressions	0	0.0
Explosives	0	0.0
Chemical products	2	4.5
Miscellaneous	0	0.0
Crime scene	22	50.0
Hit and Run	90	
Physiological evid	5	5.6
Narcotics	2	2.2
Firearms	0	0.0
Documents	0	0.0
Clothing and fabrics	4	4.4
Fragments	11	12.2
Trace evidence	83	92.2
Marks and impressions	0	0.0
Explosives	0	0.0

laboratory's involvement in between 3 percent and 4 percent of the nation's crime. At an average caseload of 250 cases per year, this would require almost 4000 criminalists, or a fourfold increase over the current number of practitioners. If improved crime scene search measures are set in motion, and administrators and command staff reinforce and support the effort, existing crime laboratories would soon be inundated by physical clue material and faced with critical shortages of trained laboratory personnel. Improved crime scene search must be coupled with increases in laboratory capability. Both academic and on-the-job training programs are needed.

4. *Quality of service must be maintained.* There are few sources for training in criminalistics; thus, people with little or no preprofessional training are entering this field, with the potential of endangering the credibility and accuracy of the results of laboratory examinations. Quality control measures of both intra and interlaboratory operations are required. Due to staff shortages, too little attention has been given to individual professional development. Short courses, seminars, and formal academic programs at the graduate level should be encouraged.

5. *Existing crime laboratory resources are largely devoted to non index crime.* Statutory tests (drugs, blood alcohol) reach the laboratory in both high percentage and quantity, pushing other evidence examination into the background. Many laboratories today become deeply involved in platter cases to the point that their heavy workload becomes so well known that it serves as a subtle deterrent to the search for physical evidence in more serious cases. Again, the whole law enforcement system must accept some responsibility for allowing such items to saturate existing capabilities. Drugs should no more be allowed to dominate the laboratory than should all police be devoted to traffic.

One solution can be the development and adoption of automated analyses for commonly recurring materials. The second might be to further encourage the acceptance of laboratory reports at lower levels of the court system and in hearings without live testimony.

6. *The crime laboratory should be in the main stream of law enforcement activity.* Instead of merely being a captive service group, the crime laboratory should have a position in and a rapport with the agencies it supports. The laboratory should be situated in the organization so that it has some voice in its budget, personnel policies, and other management decisions. In organizational structures where the laboratory reports to a non-technical supervisor, there is often a complete breakdown in ability to translate to the budget-making body the exact needs of the laboratory.

7. *Crime laboratories must be planned and integrated into the criminal justice system.* The development of crime laboratory capabilities must proceed hand in hand with crime scene search and awareness of the existence of this resource. The law enforcement investigator, the prosecutor, and other members of the legal community must be brought into any planning process to assure that the capabilities provided will, in fact, be used. This awareness and use cannot occur overnight, nor should anyone expect a crime laboratory to develop other than through an orderly, phased planning process which integrates the laboratory into the total law enforcement system. The laboratory planning model developed in this study can provide significant assistance in these areas.

8. *A crime laboratory should serve an entire standard metropolitan statistical area.* The physical, economic, and social interdependence of the cities and counties which comprise an SMSA also influences the pattern of crime in that area. A crime laboratory with a specific charter to serve an entire SMSA and

multiple-source funding can be responsive to the needs of all of the law enforcement departments in that area.

9. *Crime laboratories should maintain and exchange management information.* Currently, there are few or no data on which to base an evaluation of the performance of a crime laboratory. The development of a system for the exchange of management information would have an impact on criminalistics which would provide greater insight into each laboratory's own operations and also a comparison with the operations of other laboratories. By establishing a mechanism for obtaining results of the use of the laboratory, initial measures of effectiveness could be established.

NOTES

(1) Final Report, 30 June 1969—28 June 1970, Grant NI-044 MRI, Project No. 3333-D, Law Enforcement Assistance Administration, U.S. Dept. of Justice, Washington, D.C.

(2) "Crime Laboratories—Three Study Reports," LEAA Project Report, U.S. Department of Justice, 1968.

(3) "Standard Metropolitan Statistical Areas," Executive Office of the President, Bureau of the Budget, 1967.

(4) Hoover, J. E., "Uniform Crime Reports—1968," *Crime in the United States*, Washington, D.C., U.S. Government Printing Office, 13 Aug. 1969.

(5) Parker, Brian et al, "Physical Evidence Utilization in the Administration of Criminal Justice." School of Criminology, University of California, March 1970.

(6) Hoover, J. E., "Uniform Crime Reports—1967," *Crime in the United States*, Washington, D.C., U.S. Government Printing Office, 27 Aug. 1968.

(7) Kingston, C. R., *A National Criminalistics Research Program*, John Jay College of Criminal Justice, New York, 1969.

(8) Kirk, P. L. and Bradford, L. W., *The Crime Laboratory: Organization and Operation*, 1st ed., Charles C. Thomas, Springfield, Ill., 1965.

(9) "The Next Move—Planning for Less Crime," Metropolitan Atlanta Council of Local Governments, Atlanta, Ga., Dec. 1968.

(10) Needham, D. V., detective chief superintendent, "The Potential of Enhanced Resources in Scenes of Crime Work. Report No. 4/69," Home Office Police Research and Development Branch, London, England, 1969.

(11) Cohn, S. I., Ed., "Proceedings of the Second National Symposium on Law Enforcement Science and Technology," *Law Enforcement Science and Technology*, Vol. 2, Port City Press, Inc., 1968.

(12) "Trace Evidence," Department of the Army Technical Bulletin TB PMG 13, Headquarters, Department of the Army, Washington, D.C., 17 April 1967.

(13) "First Annual Report of the Law Enforcement Assistance Administration," U.S. Department of Justice, Washington, D.C., 1969.

(14) "How to Prepare Uniform Crime Reports," *Uniform Crime Reporting Handbook*, Federal Bureau of Investigation, U.S. Department of Justice, Washington, D.C., July 1966.

(15) Willmer, M. A. P., "The Criminal as a Transmitter of Signals (SA/PM 12)," Police Memorandum, Home Office Scientific Adviser's Branch, London, England, Dec. 1966.

(16) The President's Commission on Law Enforcement and Administration of Justice," The Challenge of Crime in a Free Society, General Report. Task Force

Report; Science and Technology," U.S. Government Printing Office, Washington, D.C., 1967.

(17) Osterburg, J. W., "The Crime Laboratory," *Case Studies of Scientific Criminal Investigation*, Indiana University Press, Bloomington, Ind., 1968.

(18) Blumstein, Alfred et al, "A National Program of Research, Development, Test and Evaluation on Law Enforcement and Criminal Justice," Institute for Defense Analyses, Arlington, Va., Nov. 1968.

(19) Borkenstein, R., "The Administration of a Forensic Science Laboratory," *Methods of Forensic Science*, A. J. Curry, Ed., Vol. III, Interscience, New York, 1964.

PLANNING A FORENSIC SCIENCE LAB

John W. Gunn
Richard S. Frank

An important function of the Bureau of Narcotics and Dangerous Drugs is to assist state and local enforcement agencies in their attempts to enforce narcotic and controlled drug laws. The laboratories of BNDD not only provide cost-free analysis and expert testimony, but also stand ready to offer expertise in the formulation and management of forensic laboratory programs.

The authors have been frequently contacted by personnel from state, local, and other federal agencies for information and advice regarding design and management of forensic science laboratories. Requests for assistance have increased over the past year due in large part to the financial aid received by state and local law enforcement agencies from the Law Enforcement Assistance Administration, U.S. Department of Justice.

Dr. Joseph,(1) in his study of crime laboratories, indicated a model regional crime laboratory would serve an area with a population of 500,000 to 1,000,000 people, where 5,000 Part I offenses per year occur. Benson, *et all*,(2) in a study for LEAA, developed a concept that a crime laboratory should serve an entire Standard Metropolitan Statistical Area (SMSA).

It is the premise of this paper that the laboratory exists and is expanding or a decision has been made to establish a forensic laboratory.

Once the decision is made to expand or establish a laboratory, the mission and goals of the laboratory program must be defined. The mission of a forensic laboratory is to provide scientific examination of physical evidence; the goal is to provide the service in the most expeditious and efficient manner. Economic factors to consider are: staff, operating budget, facility, and equipment.

It has been the experience of the authors that requirements should be set up on a modular basis, as much as possible. This enables planning to be readily adjusted for changes in staffing, which is the basis for .evaluating facility, equipment, and operational requirements. Modules must, however, be so designed that they can be used with freedom. Adjustments for special requirements must always be considered.

The forensic laboratory that will be discussed is a laboratory that is involved in the analysis of narcotics and dangerous drugs. This laboratory, however, could easily be a section of a full-service forensic laboratory with the equipment and instrumentation having much greater use than only for narcotic and drug analyses.

It is most desirable that any new laboratory be a full-service crime laboratory equipped to handle all but the most specialized phases of examining physical materials in criminal investigations. Kirk,(3) Lucas,(4) and Guttenplan(5) discuss various aspects of the full-service forensic laboratory.

STAFF

The project of staffing the laboratory with an adequate number of qualified professionals is a very important job. The literature (3,6) contains some extremely useful information.

The size of the staff of the laboratory is predicated by the workload, or by the number of pieces of evidence to be processed or examinations required to be performed by the laboratory. In determining the number of chemists required to handle the workload, the following factors must be determined: 1. Total working hours per chemist per year, 2. Non-analytical hours per chemist per year, 3. Analytical hours per chemist per year, 4. Number of examinations to be performed per chemist per year, and, 5. Total number of examinations per laboratory per year.

The total working hours may be established by a procedure similar to the following:

		Balance
Days per year 365		
Less Saturdays-Sundays per year 104		261
Less vacation per year 20		241
Less illness per year 7		234
Less legal holidays . . . . ' 7		227
Times hours per day x8		1,816

Elements contributing to the non-analytical time of laboratory personnel must be deducted from the total working hours and include review of scientific literature, research, court testimony (including travel), training received, training conducted, assisting enforcement personnel and miscellaneous duties.

The amount of time relating to each of these non-analytical elements will vary greatly between organizations. Court testimony time, for instance, will be greatly affected by the distance of laboratory from court; training received will vary with the number of new personnel and with the emphasis placed upon keeping current with new techniques; training conducted varies with the responsibility for training other personnel. It is estimated that between one-third and one-half of available chemist man-hours are devoted to these non-analytical duties.

With the estimated number of non-analytical hours established, the number of analytical hours would be the balance of the total working hours per chemist per year; for example, if the non-analytical time is estimated as one-half, the analytical hours would be: 1816 hours minus 908 hours non-analytical equals 908 analytical hours per year per chemist.

The number of examinations to be performed per chemist per year is determined by dividing the average time of an analysis into the number of analytical hours per year per chemist. For example, if the average time for an examination is two hours, and 908 analytical hours are available to a chemist, a chemist could perform 452 examinations per year.

The average time for an examination is greatly affected by the depth of the analysis that is to be performed. If only a qualitative examination is performed on the average exhibit, the average time will be considerably less than if a quantitative examination is also performed. Factors affecting the average time of an examination include: size of exhibit (i.e., number of tablets to examine), background information supplied, suspected drug, excipients, quantitation and expertise of personnel.

BNDD's experience indicates that approximately two hours are required to perform the examination of an average exhibit submitted to its laboratories. This figure is derived not only from BNDD evidence, but from evidence submitted by all other agencies for analysis and it includes quantitative analyses in the majority of cases.

In determining the necessary number of examinations to be performed by the laboratory in a year's time, enforcement personnel must be relied upon to provide the laboratory programs with information regarding changes in the staffing ceiling of enforcement. This information, along with past history of evidence collected, is utilized to establish future laboratory workloads.

By relating the number of total examinations required to be performed by the laboratory to the number of examinations each chemist can be expected to perform during the year, the size of the staff of the laboratory necessary to properly support the enforcement effort can be established.

A useful modular concept, to utilize in monitoring future staffing requirements, is the relationship of the number of enforcement personnel each chemist can support. If, for example, workload data shows that one chemist can support twenty enforcement personnel, to which forty are being added to the staff the next year, it can be easily justified that two additional chemists must be added to the staff of the laboratory.

As indicated earlier, when modular concepts are used to support staffing requirements, the modules must be constantly monitored and updated. When no previous data exist, and estimates are made, sometimes relying on data of other organizations with similar missions, the modules are particularly subject to change, and must be constantly updated to keep their information valid.

The position of the Laboratory Director is the most important in the laboratory and the selection of the individual to fill this position should be made as early as possible when a new laboratory program is being formulated. Since this individual is to be responsible for supervising the entire laboratory, he must be given the authority and responsibility to fill all the positions which report directly to him. He, in turn, must do the same with any subordinate supervisory positions. It is also beneficial to have the Director's advice and experience when planning equipment purchases, laboratory layout and formulating operating policies and procedures.

The Director's qualifications should include scientific background with experience in the forensic field, but technical ability alone must not be the basis of the selection for this position. Too often an individual is placed in an administrative capacity because of outstanding technical ability, and the result proves extremely unfavorable. The Director's primary responsibility should be to manage the laboratory's operation, which requires someone with ability to do just that. In small laboratories the staff may be such that the Director may be required, on occasion, to perform examinations of evidence, but in a laboratory with sufficient staff this should not be the case. The Director is responsible for staffing, budgeting, planning and coordinating operation of the laboratory and establishing and maintaining liaison with the scientific and enforcement community. To accomplish this effectively, he must be able to devote his entire efforts to administration.

The laboratory's professional scientific staff is responsible for accomplishing the mission of the laboratory. To this end, the scientist is established as an expert witness in court and must have the education and experience to support this. The recognized educational requirement is a Bachelor of Science degree; without this minimum degree the individual must be considered to be a forensic technician, regardless of the number of years of experience.

Experience is a difficult area to qualify. When forming a new laboratory, it is necessary to gather some forensic scientists with sufficient experience to handle not only the laboratory's caseload, but also to train inexperienced personnel.

In order to obtain high-caliber personnel, the organization must be made attractive. The primary factor in attracting such individuals is salary, which must be competitive with similar positions in both private industry and government. The American Chemical Society regularly publishes detailed salary and information that may be used as a guide in identifying salary trends.

Maslow(7) and other behavioral scientists have indicated that man is a wanting animal and as soon as one of his needs is satisfied, another appears in its place. Salary will attract high-caliber personnel in an organization, but that organization must satisfy his other needs also; the point being that while salary is the initial satisfier, emphasis on satisfying other needs, such as continued self-development and challenge, will not only keep existing employees content, but can act as an attractive recruiting agent, particularly when salaries may be somewhat unfavorable in comparison to similar employment. Satisfaction of needs must not only be discussed, but planned for and accomplished in the day-to-day operation of the laboratory so each chemist has opportunity for professional development. The laboratory must encourage participation in professional societies, opportunities to attend short courses, and graduate school is a must for a viable laboratory.

Once staffing problems have been worked out, the actual operation of the laboratory must be planned. Factors that must be considered include organization, funding requirements and standard operating policies and procedures. Organization must be considered in two aspects: where the laboratory fits into the overall agency structure and within the laboratory itself.

It is important that the Laboratory Director be directly involved in overall policy decisions. Since the laboratory is greatly affected by enforcement programs, there is a need for close coordination between the related programs of enforcement and laboratory support. However, it is equally as important that the laboratory not be directly under the supervision of the enforcement director. The reason for this may be seen in drawing an analogy between this situation and the relationship between a product control department and production department in a manufacturing operation. Since their individual responsibilities differ in accomplishing the overall mission, i.e., maximum profit for company, the production head should not be in a position to exert undue pressure upon the control department which may adversely affect the quality of the product. Overall management of both departments can best be accomplished by an individual having line authority above each, with an understanding of the entire operation.

The organizational structure within the laboratory depends largely upon the size and experience of the staff. Since the "working" chemist is considered to be an expert, the amount of technical supervision required is slight. Supervision required is largely administrative, and a supervisor can effectively supervise six to eight professionals. Trainees and chemists who have not attained the "working" level will require technical supervision as well as administrative, and the effective span of supervision will be less.

In a laboratory which is staffed totally by experienced forensic chemists, the need for a supervisory chemist, which makes the Laboratory Director a second line supervisor, is debatable when the laboratory's staff is eleven or less. To a large degree, the determining factor is the amount of duties drawing the Director's attention away from the day-to-day operation of the laboratory. If the amount is slight, the Laboratory Director may be able to administer the entire operation, and the organizational structure may be represented as:

BUILDING SPECIFICATIONS FOR
A FORENSIC CHEMISTRY LABORATORY

1. Laboratory space will be divided into (   ) 500-square-foot sections. Each will provide laboratory space for two chemists and/or technicians. Each section must be provided with the following:

  A. One laboratory bench to be provided with: 1. Seven duplex convenience outlets (110V) on a separate 30-amp circuit, 2. ½″ cold water supply line for 3″x6″ cup sink of Durcon 2A construction, 3. 3/8″ vacuum and air pressure supply lines capable of providing 40 psi, and 4. All under-table drain lines shall be 1½″ modified epoxy resin (Durcon 2A or equal). Three drain lines for each two benches will be required with "P" traps.

  B. Table sinks—one per section and must be provided with: 1. ½″ hot and cold supply lines, 2. ¼″ aluminum distilled water supply line, and 3. 2″ modified epoxy resin drain line with "P" traps.

  C. Fume hood—one per section and must be provided with: 1. ½″ cold water supply line 1½″ modified epoxy resin drain line for a 3″x6″ cup sink (Duron 2A or equal construction), 2. 3/8″ natural gas supply line, 3. Exhaust duct—10″ diameter to run to the outside, 4. Power required: 115/230V 60-cycle single phase separate circuit for ½ HP blower motor, 2 duplex convenience outlets (115V, 15 amps) and 2 230V, 30-amp outlets for each hood, 5. 3/8″ steam supply line to be run from a central distiller, and 6. Air pressure and vacum lines as described in laboratory bench above.

  D. One ceiling-mounted emergency shower. ½″ cold water supply required.

  E. One emergency eyewash. ½″ cold water supply required.

  F. Floor tile shall be of chemical-resistant construction.

2. Three instrumentation rooms—200 sq. ft. each. Each room to have facilities described above for one laboratory bench and one fume hood. Special power requirements for each room:

  A. One 115 V, 30-amp separate circuit.

  B. Two 115 V, 15-amp separate circuits.

  C. One room will also need an additional 115V, 15-amp separate circuit.

3. Chemical storage room—200 sq. ft. Must be constructed so as to provide a 2-hour fire barrier from all other areas.

4. Solvent storage room—200 sq. ft. Must be constructed of 6" cinder block walls, plastered and painted, and must be provided with an explosion-proof door.

5. Glass washing and disposal room—250 sq. ft. To be provided with the following facilities:

  A. ¾″ hot and cold water supply lines.

  B. ½″ steam supply line to be run from a central distiller.

  C. 1½″ drain line.

  D. 115V, 15-amp separate circuit for dishwasher.

  E. A 2′x2′ stainless steel sink together with a 2′-wide stainless steel table that drains into the sink. Both must have a 6″ splash board and 6″ ledge (stainless steel). The waste line must be equipped with a suitable trap to keep odors from entering the area. The sink must be equipped with a running cold water faucet, a 6′ hose attachment and a 1½ HP disposal unit.

6. Glass and equipment storage room—300 sq. ft. No special requirements.

7. Evidence Vault—6″ cinder block construction, plastered and painted on the outside, painted on the inside. To be provided with Class 5 vault door with a hand change combination lock and day gate. Vault must also be provided with electrical protection device.

8. Library, conference and training room—300 sq. ft. Necessary ventilation and air-conditioning must be furnished for a maximum occupancy of 20 people at one time.

9. Locker rooms (male and female)—100 sq. ft. each. Complete with shower, commode and lavatory.

10. Floor load. 70 lbs. per sq. foot will be adequate. Special requirements may exist for specific instruments, such as NMR, mass spec., etc.

11. The total power required to this lab may be computed by adding specific requirements for sections, special purpose rooms, and specific instruments.

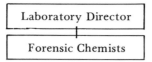

If, however, the Director must direct considerable attention away from day-to-day operation and/or the number of personnel exceeds effective supervision, first line supervisors should be used, and the organizational structure may be represented as:

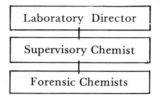

The number of supervisory chemists and groups will depend upon the total number of forensic chemists and the number of forensic chemists that it is decided can be effectively supervised. The Bureau of Narcotics and Dangerous Drugs has established six to eight as the optimum number to be supervised in one group. Therefore, if the staff of a laboratory reaches twelve forensic chemists, two groups are formed.

Adequate support personnel must be included in the staffing for efficient operation. At a minimum, two clerk/typists, one evidence technician and a laboratory helper are necessary for a five- to ten-man laboratory.

TABLE 1

Laboratory Space:
    250 sq. ft./chemist x   chemists =   sq. ft.
Instrumentation Rooms:
    200 sq. ft./room x   rooms =   sq. ft.

Chemical Storage Room	= 200 sq. ft.
Solvent Storage Room	= 200 sq. ft.
Glassware and Equipment Storage	= 300 sq. ft.
Evidence Vault	= 250 sq. ft.
Glassware Washing Room	= 250 sq. ft.
Library	= 300 sq. ft.
Conference Room	= 300 sq. ft.
Office Space	= 500 sq. ft.
TOTAL	= sq. ft.

OPERATING BUDGET

Funds to allow the laboratory's day-to-day operation to exist can be established on a modular basis. Items to consider in this category include glassware breakage, chemical reagents, solvents, instrument parts and repairs, training of personnel, travel and other miscellaneous supplies and requirements. Amount of travel will vary greatly from one organization to another, as will amounts paid for supplies; therefore, it is difficult to discuss exactly how much funding is required. Once an amount is projected for each chemist, however, the total funding required for the laboratory's operation can be readily determined by multiplying by the total number of chemists. The particular value of this operating module for budgeting purposes is the ease in altering funding requirements when staffs are being increased.

TABLE 2

BUILDING REQUIREMENTS

1. Floor Load
2. Elevators (Freight and Passenger)
3. Partitions
4. Doors
5. Ceiling
6. Flooring
7. Lighting
8. Air Conditioning
9. Heating
10. Fire Extinguishing System
11. Washrooms
12. Stairs

MECHANICAL SERVICE REQUIREMENTS

1. Cold Water
2. Hot Water
3. Distilled Water
4. Electricity
5. Steam
6. Vacuum
7. Air Pressure
8. Gas
9. Drains
10. Fume Exhaust
11. Emergency Eyewash and Shower

Future needs for things such as reagents, supplies, training, etc., are relatively easy to establish compared to replacement of instruments, and acquisition of new instrumentation. Since it is almost impossible to know when an instrument will require replacement, replacement cycles must be established. Many individuals use this basic idea for replacing automobiles. At a certain age, it becomes more economically efficient to replace an item with a new one. Replacement cycles should be established for each of the major instruments in the laboratory, and worked into the laboratory operating fund.

Training (night school, short courses, attendance at meetings, etc.) and career development are extremely important factors in the operation of a laboratory program. Technology is rapidly changing, and unless an effort is made to keep up with the changes, an organization will rapidly become outmoded and decay. The majority of qualified individuals today are looking for organizations which are making efforts to keep advanced in addition to paying sufficient salaries. The interest an organization takes in developing its scientific personnel will pay many dividends in accomplishing the final mission.

FACILITY

Overall space requirements for a laboratory facility will vary according to the number of actual laboratory personnel. Each forensic chemist should have approximately 250 square feet of laboratory work space. In addition, there are requirements for specialized laboratory space, storage space, and office space that will not vary to as great an extent with the number of chemists as laboratory space per se. *Table I* shows a requirement list.

Thus, for a five-man laboratory with two instrumentation rooms, approximately 3,900 square feet of net space will be required; for a ten-man laboratory with three instrumentation rooms, 5,350 square feet will be required.

The cost of preparing a facility will vary greatly from building to building, and from area to area. Factors that must be considered are listed in *Table 2.*

Laboratory furniture must also be considered in the cost of the facility. Important factors here include: casework, bench tops, service shelves, wall cabinets, table units, service fixtures (gas, air, vacum, electricity, water), table sinks, cup sinks, fume hoods (superstructure, base cabinet, motor-blower).

Costs vary greatly according to the type of material which is chosen. Bench tops are available in wood, stone, asbestos, fiber, stainless steel, plastic laminate, and epoxy resin, the latter being extremely resistant to chemical and physical abuse, but also being the most expensive. Thus, the material utilized will affect the final cost.

Experience has shown that a reasonable figure to use for planning purposes is approximately $55 per square foot for laboratory space and $10 per square foot for office space. This should enable the acquisition and installation of high-quality equipment, and provide for a complete laboratory facility.

EQUIPMENT

Necessary glassware, balances, scientific instruments, etc., must be procured to enable the laboratory to function efficiently and properly. A suggested basic equipment module is contained in *Table 3.*

The cost of equipment will vary according to the quality and manufacturer. The unit costs identified for items in *Table 3* are intended to be representative of

TABLE 3

EQUIPMENT	AMOUNT PER CHEMIST	UNIT COST	COST PER CHEMIST
Ultraviolet Spectrophotometer	1/10	13,000	1,300
Infrared Spectrophotometer & Accessories	1/7	11,000	1,575
Gas Chromatograph	1/5	9,000	1,800
Fluorimeter, Recording	1/10	9,000	900
Spectropolarimeter	1/10	6,500	650
Balance, Analytical	1/2	900	450
Balance, Top-Loading, Two Ranges	1/5	1,500	300
Balance, Micro	1/5	1,300	260
Melting Point Apparatus	1/10	300	30
Microscope	1/5	500	100
Microscope, Compound	1/5	1,000	200
Microscope, Polarizing	1/5	3,000	600
Glassware, Laboratory	1/1	500	500
Ultraviolet Cabinet	1/5	150	30
Glassware Washer	1/10	2,500	250
Distilled Water Still	1/10	1,200	120
Oven, Vacuum	1/5	250	50
Oven, Convection	1/5	1,000	200
Stool	1/1	15	15
Refrigerator, Explosion Proof	1/10	700	70
Water Bath, Heating and Refrigerating	1/10	700	70
Centrifuge	1/5	200	40
Hot Plate	1/1	100	100
Shaker	1/10	400	40
Thin-Layer Chromatography Equipment	1/10	400	40
Vacuum Pump	1/5	200	40
Evaporator, Flash	1/10	600	60
Weights, Analytical	1/10	100	10
Calculator, Electronic	1/5	1,000	200
Miscellaneous Chemicals, etc.	lot	1,000	1,000
TOTAL		$11,000	

what will be needed for good quality equipment.

The specified dollar amount per chemist is intended to be an approximation and should be utilized in that manner. For instance, for a ten-chemist laboratory, one ultraviolet spectrophotometer will usually be capable of efficiently handling the workload; whereas, one infrared spectrophotometer will often be used to its capacity and a second instrument should be considered. Having "back-up" instrumentation for utilization in periods of heavy workload and also while maintenance is being performed on the primary instrument is desirable, but may not be economically feasible for all instrumentation. It should be considered when an instrument is one which is utilized in the majority of examinations, and maintenance or replacement of parts frequently result in abnormally long down time.

In addition to the Basic Equipment Module, other highly sophisticated instrumentation with application in forensic science should be considered. This supplementary instrumentation is not routinely used by the forensic chemist when performing the majority of examinations; however, its use is invaluable in situations where the "basic" instruments do not provide sufficient analytical information. Such instrumentation includes: Nuclear Magnetic Resonance Spectrometer, Mass Spectrometer, X-ray Diffraction Apparatus, X-ray Fluorescence Apparatus and Atomic Absorption Spectrophotometer.

All the above equipment, both Basic Equipment Module and Supplementary Instrumentation, has much wider application than just forensic drug analyses. The same equipment can be used for toxicology, arson examinations, and other general chemical examinations. When equipping the forensic chemistry laboratory, it is important to consult with other departments to establish their requirements and workload. Whereas an item listed on the supplementary list may not be justified only for the forensic chemistry laboratory, overall use by the total laboratory may warrant its acquisition.

STANDARD OPERATING PROCEDURES

A manual containing S.O.P. which outlines areas of responsibility and administrative procedures to follow in the laboratory's operation is an invaluable tool in providing all personnel with information of policies and procedures, thereby assuring as efficient an operation as possible.

Standard procedures for the handling of evidence are extremely important for the laboratory. Kirk and Bradford(3) state: "Because it is the most important single function of the operation to deal adequately and properly with the evidence, its proper handling is of the utmost importance and the major item of routine in the laboratory ... It is important that a routine be established by which physical evidence will pass through the laboratory in a regular and predictable manner so that there will be no loss, confusion or breaks in its custody."

In establishing a routine procedure, the planning should be followed by an examination of the planned procedure by a legal expert. This expert will be able to review the entire procedure and point out areas that could be questionable in a court of law. Procedural steps in the laboratory evidence handling include: receipting in laboratory, indexing, storage prior to analysis, breaking of seals, custody during analysis, sealing after analysis, storage after analysis, and production in court.

An exact procedure to follow in handling evidence in the laboratory is difficult to suggest without knowing what security is available for the evidence, what other operating procedures are, etc. Valuable points to keep in mind in any procedure, however, are: 1. Provide for a continuous, documented chain of custody, 2. Keep chain of custody as short as possible, 3. Assure that safe or vault meets minimum security standards, and 4. Assure that when seals are broken, analyzing chemist has sole access to evidence.

SUMMARY

The factors to be considered, once the decision to expand or to establish a forensic laboratory has been made, are staff, operating budget, facility and equipment. It is recommended that most requirements should be set up on a modular basis; examples of these modules are given. The staff of the laboratory is the most important ingredient in the planning. A manual containing standard operating procedures is suggested. The assistance of the BNDD Laboratories is available to all law enforcement agencies who are planning forensic laboratories.

NOTES

(1) Joseph Alexander: "Study of Needs and Development of Curricula in the Field of Forensic Science" "Crime Laboratories: Three Study Reports." LEAA Project Report, Washington, D.C., U.S. Department of Justice (April, 1968).

(2) Benson, W. R., Story, John E., and Worley, M. L.: "Systems Analysis of Criminalistics Operations," Final Report Midwest Research Institute Project No. 3333-D, LEAA Grant NI-044, U.S. Department of Justice, Washington, D.C. (June, 1970).

(3) Kirk, P. L., and Bradford, L. W.: *The Crime Laboratory*, Charles C. Thomas, Springfield, Illinois (1965).

(4) Lucas, D. M.: "Criminalistics—The State of the Art." Paper presented at the 22nd Annual Meeting of the American Academy of Forensic Sciences, Chicago, Illinois. February 25-28 (1970).

(5) Guttenplan, H. L.: "The National Institute on Police Laboratory Operations," *Police*, Vol. 14, No. 4, pp. 38-49 (March-April, 1970).

(6) Borkenstein, R. F.: "The Administration of a Forensic Science Laboratory," Curry, A. S. (Ed.): *Methods of Forensic Sciences*, Vol. III, pp. 155-168, Interscience Publishers, New York (1964).

(7) Maslow, A. H.: *Motivation and Personality*, Harper & Row, New York (1954).

VI.

The Impact of Science on the Criminal Justice System

INTRODUCTION

One principal point which emerges from the previous readings is that science plays a supportive role in the criminal justice system. It aids the investigator in establishing the *corpus delecti* of a crime, in reconstructing an incident, in identifying likely suspects, and in proving or disproving the association of particular physical evidence with a suspect. Laboratories also assist the police and prosecutor in the presentation of evidence during the actual prosecution of a case. Just as important, a defendant in a trial may be helped by the laboratory in which examinations show no connection between physical evidence and the suspect or which implicate another person altogether.

Any service like a crime laboratory must routinely examine its contributions to those who use its capabilities. To what degree are laboratories utilized by agents of the criminal justice system, and what is the impact of this usage? Are forensic science laboratories upholding their scientific commitment to objectivity and neutrality? Do scientific crime laboratories materially improve the quality of justice dispensed in the United States?

Brian Parker of Sacramento State University was one of the first forensic scientists to attempt to provide answers to such questions when in 1963 he surveyed crime laboratories in the United States and throughout the world to determine their level of utilization. The findings were discouraging: criminal investigators made no use of scientific services in over 98% of their cases. Also, an overwhelming tendency was discovered to concentrate laboratory services on homicides which account for less than 0.1% of all known violations.

A selection from Harry Kalven, Jr. and Hans Zeisel's book, *The American Jury*, offers another perspective on the use of scientific evidence by the criminal courts. This study, published in 1966, describes the types and degrees of usage of evidence by the prosecution and the defense. It becomes apparent that an imbalance exists between the prosecution's and defense's use of expert witnesses. This imbalance will be addressed in greater detail in the following section.

Willard Lassers examines the use of physical evidence in capital cases which would, one would expect, require greater utilization of scientific evidence. He found that approximately one-fourth of the capital cases involved some form of physical evidence, but that most of it was rather elementary and restricted to fingerprints, ballistics and blood. Lawyers still heavily relied upon confessions, the testimony of witnesses, and other traditional forms of proof; science played a clearly secondary role. A serious concern is expressed over the availability of scientific services to defendants, and especially indigent ones.

The final article is a presentation of results from a study sponsored by the National Institute of Law Enforcement and Criminal Justice. Brian Parker and Joseph Peterson examine and document the availability of physical evidence at the scenes of some Part I crime scenes. If it were shown that few crime scenes yield such physical evidence, then the lack of evidence would explain the low percentage of cases in which evidence was eventually analyzed and introduced into court. To the contrary, the study determined that physical evidence was present in over 80% of the 750 crime scenes investigated and merited scientific attention. Actually, only about six percent of the cases involved a laboratory examination of physical evidence and the overwhelming majority of these cases involved the identification of illicit contraband seized by the police.

THE STATUS OF FORENSIC SCIENCE

IN THE ADMINISTRATION OF CRIMINAL JUSTICE

Brian Parker

In crime investigation, scientific knowledge is commonly recognized as useful. Indeed the areas covered draw upon all scientific disciplines(2) and, in all probability, no species of criminal violation is outside a profitable application of scientific technique on occasion.(3) This recognized value can be seen around the world in the establishment of scientific laboratories in police departments, justice departments and other governmental agencies devoted to service in the administration of criminal justice.(4) The wide development of scientific laboratories involved in crime detection is particularly marked in the United States over the last thirty-odd years.(5)

While this ill-shapen innovation(6) has proven, with little doubt, its use, there remains a legitimate question as to the extent of its use. The scientific examination and interpretation of the physical tracings left in a criminal passage is only *one* of the investigator's tools.(7) The fascination that attaches to scientific operations(8) obscures the fact "that the ultimate responsibility in all criminal cases rests upon the [i] nvestigator"(9) who decides whether or not this particular tool is to be used. If the investigator thinks that "in a high percentage of criminal cases reference of material to the expert is unnecessary. ."(10) and that "in a good percentage of the cases it will be found that there is no physical evidence. . ."(11) the actual utilization of scientific aids would reflect this view.

Two other administrative decisions affect the extent of use made of this tool. One of these is the organizational structure of the forensic science laboratory with regard to the types of services to be rendered, to its eductional and public relations duties, and to research and development on new problems and improved techniques.(12) The second is the presentation of scientific evidence by prosecutors(13) and the competent questioning of this evidence *or the lack of it* by defense counsel.(14) A first approximation to knowledge of these effects is gained from a study of the fiscal support given to forensic science laboratories.

The use and cost data for scientific examinations was requested in 1962 of various agencies in 50 U.S. states, in 50 U.S. cities and in 15 foreign countries. Each was asked to provide information on local scientific facilities in respect to annual expenditures, laboratory personnel and work load distribution. In addition to information received on forensic science laboratories engaged in aiding criminal investigations, medical examiner and coroner systems provided similar information on their operations.

EXTENT OF REPLIES

Over ninety percent of the U.S. sources answered, which covers better than ninety-five percent of the U.S. population. The U.S. cities queried are the fifty largest in population; those forty-seven that answered represent over sixty percent of the total population in standard metropolitan statistical areas.(15) Table I shows the breakdown on returns.

TABLE I

REPLIES

Area	Uses City System	Uses State System	Uses F.B.I.	Insufficient Information	Total Replies	No Reply
States		24	16	6	46	4
Cities	24	10	5	8	47	3

Of the fifteen foreign countries queried, nine answered. Suitable information for this study was received in six of these nine replies.

UTILIZATION OF FACILITIES

The recording of known criminal violations is a very complex operation. The legal system in each country by its definitions of what constitutes criminal violations greatly affects any method of recording. Thus a comparison between countries as to the utilization of scientific laboratory facilities is best approximated by examining the percentages of total known criminal violations that are processed. Table II compares estimates for three countries with legal systems of similar origin.

TABLE II

GENERAL UTILIZATION OF LABORATORIES

Country	Percentage of Total Criminal Violations Examined
United States	
Local	Less than 1.0
F.B.I. (local)	Less than 0.5
England and Wales	1.5
Ontario, Canada	1.3

Within the United States forensic science laboratories vary in the methods of recording their own work. Statistical information may be compiled according to categories of criminal violations, of specimen submitted and/or of scientific examination employed. The first category is represented in Table III.

TABLE III

SPECIFIC UTILIZATION OF LABORATORIES

Criminal Violation(s)	Number of Laboratories	Percentage of Total Violations Examined			
		Median	Average	Range	Middle 2/3rds of Range
Criminal Homicide	9	2.0	2.1	0.4— 5.0	1.3— 2.9
	9	22	26	20 —35	20 —33
Burglary	3	3.5	3.6	1.8— 5.6	
	15	22	32	10 —80	18 —55
All violations other than those in the Crime Index[16] ...	18	30	40	0.0—94	10 —79

COST OF FACILITIES

The cost of local forensic science laboratory (FSL) facilities in the United States appears in the following four tables. Table VI takes into account that 60% of the total expenditures are for examinations of violations within the Crime Index classifications.(17) Tables IV, V and VI include the costs of medical examiner and coroner (ME&C) facilities as well; for Tables IV and V these inclusions represent total cost, while Table VI pertains specifically to an estimate of cost for that proportion of criminal violations involving the services of the medical examiner or coroner.(18)

The expenditures of foreign countries on forensic science laboratory facilities are difficult to relate due to currency differences and costs of living. The following table, Table VIII, lists for these reasons the expenditures in foreign currency as well as conversions to dollars.

TABLE IV

EXPENDITURE PER 100,000 POPULATION

Nmber & Type of Facilities	Median	Average	Range	Middle 2/3rds of Range
FSL				
24 States[19] ...	$ 2,360	$ 3,660	$ 500—16,000	$ 1,150— 5,500
24 Cities[20] ...	3,650	4,730	500—10,000	2,200— 8,700
24 Cities[21] ...	7,410	9,800	2,100—24,000	4,500—16,500
ME&C				
23 Counties and States[22]	8,670	10,700	2,250—32,900	4,500—13,550

TABLE V

EXPENDITURE PER CASE

Number & Type of Facilities	Median	Average	Range	Middle 2/3rds of Range
13 FSL[23] ...	$ 45	$ 51	$ 22—110	$ 35—54
20 ME&C[23] .	57	63	16—188	33—84

TABLE VI

FUNDS AVAILABLE PER CRIMINAL VIOLATION

Number & Type of Facilities	Median	Average	Range	Middle 2/3rds of Range
FSL[24]				
24 States[25] ...	$ 2.1	$ 2.6	$ 0.4— 7.5	$ 1.0— 4.1
24 Cities[26] ...	2.0	2.0	0.3— 4.5	1.1— 3.2
24 Cities[27] ...	3.8	4.1	1.0— 7.7	1.9— 6.5
ME&C[28]				
23 Counties and States	104	168	19 —575	44 —445

TABLE VII

PERCENTAGE EXPENDITURE OF REVENUE[29]

FSL Facilities	Median	Average	Range	Middle 2/3rds·of Range
States	0.013	0.017	0.004—0.049	0.006—0.027
Cities	0.06	0.08	0.01 —0.19	0.04 —0.12

TABLE VIII

FOREIGN EXPENDITURES

Country or Subdivision	Average per 100,000		Population	Average per Violation
	Foreign	Currency	Dollars	Dollars
England and Wales	£	638	1,800	76
Canada				
R.C.M.P.			1,555	145
Ontario			5,420	85
Japan	Y	31,000	93	110
Australia				
New South Wales	£	1,215	2,370	
Victoria	£	1,560	1,075	
New Zealand	£	590	1,320	
Switzerland				
Zurich		65,000 Sfrs	15,300	

DISCUSSION

The estimates in Table II would seem to indicate that scientific aid in criminal investigation is a tool of negligible utility. There is no use made of this tool by investigators in over 98% of the known criminal violations.

However, this statistic neglects the question of how many known criminal violations could be constructively examined by scientific methods. Constructive examination denotes that examination which substantially advances the progress of an investigation. Scientific method excludes those techniques which, while possibly and properly under laboratory administrative control, are not under direct personal scientific supervision at the time of use, e.g. breath tests for alcohol.(30)

Besides these restrictions in definition, many times a particular criminal violation may not be a subject for the application of scientific aids. Such might be the case in a criminal violation involving a considerable time lapse between the occurrence of a violation and its official discovery. The physical tracings in this period may be lost, obliterated or adulterated irretrievably depending on the environment while possible general access to the area will reduce the legal effect of recoverable tracings. The limitation may be even more serious in that adequate development in fundamental research is lacking thereby severely restricting the examination of tracings.(31)

In the 1938 *Home Office Report* the members of the "[s]ub[c]ommittee who have had wide experience consider[ed] that, when the work is more fully developed, the number of cases in which materials requiring scientific examination may be encountered may well prove to be of the order of 4 percent of the total number of indictable crimes reported to the police."(32) In contrast, the Attorney General's Laboratory of Ontario, Canada, has shown a steady 25% to 35% increase in service demands each year for the past eleven years without any visible diminishing of this growth rate.(33) My survey did not disclose an operating system which has reached 4% and the meagerness of compiled data on operating systems leaves this question of the scope of general use open to speculation.

Utilization of scientific aids by the U.S. crime investigator in specific categories of criminal violations is somewhat easier to examine. From Table III it can be seen that roughly one-third of the forensic science laboratories compile statistical data on use as related to categories of criminal violations. Among the seven categories included in the Crime Index, criminal homicide and burglary violations make up the bulk of the work for most laboratories. In the few instances where investigators have found available a broader service the categories outside those of the Crime Index have furnished 80-90% of the work. The wide range as to service in the criminal homicide category is often related to the availability of a medical examiner or coroner system.

A most interesting fact in Table III is the tendency to concentrate forensic science laboratory services on the seven categories of the Crime Index. As calculated from available data (34) the rate per 100,000 population for total known violations in the United States is over 7,000. The total rate for those categories of the Crime Index is 1,053 or somewhat less than 15% of all categories. Table III shows that about 60% of the cases examined in forensic science laboratories are within the seven Crime Index categories. Thus less than 15% of all known violations constitute over half of the violations examined scientifically. Equally interesting is that, for half of the laboratories tabulated, criminal homicide violations represent over 20% of their examinations while criminal homicide violations make up much less than 0.1% of all violations.(35)

These statistics must be viewed with proper caution. To treat all known criminal violations as equally important biases the results. Then, too, the percentage of violations is not proportional necessarily to the percentage of time taken in examination and interpretation. Nevertheless, these statistics do point up a tendency on the investigator's part to channel and limit his call on scientific aids.

Non-utilization of scientific aids by the investigator has many causes—possibly equal to some multiple of the number of investigators! Two of particular interest are the confusion of professional roles and the lack of knowledge.

The investigator from the position of rookie patrolman to the position of homicide detective is dealing with all the known criminal violations. His expertise consists in the ability to gather in all varieties of data and the capacity to extract and correlate the *significant* data. He must have at his disposal in reference to the latter capacity scientific and medical professionals to help him determine the significance of physical tracings. If the investigator attempts to determine the significance of the physical traces in contrast "to ascertain[ing] whether there is any material or trace which looks as though it may be significant. . . ,"(36) he has exceeded his professional role and is intruding on the roles of other professionals. It is likewise unfortunate when scientific or medical professionals seek or are given the role of the investigator.(37) These professionals are too often blind to their own limitations.(38) The administrative control(39) over the investigation should remain in the investigator's hands as coordinator.

The proper action of the investigator in the utilization of scientific aids depends on the breadth of his knowledge. He must be able to recognize the possibility of significance in physical tracings. Since his education as to science many times may be rudimentary or non-existent and as to forensic science most times will be non-existent, the training of the investigator must be undertaken by the forensic science laboratory staff.(40) This training must develop in the investigator the ability to see possible significance in physical tracings.(41) The efficiency and the evolution of such a training program needs a constant re-evaluation both from the viewpoint of the investigator and of the forensic scientist. The investigator needs to know precisely in what categories of criminal violations and for what types of tracings the laboratory is presently of the most help. With this knowledge, he can better allocate his time and energy. The forensic scientist needs this same knowledge to correct weaknesses in training program and to discern those areas where fundamental research is urgently required.(42)

Along with the need for precise information on specific utilization of scientific aids more attention must be directed towards the administrative organization of the forensic science laboratory and the legal attitude regarding its product.(43) As the specific utilization of scientific aids involves interprofessional responsibilities between investigator and forensic scientist(44) so does the structure of a scientific service involve interprofessional responsibilities between forensic scientist and lawyer. The lawyer from his positions in the courtroom and in the legislature molds this structural organization within the restrictions delineated by the forensic scientist. The balance point depends upon the resources and the interest of the community.

In the United States, the average cost for the scientific examination of a violation is about $50.(45) The average number of violations examined by each staff member is 250.(46) In Ontario, Canada, the average cost is $85 per violation(47) with the average number of violations examined per staff member being 100.(48) In England the average cost per violation is $76(49) by direct currency conversion but considering the cost of living to be half that of the U.S. this cost would be roughly $150.

It has been estimated(50) that the average cost per violation should be $150 while the average number of violations examined per staff member should be 50.(51) On the basis of these annual estimates the forensic science laboratory in the United States must handle five times the normal work load with but one-third the necessary funds. The quality of the scientific examination can only suffer under such conditions as will the training program for investigators and the contributions to fundamental research.(52) The situation is becoming worse each year with increasing work loads.(53)

U.S. cities in contrast to the states are spending five times as much of their revenues on scientific aid facilities(54) and better than twice as much per capita.(55) For forensic science laboratories the latter amounts to about seven cents per citizen. Table VI illustrates as a further comment the amount of money that would be available if each and every criminal violation in the Crime Index categories was to be submitted for scientific laboratory examination.

An operating annual budget for a city laboratory serving a population of 100,000 in the United States can be calculated from the figures given in this paper.(56) At a utilization level of 1.5% the average expenditure should be $15,750; at a utilization level of 4% the average expenditure, $42,000. Table IV in contrast gives the present average expenditure as $9,800. The laboratory staff should be two at a utilization level of 1.5% and six at a utilization level of 4%. At present one member handles the work load recommended for six.

Funds alone will not provide an adequate forensic science service. This can be seen by comparing the development of such a service in two similar countries. In 1930 the United States and England had no appreciable services in this field.(57) Today England(58) has one of the finest systems of forensic science laboratory services in existence. The situation in the U.S. has less to commend it.(59) The English service is administratively independent of the investigator and of the prosecutor and is under the scientific control of the staff(60) as recommended in 1938.(61) U.S. services are usually administrated by police departments or district attorneys' offices which have direct concern with individual cases. The scientific officer in England has higher academic degree standing.(62) Indeed this policy requirement of university academic preparation needs to be relaxed somewhat so that technical college graduates may be used for staff expansion. In the U.S. it is not uncommon for scientific examinations to be conducted by high school level personnel. The English system does not yet have a Forensic Science Centre as originally proposed(63) although the system has produced work worthy of a research center.(64) The F.B.I. Laboratory in the U.S. performs some of the functions of such a center.

The best commentary on a system that works is its actual performance. *Regina v. Barlow*(65) is destined to be a classic in scientific crime detection. Here the investigators, the forensic scientists and the lawyers combined in an interprofessional, interdisciplinary operation to prove the first recorded murder by insulin injection. A statement attributed to one of the principal forensic scientists was to the effect that this operation was *not* the result of teamwork but rather the result of a highly integrated organism.

NOTES

(1) All statements and conclusions in this paper are those of the author and do not indicate the views of any school or organization.

(2) Patterson, *Science and the Courts*, 1 J. For Sci. Soc. 5 (1960).

If, for the sake of convenience, we do divide science into pure and applied subjects, then one of the characteristics of the applied sciences is that they are no respecters of the conventional boundaries of the pure sciences. Forensic science is a good example of this, drawing among others on chemistry, physics, biology statistics, medicine, pathology, photography, law and engineering. I hope that no one is offended by my omission of his own specialty, but the point is that incomplete though this list is, it includes some pure and some applied sciences, so that in considering the content of forensic science, the artificial boundaries are doubly recrossed. *Id.* at 6.

(3) Home Office Report of the Departmental Committee on Detective Work and Procedure, vol. 5 § 409 (1938 reprinted 1954).

[I]t [scientific work] has an important contribution to make in the investigation of many branches of crime. This contribution is more important in some offenses than in others, but it is difficult to think of any branch of crime in which scientific technique and laboratory examination of materials may not on occasion afford useful, and perhaps vital, assistance . . . *Ibid.*

(4) Madras State Forensic Science Laboratory (India); Scientific Police Research Institute (Japan); Dominion District Laboratories (New Zealand); Laboratorio Criminalistico (Perú); etc. See The Forensic Science Society (London), World List of Forensic Science Laboratories (1963).

(5) Address by C. M. Wilson, *First Inter-American Conference on Legal Medicine and Forensic Science*, San Juan, Puerto Rico, December 1, 1962 (hereinafter referred to as *Inter-American Conference*). These proceedings will be published in book form by Charles C. Thomas Co.

(6) Bacon, *Essays 24 Of Innovations.*

As the births of living creatures at first are ill-shapen, so are all innovations, which are the births of time. *Ibid.*

(7) O'Hara, Fundamentals of Criminal Investigation ch. 1 (1956).

(8) Although the precinct detective may perform 95 percent of the work in a homicide investigation, it is the remaining 5 percent contributed by the medical examiners and other technical experts which often receives the publicity and which impresses the uninitiated. *Id.* at 11.

(9) Gross, Criminal Investigation 78 (4th ed. Howe 1950).

(10) *Id.* at 78.

(11) O'Hara, *op. cit. supra*, note 6, at 12.

(12) (a) Home Office Report, *op. cit. supra*, note 2, § 412.

The main branches of this work which need to be provided for in one way or another can be summarized as follows: 1. The instruction of the rank and file in the subject generally; 2. The further instruction of detectives, especially in certain branches of police technique and scene of crime work; 3. Laboratory work, including (a) routine examinations; (b) specialist examinations; (c) research; and 4. Work in the interests of the service as a whole which could best be provided for by a Forensic Science Centre embodying a research laboratory, a library, a museum of specimens of various kinds, and machinery for the coordination of the work going on in the different laboratories and for disseminating information to these laboratories and throughout the Police Service. *Ibid.*

(b) *A Preliminary Survey of Education and Research in the Forensic Sciences in the United Kingdom*, 2 J. For. Sci. Soc. 2 (1961). There is nowhere any formal course aimed at producing forensic scientists and their training appears to be based on the apprentice system. Id. at 2.

It is disquieting to find that the Home Office and Other Government Laboratories are unable to make the contributions to fundamental research in forensic science which might be expected from their great practical experience in this field. This presumably reflects a lack of appreciation by the authorities concerned of the value and necessity of fundamental research in the field administered by them. *Id.* at 4.

(13) Gardner, *Need for New Concepts in the Administration of Criminal Justice*, 50 J. Crim. L., C. & P. S. 20 (1959).

> Even today, with all the facilities available to prosecutors, in probably ninety-five percent of the cases prosecuted, scientific evidence which should have been available has either gone undiscovered, has been so contaminated as to be useless, or has entirely escaped the attention of the police and the prosecutor. *Id.* at 25.

(14) Defense counsel do not necessarily have to produce scientific proof themselves that the defendant is innocent; it is sufficient if they can make the court and jury realize that there was scientific proof available to the prosecution and that consequently it is an insult to the intelligence of judges or jurors to ask them to act upon surmise or upon the eloquence of a prosecutor when by proper investigative work scientific proof could have been presented to them. . . . *Id.* at 25.

(15) FBI, U.S. Dep't. of Justice, Uniform Crime Reports—1961 (1962).

> *Standard metropolitan statistical areas* are generally made up of an entire county or counties having at least one core city of 50,000 or more inhabitants with the whole meeting the requirements of certain metropolitan characteristics. Id. at 26.

(16) *Excluded* from this grouping are those classified as: criminal homicide, forcible rape, robbery, aggravated assault, burglary, larceny $50 and over, and auto theft. These seven classifications make up the Crime Index. *Id.* at 32.

(17) See Table III and note 16 *supra*.

(18) Five percent has been taken as probably the maximum proportion of medical examiner or coroner cases to involve criminal charges. Similarly five percent of the total cost of these systems has been attributed to the administration of criminal justice.

(19) The populations of standard metropolitan statistical areas were excluded from these calculations if a forensic science laboratory facility existed in the core city of the area.

(20) The populations used were those of the standard metropolitan statistical areas for the core cities concerned.

(21) The populations used were those of the city areas. These populations are more likely the ones paying the cost.

(22) This is total cost for both criminal and non-criminal cases.

(23) The number pertains to agencies reporting total cases.

(24) These figures represent the funds that could be used in examinations of

the violations classified within the Crime Index. See note 16 *supra.*

(25) See note 19 *supra.*

(26) See note 20 *supra.*

(27) See note 21 *supra.*

(28) As homicide cases are the major portion of criminal cases involving the services of medical examiner and coroner systems, these expenditures are per homicide case. See note 18 *supra.*

(29) These calculations represent that portion of local revenue used for forensic science facilities. Golenpaul Associates, 1962 Information Please Almanac 363-398 (1961).

(30) Address by Robert Borkenstein, *Inter-American Conference* see note 5 *supra.*

(31) *Supra,* note 12 (b), at 3.

(32) Home Office Report, *op. cit. supra*, note 3, § 411. A recent interview by the author with Dr. F. G. Tryhorn, Forensic Science Adviser to the Home Office, indicated that this figure of 4% still is considered a reasonable level of attainment.

(33) Address by H. Ward Smith, *Inter-American Conference* see note 5 *supra.*

(34) Crime Index rate for 1961 was 1,052.8. FBI, U.S. Dep't. of Justice, *op. cit. supra*, note 15, at 33. Arrest rate for 1961 in the Crime Index categories was 531.3. *Id.* at 92. Arrest rate in all categories for 1961 was 3,652. *id.* at 92. If the latter two figures are assumed to be representative of the total U.S. population (figures are based on a population of over 115 million), then a rough calculation would give a rate for total known violations as 3,652 times 1,053 divided by 531 or over 7,000.

(35) Criminal homicide rate for 1961 was 4.7. *Id.* at 33. 100 times 4.7 divided by 7,000 is 0.067%.

(36) Home Office Report, *op. cit. supra*, note 3, § 423.

(37) It is important to remember that scientific professionals are concerned with less than 1.5% of all known criminal violations and that medical professionals, with less than 0.1% of all known criminal violations.

(38) Parker, *Scientific Proof*, 32 Rev. Jur. U.P.R. 201 (1963).

(39) The problem of administrative control is a difficult issue often clouded by related issues of merit. Even within the fields of science, interprofessional activity conflicts arise as exampled by disputes between medical and non-medical professionals. The medical professional thinks, quite correctly, that a medical problem cannot be decided by non-medical professionals. This is the same for any professional problem. However, some medical professionals extrapolate from this fact the position that any interprofessional activity which includes medicine must be administratively controlled by a medical professional. The futility of this position can be visualized by noting that if all professions took this stand no administrative control would be possible where more than one profession was involved. See also Chemical and Engineering News, July 15, 1963, p. 102. In the administration of criminal justice in the U.S. the coordinating agency for scientific aids should be the courts. Richardson, Modern Scientific Evidence 28 (1961). Parker *supra* note 38.

(40) Members of the Home Office Forensic Science Laboratories take part in the training programs at Police Training Centres in England. Newsam, The Home Office 42 (2d ed. 1955); Address by Alan S. Curry, *Inter-American Conference* note 5 *supra.* Similar participation by forensic scientists in training programs is a common feature of the more noteable systems. Smith, Laboratory Aids for the Investigator (Attorney General's Laboratory, Ontario, Canada); Green & Burd, Collection, Identification and Examination of Evidence (California Peace Officers' Training Publication no. 15); Appendix materials to *Inter-American*

Conference note 5 *supra* (Wisconsin State Crime Laboratory).

(41) This training will emphasize that the type of violation does not limit the type of physical tracings to be found. The investigator has only himself to blame if he misses in a burglary case a type of physical tracing more commonly found in a murder case.

(42) Kirk, *The Ontogeny of Criminalistics*, 54 J. Crim. L., C. & P. S. 235 (1963).

> *Research,* so essential to an active science, cannot remain undefined in its objectives, nor limited to technical progress alone. The most important objective of all is still receiving the least attention, *viz.*, the interpretative. The physical properties which serve for identification and for individualization are not all equivalent in kind or in value, nor uniformly effective under varying circumstances. Applications of theories of probability to evidence interpretation remain inadequate for the need. Related statistical studies have been limited and unsatisfactory for the most part. . . *Id.* at 238.

(43) Parker *supra* note 38.

(44) Wilson, *op. cit. supra* note 5.

(45) See Table V.

(46) Based on reports from 13 forensic science laboratories.

(47) Smith, *op. cit. supra* note 33.

(48) 1961 Ann. Rep. Att'y Gen. Lab., Province of Ontario, 76.

(49) See Table VIII.

(50) *Op. cit. supra* notes 47 and 48. Estimates by other forensic scientists are in substantial agreement. International City Managers' Association, Municipal Police Administration 291 (1961). C. M. Wilson, private communication.

(51) The forensic scientists in examining an individual violation must separate the physical tracings, prepare the equipment and supplies, examine the tracings, interpret the results and write a report. In the space of 52 weeks for the year, 6 weeks can be lost through vacation time, holidays and sickness. A conservative estimate for court attendance would be 16 weeks. For a 40 hour week, the remaining 30 weeks amounts to 1200 hours. 50 examinations gives 24 hours per violation or 3 days. 250 examinations means less than 5 hours per violation or half a day.

(52) *Supra* note 12 (b).

(53) Statements by Charles Umberger in Panel Discussion, *Inter American Conference* note 5 *supra*.

(54) See Table VII.

(55) See Table IV.

(56) Total known violations taken as 7,000 per 100,000 population. Note 34 *supra*. Percentage of total criminal violations examined in forensic science laboratories is about 1.5% at best. See Table II. A reasonable percentage of total criminal violations to be examined in forensic science laboratories would be 4%. Note 32 *supra*. Estimates for expenditure per violation and work load per forensic scientist respectively $150 and $50. Note 50 *supra*.

(57) Wilson, *op. cit., supra* note 5; Goddard, *Scientific Crime Detection Laboratories in Europe*, 1 Am. J. P. S. 125, 128 (1930); Newsam, *op. cit. supra* note 40.

(58) The Home Office Forensic Science Laboratories are eight in number serving England and Wales. Curry, *Inter-American Conference* note 5 *supra*. Geographically the area served is almost that of the state of Georgia while the population served is almost the combined total of the populations of the states of New York, California, Pennsylvania and Illinois. Hammond's World Atlas 1-3 (1959).

(59) Wilson, *op. cit. supra* note 5.

(60) Newsam, *op. cit. supra* note 40.

Closely though the Home Secretary is concerned with the administration of justice, the treatment of offenders convicted by the courts, and the merits of individual cases brought to his notice, he has no significant concern with prosecutions . . .

. . . Nowadays it is well recognized and has frequently been stated in Parliament that the Home Office is not a prosecuting authority. *id.* at 133-134.

(61) Home Office Report, *op. cit. supra* note 3, § 432, 435.

(62) Curry, *op. cit. supra*, note 5.

(63) Home Office Report, *op. cit. supra*, note 12 (a).

(64) Harrison, Suspect Documents (1958); Curry, Poison Detection in Human Organs (1963).

(65) Before Mr. Justice Diplock, Leeds Assizes, December, 1957. See also Birkinshaw et al, *Investigations in a Case of Murder by Insulin Poisoning*, British Medical J. vol. ii, p. 463 (1958); Price, *Post Mortem Technique in Homicide Cases*, 2 J. For. Sci. Soc. 94, 99 (1962); Price, Oakley & Byford, *Regina v. Robinson-Brannan*, 2 J. For. Sci. Soc. 51 (1961).

THE ANATOMY OF THE EVIDENCE

Harry Kalven, Jr.
Hans Zeisel

By presenting descriptive data on the composition of the evidence in the variety of criminal trials, this survey offers a unique opportunity for a systematic inventory of the patterns of evidence.

The data are of two kinds: first, specific details as to the number of witnesses, the types of witnesses, the presence or absence of a criminal record, with other details; and, second, an over-all view of the evidence in terms of a single simple question put to the judge as to whether the case on all the evidence was clear or close.

We begin in Table 1 with the over-all view. In a rough form, the judge's answer to the clear-close question serves to provide a map of the evidence in the cases that come before a jury.

Table 1 gives an important first impression of the range of doubt in the criminal trial. Only 43 percent of all cases are rated by the judge as close to the reasonable doubt threshold(1) or, in our terms, as presenting evidence problems of any substance. The majority of cases are rated as clear, and of these the majority are clear in the direction of conviction.(2) We can see at the outset that insofar as the jury is having trouble with issues of fact in criminal cases and may thus be moved to disagree with the judge, the trouble is confined to this 43 percent of the cases.

From the over-all view we turn to the details of the evidence and begin with the number of witnesses in the criminal case. Table 2 shows the number of

The two tables taken together underscore once again the imbalance in the evidence marshalled by defense and prosecution. Apart from the two more cogent categories, eyewitnesses and experts, which appear in but 11 and 6 percent respectively of the defense cases, the defense evidence is seen to consist overwhelmingly of the defendant himself, his family and friends, and his character witnesses.

Tables 3 and 4 also answer two questions of great interest to the administration of the criminal law. Table 4 shows how often a defendant in a criminal trial elects to exercise his privilege of not testifying on his own behalf. He testifies in 82 percent of the cases, thus claiming his privilege not to testify in only 18 percent. Again, Table 3 shows how often the prosecution introduces into evidence an alleged confession: it does so in 19 percent of the cases.

One may focus more closely on the distribution of particular categories of witnesses. The eyewitness, as we know from Tables 3 and 4, appears in 25 percent of the prosecution cases and in 11 percent of the defense cases. Table 5 completes the pattern.

TABLE 5

Eyewitnesses

Percent

Neither side	69	
Defense only	6	} Total defense, 11%
Both sides	5	} Total prosecution, 25%
Prosecution only	20	
Total*	100%	

*Sample II only.

It is a commentary on the difficulties of proof in the ordinary criminal case that in some 69 percent of all trials neither side has an eyewitness.(5) In only one out of five cases in which the prosecution has an eyewitness does the defendant have one too, but in half the cases in which the defendant has an eyewitness the prosecution has one to oppose him. In only 5 percent of all cases do both sides have eyewitnesses, making possible the confrontation of conflicting eyewitness' testimony.

The analogous statistics on the expert witness read very much the same. The expert witness, it will be recalled, appeared in 25 percent of the prosecution cases and in 6 percent of the defense cases. Table 6 sets out the data.

Again, the imbalance between prosecution and defense appears. In 22 percent of the cases the prosecution has the only expert witness, whereas in only 3 percent of the cases does the defense have such an advantage. And while in 69 percent of the trials there are, as we saw, no eyewitnesses, it appears that in 72 percent there are no experts. Finally, Table 6 puts into focus the celebrated

TABLE 6

Expert Witnesses

Percent

	Percent	
Neither side	72	
Defense only	3	Total defense, 6%
Both sides	3	Total prosecution, 25%
Prosecution only	22	
Total*	100%	

Sample II only.

"battle of experts." In only 3 percent of the cases do both sides present experts, and even this figure must overstate the frequency of the battle, since in some of these cases the experts are in different fields and are testifying on different issues.

It may not be without interest to carry the description of expert testimony one step further and show in Table 7 the variety of experts.

A medical expert appears in little less than half the cases in which there are experts, or in 12 percent of all cases. In view of the widespread contemporary interest in the role of psychiatry in criminal law, it may be somewhat surprising to see how infrequently the psychiatrist makes an appearance in court. As we can infer from Table 7, a psychiatrist appears in less than 2 percent of all cases, and slightly more often for the defense than for the prosecution.(6)

A somewhat different perspective on the evidence is obtained by observing how this profile of evidence changes for different types of crimes. Six crime categories have been selected for this comparison: homicide, simple and aggravated assault, rape, burglary, drunken driving, and narcotics.(7)

By retracing the various descriptive steps one can see how each item varies over these six crimes. Table 8 begins with the number of witnesses presented by both sides.

The variation is perhaps less than might have been expected, but the total number of witnesses is clearly larger for murder cases than, for example, for narcotics cases. Further, the imbalance of witnesses between prosecution and defense varies by crime from a 3 to 1 ratio in narcotics to a 1 to 1 ratio in drunken driving.

Table 9 sets forth the details of the various types of evidence offered by the prosecution in the six crime categories. Several points are worthy of comment. First, the frequency of confession, 19 percent over-all, varies considerably by crime; there is one in almost half the homicide cases (43 percent) but virtually none in drunken driving and naroctics cases (1 percent and 3 percent). Again, the expert witness, present in 77 percent of the narcotics cases and in 58 percent

TABLE 7

Type of Expert Witnesses

(In percent of the 291 cases with experts)

	Prosecution (Percent)	Defense (Percent)
Medical, general**	43	9
Medical, psychiatric	4	5
Chemical	22	*
Intoxication	5	*
Handwriting	10	1
Firearms	9	*
Misc. Laboratory Technicians	4	—
Accountants, appraisers	11	1
Narcotics	2	—
Misc. other sciences (fire engineers, opticians, etc.)	6	4
Misc. police, FBI	6	—
Other	2	4

* Less than one half of 1 percent.

** Not all categories in Table 7 are mutually exclusive. Experts on "Intoxication," for example, might also be "Laboratory Technicians"; occasionally it was impossible to clarify the function further.

of the homicide cases, is found in only 5 percent of the burglary cases. Finally, as would be expected, a dominant witness group in each crime category is the police.

Table 10 gives a comparable breakdown for the kinds of evidence presented by the defense.

In concluding this description of the lay of the evidence in the criminal trial, we turn to an item of special interest and complexity: the defendant himself as a witness. Whether or not he testifies depends on several factors. It is a characteristic of American law that it allows the defendant to decide for himself whether he will testify and gives him the privilege of not testifying if he so wishes. This privilege, a variant of the constitutional privilege against self-incrimination, has been a celebrated point of legal controversy since the days of Jeremy Bentham. In recent years it has become the focus of public controversy as witnesses before Congressional committees have claimed the privilege.(8) In general, the legal rule not only protects the defendant from testifying, but also says that no interference may be drawn from his failure to do so.(9) Critics of the rule have stressed that this is quixotic and self-defeating, since the trier of fact cannot avoid drawing a negative inference when the defendant refuses to testify, no matter what the formal rule is. The defendant, it

TABLE 8

Number of Witnesses for Selected Crimes

Number of Witnesses	Homicide Prosecution %	Homicide Defense %	Assault Prosecution %	Assault Defense %	Rape Prosecution %	Rape Defense %	Burglary Prosecution %	Burglary Defense %	Drunken driving Prosecution %	Drunken driving Defense %	Narcotics Prosecution %	Narcotics Defense %
0	—	6	—	2	—	9	—	17	—	4	—	16
1	—	17	1	26	—	19	—	31	3	21	—	37
2-5	21	39	58	52	51	45	56	44	82	60	54	46
6-10	41	24	31	15	39	18	28	8	14	11	45	1
11 or more	38	14	10	5	10	9	16	—	1	4	1	—
Total	100%	100%	100%	100%	100%	100%	100%	100%	100%	100%	100%	100%
Average number of witnesses per case	11.3	5.7	6.4	3.7	6.3	2.2	6.5	2.4	4.1	3.5	6.1	1.9
Number of cases	108		107		72		79		112		68	

TABLE 9

Prosecution Evidence for Selected Crimes
Number indicates the percentage of trials for the particular
crime in which this kind of evidence is presented.

	Homicide	Assault	Rape	Burglary	Drunken Driving	Narcotics
	%	%	%	%	%	%
Police	90	72	60	91	98	86
Complainant	3	94	97	68	27	17
Eyewitness	44	29	4	20	22	8
Expert	58	18	28	5	5	77
Confession	43	16	27	30	1	3
Family or friends of victim	35	34	46	6	5	2
Accomplice	5	—	4	24	—	11
Other witnesses	5	2	3	3	4	11
*Number of Cases**	*108*	*107*	*72*	*79*	*112*	*68*

*Sample II only.

is argued, must know more about his alleged innocence than anyone else, and if he decides to withhold evidence, he must be doing so for a reason.

The data cannot decide the policy controversy. However, considerable light is thrown on the strategic game the defendant in the criminal trial often plays in deciding whether or not to testify. To begin with, it has been seen that the defendant testifies in 82 percent of all cases and elects not to testify in only 18 percent. Thus, in the large majority of cases, the defendant clearly prefers to balance of advantages and disadvantages that come from testifying. The strategic considerations may be complex.(10) There is the possibility that the defendant by his demeanor will make a poor witness and thus defense counsel prefers his silence as a better risk. The defense may want to underscore that the prosecution has the burden of proof and not complicate the jury's appraisal of the prosecution evidence by efforts at rebuttal. Finally, there is the important legal rule(11) that once the defendant takes the stand it will be possible under some circumstances to disclose to the jury his prior criminal record, for the purpose of impeaching his credibility as a witness. Against these three potential advantages to be gained by the defendant's silence is to be weighed the common-sense inference of the defendant's guilt, if he chooses not to talk.

Table 11 shows the frequency of criminal records for defendants in all criminal cases.(12)

Table 12 gives a first view of how the strength of the prosecution's case and the presence or absence of a prior record influence the defendant's decision whether or not to testify.

TABLE 10

Defense Evidence for Selected Crimes
*Numbers indicate the percentage of trials for the particular
crime in which this kind of evidence is presented.*

	Homicide	Assault	Rape	Burglary	Drunken Driving	Narcotics
	%	%	%	%	%	%
Defendant himself	79	96	85	70	90	85
Family or friends of defendant	57	55	39	39	59	24
Character witness	34	28	34	15	23	11
Eyewitness	16	18	16	4	12	3
Expert	25	1	—	—	5	3
Accomplice	1	2	—	5	—	3
Other witnesses	15	7	13	35	7	16
*Number of Cases**	*108*	*107*	*72*	*79*	*112*	*68*

*Sample II only.

TABLE 11

Frequency of Criminal Record

	Per Cent
Defendant has—	
No record	53
Record for similar crime	22
Record for different crime	25
Total	100%
*Number of Cases**	*1143*

*Sample II only; 48 no answers.

TABLE 12

Frequency with which Defendant Testifies, by Lay
of Evidence and Prior Record

	Defendant has			
	Criminal Record		No Record	
Case is—	Per Cent	Cases	Per Cent	Cases
Clear for acquittal	53	19	90	41
Close	80	187	94	303
Clear for conviction	73	331	88	262
Average all cases	74	537	91	606

The bottom row shows that the record is an important determinant of the defendant's decision to testify. If he has no record, he will elect not to testify in only $(100 - 91 =)$ 9 percent of the cases; if he has a record this percentage rises to $(100 - 74 =)$ 26 percent. Further, when the evidence is most favorable to the defendant—where the case is clear for acquittal or close—the defendant without a record testifies over 90 percent of the time. This percentage drops, even for defendants without a record, when the case is clear for conviction. Again, when the defendant has a record and the case is clear for acquittal he elects to testify only 53 percent of the time, suggesting that here counsel sees no reason to disturb a favorable situation by the disclosure of the record.

Another refinement can be added to the picture. The strategy game is complicated by the fact that it is not always true that the defendant's prior record will be disclosed if he takes the stand, nor is it always true that the record will remain unknown if he does not take the stand. Table 13 gives the pertinent information.(13)

In 28 percent of the cases where the defendant takes the stand, the jury nevertheless fails to learn of his record, and, conversely, in 13 percent of the cases in which the defendant does not take the stand, the jury learns of his record anyway. A variety of reasons, about which the judge seldom gives information, may cause either this disclosure or nondisclosure.(14)

We can give the data one more turn by asking whether the impact of a record on taking the stand varies according to whether the record is for a similar or a different crime. Table 14 sets forth the data and shows that, to some small degree, the defendant is more inhibited by the risk of disclosing a similar record. Except for the cases that are clear for acquittal, the percentage of defendants who testify on their own behalf is smaller—albeit by a very modest margin—if the prior record is for a similar crime than when it is for a different crime. The number of clear-for-acquittal cases in Table 14 is too small to warrant any inferences from the differences in percentages.

TABLE 13

Jury's Knowledge of Defendant's Record

	Defendant has a Record and—		
	Takes the Stand	*Does Not Take Stand*	*Total*
Jury	*Per Cent*	*Per Cent*	*Per Cent*
Learns of record	72	13	59
Does *not* learn of record	28	87	41
Total	100%	100%	100%
*Number of Cases**	*1199*	*335*	*1534*

*Samples I and II defendants with prior record.

TABLE 14

Frequency with which Defendant Testifies, by Lay
of Evidence and Type of Record

	Similar Record		*Different Record*		*Total Record*	
Case is—	*Per Cent*	*Cases*	*Per Cent*	*Cases*	*Per Cent*	*Cases*
Clear for acquittal	60	5	50	14	53	19
Close	78	65	81	122	80	187
Clear for convition	72	181	73	150	73	331
Average all cases	73	251	76	286	74	537

This then is the profile of evidence in the contemporary criminal trial. To inventory the various items of evidence has proved to be a relatively tractable task. However, to locate what it is in the evidence that produces judge-jury disagreement will be a far more formidable and subtle matter. The easy descriptions here may serve then as a kind of preface to the harder analysis of the jury as the trier of issues of fact.

NOTES

(1) There is perhaps an apparent paradox, when the legal test is whether the evidence places the defendant's guilt beyond a reasonable doubt, in referring to a case as "close," particularly if the term suggests an even chance either way. What is meant by "close" in a criminal case is "close to the borderline of reasonable doubt," which might be, if it were measurable, 80 percent sure or 95 percent sure, etc., depending on one's sense of the test. In any event "close" does not refer to the mere preponderance of the evidence, the test for a close case in civil negligence actions.

(2) There may be some interest at this point in a preview of a companion variable relating to evidence. The Sampe II questionnaire asked (Q.11) "Was the evidence as a whole easy to comprehend, somewhat difficult [or] very difficult to comprehend?" The distribution of comprehensibility is as follows.

	%
Easy	86
Somewhat Difficult	12
Very Difficult	2
	100%
	1191

For our immediate purposes, the interesting fact is that over fifty percent of all cases are both clear and easy.

(3) Where the defendant was accused of participating in a scheme to defraud an insurance company by presenting false fire insurance claims, the prosecution mustered 120 witnesses against the defendant's 11, for the sample's high of 131. Judge and jury agreed to convict. [II-1128]

(4) In the end, this imbalance may simply reflect the fact that the prosecution has the burden of proof. Since there will be repeated occasion to refer to imbalance, it is perhaps important to emphasize that we use the word "imbalance" as a descriptive term, referring to quantity only.

(5) The absence of relationship between the incidence of eyewitnesses and the closeness of the evidence is indicated by the following fourfold table:

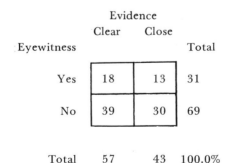

| | Evidence | | |
| | Clear | Close | |
Eyewitness			Total
Yes	18	13	31
No	39	30	69
Total	57	43	100.0%

(6) In addition to the various items reported in the text, the judge was asked to indicate whether witnesses on either side involved themselves in contradictions at any point. The question is perhaps somewhat spoiled in that it is indeterminable from these answers whether one witness contradicted himself or

two witnesses on the same side contradicted each other. The distribution of contradiction is as follows:

	Prosecution Witnesses	Defense Witnesses
Contradictions:	%	%
Major	6	13
Minor	29	26
None	65	61
	100%	100%

(7) These six crimes constitute 46 percent of all cases as follows: homicide 8 percent, assault 10 percent, rape 5 percent, burglary 5 percent, drunken driving 13 percent, narcotics 5 percent. The overall number of cases varies slightly as between Tables 8, 9, and 10, because of occasional "don't knows."

(8) For a sampling of the controversy, see Meltzer, Invoking the Fifth Amendment—Some Legal and Practical Considerations. Bulletin of the Atomic Scientists, v. 9, p. 176 (1953); Kalven, Invoking the Fifth Amendment—Some Legal and Impractical Considerations, ibid., p. 181; Meltzer, Invoking the Fifth Amendment: A Rejoinder, ibid., p. 185; Griswold, The Fifth Amendment Today (1955); Hook, Common Sense and the Fifth Amendment (1957); Packer, Ex-Communist Witnesses (1962).

(9) The Supreme Court has recently held that the self-incrimination clause of the Fifth Amendment, binding on the states by reason of the Fourteenth Amendment, forbids comment or instruction that a defendant's failure to testify is evidence of guilt. Griffin v. California 380 U.S. 609 (1965); Malloy v. Hogan, 378 U.S. 1 (1963).

(10) Table 10 above, suggests that one possible determinant is the kind of crime with which the defendant is charged. Thus in burglary and murder cases the stand is refused 30 percent and 21 percent of the time, whereas in assault cases the defendant testifies 96 percent of the time. Since the decision to testify has a high correlation to the absence of a record, and since defendants with records are not distributed randomly among the crime categories, it is likely that this variation by crime reflects in part variations in the incidence of records.

(11) As noted, the rule is complicated.

(12) Table 11 is limited to data for Sample II; there the distinction between record for a similar or different crime is preserved. The distribution in Sample I is as follows:

	%
No Record	53
Record	47
Total	100%
Cases	2385

(13) As noted, differential knowledge of a prior record as between judge and jury may become a cause of disagreement.

(14) One of the factors affecting a defendant's decision to testify will be the law concerning impeachment by means of the defendant's criminal record. Some jurisdictions bar impeachment where the conviction was remote in time, others may limit it to crimes that imply a lack of veracity, and still others bar impeachment unless the defendant has initiated evidence tending to show his good character. In addition, the record may have been revealed prior to the defendant's testimony as part of the evidence, or its sheer notoriety may obviate

any attempt at concealment. It would be interesting to learn whether defendants in states that tend to limit the scope of impeachment are more likely to testify.

PROOF OF GUILT IN CAPITAL CASES—

AN UNSCIENCE

Willard J. Lassers

To what extent do the police and prosecution, in cases where death is the sentence for murder, avail themselves at the trial of the techniques of modern science in establishing guilt? So far as we are aware, no prior investigation of this matter has been conducted.

The question is important, its ramifications extending far beyond the small number of individuals sentenced to death in any one year (60 to 80) and the still smaller number executed (7 in 1965 and 1 in 1966). If it appears that the police and prosecution do not make full use of current technology in death cases, then it seems a fair assumption that still less use is made of such methods in murder cases where the death penalty is not sought and in other non-capital criminal prosecutions. Presumably the prosecution makes the most thorough investigation and has the most positive proof of guilt in those cases where the extreme penalty is sought. If the resources of science are employed at all, one would expect them to be utilized the most where the heaviest penalty is sought.

There is another related reason for investigating the use of science in murder prosecutions. In 1964, in the *Escobedo* decision, and again in 1966 in the *Miranda* decision, the Supreme Court of the United States placed radical restrictions on the prosecution in obtaining admissible confessions from persons in custody. Few issues in law enforcement are more emotion-laden. Civil libertarians (and we include ourselves) believe that conviction by confession, among its other evils, kills inducement to good police work. Others view confessions as essential to law enforcement, claiming that in many instances there is no other way to solve crimes. We do not presume to resolve this dispute. Surely, however, data on the utilization of scientific techniques is relevant to the controversy. A showing of failure to make full use of modern methods tends to support the view that reliance on confessions has retarded growth of scientific methods of crime fighting.

There is a third reason for interest in the topic: it throws some light upon a related, but different question, that is, the extent to which the police and prosecution avail themselves of scientific techniques in ascertaining the identity of the criminal, apart from the use of such evidence in the courts. The state of the art as used to convict may reflect the state of the art as used to catch the accused. We are concerned here, however, solely with scientific evidence in court.

Let us stress an important point. Our attention is directed solely at the use of scientific evidence to determine the identity of the individual responsible physically for the death of the victim. We were not concerned with scientific testimony as to the numerous "state of mind" issues that arise in a murder trial, such as mental capacity, ability to form an intent to kill, the "voluntary" character of a confession, etc. These issues are beyond the scope of this paper.

We think our study shows an incredible lag in the employment of modern methods. The prosecution does use scientific evidence in upwards of 25% of all cases, but it relies almost exclusively on three forms of such evidence, the newest of which is 40 years old; firearms identification (so-called "ballistics"), blood typing, and fingerprint comparison. We deem this fact highly disturbing, not because of the percentage (since there is no standard for judging whether it is high or low), but because it indicates stagnation. And it indicates something more and worse; that the scientific process stands at the periphery of the judicial fact finding inquiry, not integrated as it ought to be in every step of the investigative and prosecution process.

Regarding the defense, the record is dismal. It hardly ever uses scientific evidence, and then its efforts generally are limited to helpful admissions on cross-examination from prosecution experts. We shall comment below on the reason for this situation.

These conclusions are based on a review of substantially all Illinois capital cases decided by the Supreme Court of Illinois since 1950, and all capital cases in the United States for 1963, 1964, and 1965 which have been reviewed by state or federal appellate tribunals. Sentences imposed in 1966 have not yet been reviewed by higher tribunals.

We chose, for several reasons, to study capital cases—cases tailor-made to appraise the use of technology by the prosecution: 1. As previously stated, scientific evidence is more apt to be used in capital cases than in other cases; 2. The limited number of such cases per year permits examination of every case. Hence we need not rely on a sample; and 3. Because of the penalty, almost every capital case is appealed, usually to the highest court of the state. Hence, there are prepared a verbatim record of the testimony, or a full summary; briefs by the prosecution and defense; and a written opinion by the court. The latter is nearly always published; it usually contains a detailed recital of the facts, and is readily available in law libraries.

We became interested in our topic during the course of another study. During 1964-1965, for other purposes, the Illinois Division of the American Civil Liberties Union conducted a survey of all cases in Illinois since 1950 where the defendant was sentenced to death. Upon reading the court opinions, it seemed to us that there was heavy reliance in these cases on confessions, witness testimony, and other traditional modes of proof. Science seemed to play a subordinate role. Our interest piqued, we decided to restudy the cases, adding the cases decided subsequently. Our procedure was as follows: we read all of the court opinions (in some cases there were both state and federal court opinions or more than one state court opinion), and, in addition, we examined the "abstract of record" which contains substantially all of the trail testimony in narrative form.

During the period 1950-1966, there were 42 capital cases that came before the Supreme Court of Illinois. The decision on the initial appeal to that court, and the subsequent disposition, are shown in Table I. Three cases of the 42 had to be excluded because there was no published opinion by the Supreme Court of Illinois or by any other court. One defendant died while his case was pending on review, and two individuals were executed without any appellate review of their decisions because Illinois law at the time granted review in the Illinois Supreme Court to those convicted of non-capital felonies, but made review in capital cases discretionary. In these two cases, review was denied by the court. Further, in these two cases, no abstract was available.

Now to the meat of the matter: Of the 39 cases, some form of scientific evidence was introduced in 15 cases (38%). In these such cases, firearms identification (ballistics) testimony was introduced on 11 occasions. In two cases there was testimony from an expert that because of the condition of a bullet, no such examination was possible. Blood type evidence was introduced on two occasions, and fingerprint evidence on two occasions. (We have considered one palm print as fingerprint evidence.) No other form of scientific evidence was introduced in any case by the prosecution.(1)

There was but a single case where scientific evidence was introduced by the defense. Seven years after the initial state court trial, the defendant was granted a federal court hearing. In these proceedings, for the first time, the defendant had an opportunity to have a defense expert examine a pair of shorts which the prosecution contended were stained with the blood of the victim. The victim, aged 8, had been sexually attacked and murdered. At the hearing, this expert testified that the stains were paint and not blood as the prosecution had claimed in the original trial. Further, in this proceeding it was shown that the prosecution had not revealed to the defendant, at the original trial, a crime lab report that a hair found in the vagina of the child was not defendant's. The conviction was set aside by the Supreme Court of the United States because of the suppression of evidence regarding the paint.

TABLE I

Capital Cases in Illinois 1950-1966

Judgment affirmed by Illinois Supreme Court

Executed	11*	
Sentence commuted	2	
Died of natural causes	1	
Suicide	1	
Further legal proceedings or commutation pending	7	
Discharged by federal courts	1	
Total	23	23

Judgment reversed and new trial granted

No capital sentences subsequently imposed	17	
Not yet retried	2	
Total	19	19
		42**

* Includes two cases where Illinois Supreme Court refused review. See text.

** Excluded are 10 cases where the trial court has imposed the death sentence but the case has not been reviewed. Among the 10 is one woman.

We were taken aback by our findings. Illinois is a leading urban, industrial state and yet the foundation of all methods of scientific evidence employed by the prosecution in these cases was established 40-60 years ago. Fingerprinting dates from the development of a workable system of classifying the prints in the 1890's and firearms identification in the middle 1920's. Blood groups were discovered in the 1900's.

These methods are not only old, but all three suffer defects. Firearms identification, of course, is of value only where the weapon is a gun and both bullets (or shells) and the alleged murder weapon are found by the prosecution. But firearms identification does not enlighten us on the crucial question, namely, "Who fired the gun?" True, in the context of a specific trial, it may be a link in a chain leading to the defendant.

Fingerprints where found can be almost conclusive, but in some situations they are valueless. Thus, if the defendant is accused of murdering his wife with his own gun, his fingerprints in the house are meaningless. His fingerprints on his own gun are scarcely more important.

Blood grouping evidence, as presented, suffers its own defect. In the usual case, the prosecution's evidence is that the victim had blood of a specific type (A, AB, B or O), that blood of that same type was found, say, on the defendant's garments, and that defendant has blood of another type.

The weakness of this evidence is that among white Europeans about 45% have Type A, 10% Type B, 5% Type AB and 40% Type O. In the usual case, victim and defendant have either Type A or O. Hence, if the defendant has any blood on his garment, there is nearly a 50% chance that it is of the same type as the victim.

After analyzing the Illinois data, we asked ourselves next whether the Illinois cases represented an isolated phenomenon. Perhaps if we reviewed the national picture for recent years the results would be different. We regret to say that the pattern is essentially the same. An initial problem was to determine the cases for study.

There is essentially no coordination between the records of the police, the prison, and the court, nor is there uniformity among the states regarding the stage in the trial process at which a death sentence is imposed, and, thus, becomes reportable as such. We decided to employ the federal records as the reliable starting point. We obtained from the Bureau of Prisons copies of the work sheets for the years 1963, 1964 and 1965 which were used in the preparation of its publication *National Prisoner Statistics—Executions.* These work sheets gave us the name of every individual sentenced to death during each of these years, the date of sentencing, offense, sex, race, and date of birth. We disregarded all cases where death sentences were imposed for crimes other than murder but included cases where an individual was sentenced to death for rape and murder.

The next step was to examine the decisions in all cases which have been taken to a higher court and decided by that court. Cases not appealed, or pending an appeal, were not included in our analysis.

There were, altogether, 230 individuals listed on the government work sheets for the years 1963, 1964, and 1965; 81 cases in 1963; 89 cases in 1964; and 60 cases in 1965. (See Table II for disposition on those cases on review.)

The next step was to find, photocopy, and read all available court opinions. For this portion of our study, we had to rely on the court opinions. We could not, as we did in the Illinois cases, read the "abstract" which contains, somewhat condensed, the testimony of each witness. There may be cases where scientific evidence was presented at the trial by the prosecution or defense but such evidence was not mentioned in the court opinion. For this reason, we must be circumspect in our conclusions in this portion of the study. But we feel justified in drawing some conclusions, and particularly when we know that the defense presents a written brief to the court containing a statement of facts. This statement is subject to comment by the prosecution in its brief. There is oral

TABLE II

Individuals Sentenced to Death for Murder 1963-1965
Disposition of Cases
(Source: National Prisoner Statistics 1963-1965,
published court decisions and correspondence

	1963	1964	1965
Total cases reported by Bureau of Prisons	81	89	60
Affirmed	38	42	16
Affirmed, sentence reduced	6	2	
Affirmed as to guilt, reversed and remanded			
as to penalty only	7	2	
Reversed and remanded	22	13	4
TOtl decided on merits	73	59	20
Not decided on merits:			
Pending in reviewing court	8	18	37
Duplicate entry of prior year		6	1
Reversed or remanded without opinion		1	1
Facts not stated		1	
Deceased before decision of reviewing court		1	
New trial granted by trial court—			
Followed by life sentence		1	
New trial granted by trial court—			
Pending		1	
Remanded, decision reversed		1	
Declared insane. No appeal			1
Total not decided on merits	8	30	40
Total decided on merits	73	59	20
Facts not stated in opinion	16	5	2
Cases available for analysis	57	54	18

argument before the higher court and then a study of the case by the court. Because it is a capital case, we assume a thorough study of the matter by the court.

In this light, our approach to the opinions was as follows: If the court decided a case on an issue which did not require a full statement of facts, or if the court did not attempt to state the facts fully, we did not include the case for analysis. We included only those cases where the court purported to give complete statement of the facts. To us it seems unlikely that there were many cases where evidence seriously pressed upon the court by prosecution or defense, scientific or otherwise, would escape mention by the court. Further, to the extent that such evidence did go unmentioned, there is no reason to believe it differs as to type from such evidence which was mentioned.

Let us look first at the 1963 data which is the most complete. Of 81 cases, 8 are still undecided. We eliminated from our study 16 cases, because the reported decision failed to include a complete statement of facts. Thus, we were left with 57 cases subject to analysis. Of the 57 cases, the prosecution relied on confessions in 31 cases (54%).

We found that scientific evidence of one form or another was introduced in 15 of these 57 cases (26%) and that there were 22 instances in all where scientific evidence was presented.(2) The breakdown as to type of evidence is as follows: blood typing: 5 cases; firearms identification (ballistics): 5 cases; fingerprint identification: 3 cases; and other: 9 cases. There were 19 California cases included among the 57. Of the 15 cases throughout the entire country in which scientific evidence was introduced, 10 were from California. Thus there were only 5 cases from other parts of the country. These included 2 cases (companion cases) from the District of Columbia, 1 from Georgia, 1 from Massachusetts, and 1 from Texas.

Let us consider these 5 cases first: In the District of Columbia cases, the scientific evidence employed consisted of blood type testimony, plus testimony that a bloodstained heel mark found on the deceased had been made by the heel of the boot of one of the defendants. In the Georgia case, the scientific evidence was a firearms identification test of a shotgun shell. In the Massachusetts case, the prosecution, in addition to the introduction of firearms identification testimony, introduced the testimony of a medical examiner as to the course of a bullet. In the Texas case, the scientific evidence was that a gas line had been cut by defendant's pipe cutters.

Based upon these cases, our conclusion is that the scientific evidence introduced by the prosecution in the 1963 cases, while more varied than in the Illinois cases, was nevertheless limited in scope and imaginativeness.

In the California cases there was a more sophisticated approach. In addition to blood typing, firearms, and fingerprint testimony, other forms of scientific evidence were introduced in 6 cases. These decisions give an indication of what might be done generally.

In one case, defendants were convicted of murdering a bartender in their car, there was evidence that numerous fibers taken from the victim's shoes matched those found in the defendants' automobile, that hairs found in the automobile matched those of the victim; and that red paint found on the floor mat of the defendants' automobile came from the shoes of the victim.

The other five cases involved a typewriter comparison, 2 forensic medicine cases (presence of semen), one soil matching case, and one matching of bloody footprints.

For 1964, there were 89 cases, of which 54 were subject to analysis (See Table II). Six cases were eliminated as duplications of names previously entered by the Bureau of Prisons for 1963.(3)

Confessions were relied on in 31 cases (57%). Scientific evidence was employed in 18 cases (33%) representing, in all, 10 states. California contributed scientific evidence in 3 of these cases.

Again nearly twenty, or half of the cases fell within the traditional pattern: blood typing: 2; firearms identification (ballistics): 5; fingerprint identification 3; other: 10.

The "other" cases, as for 1963, reveal what evidence can be found when the police are prepared to approach an investigation scientifically. Texas identified the hat of a defendant by hair comparison. Pennsylvania presented evidence that the pants of a defendant, accused of murder of a boy, were splattered with brain tissue. Pennsylvania also, in a murder and possible rape case, presented evidence the victim had had intercourse within 10 days of death and that there were semen stains on the defendant's shorts. No semen was found in the vagina of the victim, however. California brought in a handwriting expert to testify that a defendant had made a sketch of a savings and loan association. The defendant was charged with murder committed during a robbery of the association. California also produced expert testimony as to the course of a bullet in a grocery robbery-murder. Arkansas produced the cast of a footprint at a murder scene which matched the defendant's. In another case it identified liquid found in a car as kerosene. The defendant was charged with the murder of several members of his family and setting the home on fire with kerosene. Alabama charged a defendant with the rape of a girl and the murder of a conservation officer who came to her aid. There was testimony that there was blood and fatty materials of human origin on a knife and that the tall light assembly of the defendant's car had paint on it which matched the paint of the car of the deceased. This evidence was significant because of other evidence that the defendant's car had collided with the car of the deceased.

One case of particular interest was from Arkansas. The defendant was accused of the rape-murder of a housewife surprised in her home while ironing. There was testimony as to the presence of semen in the vagina of the deceased, but the most dramatic evidence, even though not "scientific" in character, was a burn mark on defendant arrested shortly after the crime. The victim had put up a struggle and the outline of the burn matched exactly the impression of her iron.

Unquestionably the most bizarre and fascinating case arose from Ohio. Defendant and one Riddle checked into a motel in Stark county. Subsequently, Riddle's body was found in a burned auto, some distance from the motel in Wayne county. At the defendant's trial for murder in Stark county, he testified that, upon returning to the motel room after a brief absence, he found Riddle dead. He placed the body in his car and drove around for two days. Defendant chose County Line Road, which divides Stark and Wayne counties, for the final scene. At the top of a hill he soaked the body and car interior in gasoline, ignited it and started the car, in flames, down the hill. The state claimed Riddle was alive when incinerated. This certainly cast grave doubt on the reliability of defendant's tale and his unusual behavior, and it counted heavily against him.

Scientific evidence in two crucial areas supported his strange version. Both the State and the defense established by expert testimony that Riddle had severe heart disease—his life expectancy, according to his doctor, could only be foretold from day to day. Further, there was expert testimony by the defense, largely concurred in by the State, that carbon monoxide is present in bodies of victims burned while alive and that the blood of Riddle contained no carbon monoxide. The Ohio Court of Appeals reversed the conviction and granted a new trial in part on the ground guilt was not proved beyond a reasonable doubt, and in part on the ground (intriguing to lawyers) that venue did not lie in Stark County.

In this case, but for scientific evidence, an innocent man might well have been convicted, because of grossly incriminating circumstances and his own odd behavior.

For 1965, the data is still fragmentary. Of 60 cases, 37 cases remain undecided and 5 had to be rejected for many of the same reasons that compelled rejection of cases in 1964. Included among the 5 was one duplicate from a prior year. Thus, only 18 cases could be analyzed. Of these 18 cases, confessions were presented in 7 cases (39%). Scientific evidence was introduced in 6 cases (33%). In three instances (two in Georgia and one in South Carolina) firearms identification testimony was introduced. In one California case, defendant's palm print was found in the cab of a taxi driver he was accused of murdering. In a Texas case, defendant was accused of murdering a woman in her home at night. A hair, found on defendant's pistol, matched the victim's; defendant's shoes had mud on them like that in victim's yard, and plaster casts of footprints in the year matched defendant's shoes. In one New Jersey case, the prosecution charged robbery and murder, followed by burning the corpse. To prove the robbery, there was scientific testimony that no gold was found among the remains, whereas there was testimony that deceased customarily wore a gold ring.

All in all, we think the record is dismal. True, there are occasional cases where evidence out of the ordinary is presented, but on the whole, it seems clear that scientific evidence is presented in a minority of the cases. And, when it is presented, almost without exception it consists of one of the three standbys used for decades.

Thus, during a 3-year span, we could study 129 cases (57 + 54 + 18). In all, there were 50 occasions (22 + 20 + 8) where scientific evidence was introduced in 39 cases (15 + 18 + 6). Of the 50, the old standbys accounted for 26 instances (13 + 10 + 3) or about 50%. Most of the 24 remaining instances employed unsophisticated or even elementary techniques. The only instances we consider as exceptions are those 7 cases: Texas pipe cutter case, the impressive array of facts in the California bartender case, and the California soil matching case, the Texas hat case, the Pennsylvania boy murder case, the Alabama conservation officer murder, and the Texas array of facts in the cab driver case.

The "array" cases such as the two mentioned above illustrate that once scientific evidence is sought more than one item of evidence may be found.

In reading the cases we were struck by the fact that in almost every instance there was no attempt to conceal the fact that murder had been committed. In fact, we recall only two exceptions: in a California case, the murderers concocted an elaborate plot to murder the husband-wife motel keepers, mask their disappearance, hide the bodies, and assume ownership of the motel. In one Illinois case (Vincent Ciucci), a husband shot his wife and children and then set the house afire to make the deaths appear as if due to fire. All this, because he had a girl, named by a strange trick of fate, Carol Amora.

Perhaps murder masked as natural death is rare. Or perhaps when discovered, capital sentences are not imposed. But we suspect that given the lack of sophisticated techniques in convicting the murderer where murder is obvious many murderers successfully conceal their crimes.

We have shown that the defense almost never utilizes scientific evidence. For the indigent defendant, the reasons are obvious. Even if he is given competent counsel, he is not provided an investigative staff and funds. Even the defendant who has funds has problems. By the time counsel is retained, the trail is usually cold. The key evidence frequently is in the hands of the prosecution, it may be impossible for the defense to obtain access to it. Finally, a truly scientific study of a criminal case requires a broad spectrum of experts and a coordinator who knows what can be done and who can do it. Such individuals and galaxies of specialists exist only in the largest cities.

The Ohio motel case is the outstanding illustration of the use of scientific evidence by the defense. There, it was a significant fact in the reversal of a capital sentence. It was achieved by bringing in Dr. Milton Halpern, Chief Medical Examiner of New York City to testify. The prosecution sought to counter the defense, but its presentation was flawed by an omission of a key fact from the report of one of its experts.

We do not suggest for a moment that scientific evidence can or should replace traditional modes of proof. Thus, for example, the California motel keepers' case demonstrates the value of careful, patient police work in assembling a massive case. Only a small part of the evidence was "scientific" as such, but in a broad sense, the presentation was truly scientific.

Nevertheless, factual determinations can be exceptionally complex. Consider for example, the storm of controversy on the issue whether the bullet which hit President Kennedy also struck Governor Connally. We should bring to bear every resource, including traditional techniques, to resolve these issues.

Modern technology ought to play a much greater role than it does now. We have the capacity to investigate the most distant reaches of the universe, and to tear apart the atom, yet, when we put men on trial for their lives we bring to bear almost none of this vast scientific capacity.

If we are to make full use of science and be *truly* scientific—and *fair to the accused*, the task will be hard for several reasons. We cannot simply establish a super laboratory in Washington to which police throughout the country can send material for analysis. A national laboratory, far beyond the scope of the FBI laboratory would be a forward step, but to be truly effective, it must draw upon a national spectrum of experts. Beyond this we must have well trained local investigators of technical knowledge and imagination. The national laboratory can scarcely rise above the material sent to it and this in turn will depend upon the skill of the local investigators.

There is another dimension to the problem. Science must be used not merely to convict the guilty, but to free the innocent. It is inevitable that the police, being first on the scene, will marshal the evidence. Road blocks which bar examination of the physical evidence by the defense must fall. And, even today, the prosecution—how often no one knows—engages in the scandalous practice of concealing exonerating evidence, permitting its expert to tell half truths and engaging in similar disreputable practices. We do not make this charge lightly. It is based upon case after case documented in the courts. Despite repeated denunciation of such practices by the courts, they have continued, and we fear they will continue.

If we are to really use science to solve crime, we must not mar the achievement by the stain of dishonest methods which are the antithesis of science. A growing professional spirit among investigators may lessen the problem. Yet, so long as men's advancements and reputations depend on results, there will be the temptation to trifle with the facts. The criminal prosecution is an adversary process. Largely, this process serves us well. But when the prosecution stoops to suppression and misrepresentation of evidence, it hides the truth the trial is designed to elicit. Suppression and misrepresentation occur, moreover, not only because of calculation or malice, but also because every investigation must proceed not upon a witless collection of facts, but also upon a hypothesis. We like to see our hypotheses proved right and as we become more committed to them the less easy it is for us to admit their error or even to see the possibility for error. Hence, the manifest importance of countering this inevitable tendency. For this, the defense must have full and unrestricted access to the facts. It must have well paid, competent investigators and it must have full access to scientific laboratories. Only then will we bring the potentialities of our technology to the service of justice.

NOTES

(1) In one robbery-murder case, the defendant was convicted of robbery. A sawed-off shotgun "similar to" the murder weapon was found in the possession of an accomplice, together with a length of gun barrel and portion of a stock. Scientific evidence was introduced that the barrel and the stock had been sawed off the gun. Since the murder case is not yet decided by the Illinois Supreme Court, the case is not included.

(2) In two Arizona cases (companion cases) there was testimony that bloodstains and hair were found on a rock, but it is not clear that the blood and hair were identified as such by expert testimony. These cases are not included.

(3) This was evidently due to an oversight since it is the announced policy of the Bureau to list an individual only once on its annual report and then in the year in which he is first sentenced to death. If the conviction is set aside and he is subsequently sentenced to death, he is not supposed to be included in the figures for the later year.

PHYSICAL EVIDENCE UTILIZATION

IN THE ADMINISTRATION OF CRIMINAL JUSTICE

Brian Parker
Joseph Peterson

Human activity necessitates changes in the real world in every instance. A thought involves a change in a neuron network. A movement involves a change in the molecular states of muscle fibers. A sound involves a change in the vocal passages. A spoken word involves these changes and a change in the molecular distribution of air. These changes in matter-energy configurations and relationships constitute physical links between an activity and its human agent. If these changes can be established, they provide a basis for inferring specific human intent to engage in the particular activity as well as direct physical connections. Through documenting those changes, the sequence of events can be proven which relate a given activity to a specific actor.

The conviction of the guilty and the exoneration of the innocent in the investigation of criminal activities has occurred time and again when attention was focused on material reality as extrinsic evidence. Success in this sense of criminal investigation is amply demonstrated in the annals of detection. Such cases as Dr. Webster's murder of Mr. Parkman, the St. Valentine Day multiple murders, and the English insulin murder have shown the value of scientific examination and interpretation of the physical traces left in the wake of human violence. From the beginnings of this century in the endeavors of such men as Gross, Reiss, and Niceforo, the contributions of scientific crime detection have been recognized as useful, and often essential, to most areas of criminal investigation. More recently, the task force report on the police stated that "success in complicated investigation may depend in large part upon the scientific evaluation of pertinent data" and that Supreme Court decisions suggest "the necessity of a more adequate police crime scene searching and painstaking laboratory review."(1)

The demonstration that "each criminal violation must be shown to be in fact a breaking of the law, and must be linked to a specific individual" is the functional service of "crime" laboratories.(2) Performance in fulfilling this functional responsibility on a local basis is conceded to be minimal in most law enforcement operations.(1) The need for increasing such scientific services has been expressed in a number of technological and administrative terms such as proximity of services, timeliness of services, education and training of law enforcement personnel, education and training of experts, certification of experts, research and development in techniques, standardization of methods, environmental reference standards, and local support.(1, 3, 4) This stress on prerequisites for increased performance assumes the performance to be vital in the administration of criminal justice. The record of individual successes is an insufficient support for this assumption. Relevance is not guaranteed by mere expansion and increased involvement.

For the "crime" laboratory, "there remains a legitimate question as to the extent of its use."(5)

Behind the operational needs there is, as stated by Dr. Blumstein, "the fundamental need to discover the impact on crime of the many actions taken to control it. Very little is known to even a rough approximation about how much any prevention, apprehension, and rehabilitation program will reduce crime. And without such knowledge, how can we intelligently choose among them?"(3) The fundamental need pertains not only to know what exists, but also to know what could exist and what should exist in the relationship of the "crime" laboratory to the administration of criminal justice. "There comes a time when an expanding scientific profession needs to stop and examine its foundations and modes of operation."(6)

THE "CRIME" LABORATORY AS A SUBSYSTEM

In a physical sense, the effect of a criminal upon the site of his activity, and, conversely, the effect of the site upon the criminal constitute the "pertinent" sources of information to the investigative process. This nonverbal information, however, must be retrieved before any value in the way of an interpretation can be assigned. When the interpretation is communicated to the investigative process, the value conveyed is subject to a reinterpretation by each decision maker involved. These reinterpretations are affected by the extent to which the retrieved information is part of the interpretative message and by information from other sources. The response engendered is the investigative assessment of the criminal incident. In turn, the criminal justice system generally is subject to this interplay of information, interpretation, and reaction. Problems in measuring "crime" laboratory impact occur all along the communication channels in the administration of criminal justice. This study was directed at the problem of retrieval which can be viewed in two aspects: documentary and technical.

The informational output of a "crime" laboratory, both relevant and irrelevant, depends upon the input—the documentary retrieval. This aspect is the collecting of physical objects ("Collecting" is used in the sense of physical removal and locational coordinates relative to the site.) from the site of the crime which might determine the event sequence for a given violation and connect the criminal to that event sequence. Figure I is a schematic diagram of physical retrievals from crime sites and suspects and subsequent processes.(7) The diagram shows only networks for physical objects and suspects with but two of the informational channels in that network. Operational delays in movement along the networks are included. This simple model emphasizes the critical nature of documentary retrieval as a laboratory input. Stated in Willmer's conceptual terms,(8,9) the physical interaction of the site environment and the criminal during the course of a violation produces a number of constituent signals. "The total signal is made up of a number of different messages that have

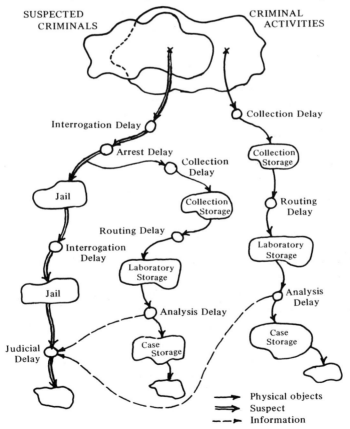

Figure 1 – Pathways for Physical Evidence Retrievals

different frequencies and similar interdependencies."(6) Since the choice of those physical objects bearing relevant signals from a crime site or a criminal is a unique selection, it is desirable to minimize the error of not collecting a significant object. Additionally, since the distribution at a site of physical objects bearing relevant signals is unknown, several objects collected may yield the same signal. This redundancy in collection must be tolerated. The collection, or documentary retrieval, is further complicated by "physiological shortcomings of investigators, such as vision, and psychological ones including perception."(6)

Technical retrieval of nonverbal information from a physical object is, within a laboratory operation, a selection of strategies. The choice of a strategy, or a combination of strategies, rests upon the query posed by the individual case. Within a given strategy, the search plan is a set function. For example, the finding of an unexpected stain at a crime site will raise the query as to what it is and how did it get there. In the absence of additional information as to the suspected violation, a general retrieval strategy would be necessary. This is the most difficult type of analysis to perform since the content of nonverbal information could be present in a variety of forms. During an abstraction, the recovery of one form may change or obliterate another form. The decisions on strategies to use in technical as well as documentary retrievals are extremely critical because of this potential loss in informational content. In such circumstances, the general retrieval strategy must so order the analyses that the maximum amount of nonverbal information is recovered. Where additional information is available, e.g., a suspected homicide, and identification of the stain as blood and the determination of the direction of travel by the blood drops that produced the stain are types of possible abstracted information. Two retrieval strategies, one chemical and one physical, would be used. A simple removal of the stain would preclude the physical analysis; a photograph alone of the stain would preclude the chemical analysis. Another example of a technical retrieval strategy is cyclic in nature wherein subsequent steps in the series are determined by the preceding abstractions. One such series is where a liquid is first determined to be blood; then, of human origin; then, of a particular group; then, of a particular type; and then, possibly, to fall within various classifications of additional seriological factors. This aspect of technical retrieval of nonverbal information from physical objects has occupied much of the laboratory involvement in the administration of criminal justice. The allocation of resources to explore and develop this scientific examination and interpretation of nonverbal information is of basic importance. However, this necessary component of the "crime" laboratory function remains irrelevant unless physical objects are brought in for analyses.

A MEASUREMENT OF DOCUMENTARY RETRIEVAL

The documentary aspect of retrieval, or laboratory input, is the level which this study sought to measure. Since a relatively small proportion of offenses actually arrive at the doors of "crime" laboratories(1,5) a measure based on laboratory receipts is biased strongly by the decision criteria employed in selecting cases for "laboratory review." The use of offense reports on cases as a basis was rejected also as subject to some of the same criteria. An ideal basis would be an independent measure of all physical characteristics at a site of criminal activity. As a practical matter this ideal could be approached by placing a suitable observer at the site as close as possible to the time of first official notice of the crime. From the records of such observers in a number of cases there could be constructed a frequency profile of the potential input to a "crime" laboratory function. This profile would represent a maximum input against which actual operations and possible alternatives could be viewed.

An assumption was made that scientists with substantial backgrounds in dealing with physical objects, particularly those experienced in forensic applications, would be most likely to recognize the possible significances of relevant physical objects. These observers, with the cooperation of a law enforcement agency, could make site visits to crime scenes and record each physical object thought to contain information relative to the pattern of criminal activity. A saturation coverage of major felonies within a given study period would provide sufficient data for a frequency profile.

A total recording of all physical characteristics in an area of violence would, in essence, mean an identical reproduction. Such a reproduction, even if possible, would not materially advance the study purpose. As reasonable boundaries for recording, all possible entrances, all possible exits, and all possible foci of violence were used. This set of boundaries did not exclude examining the possible routes connecting boundary areas nor observing any apparently unusual state of the general environment.

Perception within this framework while reducing somewhat the total reproduction of a site still requires a means of directing attention to significant objects. A categorizing model of six parts was taken for this purpose. The six categories were: position, transfer, impression, break and tear, dispersion, and physiochemical nature. Position included orientation of the physical object where the shape offered that possibility. Transfer referred to material originally on one object which remained on a second object after contact was broken between the two objects. Impression was the result of pressure imprint during the contact of two physical objects which might or might not involve relative movement of the two objects during the contact. Break and tear described the splitting apart of an object by forces involved in a contact. Dispersion was the result of an object breaking into parts which are then scattered by the disintegrating force. These five categories cover the production of patterns as the consequence of energy changes, and are not limited by the nature of the objects involved. The sixth category covered the inner structure and composition of an object itself. This categorizing model did not require that the observer have in mind any specific types of physical objects thereby allowing time to consider as an inclusion any material aspect in an area of violence.

The records resulted in a reasonably low scale of abstraction. Each field report consisted of free narrative(10) loosely-structured by the mentioned relevance, boundary, and category constraints. For each report an itemized list of physical objects was prepared on a McBee "Keysort" card along with follow-up data on the administrative processing of each case. Subsequent analyses of the complete field reports produced the frequencies of relevant physical objects. Service requests to laboratories during the study period provided another dimension of data relative to other major felonies committed but not covered by the field work.

OPERATIONS AND ANALYSES

In the choice of a field area for conducting the study, several assumptions were made. First, the types and frequencies of physical objects possibly involved in violent acts would be similar throughout a metropolitan region. Secondly, the cooperation of a law enforcement agency interested in the purposes of the study and willing to adjust to the presence of observers in the daily operations would be essential. Thirdly, the attempt to cover the bulk of serious crimes would limit the area for study to a population size commensurable with the use of six observers, i.e., an estimated field area population of 100,000. Several conferences with officials of the Berkeley Police Department culminated in an agreed upon plan of cooperation for carrying out the desired study in that city over a three month period.

Logistically the study goal was to place an observer at as many crime sites as possible during his particular shift. A variety of arrangements were tried and tested keeping this goal in mind. Most misdemeanor violations were judged not to be as potentially high in physical evidence content as most felonies. However, any situation that even seemed remotely possible of yielding information was considered to be potentially productive. Family disturbances, narcotic street arrests, shoplifting and petty theft, and miscellaneous "advice-giving" situations were, for the most part, avoided. Operating with the I.D. officer and traveling with him to the crime scenes proved to be the best way to get at the greatest number of sites, within the shortest span of time. Two other alternatives were used to place an observer at a crime site; these were traveling with the evening patrol sergeant and monitoring the police radio communications.

Each field report was considered repeatedly along with the observer's sketch of the site in itemizing every physical aspect thought likely to be involved in the criminal activity. On each McBee Keysort card representing an offense, this itemized list was placed along with a Departmental case number, the observer's name, the suspected offense classification, and, after a minimum period of two months lapse time, follow-up data on the departmental processing of the case. Codes were constructed for these informational characteristics and each card was then punched accordingly. The physical objects itemized from the field observations were categorized case by case. Every physical object was assigned to one category; multiple entries were not counted for individual cases.

TABLE I

Proportion of Cases with No Retrievable Physical Objects

Suspected Offense	Number of Cases	No Objects	Adjusted*	Percentages	
				No Obj.	Adj.*
Burglary					
Residential	355	47	18	13	5
Non-Residential	114	7	7	6	6
Auto	78	9	8	12	10
Total	547	63	33	12	6
Auto Theft	85	5	5	6	6
Theft	45	12	12	27	27
Robbery	26	5	4	19	15
Rape	6	0	0	0	0
Assault/Battery	6	1	1	17	17
Murder	5	0	0	0	0
All Others	29	7	7	24	24
Total	749	93	62	12	8

*Totals adjusted for cleaned sites, inaccessible sites, and minimal disturbance.

RESULTS

The number of cases where no physical objects could be retrieved were few in most offense classes. In the 63 suspected burglaries where this happened, five cases involved cleaned-up sites, four cases involved sites inaccessible to an observer, and 21 cases involved situations where it was thought the entry was by key or through an unlocked door coupled with removal of a single item prominently displayed, i.e., a portable color television. For one robbery there was an inaccessible site. This data is presented in Table I with totals and adjusted totals for cleaned sites, inaccessible sites, and minimal disturbance.

Table II indicates the number of physical object categories filled for all cases in a suspected offense class with median values considering all cases and cases where physical objects were retrievable.

The distribution about the median values for the physical object categories within given suspected offense classes can be seen in Table III.

Table IV presents the total number of offenses in each physical object category for each suspected offense class.

The rate of occurrence of each physical object category within various suspected offense classes appears in Table V.

Comparisons of field observation data with certain follow-up data on those suspected offenses are made in Table VI along with known offenses as tabulated by the Berkeley Police Department.

Table VII illustrates the offenses as officially reported, field observed and

TABLE II
Physical Object Categories Per Case

Suspected Offense	Number of Cases	Number of Physical Object Categories Filled	Median for	
			All Cases	Cases with Retrievable Objects
Burglary				
Residential	355	1002	3	3
Non-Residential	114	479	4	4
Auto	78	168	2	2
Total	547	1649	3	3
Auto Theft	85	282	3	3
Theft	45	87	2	3
Robbery	26	47	1	2
Rape	6	31	4	4
Assault/Battery	6	15	3	3
Murder	5	22	6	6
All Others	29	85	2	4
Total	749	2218	3	3

TABLE III

Distributions in Physical Object Categories

Suspected Offense	Number of Physical Object Categories Filled Per Case											
	0	1	2	3	4	5	6	7	8	9	10	11
Burglary												
Residential	47	54	68	75	48	31	12	9	2	2	6	1
Non-Residential	7	6	14	22	21	10	12	11	5	4	2	—
Auto	9	23	16	17	7	4	1	—	1	—	—	—
Auto Theft	5	10	19	12	18	9	7	3	—	2	—	—
Theft	12	7	8	11	4	3	—	—	—	—	—	—
Robbery	5	8	4	5	4	—	—	—	—	—	—	—
Rape	—	—	1	1	2	—	—	—	—	2	—	—
Assault/Battery	1	1	—	2	2	—	—	—	—	—	—	—
Murder	—	2	—	—	—	—	1	2	—	—	—	—
All Others	7	4	4	3	4	1	4	—	—	1	1	—
Total	93	115	134	148	110	58	37	25	8	11	9	1

TABLE IV

Physical Object Categories Per Suspected Offense

Suspected Offense	1	2	3	4	5	6	7	8	9	10	11	12	13	14	15	16	17	18	19	20	21	22	Misc	Total
Burglary																								
Residential	111	125	107	50	72	65	51	63	62	27	23	43	47	15	26	15	9	7	4	7	10	11	26	1002
Non-Residential	73	49	20	41	33	25	10	34	14	20	20	10	15	24	17	18	4	3	11	5	10	8	8	479
Auto	37	28	7	22	3	6	11	4	5	4	7	3	6	3	1	2	1	–	1	–	–	1	8	168
Total	221	202	134	113	108	96	72	99	80	52	50	56	65	45	35	40	36	24	23	33	33	20	42	1649
Auto Theft	31	36	25	12	8	19	16	3	8	25	18	18	1	7	5	3	8	7	4	2	4	1	11	282
Theft	18	15	6	6	3	4	3	–	6	7	5	1	1	1	1	2	4	5	1	1	3	–	3	87
Robbery	2	6	2	–	2	4	4	2	1	3	4	1	–	3	–	–	1	3	3	2	3	1	–	47
Rape	0	2	3	2	2	3	5	2	2	1	2	1	1	4	1	–	1	–	3	3	1	–	1	31
Assault/Battery	1	2	1	3	2	1	–	–	–	–	1	3	–	1	–	–	1	–	–	3	–	–	–	15
Murder	2	2	2	1	3	–	1	–	1	2	3	1	–	–	–	–	–	–	–	–	–	1	3	22
All Other	7	6	4	4	1	1	4	2	–	3	5	–	3	7	1	7	5	3	–	–	5	2	2	85
Total	282	271	177	141	129	130	106	106	98	96	88	81	71	65	48	46	48	47	35	33	33	25	62	2218

Key to Table IV

1. *Toolmarks* – This category includes all physical evidence where it was evident that one object, serving as a tool, acted on another object creating impressions, friction marks, or striations. A screwdriver, pipe, pry bar, fender of an automobile, or barrel of a gun could all produce toolmarks.

2. *Fingerprints and Palmprints* – All prints of this nature, latent or visible, are included. Bare foot prints, glove or other fabric prints would be included in this category also.

3. *Organic, botanical, zoological material and unknown stains* – Cases where matter of organic origin or stains of nonorganic nature were discovered. Excreta, all residues from trees and shrubs, and food items were typical examples.

4. *Glass or plastic fragments* – The presence of broken or chipped glass or plastic in an area suggesting it was the result of the responsible's actions or it might have been transferred to person(s) involved in the offense.

5. *Tracks and Impressions* – Includes skid and scuff markings, shoe prints, depressions in soft vegetation or soil, and all other forms of tracking. Conventional tool marks would not be included in this category.

6. *Paint* – Liquid or dried paint in positions where transference would be possible to persons in that area. Freshly painted locations, cracked and peeling paint on window sills, and automobile collisions are leading examples.

7. *Clothing* – Instances where items of clothing are left, carried, removed or discarded by persons. Individual fiber characteristics are included in a separate category.

8. *Wood fragments* – Cases where forces have created fragmenting or splintering in areas where transference was likely. Prying, kicking, and chopping attempts at entry points were the most frequent examples.

9. *Dust* – All cases where "dust" (all types of surface contamination) was noticeably disturbed by someone.

10. *Cigarettes, matches, related ashes* – Discovery of any of these combustible items which were in such position that their relationship to responsibles was likely.

11. *Paper*, in various forms – There are two basic areas of identification of paper. First, where the paper itself might be traced to its original position or orientation, and second, where external information including latent prints and other contaminating substances might be present on the paper.

12. *Soil* – The presence of soil or soil-like material in locations where identification or individualization seemed possible.

13. *Fibers*, natural or synthetic – Fibers were often found near crime scenes or edges, or on objects where electro-static or mechanical forces caused a transfer.

14. *Tools and weapons* – Cases where tools and weapons were found at crime scenes or in automobiles and there was a strong likelihood that they were involved in this or another criminal offense.

15. *Grease and oil* – Any lubricant or fatty substance, often possessing environmental contamination, that was in a position to suggest involvement in the crime.

16. *Construction and packing material* – All those substances commonly found in construction or packing areas, which don't belong in any of the other classifications.

17. *Documents* – Of such quality that their origin may be traced to a person or instrument. Suicides, and robbery notes would be of this type. Also cases where instruments were stolen (check protectors) that could be traced back to a product of that particular instrument, in possession of rightful owner.

18. *Containers* – All bottles, boxes, cans and other containers which might hold residues or material of helpful nature.

19. *Metal fragments* – Industrial machining areas, scenes or objects of collisions, and other scrappings that would probably result in transfers to persons or objects in the vicinity.

20. *Hair* – Any animal or human hair discovered in an environment which could link a person with that particular area.

21. *Blood* – All suspected blood, liquid or dried, animal or human, present in a form to suggest a relation to the offense or persons involved.

22. *Inorganic and mineralogical substances* – All substances, and otherwise not belonging in another category, that could be classified under one of these headings, and bearing a relationship to the offense or offender.

Misc. *Other* category – Miscellaneous.

TABLE V

Rate of Occurrence of Physical Object Categories By Suspected Offense Class

Number of Categories Per Number of Cases in Each Category

Physical Object Category	Burglary, Residential	Non-Residential	Auto	Total	Auto Theft	Theft	Robbery	Rape	Assault/ Battery	Murder	All Others	Total
Toolmarks	.39	.68	.54	.46	.39	.24	.10	.0	.2	.4	.32	.43
Fingerprints	.41	.46	.41	.42	.45	.45	.29	.3	.4	.4	.27	.41
Organic Substance	.35	.19	.10	.28	.31	.18	.15	.5	.2	.4	.14	.27
Glass	.16	.38	.32	.23	.15	.06	.00	.2	.2	.2	.50	.21
Track	.23	.31	.04	.22	.10	.09	.10	.3	.2	.2	.18	.20
Paint	.21	.23	.09	.20	.24	.12	.00	.5	.0	.2	.32	.20
Clothing	.17	.09	.16	.15	.20	.09	.19	.8	.2	.2	.18	.16
Wood	.20	.32	.03	.20	.04	.00	.05	.0	.0	.2	.09	.16
Dust	.20	.13	.06	.17	.13	.09	.10	.3	.0	.0	.05	.15
Cigarette	.09	.19	.07	.11	.29	.18	.38	.5	.0	.2	.14	.15
Paper	.07	.19	.10	.10	.31	.12	.19	.2	.0	.0	.18	.13
Soil	.14	.09	.04	.12	.23	.03	.05	.2	.2	.4	.05	.12
Fibers	.15	.14	.04	.13	.01	.03	.14	.0	.0	.0	.05	.11
Tools	.05	.22	.09	.09	.09	.09	.19	.2	.4	.4	.05	.10
Grease	.05	.16	.04	.07	.09	.12	.00	.2	.0	.0	.05	.07
Construction Material	.08	.11	.03	.08	.04	.00	.00	.0	.0	.0	.14	.07
Document	.05	.16	.03	.07	.10	.06	.05	.0	.0	.0	.05	.07
Container	.05	.04	.06	.05	.09	.12	.00	.0	.2	.2	.41	.07
Metal	.03	.10	.04	.05	.05	.09	.00	.2	.0	.2	.14	.05
Hair	.06	.05	.01	.05	.03	.03	.10	.5	.0	.0	.09	.05
Blood	.02	.06	.00	.03	.05	.03	.14	.2	.6	.6	.23	.05
Inorganic Substance	.03	.09	.00	.04	.03	.00	.00	.0	.0	.0	.14	.04
Miscellaneous	.09	.07	.12	.09	.14	.09	.05	.2	.2	.2	.09	.10

TABLE VI

Comparison of Field Observation Data with Departmental Data

Offense Class	Suspected Offense, Field Observed			Offenses Tabulated		
	Number	Arrests	Known Suspect	Number	Cleared	Percent Cleared
Burglary	538*	78	61	875	260	30
Auto Theft	81*	15	3	328	83	25
Theft over $50.00	44*	7	3	1679	332	20
Robbery	26	10	3	209	36	17
Rape	6	1	0	101	51	50
Assault (Battery)	6	1	1	26	17	65
Murder	5	2	1	292(60)	224	83
				2	2	100
Subtotal	706	111	74	3303	989	30
All Others**	28*	5	11	4900	4081	83
Total	734*	119	83	8203	5070	62

*In 9 cases no follow-up was possible and in 6 no follow-up information was available.

**Part II Crime Classes (Miscellaneous Offenses).

TABLE VII

Laboratory Input During Study Period

Offense Class	Official Tabulation	Field Observed Suspected	Received by Laboratory
Burglary	875	538	0
Auto Theft	328	81	0
Theft	1679	44	0
Robbery	101	26	1
Rape	26	6	0
Assault/Battery	292	6	1
Murder	2	6	2
Subtotal	3303	706	4
All Others*	4900	28	485
Total	8203	734	489
*All Others Forgery/			
Counterfeiting	165	0	6
Narcotic Drug	532	0	452
Drunk Driving	35	1	25
Remainder	3413	27	2
Total	4900	28	485

presented for laboratory review.

Of the 119 arrests made for offenses covered by field observation, Table VIII gives the number of physical object categories filled for each offense.

The total number of arrests in each physical object category is shown in Table IX.

Among the field observations, those cases where a suspect was connected to the crime scene through a latent fingerprint numbered 17 out of the 119. This type of identification was made in 8 residential burglaries, 3 auto burglaries, 3 auto thefts, 2 non-residential burglaries, and 1 hit-and-run case. The proportion of adult to juvenile suspects was 67 to 52 respectively among the 119 arrests.

In 83 cases, a suspect's identity was known although no arrest had been made. Table X presents for these 83 cases a breakdown as to the absence or presence of physical objects in the various categories.

Table XI presents the total number of cases where a suspect is known for each physical object category.

DISCUSSION

In the structure of the criminal justice system, the impact of scientific services could affect a number of decision points. At the beginning, a citizen's decision to notify his law enforcement agency of inflicted injury or damage can be influenced by that citizen's knowledge or misknowledge about scientific

TABLE VIII

Distributions in Physical Object Categories for Arrest Cases

Suspected Offense	Number of Arrests	Number of Physical Object Categories Filled Per Case													Total Cases With Objects
		0	1	2	3	4	5	6	7	8	9	10	11	12	
Burglary															
Residential	54	6	5	10	14	7	5	4	1	0	0	2	0	0	48
Non-Residential	13	2	2	0	2	2	2	0	1	0	1	1	0	0	11
Auto	11	2	4	2	3	0	0	0	0	0	0	0	0	0	9
Auto Theft	15	1	1	2	3	6	0	1	0	0	1	0	0	0	14
Theft	7	2	0	2	2	1	0	0	0	0	0	0	0	0	5
Robbery	10	0	4	1	3	1	1	0	0	0	0	0	0	0	10
Rape	1	0	0	0	0	1	0	0	0	0	0	0	0	0	1
Assault/Battery	1	0	0	0	1	0	0	0	0	0	0	0	0	0	1
Murder	2	0	0	0	0	0	0	0	2	0	0	0	0	0	2
All Others	5	0	1	0	0	1	0	2	0	0	1	0	0	0	5
Total	119	13	17	17	28	19	8	7	4	0	3	3	0	0	106

TABLE IX

Physical Object Categories Per Arrest

Suspected Offense	No. of Arrests	Physical Object Category																							Total	Total Cases With Objects
		1	2	3	4	5	6	7	8	9	10	11	12	13	14	15	16	17	18	19	20	21	22	Misc.		
Burglary																										
Res.	54	15	61	18	12	7	11	9	11	9	3	4	6	9	3	1	4	2	4	0	3	3	2	3	200	48
Non-Res.	13	7	11	4	4	1	2	1	4	0	2	4	1	1	2	3	1	2	0	0	1	1	1	2	55	11
Auto	11	2	11	0	0	1	1	2	0	0	1	0	0	0	1	0	0	0	0	1	0	0	0	1	21	9
Auto Theft	15	6	9	5	3	2	3	3	1	2	4	3	3	0	0	2	0	2	1	2	2	0	0	2	56	14
Theft	7	2	3	1	0	0	0	1	0	0	2	1	0	1	1	0	0	1	0	0	1	0	0	2	15	5
Robbery	10	1	3	1	0	1	0	2	0	0	3	2	1	2	3	0	0	0	0	0	2	2	0	0	25	10
Rape	1	0	1	0	1	0	0	1	0	0	0	0	0	0	0	0	0	1	0	0	1	0	0	0	4	1
Assault/Battery	1	0	1	1	0	0	0	0	0	0	0	0	0	0	0	0	0	0	0	0	0	1	0	0	3	1
Murder	2	1	1	1	0	1	0	0	0	1	1	0	0	0	0	1	0	0	0	1	2	1	1	0	9	2
All Others	5	1	2	0	0	0	4	1	1	1	1	0	1	0	0	0	0	0	0	1	1	1	1	0	24	5
Total	119	35	104	31	20	17	21	21	17	13	17	15	12	14	12	5	5	8	5	4	10	12	4	10	412	106

TABLE X

Distributions in Physical Object Categories for Known Suspect Cases

Suspected Offense	Number of Cases	Number of Physical Object Categories Filled Per Case													Total Cases With Object
		0	1	2	3	4	5	6	7	8	9	10	11	12	
Burglary															
Residential	38	2	12	3	7	7	3	1	2	1	0	0	0	0	36
Non-Residential	14	0	1	1	1	4	1	4	0	1	0	1	0	0	14
Auto	9	1	1	2	4	1	0	0	0	0	0	0	0	0	8
Auto Theft	3	1	0	0	0	0	1	0	1	0	0	0	0	0	2
Theft	3	1	1	1	0	0	0	0	0	0	0	0	0	0	2
Robbery	3	0	2	1	0	0	0	0	0	0	0	0	0	0	3
Rape	0	0	0	0	0	0	0	0	0	0	0	0	0	0	0
Assault/Battery	1	0	1	0	0	0	0	0	0	0	0	0	0	0	1
Murder	1	0	1	0	0	0	0	0	0	0	0	1	0	0	1
All Others	11	4	1	2	1	2	0	0	0	0	0	0	0	0	7
Total	83	9	20	10	13	14	5	5	3	2	0	2	0	0	74

TABLE XI

Physical Object Categories Per Known Suspect Case

Suspected Offense	No. of Cases	1	2	3	4	5	6	7	8	9	10	11	12	13	14	15	16	17	18	19	20	21	22	Misc.	Total	Total Cases With Objects
Burglary																										
Residential	38	14	20	7	3	3	7	3	11	10	4	3	2	7	3	2	3	2	2	1	2	2	1	2	114	36
Non-Residential	14	11	9	3	4	6	4	0	7	1	3	3	2	1	6	3	0	2	1	3	1	0	0	1	71	14
Auto	9	7	3	0	4	0	1	1	0	0	1	2	1	1	0	0	0	0	2	0	0	0	0	0	23	8
Auto Theft	3	1	1	2	0	0	0	0	0	0	1	1	1	0	1	1	0	0	0	0	1	1	0	1	12	2
Theft	3	1	1	0	1	0	0	0	0	0	0	0	0	0	0	0	0	0	0	0	0	0	0	0	3	2
Robbery	3	0	2	0	0	0	0	0	0	0	3	0	0	0	0	0	0	0	0	0	0	0	0	0	5	3
Rape	0	0	0	0	0	0	0	0	0	0	0	0	0	0	0	0	0	0	0	0	0	0	0	0	0	0
Assault/Battery	1	0	0	0	0	0	0	0	0	0	0	0	0	0	1	0	0	0	0	0	0	0	0	0	1	1
Murder	1	0	0	0	0	0	0	0	0	0	0	0	0	0	0	0	0	0	0	0	0	0	0	1	1	1
All Others	11	2	3	2	1	0	1	2	1	0	0	2	0	0	1	0	0	1	4	1	0	2	2	1	26	7
Total	83	36	39	14	13	9	13	6	19	11	12	11	6	9	12	6	3	5	9	5	4	5	3	6	256	74

crime detection. The patrol response to that report and subsequent evaluation will decide the possible engagement of the services by a "crime" laboratory. Where the patrol evaluation, in effect, refers the matter to the detective division, the question will again arise. If the assessment is to seek scientific involvement, the choice of physical objects to be collected may be made by the patrol officer, the detective, a specialized evidence technician, or laboratory personnel. On the arrest of a suspect, discretion must be exercised to collect physical objects from, or in the possession of, that individual. The laboratory operation excerpts the nonverbal information and offers an evaluation of its meaning with respect to the specific case. The law enforcement agency's decision to release or to seek a complaint can be influenced by the laboratory's evaluation. The office of the prosecutor in reviewing the case for a dismissal or a prosecution action is affected by the laboratory report. A defense response must weigh the scientific evidence against or for the defendant. If a pretrial conference takes place, scientific evaluation can qualify the route of pleading. During a trial, laboratory findings and interpretations can convince a judge or jury on the issue of guilt or innocence. In appeal, the presence or absence of a scientific report may well relate to the questions of due process and other constitutional issues.

The impact of forensic science has been traditionally one of individual outstanding cases rather than significant quantities of cases where analysis of physical evidence has contributed to the administering of justice. For this study the major purpose was to examine the potential input into a laboratory by actually going to the crime sites and measuring the available material. The task was to examine the day after day case load in a community to establish if criminalistics could become more of a working aid, rather than a last resort where all else has failed. That decision point where private knowledge becomes public notice in the structure of the criminal justice system was the focus for learning if broad patterns of physical evidence existed that could be helpful in apprehension.

The fact that only 12% of all the burglaries investigated had no potential physical evidence was quite impressive. Burglaries are often an offense class where few service requests are made of a laboratory, i.e., about 5% or less of known offenses.(11,12) It should also be considered that the reports were limited to 10-15 minutes for the average investigation. Those crime categories which often do not involve a physical interaction between the responsible and the victim or his property (petty thefts, robbery) proved to be the largest categories where no physical evidence was reported. The inaccessibility of certain crime sites prevented adequate investigation, therefore adding to the cases where nothing was retrieved.

It is also significant that for all cases, physical objects were not usually confined to one particular type. The median number of physical object categories for burglary was, 3; for robbery, 1; and for murder, 6. That is, evidence is not only present, it is present in usually more than one form. This might prove to be a strategic aid, for if there were a tendency for officers or investigators to terminate their search after one type of evidence was recovered, these figures indicate they should not do so. Operationally, it might be impossible to recover and evaluate each form, therefore, it seems even more important to identify the types, so that priorities may be established. Because burglaries proved to be such a large category, it was broken down into subtypes, selected as residential, non-residential, and auto.

Non-residential burglaries seemed to yield consistently more physical objects than residential or auto burglaries. This can probably be explained by the security precautions of non-residential structures, their overall size, and the inside conditions. That is, quantity of evidence types apparently depend more on the structure and its contents than the persons committing the offense. More non-residential buildings required an actual "breaking and entering" while homes and autos, even if they were locked, did not prove to be as secure. The larger the burglary site, the more surface area the burglar usually covered. In a restricted environment like a car there was less for the person to disturb. Residences were usually cleaner and freer from quantities of dirt, grease, and machine waste material.

With the unadjusted proportions represented in Table I, physical objects from 7 out of every 8 criminal activities would appear as a likely laboratory input. An adjustment for cleaned or inaccessible areas increases the potential input to objects from 9 out of every 10 criminal activities. While subject to constraints resulting in smaller proportional input, as a practical matter this boundary is important to remember since it supports the contention that few criminal activities leave no physical record and implies a necessity for comprehensive documentary retrievals.

Among the constraints diminishing the potential input to a laboratory are those which estimate the extent of damage as minimal and those which construe the activity as minor. Examples would be theft under $50 and disorderly conduct respectively. A third constraint reducing the input would be transitory changes unlikely to leave a substantial record, e.g., a verbal assault. On applying these constraints along with the *unadjusted* proportional results from the field observations to the total offenses tabulated for the study period, the approximate laboratory input drops to physical objects from 1 out of every 4 criminal activities. This outcome is presented in Table XII. Within the first seven offense classes the approximate input proportion is 2 out of every 5 criminal activities (1397 in 3303); for all other offense classes the forgeries, narcotic drug violations and drunk driving represent an approximate input of 1 out of every 7 criminal activities (732 in 4900). The 1 in 4 ratio would have produced a laboratory input of 2129 cases in the three-month study period.

Physical objects are not equal in probative value and this fact places another limit on "laboratory review." Since the evidential worth is correlated closely to a specific case circumstance, this limit would be assessed better in a pilot operation of a "crime" laboratory. However, with physical objects from three categories occurring in half the offenses observed (Table II), this limit is thought to be small for two reasons. First, the technical retrieval of information will be necessary in many instances to know what is knowable. Secondly, the physical

TABLE XII
Approximate Laboratory Inputs, 3 Months

Offenses	Offenses with Retrievable Physical Total	Offenses Classed as Objects	Major
Burglary	875	775	775
Auto Theft	328	309	309
Theft	1679	1230	–
over $50	209	153	153
Robbery	101	82	82
Rape	26	26	26
Assault/	292	243	–
Battery	60	50	50
Murder	2	2	2
Subtotal	3303	2667	1397
Forgery	165	165	165
Narcotic Drug	532	532	532
Drunk Driving	35	35	35
All Others	3413	–	–
Subtotal	4900	732	732
Total	8203	3399	2129

objects observed include a substantial number of items with high probative value. In this latter connection it is worth noting that the two categories of toolmarks and fingerprints account for one-quarter of all category entries (Table IV).

The use of scientific review as exemplified by the 489 cases received by laboratories (Table VII) from the 8203 reported cases in Berkeley appears very limited. A current crisis in narcotic drug violations accounts for 452 of the 489 cases with only 4 cases arriving at a laboratory from among the first seven offense classes. Since the full resources of a laboratory could be engaged in correlating documentary retrievals from both crime site and suspect, the field data is restructured below for the first seven offense classes (Table XIII). An extrapolation of the data in Table XIII to the total offenses in the three-month study period (Table VI) would show a possible input of 1190 cases and a potential input of 305 cases compared to the actual input of 4 cases to a laboratory operation. Adding the cases from forgeries, narcotic drug, and drunk driving cases would give possible and potential inputs of 1922 and 1037 respectively. (Thefts under $50 and assaults other than batteries were excluded in this extrapolation.)

The 489 cases received by laboratories from among 8203 reported cases in Berkeley is of the order of magnitude previously noted,(5) around 2% nationally in 1961. A question asking how many cases were referred to laboratories by police departments in 1968 was sent to cities in the population bracket of 50,000 to 250,000. Replies from 316 cities included 56 which answered that question. Of the 39 responding cities with populations from 50,000 to 99,000

TABLE XIII

Laboratory Inputs From Field Observed Offenses*

Suspected Offense	Possible Input	Arrests	Potential Input Known Suspects	Total	Actual Input
Burglary	484	68	58	126	0
Auto Theft	80	14	2	16	0
Theft	33	6	2	7	0
Robbery	21	10	3	13	1
Rape	6	1	0	1	0
Assault/Battery	5	1	1	2	1
Murder	5	2	1	3	2
Total	656 **			168	4

*The figures for suspected offenses, arrests, and known suspects are based on the field observations where physical objects were noted in individual cases. The actual input figures are based on all tabulated offenses for the study period.

**749 cases minus 93 cases, Table I.

the median submission rate per year was 414 cases per 100,000 population; the 17 responding cities with populations from 100,000 to 250,000 reported a median submission rate per year of 428 cases per 100,000 population. For all 56 cities replying to that question, the median submission rate per year was between 428 and 455 cases per 100,000 population. The Berkeley data extrapolated to a year basis would give a submission rate of 990 cases per 100,000 population. This crude measure suggests the general use of scientific review in the administration of justice is on a level similar to that of the Berkeley Police Department. Moreover, since each case submitted involves an allocation of resources, primarily man-hours, the administrative processing is an important constraint on "laboratory review." In this light, the submission rate and the related proportion of cases may be determined largely according to resource allocation as influenced by prevailing policies on what constitutes serious enough crime, i.e., currently the problem of drug abuse.

Webster's study(13) on the patrol duty time accorded to evidence collecting indicated a 3.3% allocation. The results of a recent study in New York for three counties demonstrated a request for "laboratory review" in 3.8% of reported cases (1102 out of 28,795).(11) This places the actual laboratory input from Berkeley, 6.0% (489 out of 8203), in a different perspective. In drawing together the various estimates based on the field study, the contrast of the actual laboratory input, 489 cases, to these amplifies the difficulties of various administrative responsibilities (Table XIV). If leads to suspects are desired from physical evidence, i.e., active information in Willmer's terminology,(14) then an input four times greater than actual would be required (2129 relative to 489). An affirmation or negation of a suspect's involvement as the yield from physical evidence, i.e., passive information in Willmer's terminology,(14) would require

TABLE XIV

Levels of Laboratory Input—3 Month Period

Number of Cases	Administrative Responsibility
8203	Total cases to be investigated (Table VI)
7220	Laboratory review of every case with retrievable physical objects (Tables I and VI)
2129	Laboratory review of major cases with retrievable physical objects (Table XII)
1922	Laboratory review of field observed cases (major cases with retrievable physical objects plus cases of forgery, narcotic drug violations, and drunk driving) (explanation of Table XIII)
1037	Laboratory review of field observed cases where an arrest was made or a suspect known (explanation of Table XIII)
489	Actual laboratory review of cases (Table VII)

over a two-fold increase in the actual input (1037 relative to 489). Physical evidence to be used as passive information would require documentary retrieval in as many cases as where physical evidence was used as active information (2129 relative to 489) since the discovery of a suspect in a given case is unpredictable.(15) The interrelating of separate offenses by the use of physical evidence also would require documentary retrieval in more cases for certain classes of offenses, e.g., burglaries involving toolmarks.

The conclusions reached in this study on input for "laboratory review" are that:

1. most offenses will have some type of physical evidence, particularly with intensive or extensive physical contact between the responsible and the crime site (Table II), 2. the variety in types of physical evidence suggests systematic samplings of a crime site and a suspect are essential (Table IV), 3. record systems are largely inadequate for the purpose of measuring input, 4. potential input based on arrests and/or known suspects is largely unrealized (Table XIII), 5. possible input, where leads to a suspect might be developed or the interrelationship of separate offenses might be established, is even less utilized (Table XIII), and 6. system limitations, i.e., resources for documentary and technical retrieval, appear to be major factors in the low utilization of scientific

knowledge in the administration of criminal justice.

NOTES

(1) President's Commission on Law Enforcement and of Justice, *Task Force Report: The Police*, 51, 90 (1967).

(2) Parker, B. P., "Government Review—Science and Crime," *Technology Review* (M.I.T.) *70* 10 (1968).

(3) Subcommittee on Science, Research, and Development, Committee on Science and Astronautics, U.S. House of Representatives, 90th Congress, 2nd Session, *Utilization of Federal Laboratories* 289, 335 (1968).

(4) Wilkins, L. T., "Priorities," Discussion Paper, National Council on Crime and Delinquency, 34 (1968).

(5) Parker, B. P., "The Status of Forensic Science in the Administration of Criminal Justice," *Revista Juridica de la Universidad de Puerto Rico 32* 405 (1963).

(6) Peterson, J., "Forensic Science and Information Theory," Graduate Seminar Paper (unpublished), School of Criminology, U.C. Berkeley (1969).

(7) Forrester, J. W., *Industrial Dynamics* 139 (1961).

(8) Willmer, M. A. P., "The Criminal as a Transmitter of Signals," Home Office (England) SA/PM 12 (1966).

(9) Willmer, M. A. P., "On the Measurement of Information in the Field of Criminal Detection," *Operational Research Quarterly 17* 335 (1968).

(10) Bross, I. D. J., et al, "Feasibility of Automated Information Systems in the Users' Natural Language," *American Scientist 57* 193 (1969).

(11) Rosenthal, P., *Planning Study for Evaluation of Forensic Laboratory Services in Erie, Niagara, and Wyoming Counties, New York*, 50 (1969).

(12) Smith, H. W., "Forensic Science in Canada," in *Law, Medicine, Science—And Justice* 448-458 (Bear, L.A. ed., 1964).

(13) Webster, J.A., *Police Task and Time Study*, D. Crim. thesis, School of Criminology, U.C. Berkeley (1968) 211.

(14) Willmer, M. A. P., "Criminal Investigation From the Small Town to the Large Urban Conurbation," *British Journal of Criminology 8* 259, 261 (1968).

(15) Ostler, R. D., "Criminals Incorporated," *The Police Journal 38* 161 (1965).

VII.

The Availability of Science in the Administration of Criminal Justice

INTRODUCTION

The American system of justice is an adversary one in which opposing advocates present evidence in the presence of a judge or jury to determine the guilt or innocence of an accused party. The use of adversaries is thought to be a fair and effective means for presenting and refuting information. The prosecution has the fundamental responsibility of showing the guilt of an alleged offender beyond a reasonable doubt. Although a defendant is not technically obligated to *prove* innocence, a defendant is required to refute that evidence of the prosecution which indicates either criminal intent or criminal conduct. To maintain a reasonable balance between the governmental machinery of the prosecution and the resources of the defense, special safeguards and rights are provided to the accused.

Readings in the last section primarily examined the use of physical evidence and of the crime laboratory by police and the prosecution. However, the article, "The Anatomy of Evidence," discussed the use by the defense of scientific evidence. This section will examine the uses of physical evidence involving first some practical considerations with which attorneys for the prosecution or defense must be familiar and secondly, involving some provisions of law which theoretically give the defendant equal access to the prosecution's scientific resources but which in fact often do not.

The first article by Wilkaan Fong, which appeared in *The Prosecutor's Sourcebook*, is an excellent discussion of the proper use of criminalistics services by the prosecutor. It offers clear guidelines to a prosecuting attorney on the proper use of an expert witness. The prosecution must respect and tolerate the neutrality of a scientist when the results of his tests are inconclusive or conflict with the government's theories. The paper explores the "communications gap" which often develops between a scientist and an attorney and notes the differences in their respective definitions of "proof" in the courtroom. The paper also covers the need for pre-trial conferences in major cases to completely familiarize the prosecution with the tests and findings of the expert.

The next three articles discuss the use of scientific services from the perspective of the defense. Julius Grant summarizes some problems of the defense expert by observing that experts called by the prosecution have the advantage of being associated with the police, have first rights to all evidence collected, and usually have more time to prepare their evidence. He also notes the problems of the defense attorney in gaining access to relevant evidence and being required to examine it in less than ideal surroundings. Joseph English summarizes the well-known problems of relying upon eye-witness testimony and the possibility that physical evidence may be misused by the prosecution unless minimum standards of training and ethics are maintained. His article concludes with nine points that he feels would lead to a higher quality of forensic science service in the criminal justice system.

Ralph Turner of Michigan State University discusses the disparity which exists between the scientific services available to the prosecution and to the defense in this country. He notes that the testimony of the prosecution's expert usually goes unchallenged by the defense attorney who either is not prepared to conduct an adequate cross-examination or lacks the resources to summon an expert. Professor Turner sees the need for forensic science institutes which would serve the defense and the prosecution equally. These institutes would examine evidence and submit to the judiciary their results which could be used by both sides in litigation.

Craig Bowman's "The Indigent's Right to an Adequate Defense," continues the debate on equal justice by analyzing several recent developments in criminal law that allow a defendant the right to view the prosecution's physical evidence and test results. Previously, this right had been forbidden in most jurisdictions. A defendant's right to "discovery" and his being guaranteed government funds to pay for required investigative services also help to equalize the judicial process.

CRIMINALISTICS AND THE PROSECUTOR

Wilkaan Fong

With the attention focused in recent years on the problem of filling the evidence void created by United States Supreme Court decisions, the role that criminalistics can play in supplying objective scientific evidence has become a matter of critical importance. This new position of prominence has been cause for both gratification and trepidation to the practicing criminalist. Gratification is felt because it would appear that the worth of investigative procedures based upon scientific methodology is recognized at long last, albeit belatedly and by imposed necessity. Trepidation exists because of the certain knowledge that in its present state, criminalistics is poorly equipped to deal with the enlarged responsibilities which have been so quickly thrust upon it.

This paper is directed at attorneys responsible for prosecuting charges in criminal proceedings. Its preparation is practical in view and based on the premise that while the attorney does not necessarily need to know all the trivial details involved in the performance of a laboratory examination, he does need to know something of the significant ideas, concepts and technological possibilities and limitations inherent in them. The reason he needs such information is all too clear. Criminalistics is plagued with "crises in communications" and "information breakdowns," awkward, sometimes hostile silences which prevent dialogue between criminalist and lawyer. This problem alone has resulted in a state of affairs in which each, in the process of pursuing his separate way, forms conceptual approaches to problems of scientific proof which conflict in ideological points of view. If in rare instances the beginnings of some form of communication are effected, immediate problems of a semantic character develop, and the most well-intentioned attempts quickly break down. Criminalistics, like all sciences, is a conglomeration of profuse ideas, principles and methodology. Its language is oftentimes guarded, abstract and pedantically detailed. Law is, in the words of Conrad(1) a symphony of empty maxims, rules, platitudes and ambiguities." Small wonder then that there is a communications gap when, by necessity, science and law must join forces. The ultimate purpose of this paper is to help bridge the gap. To do so, the approach will be to examine who the criminalist is, where he works and how he functions. Upon this foundation then, the major problem areas within the gap and suggested solutions for remedying them will be discussed.

THE PROFESSION

The prosecuting attorney can be expected to handle a variety of witnesses testifying to matters of a technical nature. Some pertinent questions might be: Who are these witnesses? What are they called? What backgrounds do they possess? Who employs them? Where are they distributed?

The answers to these questions are not easily gained. While virtually everyone recognizes the need for specialized knowledge in the resolution of judicial matters, few can define and clearly characterize the individual who performs the function of delivering technical testimony.

Workers in police laboratories are a diverse lot. There is the criminalist, educated at a university level. But there are also a host of workers performing criminalistics functions as limited technicians or specialists, commonly including fingerprint technicians, laboratory technicians performing repetitive examinations, firearms, identification specialists, document examiners, police photographers, chemists, microscopists, serologists, toxicologists, and instrumental specialists of one kind or another. In rare instances, the services of botanists, entomologists, mineralogists, physicists, anthropologists and explosive specialists, to name a few, can be sought.

It is obvious that this diverse lot must include all levels of educational backgrounds and experience. Joseph(2) reports a total of 459 civilian personnel employed in crime laboratories in the United States, 380 of whom possess bachelor of science or equivalent degrees, and twenty with doctoral degrees or the equivalent. In addition, 623 full-time police personnel are reported, only a fraction of whom hold bachelor of science degrees.

The major supplier of personnel with degrees in criminalistics has been the University of California at Berkeley. In a recent alumni survey report,(3) forty-six of its graduates were active in criminalistics. Their distribution among governmental and private agencies is as follows: municipal or local, 27; state, 9; federal, 4; and private, 6.

An additional source of graduates in criminalistics has been the School of Police Administration and Public Safety at Michigan State University, which has never had a graduate curriculum in criminalistics. Its output has been modest in number by comparison. The estimate can be made that the total number of practicing university-educated criminalists in the United States number less than seventy. Small wonder, then, that trepidation exists in the minds of criminalists when they consider this minute number in relation to the prodigious task before them.

The first usage of the term "criminalistics" is obscure but is probably rooted in Europe. It was Kirk(4) who first thought to espouse the idea that what was known as police science involved attributes differing from any other scientific discipline. He urged the adoption of the term "criminalist" to identify a separate breed of scientist whose specific purpose was the furnishing of proof for judicial purposes through the application of the scientific method to the study of physical evidence.

The idea was visionary and included a pragmatic principle of approach. Its significant meaning was that the criminalist, guided by a conceptual approach, could deal with virtually all the common problems in physical evidence. The idea that one individual could range the entire spectrum of possible physical evidence problems was daring and aroused vigorous opposition from within the technician-oriented elements of the police science fold.

While the generalist versus specialist issue has not been entirely resolved, the term "criminalistics" has been almost universally adopted, and is preferable to that of police science or criminology. In addition to the urgings of Kirk, the popular adoption of the term is due in no small measure to the highly regarded textbook entitled *An Introduction to Criminalistics* by O'Hara and Osterburg.(5) The California Association of Criminalists define criminalistics as *"that profession and scientific discipline directed to the recognition, identification, individualization and evaluation of physical evidence by the application of natural sciences to law-science matters."*

If the criminalist is an enigma to himself and others, there are certain attributes which justify his existence as a separate kind of scientist. Although he employs procedures as other scientists do, through the usage of an attitudinal philosophy that enables any scientist to extract dependable overall guidelines for use in problem solving, two principal attributes distinguish the criminalist as a separate being among scientists: 1. He must testify on the witness stand in a courtroom where his conclusions are a matter of public record and subjected to searching inspection; and 2. The significant meaning of his examination of physical evidence is realized by answering the concomitant questions: what is it? and, are the two things source related? Of the two, the latter occupies the greater amount of his time and attention. It is directed towards the problem of determining common origin between two objects. Were the two bullets (fatal and test) fired from the same weapon? Were the two shoe impressions (questioned and test) made by the same shoe? Are the two fragments of glass (questioned from the suspect's clothing and sample from scene or burglary) from the same source? The ultimate aim of the criminalist in all problems of this kind is the individualization of source. This is indeed "the name of the game," and so fundamental that Kirk(6) has suggested that criminalistics is *the science of individualization*, and is concerned only incidentally with identification in its ordinary sense. No scientist of any description is as totally committed to this problem as is the criminalist.

The hot pursuit of individualization carries the criminalist across lines into realms the cultivators of particular specialties claim delineate their private closed preserve. The "specialist" resents this intrusion by the "generalist" and queries plaintively: "How can one person be an expert in all things?" The answer is that the criminalistics individualization of source approach is, like all sciences, attitudinal in character and based on relatively simple concepts of approach. These will be discussed later under the heading "Criminalistics, Evidence and Proof."

While criminalistics is based on the application of the natural sciences, its professional practice is an art. In this it is like the practice of medicine. The physician, for instance, establishes as a first step a doctor-patient relationship which gathers information setting forth the problem, thus providing the basis for a practical, artful approach to a solution. The criminalist must establish a similar information-gathering relationship with the clientele that he serves for the same reason. This is not easily accomplished, for as in criminalistics, as it must be in medicine, the clientele are not necessarily informative and do not always tell the whole story for various reasons.

An additional parallel which can be cited between medicine and criminalistics is that historically the medical doctor was a general practitioner treating a wide variety of medical problems, but the increasing complexities of medical science necessitated the proliferation of narrow medical specialties, and even sub-specialties. Is it not likely that criminalistics will take the same course? The answer is probably affirmative. The urgencies for specialization which complexity compels afflict criminalistics as they do all other sciences. Higher degrees of specialization will take place in the future, not only because of increasing technological complexities, but because of the increasing crush of daily case work. This trend will not invalidate the criminalistics concept that the application of a few basic principles, coupled with the strong attitudinal approach which is characteristic of all scientists, can offer practical solutions to the greatest number of law-science problems.

Criminalistics has had its family fights which have complicated efforts to popularize its work and educate its immediate clientele, lawyers and law enforcement personnel. The optimistic view is that this discord has had salutary effects. This is probably true, for there is now the realization that both sides must yield a good measure of their own dogmatism and relinquish needless pretenses that theirs is the only way. Whatever the view the practitioner of police science holds, few can take exception to the thesis that to function effectively the criminalist must understand enough of science to be able to follow its principal advances in the major fields applicable to the forensic scientist. Along with this must come the governmental realization that perhaps the solution lies in improving the education and the general lot of the criminalist so that more and better quality personnel will be attracted to his ranks.

Laboratories engaged in the application of the natural sciences to law-science matters are known by as wide a variety of labels as the workers in them. Examples of some are: police crime laboratory, crime laboratory, criminalistics laboratory, forensic criminalistics laboratory, forensic science laboratory and crime detection laboratory.

Joseph(7) reports that there is a total of 105 non-federal laboratories engaged in police science in the United States. For the purpose of his report a laboratory was defined as one which performed at least "wet chemistry." This reduced the number to approximately 100. About sixty of these operated at a local level and the remainder at a state level.

Dillon(8) points out that "the first criminalistics laboratory in police history in the United States was established in California (1930), the most influential academic training in criminalistics has been given at the University of California, and the largest concentration of criminalistics laboratories and criminalists are located here (California)." His report takes singular exception with the popular notion that criminalistics had its beginnings in the Midwest as an outgrowth of the 1929 St. Valentine's Day massacre in Chicago.

In virtually every instance, the genesis of a criminalistics function, whether local or state, has been either the outgrowth of a need laid bare by a major crime of violence, or a series of such crimes occurring at a particular locale. The notoriety which attends such cases, and the ensuing public outcry against the apparent deficiencies of the investigative effort, focused attention on possible avenues of improvement. The laboratory examination of physical evidence involved in all these cases was a natural result.

The common arrangement in which the criminalistics laboratory's place in the governmental structure is that of subservience to police administrative or line personnel can be traced back to these informal, often hurried beginnings arising out of need. Despite the fact that there are criminalistics laboratories that have operated with outstanding success under a police agency of one kind or another, this type of arrangement is defective and has led to serious problems.

Uniformed police personnel view the criminalist as a rather incomprehensible, condescending breed, occasionally arrogant and afflicted with a prima donna complex. As one officer was overheard to say, "You have to be a little crazy to be one of those crime lab guys!" The criminalist, in turn, complains that many police officials are illiterate about science and far too misinformed in their expectations.

When the law enforcement agency, which is a quasi-military organization, is composed of police administrative and line personnel who have a university-trained orientation to forensic science, a common ground in professional attitudes exists upon which dialogue can be based leading to an amicable, effective working relationship. When this is not true, serious problems will inevitably develop.

There is first the necessity to fit the criminalistics function into an existing administrative and salary structure. Petty jealousies on an intradepartmental level are certain to develop among the experienced officers of line rank when the relatively inexperienced but university-educated criminalist succeeds in commanding a salary and professional position commensurate with his educational background and responsibilities. Other problems which have been experienced are: 1. The lack of understanding of the role that the scientist must play if he is to maintain his identity and effectiveness as an expert witness. 2. The inability of police administrators to comprehend the distinction between a technician and a criminalist. 3. The desire to use the laboratory as either a status symbol for public relations, or as a "front" to gain funds which if gained are then diverted to other uses. 4. The "creation" by administrative decree of laboratory workers from the ranks of police personnel because of low salaries or meager supply of criminalists. 5. The "prosecution mindedness" and attendant lack of objectivity which can be the cause of serious friction, especially in major cases, when the "heat is on" for a quick solution. 6. The misuse of highly trained criminalistics personnel for duties which are more appropriately performed by departmental personnel at lower levels of ability.

Close physical proximity can be an additional problem. A location within earshot of ugly epithets shouted by recalcitrant prisoners being dragged in by uniformed police officers for booking offends the finer sensibilities of the criminalist and affords a poor atmosphere for a scientific laboratory. The meaning is clear: compelling reasons exist for placing the criminalistics function outside the confines of the immediate law enforcement tent. However, the question arises, if criminalists are not placed under police agencies, then what will be done with them? The answer is that the criminalistics laboratory should be a separate entity with strong university ties. Its necessary relationships with the police, prosecutor, coroner, or medical examiner are matters of administrative policy and procedures which can be worked out to mutual advantage. Like relationships already exist, with success among the three separate parties named. A similar proposal in principle has been advanced by Bradford and Kirk(9) with refinements directed toward the trend to centralize rather than to fragment governmental functions. These authors advocate the formation of regional laboratories equipped with sophisticated instrumentation and staffed with top level scientific personnel to handle major technological problems. Common problems could then be handled by local level, satellite laboratories with the advantages of economy, close contact with law enforcement personnel and speed.

INVESTIGATIVE ROLE OF THE LABORATORY

The laboratory's role in the investigation of crimes can be played in many ways. Osterburg(10) sums them up as follows: 1. Link the crime scene or victim to the criminal. 2. Establish an element of the crime. 3. Corroborate or disprove an alibi. 4. Induce an admission or a confession. 5. Exonerate the innocent. 6. Provide expert testimony.

The depth and scope of the assistance supplied by a criminalistics laboratory, which allows it to fulfill this role, are determined by many factors. There are the obvious ones: number and capabilities of personnel, instrumentation available and space allowed for physical facilities. However, a high standard of personnel qualifications and an impressive array of the latest scientific instrumentation do not insure that the role of a laboratory will be fully and effectively played. The criminalist is totally dependent upon the quality of understanding applied in · gathering the evidence he examines. Failure of the investigator to recognize, record, preserve, identify and transport physical evidence will most certainly hamstring the efforts of the workers in the most sophisticated of laboratories. Some of the most potentially useful evidence is of a relatively uncomplicated nature and well within the capabilities of the most modestly equipped laboratory, provided intelligent understanding of fundamental and simple investigative principles is applied.

In many jurisdictions field investigative services are provided under the supervision of the criminalistics laboratory. In larger departments, these services are supplied by either photographers or specialists in the development of fingerprints. In many smaller departments, they are either non-existent or are provided at a very rudimentary level by investigative personnel. Field services provided by criminalists are not necessary except in the most demanding cases. Experience has shown that a properly motivated, intelligent, resourceful investigator, who has had the benefit of intensive training with strong criminalistics orientation, can supply a thoroughly competent field service.

Police training programs have greatly expanded in recent times, and many training officers have sought to tack scientific prestige onto their efforts by offering faulty lecture content under the banner of police science. The result has often been an overselling of laboratory capabilities with no emphasis given to limitations. These practices and their results rankle the criminalist who is subsequently called upon to "pull the rabbit out of the hat." The delivery of lecture content beyond rudimentary levels to police recruits offers low return for the amount of criminalistics effort expended. Outstanding results accrue when intensified seminar sessions are held for experienced investigators or specialists who have direct responsibility for crime scene processing.

A balanced criminalistics function should be prepared to offer a wide variety of services which will insure the effective performance of its role in the investigative process. An enumeration must include the following:

1. *In Crimes Against Persons.* The identification and comparison, as appropriate, of all varieties of trace evidence such as blood, semen, hair, fibers, soil, plant debris, insect remains, tissue, wood, cordage, weapons of all varieties; the comparison of bullets, cartridge cases, shotgun shells; the determination of the general condition of a firearm, and estimation of the distance from which a firearm was fired.

2. *In Crimes Against Property.* The examination and· comparison of paint, metals, safe insulation, shoeprints, tire prints, glass, toolmarks, etc.; the restoration of obliterated serial numbers; the detection, comparison and identification of flammable liquids in burned debris from fire scenes.

3. *In Drinking Driver Law Enforcement.* Quantitation of alcohol from blood,

urine and breath; the delivery of opinion testimony correlating levels of alcohol concentration with brain impairment.

4. *In Narcotics and Dangerous Drug Law Violations.* The identification from seizure materials, narcotics and dangerous drugs, as well as their detection in blood and urine.

5. *In Forgery Cases.* The examination and comparison of handwriting, handprinting, typewriting; restoration of obliterated writing; identification of paper; identification and comparison of inks; restoration of indented writings.

Geographical and jurisdictional peculiarities can profoundly influence whether or not the criminalistics laboratory may offer a balanced service. The exigencies in some locations occasioned by a high incidence of narcotics arrests demanding immediate laboratory answers to meet the requirements of reasonable cause and due process are an example.

CRIMINALISTICS, EVIDENCE AND PROOF

The prosecuting attorney will be presented with investigative information from which he must determine the course of legal action to be taken against a suspect. In his study of this information, the problems of proof he can expect to encounter will become evident. If the investigative results are incomplete, the quality of the prosecution will surely be impaired. If elements of proof required by law are lacking, charges must be dropped.

The information which guides the prosecutor will be provided by various members of an investigative task force. This force will surely include the criminal investigator, members of the medical profession, the criminalist and specialists of one kind or another. Coordination of the major investigative efforts, then, becomes a matter of paramount importance.

The ultimate responsibility for a successful prosecution of a criminal case rests with the prosecuting attorney. If a study of the investigative data presented reveals details of proof which are incomplete, remedies should be sought through discussions with the appropriate members of his fact-finding team. This is particularly true in jurisdictions where the investigative agency is small, poorly funded, and its members untrained and inexperienced. Further, in all jurisdictions major cases can arise in which the complexities of the problems of proof are interwoven among several separate members of the fact-finding task force. It is appropriate for the prosecuting attorney to assume the role of the coordinating authority.

The prosecuting attorney wants a full report from the criminalist. He needs to know what the criminalist did, what his results were, and in a general way the basis for the conclusions reached. He is often frustrated when the report tends only to record results without thoughts toward either persuasion or interpretation.

Most criminalists will admit that they are rather poor report writers. Yet, it must be said that as a group they try hard. The difficulties develop when the criminalist comes to grips with the problem of serving the lawyers needs and at the same time remaining true to the principles of scientific objectivity.

When he writes a report, the criminalist like all scientists tries to maintain an objective tone. His reports are couched in passive rather than the generally preferred active construction, a reflection of his desire to maintain a tone of objectivity by remaining out of sight. The criminalist is instinctively wary of flat assertions. The lawyer, on the other hand, is impatient with wariness and demands: "Is it or isn't it?," and tolerates with difficulty the cagey assertion, "it could be." Herein are the beginnings of the departures in understanding between the lawyer and the criminalist.

At this point it seems pertinent to analyze the various steps by which the criminalist arrives at a conclusion. The virtues and limitations of processes which are applied — their broad implications — go directly to what the criminalist reports.

The stepwise narrowing process which leads the criminalist to a conclusion begins with examinations that are convenient, sensitive, reliable and eliminative in character.

When the problem is one of identification in its ordinary sense, many preliminary screening tests are available. Some examples are chemical color tests for blood, semen, narcotics, dangerous drugs, trace metals; application of solvents to plastics, paints, resinous materials and a wide variety of chemical substances; scans throughout the various regions of the electro-magnetic spectrum through the use of spectro-photometers; microscopic examinations; and injections of volatiles or substances capable of volatilization into a gas chromatograph.

When the aim is the common problem of individualizing source, the criminalist can apply many of the screening tests enumerated above, but there is an additional approach which is especially important — the consideration of class characteristics. Such characteristics are those common to like things, for example, manufactured items: patterns, size and forms of shoeprints; diameter, direction of twist and number of lands and grooves on a bullet; and color and layered makeup of paint.

Assuming reliability in the methods used, a lack of coincidence in properties at the preliminary examination level permits the unequivocal elimination of the possibility raised by the question at hand. An agreement establishes only a presumption with varying degrees of significance, and additional examinations are required.

The criminalist fruitfully employs the attitude of all scientists in the methods he uses. He observes and compares like objects under like conditions. He applies internal controls that allow the detection of gross errors in the examination process. He insures, insofar as it is possible, the acquisition of adequate and authentic standards for comparison. He preserves the integrity of the evidence at every step by applying procedures which guard against contamination, alteration, and misidentification.

As the step by step narrowing process proceeds, finer and finer differences are distinguished. At each step, the criminalist collects pertinent evidence, evaluates its significance, and performs additional confirmatory tests as required. Finally he reaches a point where he can begin to construct a conclusion. At this point, he will go through a process of intensive criticism. If the construction amounts to a conclusion relative to specific identification of nature or source, he must consider the universal validity throughout the extent of things. This is true despite the fact that legal requirements do not demand absolute proof. If his construction cannot withstand his self-imposed criticism, he must modify or reject it entirely. This is the stern discipline of the criminalist and is designed to keep his profession sound and rigorously honest.

The thought processes involved in the construction of a conclusion require several considerations. Mention has been made that when the criminalist is faced with the problem of individualizing source he considers class characteristics as a first step. If these correspond he moves to features which make use of individual characteristics. A class of characteristics intermediate between the two exists.

Individual characteristics are those which result from history of wear and usage. In addition to class characteristics, a tire imprint can have markings in the form of scratches, cuts and localized areas of wear resulting from the unique history of its source. Similar considerations apply to the sides of a bullet and a toolmark.

In the examples given, if class characteristics are in agreement between the evidence and suspect source along with a sufficient number of individual characteristics, the conclusion "specific identity of source, to the exclusion of all other sources," is justified. In the absence of a sufficient number of individual identifying characteristics this conclusion, which is absolute in its meaning, cannot be claimed.

When individual characteristics are either low in number or poor in quality, but class characteristics are in agreement, conclusions such as: "the   could have had a common origin," "a high probability of common origin is established," and "the results would serve to support a belief that   have had a common origin" can be given.

A commonly practiced approach allowing for convenient and accurate decision making is that based on a comparison of patterns, charts, forms and the like. Some common examples are 1. bullet and cartridge case markings as revealed through juxtapositioning through a comparison microscope, 2. handwriting and typewriting, 3. density distributions of mineral constituents in soil through flotations in a glass tube containing a fluid density gradient increasing from the upper to the lower levels, 4. fingerprints, 5. shoeprints and tireprints, 6. chromatograms resulting from a variety of sophisticated instrumental methods which serve to separate the constituents of complex mixtures, 7. absorption spectograms resulting from the passage of energy throughout a wide range of the electromagnetic spectrum through samples in solution, 8. emission spectrograms obtained from spectrographic analysis, 9. x-ray diffraction patterns, and 10. gamma ray spectrograms resulting from neutron activation analysis. Kirk(11) has called attention to this extremely useful approach.

In its present state, the art of individualizing source suffers serious limitations. In many instances the nature of the evidence itself declares against the likelihood of a specific claim of source to the exclusion of all others. Building materials like paint, glass, wood, plastics and metals, and personal clues like fibers, hairs, blood and semen are examples. Further, the criminal in the commission of his unlawful acts is not especially considerate of the sample needs of the criminalist. Thus, both the quality and quantity of the evidence samples are usually poor.

When the sample situation is unfavorable as to nature, quantity and quality, the likelihood of differentiation leading to individualization of source is precluded from the beginning, examinations are justified if there exists the possibility of providing information which has supportive or eliminative value within a given context.

When the sample situation is favorable, greater possibilities for providing useful information exist. Wood on clothing or tools of a suspect has low value if it is present as tiny bits and as single common variety. In a case involving the arson of a lumber milling company, wood became of great probative value when it was shown to be present on a suspect's clothing, not only as curled shavings, some partially charred, but also in several varieties. The varieties included less common woods and their number and relative amounts paralleled those from piles of shavings at the fire scene.

Specific identification of source involving wood was possible in a case of the cutting down of a valuable blue spruce tree from a public park. Despite the absence of a short length between the trunk found in the possession of the suspect and the stump remaining at the park, it was possible to match the two remaining ends through growth rings demonstrating structural variations because of compression wood.

Numerous other examples can be cited to demonstrate the interrelationships of nature, quality and quantity of evidence to degrees of proof possible. Further, it is clear that the amount of success to be achieved is directly related to the imagination and resourcefulness of the investigator in the field as well as to that of the criminalist in the laboratory.

But some examiners in police science laboratories are of the mind that unless evidence lends itself to specific individualization of source it has very little if any value as evidence. This "it is" or "it isn't" attitude does not countenance "in-between," "maybe" or "probable" conclusions. This approach is incomprehensible to the criminalist. If valid, its significant meaning would be that the broad category of evidence often referred to as trace evidence should be deemphasized to a point of little, if any, utilization.

Some prosecuting attorneys have been afflicted with the same condition of attitude. Thus they greet with intolerance conclusions which can establish only roughly estimated degrees of probabilities. The author was accosted by an enraged prosecutor in the hallway outside the courtroom after delivering an opinion which established only a probability of common origin. In tones reflecting outraged disappointment, he demanded, "Why can't you say that the paint (from the defendant's car) came from the victim (auto forced off highway into river resulting in the drowning of two occupants) when I tell you where the paints come from?"

This type of demand and over-reaction fails to consider that the criminalist can include in his considerations only the results of his observations in the laboratory and not what he is told by investigating officers. Intelligent, hypothetical questioning would be a useful approach in these situations, but in the author's experience subject to objection on legal grounds in criminal matters.

Construction of a report is difficult, and the discussion given has been indulged in at length so that emphasis can be laid on an avenue of approach which can have practical value despite the fact that the variety of evidence does not lend itself to specific individualization of source.

It is seldom that physical evidence and investigative results need to stand independent of each other. Ordinarily, the findings of a criminalist are offered in support of testimony given by other members of the fact-finding task force. The strategem to be conceived is the extraction from the evidence at hand of the fullest significant meaning by fitting it into its proper relationship with other evidence. When there is available a combination of physical evidence as varieties of either the same thing or of different things, there exist the possibilities for the development of extremely significant proof. This is true despite the fact that each variety in itself establishes only an element of probability. The avenue of approach is the utilization of evidence combinations, an amassing of an array of evidence, each with its own significance in probability, either low or high, but never in itself conclusive, to the extent that when the array is considered in its totality, only one conclusion can be reached.

Combinations of physical evidence as different varieties which apply to this strategy are: 1. cross-transfers of paint, glass, metal, blood, hairs, fibers and fabric imprints between a suspect car and victim in "hit and run" automobile fatalities, 2. transfers of woods, glass, paint, safe insulation and metals to the tools, clothing and cars used by safe burglars, 3. adherent plant materials, insect debris, and soil on the clothing of suspects from their acts of effecting illegal entry, 4. cross transfers of personal contact traces, such as blood, saliva, urine, hairs and fibers in homicides, rapes and assaults.

Examples of combination evidence of the same variety are: 1. wood as mentioned in an example given previously, 2. tracking laid down by four different tires mounted on the same car, 3. paint transferred from multicolored objects such as old safes to tools, clothing and cars of suspects, 4. varieties of plant material, e.g., newly mown grass on a lawn, transferred to the person of a suspect.

It is implicit in the above discussions that the basis for constructing a conclusion is subjective in character. Intuition and cognition based upon experience are largely involved, and the degree of proof claimed will depend on an evaluation of the number of physical properties or comparison features which are in agreement, the estimated frequency of occurrence of each feature, and as appropriate, the criminalist's estimate of his ability to distinguish fine differences at each step of the narrowing down process.

The philosophical basis for interpreting physical evidence referred to as "dichotomy in interpretation," defined simply as the black and white versus the black, gray and white view, has been discussed by Osterburg.(12) The gist of Osterburg's comments, reflected by this author in the foregoing discussion, is that the gray view is the view of choice based upon the principles of logical scientific thought processes. He further calls attention to the critical need for research requirements developing basic data upon which objective criteria for evaluation of physical evidence can be based.

Examples of the process for decision making have been given by Burd and Greene(13), Englaar(14), Huber(15), Kind(16), Kingston and Kirk(17) and Osterburg.(18)

Kirk and Kingston(19) and Parker(20) have advocated the removal of evidence evaluation from a subjective basis to an objective basis through the application of statistical probability. Simply stated, the approach is to multiply the separate probabilities of occurrence assignable to each identification feature or member of an evidence combination to arrive at a probability of occurrence of all. The significant meaning is that the product of this calculation would allow a decision relative to the individual criminalist's assessment of the risk he is willing to assume. While the concept is simple, its valid application in practice rests upon the acquisition of statistically meaningful probability factors that enter into the calculations which satisfy rigid requirements.

The acquisition of data from which factors can be assigned is a very large task. *Valid* usage of such factors presupposes that a planned study incorporating stern control in the statistical data gathering process has been applied. Thus, the data must achieve as closely as possible the qualities of randomness and independence. A discussion of the conditions and limitations which need to be dealt with if maximum and valid benefit is to be derived from a statistical approach towards decision making is given by Kingston and Kirk.(21)

These authors justify the statistical approach to those who oppose its usage through three important passages:

The difference between the two approaches (intuitive and statistical) lie in the fact that means of minimizing errors, e.g., bias interjected by the examiners' prejudices) are incorporated into a proper statistical approach and can be spelled out for the experimenter, whereas such definite controls are not easily applied to the intuitive approach.

. . . [M]any opponents of the use of statistical methods in criminalistics have pronounced dogmatically that conditions (and limitations) are so limiting as to completely invalid any results. However, we know of no rational argument purported to uphold this view.

. . . [W]hen uncertainty exists, and a statistical approach possible, then this approach is the best one available for it offers an index of uncertainty based upon a precise and logical line of reasoning. It is almost incredible that this very reason for the development of statistical methods is seized upon by its opponents and used as an argument against the use of statistics. They will show that an occurrence which was deemed extremely improbable did actually happen and contend that therefore the methods by which its improbability was calculated can not be trusted. . . . Although the uncertainty involved in a situation to which a statistical analysis is applicable constitutes a limitation on the appropriateness of *any* decisions made, the fact of uncertainty validates the contention that the statistical approach offers the *best possible* solution to the problem.

Unfortunately there is the strong tendency to minimize the limitations of the statistical approach, usually through ignorance, and as a consequence misusages take place. Kingston discussed gross errors possible in a criminal case.(22) In the same article, the author makes mention of the "conservative guess" approach. Since probability factors are not easily come by, a common practice is to "select a probability of chance occurrence that is clearly much higher than the true one, using the justification that the final calculation will then be higher than it should, thus underemphasizing its importance. If such guesses are indeed conservative, this is perfectly good procedure, as long as the limitations are not forgotten."

The current model in evidence evaluation is intuitive because it is the best known, employs only the most rudimentary understanding of statistical probability, and does not require the task of gathering data upon which the statistical approach is based.

The intuitive approach involves many variables, many unknown probabilities and many unpredictables. Workable approaches allowing reasonably accurate conclusions are available and are used with accuracy and success. These approaches have been mentioned before. However, no proponent of the intuitive approach can seriously and validly argue that probability is not involved in their decision making processes, and that the surest answers are to be attained through statistically gathered data and the weighing of uncertainties. The intuitive approach is in fact a statistical approach based on experience without quantitative explicitness.

The prodigious problem to be overcome before the statistical approach begins to have common application is that of performing fundamental research directed towards the evidence evaluation by statisticians who are criminalistically oriented. Such research could exploit the lightning speed of computers enabling calculations of approximate solutions. O'Hara and Osterburg(23) as well as Kirk(24) have called for the establishment of criminalistics research centers to deal with these and other problems of a theoretical and applied technological character.

Within this context mention can be made again of the burgeoning responsibilities imposed by the importance of the role that the criminalistics must play in the administration of justice. Much talk is being bandied about the possibilities of financial assistance to allow criminalistics to play its role effectively. The problem now becomes an affair of economics, and if the efforts of creative individuals are to result in fruition, the criminalist must learn to know his way around the political arena in order to find funds to do what he needs to do.

An additional problem will be that of greater acceptance by the practicing police science examiner and the public of innovations. An optimistic view would be that there is generally a greater receptivity to serious innovation than experienced in the past. The basis of this view is the advances in all sciences that have resulted in more open mindedness and the beginnings of a refusal to cling exclusively to past methods. Studies in which statistical considerations were applied have been reported as related to fibers by Kirk and Burd(25) and firearms identification by Biasotti.(26)

THE COMMUNICATIONS GAP

The criminalist and the lawyer will find frequent occasions to join forces in the courtroom. It was stated in the beginning that one of the most harassing problems facing the criminalist is the awkward, sometimes hostile silences that prevent dialogue between the criminalist and the lawyer. It is in the courtroom that the results of these "information breakdowns" become all too evident.

Intellectually, the criminalist may have more in common with the lawyer than with the traditional police officer. But the ideological obstacles which plague their efforts in the courtroom have not been overcome by this common ground.

The neophyte criminalist quickly learns that the courtroom is the natural environment of the lawyer. He finds that the lawyer's concept of proof is not at all based upon ideas applied by scientists in their own natural habitat, the laboratory. Further, he finds that while the lawyer may indulge him by agreeing that the legal procedures are not in tune with the scientific procedure, the game is played accordingly to lawyer-made rules.

Thus the criminalist will be encouraged to be unbiased, principled and honest insofar as these desirable qualities meet the definitions laid down by the law and legal precedent. The impression of being unbiased which the criminalist would like to carry over to the jurors is suspect from the outset because he is a prosecution witness on the payroll of a law enforcement agency. If he tries to adhere to the dictates of honest principle, which is implicit in the oath he takes "to tell the truth, the whole truth, and nothing but the truth . . . ," he runs into difficulty, and his testimony can be branded as unresponsive, because whole truth, within the context of the law, has a very limited meaning. If he is honest and delivers opinions which do not carry the meaning of absolute certainty, he incurs the displeasure if not the wrath of the lawyer.

Many other obstacles stand in the way of a meeting of criminalist-lawyer minds, some of which have been dealt with in the discussions of evidence evaluation. As a practical matter, many lawyers are impatient, work under poor conditions, do not have time to gain an understanding of the criminalist's testimony, or feel that reliance on the criminalist's ability will suffice for the situation at hand. The exigencies of many legal proceedings which require prompt resolutions are an important cause of impatience.

Perhaps the greatest obstacle preventing effective criminalist-lawyer communication is the problem of semantics. The author remembers well the occasion when he was asked for the first time in court, "Do you have an opinion beyond a reasonable scientific certainty that   have had a common origin?" A look of consternation and disbelief was evident on the face of the prosecuting attorney when the answer was "Yes," followed by, "The   could have had a common origin." It was subsequently learned that the prosecutor's view was that if the witness was in the "gray" area of results to the extent of 51 percent probability in the direction of common source, an opinion of "specific identity of source" could be claimed. This view is nonsense and is rejected by all criminalists.

It would appear that the semantic problems arise out of legal precedents relating to medical testimony. Conrad(27) has called attention to this problem, stating, ". . . we find a tendency on the part of the courts to formulate the rules relating to degrees of certainty in terms of the medical witness and not the scientist generally."

Criminalistics testimony usually relates to physical evidence, the pertinent problem being one of establishing identity of nature or source. Medical testimony usually deals with cause-effect conditions involving persons.

In some instances, the problems posed to the criminalist bear all the earmarks of those of the medical witness, and similar considerations are appropriate. One outstanding example is the testimony of the criminalist relating blood alcohol content in a person (cause) to conditions of brain impairment (effect). The criminalist, assuming background qualifications, will unhesitatingly deliver an opinion of whether or not a subject was "under the influence" based on demonstrated levels of alcohol concentration, because of the great body of scientific knowledge available from studies which have been directed to this specific problem. Thus, he is greatly fortified by the knowledge that the "risk he is assuming" is negligible because of the quality of the results gained from these studies. The medical witness presumably delivers opinions based upon the same foundations.

In most instances, however, the criminalist's testimony will deal with physical things, their nature and their source. It is here that departures in concept and semantic difficulties appear. The root cause is that legal precedents dealing with medical cause-effect relationships are being applied to criminalistics fact-idea relationships.

Conrad(28) has discussed the legal concepts of "reasonable scientific certainty," "beyond mathematical doubt," and "beyond reasonable probability." He places emphasis on the latter, stating after defining the limits within which the expert is permitted to testify, that "the expert's job is to bring his testimony to or beyond the point of reasonable probability or certainty." He defines reasonable probability by citing a decision: "reasonable probability is that standard of persuasion that is in quality sufficient to generate the belief that the tendered hypothesis is in all human likelihood, the fact.(29)

Conrad further states:

> From a strictly legal standpoint, when the expert testifies to a reasonable scientific probability, he has satisfied his obligation to the court. The expert is not required to satisfy a party's burden of proof, although the expert's testimony may be quite persuasive when that question arises. Therefore, when an expert gets into the realm of mathematical probability to establish the existence or nonexistence of a fact, he is departing from the usual legal standard and is approaching the yardstick of absolute certainty. He is, therefore, undertaking an obligation which he need not assume in order to insure the acceptance of his testimony without qualification or reservation.

The criminalist's reaction to the foregoing is to ask: "At what point have I satisfied the requirements of reasonable scientific probability? What risk, if any, should I be willing to assume to make such a claim? Is the concept not dependent upon the kind of evidence being dealt with?"

The criminalist is uncomfortable and disturbed by the clear lack of legally defined objective criteria which meets the standards of scientific objectivity allowing him to answer these questions. This lack underscores the particular disturbance he experiences when he is told that from the legal standpoint as stated above, "he undertakes an obligation he need not assume" when he gets into the realm of mathematical probability.

It is the nature of the criminalist to strive for finer and finer degrees of differentiation, and to apply any method that can lead to the unattainable absolute. While it is true that at this time some evidence does not lend itself to mathematical probability, it is true only because the experience data have not been statistically gathered to allow its usage. Given the backing of scientific studies upon which he can base a conclusion in relation to an assessment of the "risk he is willing to assume," the criminalist will deliver interpretative testimony that goes beyond "reasonable probability" to the point of established fact. Given less, the testimony will be guarded and equivocal.

EFFECTIVE CRIMINALISTICS TESTIMONY

The discussions up to this point have been intended to give a small measure of insight into the nature of criminalistics, its major problems and the processes by which it serves justice. The prosecuting attorney's reaction might well be: So much for criminalistics and its problems. How do we go about getting the job done now? That which follows addresses itself to this pragmatic question.

A pre-trial conference is essential in all major cases. This is especially true when the subject matter to be offered is of a highly technical nature. Preliminary to this conference, the prosecutor must read the laboratory report to find its significant meaning, and weave it into the fabric of factual evidence supplied by other members of his fact-finding task force. If there are points which need clarification he should telephone the laboratory and seek assistance. The resolution of unsolved problems of proof should take place well in advance of the trial date, thus avoiding the pressure of "crash" efforts at the last moments before trial. In addition, steps can be taken to deal with anticipated issues and problems which can arise during the trial.

When the understanding that comes through preparation has been achieved between the criminalist and the lawyer, an easy rapport develops during the trial. This rapport is felt and entered into by the jury. The failure to arrange a pre-trial conference, or to substitute for it a hurried, whispered conference in the hallway outside the courtroom immediately before the actual appearance can only invite difficulties and risk disappointment. The pre-trial conference should cover the subjects which follow.

Timing: The criminalist's role as related to other witnesses should be considered and his order of appearance planned accordingly. Ordinarily, the criminalist will be one of the last witnesses produced by the prosecution. Little purpose is served and much time uselessly expended if the criminalist is subpoenaed to appear on the opening day of trial when it is clear that his testimony will not be required for four or five days. This is especially important when the criminalist's headquarters is distant from the trial location.

Chain of Possession: Foundation as to chain of possession of the evidence examined and its integrity must be considered. A plan should be made for the orderly appearance of witnesses needed to establish this foundation.

Qualifying Examination: The criminalist will usually prepare a set of qualifying questions, complete with answers, for the prosecuting attorney. This is designed to extract from the criminalist those essentials of background academic qualifications and experience that will serve to establish the legal foundation necessary for expert testimony. Some lawyers are opposed to the usage of a "canned" set of questions and answers. The opposition has a basis in logic as related to effect. A less limiting procedure is for the criminalist to subject a summary of his background credentials. From this the lawyer can formulate a line of questions which make psychological use of qualifications by carefully developing those areas pertinent to the evidence.

Qualifying questions should be asked one at a time and answers received the same way. Answering a general request, "tell us about your background," would risk giving the jury the impression that the witness is bragging. A practice to be avoided is the asking of a question directed to show how many times the witness has performed a particular type of examination. The effect can be poor if the number is low. If high, the most likely situation is that no accurate answer can be given since most criminalists do not waste their time keeping detailed counts of the numbers of examinations they have performed. Moreover, the number of examinations made is not a measure of ability.

If the witness is especially well qualified it can be anticipated that the defense attorney will attempt to stipulate qualifications. This is often done if the witness is well known to both attorneys as well as to the court, but cannot be considered good practice because such qualifications will not be known to the jury. Furthermore, the meaning of the term "stipulation" is not always clear to the jurors.

Direct Examination: Pre-trial discussions should include the order of direct examination questions which will most effectively and clearly bring out the significant meaning of the technical testimony being offered. A pre-planned series of questions based on an understanding of the subject matters to be developed should be discussed, and if neccessary eventually prepared. The lawyer should do the preparation with advisory assistance from the criminalist. Such a set is essential if the subject matter of testimony is either unusually involved from a technological point of view, or includes a complicated set of evidence combinations. The questions should be framed in such a way that no impression is given that the prosecutor is testifying.

For tactical reasons, some prosecutors prefer that the amount of direct examination in support of an opinion be minimized, holding that the mere expression of an opinion or the delivery of a conclusion is sufficient. No "pat" approach can be given to satisfy all situations and it is unquestionably the prosecutor's prerogative to determine the course he will follow.

Clarity of presentation, however, is favored by laying the foundation for an opinion during direct examination. Such a procedure does not leave to chance the jurors' full understanding of the basis for the conclusion that the criminalist has reached. In addition, needlessly lengthy cross-examination directed at a small point taken out of orderly context can be avoided.

A decision as to the advisability of engaging in highly involved technical discussions before the court should be made. Some varieties of evidence lend themselves to ease of discussion which benefits the jurors' understanding. Others do not.

The Opinion: The manner in which an opinion is to be elicited will vary according to the kind of testimony being delivered. When the evidence is of a single variety and the opinion conclusive to the extent that it excludes all other possibilities, the opinion should be elicited immediately after foundation regarding possession has been demonstrated. With the significant meaning firmly established in the beginning, the ensuing line of questions will forge the basis of the conclusion through explanation easily comprehended by the jurors.

The alternate route is to show possession foundation quickly and then proceed with a line of questioning developing in a stepwise fashion what was done, how it was done, the observations which were made, and finally the conclusion arrived at, expressed as an opinion. Most prosecuting attorneys prefer this approach, contending that the requirements for establishing legal foundations must be met before an opinion can be delivered. These requirements will differ from jurisdiction to jurisdiction, being more determined by what has become generally accepted practice in the particular locale than by the dictates of legal precedent. Either approach can be used, but clarity and thus effectiveness are favored by the first procedure.

Criminalistics testimony will more often deal either with one kind of physical evidence from which it is possible to show only a degree of probability, or several varieties of evidence developed in combination.

The significant meaning of this type of evidence is to be imparted by the stepwise discussion of the procedures used in detecting its presence, the comparisons made, the degrees of differentiation possible, and as appropriate the fact that no differences eliminative in character could be shown. Whether as one variety, or as several varieties each considered singly, there will be limitations of a problematical nature, but if the questioning and answering are presented with ordered cogency, the "in total" conclusion to be arrived at formulates in the jurors' minds.

In situations of this kind it has been common practice to elicit from the criminalist a separate opinion regarding each variety when several are available. A needlessly repetitive and near ritualistic impression is imparted to the jurors, resulting in an undesirable dilution to the testimony's overall significance.

When the combination variety of evidence has been presented with coherence and orderliness as a group, the significant meaning within the context of testimony given by other witnesses will be reached with the ease by the jurors *without a formal statement of opinion*. The same consideration can be applied despite the fact that only one variety of evidence of a probability nature is at hand.

Cross-examination in the face of an array of factual evidence is foolhardy, but if attempted upon the premise that each individual probability falls short of certainty, the criminalist will readily admit to the appropriate limitations. However, the burden of proof now lies with the defense attorney and his client to produce evidence to show that the factual combination developed by the prosecution happened by chance. This showing must meet rigid specifications, and it is extremely unlikely that it will take place.

Demonstrative Aids: If the evidence to be presented lends itself to illustration through demonstrative aids, the pre-trial conference should include a discussion as to whether or not they should be prepared, and, if so, the manner in which they can be introduced as exhibits. Evidence of a patterned character lends itself well to presentation before a jury. Moreover, great benefit is to be realized from photographs of wounds on the body; both photographs and diagrams of a crime scene are useful. A discussion of the usage of these aids has been given by several authorities.(30) Some firearms examiners have taken the position that photographs of bullet comparisons serve no useful purpose, should never be used, and that oral testimony alone will suffice. Their contentions are based on unhappy experiences in which the defense attorney was able to make much of incidental markings not in coincidence in a photograph introduced to support the claim of identity of origin of two fired bullets. Further, it is contended that the courts will come to expect photographs of bullet and cartridge case matches in all cases, and such an expectation, if met, would necessarily require great expenditures of time.

Photographs can lay the basis for a critical cross-examination. However, whatever the witness says on the stand is basis for cross-examination. If there is justification for non-usage of photographs on this basis, a similar line of reasoning would keep the witness off the stand entirely.

A well prepared witness will anticipate the tack cross-examination can take, and accordingly will be in a position to counter with a clearly enunciated, reasoned explanation. He should emphasize that the photograph was not the basis of his conclusion, but serves only to illustrate an isolated aspect of the total examination process.

The argument that the courts will come to expect photographs in all cases must be rejected. The scientific witness can exercise his prerogative to specify not only the extent of the conclusions he has reached, but also the manner in which he intends to illustrate his conclusions. If in his judgment, there are compelling reasons not to use photographs, they should not be used. No basis, however, exists for the policy of excluding photographs under all circumstances.

THE TRIAL

Of the criminalist's several roles, none is as demanding as the role of the expert witness. When he takes the witness stand, the criminalist carries the full knowledge of his responsibilities, the anticipation that his testimony can be subject to searching cross-examination, and the realization that his very professional future is subject to risk if he comes off poorly. The subject matter during pre-trial conference treats the considerations which can serve both criminalist and lawyer during the trial. There remains only the matters of the responsibilities of the criminalist, and cross-examination.

The criminalist has the responsibility of being well prepared to discuss and illustrate the basis of his conclusions. He must anticipate the questions that will be asked, and be in a position to answer them.

The most challenging problem will be that of persuasively expressing himself in language that the jury, composed of a cross-sectional representation of the immediate population, will understand. In doing so, the criminalist must not make the mistake of "talking down." It is rare that the jury is drawn which is entirely unreceptive to testimony presented with honesty and cogency. On the contrary, the jurors will ordinarily greet the criminalist with interested expectation, and possibly as welcome relief from the boredom of other types of testimony. If during the testimony they appear to be disappointed or confused, it is most likely because of an inept presentation by the witness.

The criminalist can be expected to be responsive. If an entirely responsive answer leaves uncertainty in the minds of the jurors, it is the prosecutor's responsibility to rectify the situation. Indifference by the prosecutor to the needs of the criminalist to explain can result in misinformation to the detriment of the case. For this reason, the criminalist may be sorely tempted to volunteer information. This cannot be accepted as good practice.

The criminalist can be expected to comport himself with the equanimity of a gentleman, and will not allow goading by the defense attorney to arouse his anger. The qualities of being unbiased and honest must be conveyed to the jurors. It should be remembered that most jurors are reasonably good judges of human character and detect easily the attribute of phoniness.

The confidence of his convictions must be carried over to the court by the criminalist. While he can be expected to adhere rigorously to the dictates of honesty and conservative objectivity, he must not use these qualities as an excuse for self-effacement to the point of being ineffective.

The Anglo-American adversary system of dispensing justice is presumably based on the supposition that the adversaries, as represented by the opposing attorneys, are equally competent both as to the law and the understanding of the subject matter being offered. Experience has shown that this supposition is faulty. When the subject matter of testimony is technological in nature, the prosecutor has the means for gaining understanding of the subject matter because he can, if he chooses, avail himself of advisory services offered by the criminalistic witness. The same advantage is not available to the defense attorney. For this reason, much of the testimony offered by the criminalist is not challenged. It is probably fair to state that most criminalists would welcome the demonstration of greater degrees of erudition in technical matters by defense attorneys. The scientific witness is not free from over-zealousness in his claim simply because he is a scientist, and there are few methods of scientific fact-finding entirely devoid of deficiencies. Advocacy of greater sophistication in cross-examination may seem strange coming from a criminalist, but when an "expert" has gone through a few harrowing experiences on the witness stand he will be encouraged to improve his methods and correct any deficiencies that have been exposed. The end result can be positive in the direction of dispensing equal justice.

In the absence of a learned foundation upon which he can base a cross-examination, there remain for the defense attorney only a few courses of action. These can usually be countered with ease, assuming adequate briefing of the prosecutor has taken place. The defense attorney can choose not to cross-examine at all. This course can be taken because of the desire not to give added emphasis to direct testimony which is already damaging, or to give the impression to the jury that the witness's testimony is so unimportant that it needs no further consideration. This route underscores the importance of bringing out reasons for a conclusion during direct examination.

He can choose to show the dishonesty, lack of intelligence and incompetence of the witness. This is rarely successful unless the witness, indeed, possesses these undesirable qualities.

The tack can be taken to confuse the issues by asking questions which have no relevancy to the testimony offered under direct examination. Here, the prosecutor has an obligation to raise an objection. A favorite stratagem is to ask a question that can be answered either yes or no when either answer can be used to the advantage of the defense attorney. The prosecutor must be alert to detect this device. If interruptions are attempted when answers begin to be unfavorable, immediately, or allow him to bring out the full answer during re-direct examination. Finally, there are the reminders that the criminalist cannot ask questions, cannot object, and cannot easily protect himself from scurrilous attacks; thus the prosecutor has an obligation to protect his witness, which according to the rules of the game, only he can do.

NOTES

(1) E.C. Conrad, *The Expert and Legal Certainty*, 9 J. For. Sci. 445 (October 1964).

(2) A. Joseph, *Study Of Needs And The Development Of Curricula In The Field Of Forensic Science:* A Survey Of Crime Laboratories 16 (A Report to the Office of Law Enforcement Assistance, U.S. Department of Justice, Prepared by the staff of O.L.E.A. project No. 013 1967).

(3) W. Capune, *Criminology Alumni 1916-1967.* A Report and Statistical Summary (1968).

(4) Kirk, *The Standardization of Criminological Nomenclature*, 38 J. Crim. L.C. & P.S. 2 (1947).

(5) C. O'Hara and J. Osterburg, *An Introduction to Criminalistics* (MacMillan, N.Y., 1949).

(6) Kirk, *The Ontogeny of Criminalistics*, 54 J. Crim. L.C. & P.S. 2 (1963).

(7) Joseph, *Supra* note 2, at 12.

(8) D. Dillon, *The Development Of Criminalistics In California* (unpublished).

(9) P. Kirk and L. Bradford, *The Crime Laboratory* 22-25 (1965).

(10) Osterburg, *The Police Crime Laboratory as an Investigative Aid,* 13 Law & Order 764.

(11) Kirk, *Criminalistics*, 10 Sci. 357 (1963).

(12) Osterburg, *The Warren Commission: Report and Hearings. A Commentary on Issues of Importance in the Study of Investigation and Criminalistics*, 11 J. For. Sci. 3 (1966).

(13) Burd and Greene, *Toolmark Comparisons in Criminal Investigation,* J. Crim. L C. & P.S. 379 (1948).

(14) Enklaar, *Principles and Problems in the Process of Identification*, 14 IDENT' NEWS 4 (1964).

(15) Huber, *Philosophy of Identification*, 2 Proc. Can. Soc. For. Sci. 315 (1964).

(16) Kind, *The Nature of the Process of Identification*, 4 J. For. Sci. Soc. 162 (1964).

(17) Kingston and Kirk, *Historical Development and Evaluation of the Twelve Point Rule in Fingerprint Identification*, Int. Crim. Pol. Rev., No. 186 (1965).

(18) Osterburg, *An Inquiry into the Nature of Proof*, 9 J ³For. Sci. 413 (1964).

(19) Kirk and Kingston, *Evidence Evaluation and Problems in General Criminalistics*, 9 J. For. Sci. 434 (1964); Kingston and Kirk, *The Use of Statistics in Criminalistics*, 55 J. Crim. L.C. & P.S. 514 (1964).

(20) Parker, *A Statistical Treatment of Identification Problems*, 6 J. For. Sci. Soc.

(21) Kingston and Kirk, *The Use of Statistics in Criminalistics*, J. Crim. L.C. & P.S. 514-16 (1964).

(22) Kingston, *Probability and Legal Proceedings*, 57 J. Crim. L.C. & P.S. 93 (1966).

(23) *Supra* note 5, at 687-88.

(24) *Supra* note 6, at 238.

(25) Kirk and Burd, *Clothing Fibers as Evidence*, J. Crim. L.C. & P.S. 353 (1941).

(26) Biasotti, *The Principles of Evidence Evaluation as Applied to Firearm and Toolmark Identification,* J. For. Sci. 428 (1964); Biasotti, *A Statistical Study of the Individual Characteristics of Fired Bullets,* J. For. Sci. 34 (1959).

(27) *Supra* note 1, 447.

(28) *Id.* at 456-60.

(29) Miller and Dobrin Furniture Co. v Camden Fire Ins. Co. Ass'n, 55 N.J. Super. 205, 150 A.2d 276 (1959).

(30) Bradford, *General Criminalistics in the Courtroom*, 11. J. For. Sci. (1966); Belli, *An Introduction to Demonstrative Evidence*, 8 J. For. Sci. 355 (1963); P. Kirk, Crime Investigation 521-22 (1953).

THE PROBLEMS OF THE DEFENCE EXPERT

Julius Grant

In discussing the problems of the expert witness called by the Defence, it is as well to define just what is such an "expert witness." An all-embracing definition is difficult to achieve, because in addition to what may be described as the professional expert witness, there are also those who have this role thrust upon them. All have their problems, but they differ in nature; in particular, according as they give evidence in civil or criminal cases. If one ignores these differences, then an expert witness may be defined as an individual who gives evidence based on matters of which he has special knowledge or expertise. Such a definition is, of course, extremely wide. It covers the professional forensic scientist, from the police photographer at one extreme, to the person at the other extreme who is required to give evidence on a specialised aspect of one particular case. An example of the latter could be a university professor who might be called upon to verify the historical validity of a document.

There are also experts on the fringe of the definition, such as those who advise on highly specialised patent cases, particularly when a patent is opposed. Their evidence is usually in the form of a Statutory Declaration made as an Affidavit, and they are free from many of the problems of the witness who has to appear in person and give evidence orally. Others included in the above all-embracing definition can be experts called by their employers when they are involved in litigation, for example, in connection with a workman's compensation action. These also, strictly speaking, are experts in the sense of the above definition, but they may also usually be regarded as interested parties; this absolves them from some of the problems mentioned below, but it can raise others.

For the purpose of this paper attention will be confined to the problems of the professional expert witness dealing with criminal cases only; and this, no doubt, is the aspect most relevant to the activities of the Forensic Science Society.

It is useful to deal with the problems involved in order of importance, namely, as follows:—

COMMUNICATION

The Court, obviously, must understand fully and precisely just what the witness is talking about. This undoubtedly is the most important problem to be faced, and one of its most difficult aspects is that of semantics, or the use of words. The present-day ramified specialisation in the many different branches of expert learning has resulted in the development of scientific jargon peculiar and appropriate to the subject; and this has become an instinctive method of thinking for those involved. Members of the medical profession are often offenders in this respect, though in their case the precise explanation of a medical condition often precludes the use of terms understandable by the layman. At the other extreme is the type of jargon that is building up in computer science—such as the quite unnecessary and misleading terms "hardware" and "software".

A paper to be given at the Institution of Electrical Engineers is entitled "A Bootstrap-gauss-seidel Load Flow." When asked what this meant the author replied as follows (*Daily Telegraph*, March, 1969):—

> A pseudo or fictitious load-flow is set up by making simple changes to the power loading at every node in the network. Since these changes are dependent on the mismatch power (or error) at each node, a 'bootstrap-effect' results. Conventionally acceptable solutions are reached considerably faster than normal, since convergence is very rapid.

Where mere translation is adequate to convey the meaning clearly, then the problem is largely solved. However, the explanation of subtle scientific conceptions can present greater difficulty. Thus, for example, the concept of pH value, as distinguished from true acidity, often arises in scientific evidence and is a case in point. It is useless to describe it as "the logarithm of the reciprocal of the hydrogen ion concentration"!

The communication problem is common to all expert witnesses, whether called by the Prosecution or the Defence, and in each case there are several hurdles of communication to be surmounted. First is the solicitor who initiates the instructions to the expert. Then there is, of course, Counsel for whichever side is calling him; and finally there is the Judge, and the members of the Jury—all 12 of them. Solicitor and Counsel, especially the latter, are probably the principal hurdles; it is the latter who matters most, and fortunately he can ask all the questions he likes, free from distraction in his own Chambers. His training and experience should enable him to do this, and to put his finger on essentials. A mentally inarticulate expert can nevertheless often confuse or even mislead him in his task of extracting the information he wants the Court to hear during the course of his examination-in-chief.

There are two alternative types of technique usually adopted by Counsel in Court to elicit expert evidence. By far the more preferable is, from the expert's point of view, to allow the expert witness to explain difficult points in his own way. This method amply justifies itself if the expert is equal to the task. However, many Counsel cling to the stage-by-stage "question-and-answer" approach in the belief that the Court will be the wiser as a result; but also very often because Counsel is afraid that the witness may be carried away by his own enthusiasm or confidence and say something which will expose him in cross-examination. The real answer is a full measure of understanding between Counsel and expert but unfortunately the Time Factor problem often prevents this from being established.

Judges, like Counsel, are trained to assimilate essential facts, and they, too can ask their own questions. A Jury, however, can be very mixed in respect of both knowledge and capacity to understand, and there must be many occasions when at least one of its number has no idea of what the expert is talking about.

These are the main problems of communication, but what are the solutions? First of all it must be appreciated that after expertise, the most important qualification of an expert witness must be a capacity to make himself understood in the simplest possible terms. This can be difficult, because he has to be precise and accurate at the same time. The professional expert witness usually succeeds in this respect because he is often called upon to explain the same type of scientific idea over and over again, and he learns the technique of doing it. The occasional expert witness is also often very successful; but sometimes he is an abject failure. A good plan is to anticipate the type of explanation that will be required and the questions that may be asked, and to formulate replies well in advance, using metaphors and similies which will help; but they must be appropriate. Word for word "rehearsals" are not recommended; they are unlikely to fit the circumstances of the occasion fully, and they can then become a hindrance rather than a help.

The problem of communication should not be left without some reference to the general question of "presentation," which can be taken to include such important attributes as audibility, delivery. and even appearance. The expert witness has to make himself as convincing as possible to what in effect, is a scientifically lay audience. He is not speaking to a learned society, but to a cross-section of the public in the case of a Jury; and whether or not it is relevant to the course of justice, factors such as the above can count in ensuring that this cross-section is duly impressed. Certainly inaudibility will not help; little can be more irritating to a Judge (and indeed to all concerned) who has continually to ask the witness to speak up; and it usually happens that once does not suffice. Quiet speaking is a habit into which a speaker is apt to relapse after each admonition. Microphones and loudspeakers are the answer to this particular problem, but they are as yet far from common in all Courts.

Delivery, too, can contribute to conviction in speaking, though histrionics are undesirable; however, a confident and emphatic delivery, free from superfluous words, can add much to mere subject matter. Appearance also, should not influence the course of justice; but a neat attire is at least a courtesy due to the Court, and a careless or slovenly appearance might with reason be regarded as indicative of a mind in a similar state.

COMPETENCE

No person of integrity would wish to give evidence outside the scope of his expertise. Integrity apart, cross-examination on subject matter as distinct from qualifications should soon disclose his real position. The substantiation of claims to expert knowledge, therefore, should require no more than a statement of relevant qualifications. Counsel, during both examination and cross-examination, are seldom content with this, and qualifications are often explored in depth in such instances. Indeed, Counsel for the Prosecution and the Defence often appear to vie with one another in boosting the qualifications of their respective experts. Some dwell on his years of experience; others on his training; and fortunate is the advocate who can invoke both. This can be misleading to a Jury, if not to a Judge. For example, how can they assess the relative merits of, say a police officer who has had a few years' intensive training on fingerprint techniques, and an expert who has had no "official" training but has spent a lifetime of work on the subject?

The question of experience in specialised aspects of criminal forensic science can often be narrowed down to a very fine point indeed. Thus, as a rule, in the police forensic science laboratories different workers specialise in different branches of experimental work. For instance, one may deal with fibres, another with poisons, another with problems involving chemical analysis; and so on. In the course of his experience each carries out many types of examinations on many kinds of exhibit of the same nature in the course of a year. The private expert witness, on the other hand, has to cast his net much wider than any one of these. As a scientist he may be every bit as good as his police counterpart but he applies his experience and methods to a wider variety of subjects, and he cannot go into the witness box and say "I examined so many hundred samples of this or that last year."

As stated, by definition an expert is someone who has specialised and advanced knowledge of a particular subject. This definition does not restrict such expertise to one subject only and the branches of knowledge on which an expert is qualified to give evidence will depend entirely on the individual. A prominent scientist could know as much about, say, clocks or mediaeval art as he does about his own branch of the scientific profession; and he could give evidence on either with equal authority. There are few people whose activities run in one channel only. Conversely there are many who by study, practice and diligent application can acquire authority in a number of different fields. The proof of such authority becomes clear in the giving of evidence, and particularly in the cross-examination and, as stated, putting it to the test is often a favourite line taken by Counsel of either side.

The pitting of the qualifications of one expert witness against those of another is most undesirable; it can be unnecessarily undignified for the experts concerned, and uninformative and even misleading to a Jury. Thus, one expert may be young, but have high qualifications in his science; his opposite number may have no university degrees, but has years of experience behind him. If the two disagree then the jury is likely to be influenced by whatever capital opposing Counsel can manage to make out of the qualifications of their respective experts. Judges are more likely to be immune to such influences, but the whole situation is none the less undesirable. The answer to this problem is by no means clear, but one possibility might be that expert witnesses should state their qualifications as fully as they wish, but should not be cross-examined on them. After all, they are on oath to tell the truth.

Certain periodicals and journals which circulate among lawyers have recently been boosting their advertising revenue by trying to persuade forensic science experts to advertise the expertise and facilities they have to offer. Existing advertisements of this nature are used as a "bait" to attract the business of competing practices. There may be some justification for this in commercial or industrial consulting work (though I think it is wrong in principle); but with forensic work, and especially where criminal justice is involved, I think it most undesirable that the choice of an expert could be determined by the amount of money spent in this way. A proper register of qualified experts should be set up as in the case of other professions, and more important still, solicitors and others concerned should be made aware of its existence. At present if the Prosecution, in a criminal matter, has sought and obtained a scientific report from a government laboratory, the Home Office will not allow another scientist in that, or even another government laboratory, to carry out different or even confirmatory investigations for the Defence, unless the material is submitted through the Prosecution (Napley, 1968).

In connection with this same problem, there should be some accepted rules as to what constitutes a qualification in the academic sense. Passing an appropriate examination or acquiring a certificate or diploma in a particular branch of science should obviously qualify. However, membership of societies, however learned (and this can include even the Forensic Science Society) should not be advanced as a qualification. It is sometimes difficult to discourage Counsel for the Defence from taking such a course, especially if the more valid qualifications are rather thin. This can be a source of embarassment to the expert witness; and the Defence expert is more likely to be affected than his opposite number called by the Prosecution, whose Counsel will probably have a better appreciation of the conventions involved.

THE TIME FACTOR

This is an ever-present problem in all legal work, and from the point of view of the expert for the Defence, it so often takes the form of long delays followed by frantic last-minute action. In criminal cases experts called by the Prosecution have a starting advantage in that they are privileged in a sense by being associated with the police: they are the first on the scene and can make their own investigations fully and undisturbed, and in their own way; and, within reason, they have adequate time for any experimental work required, since the decision to prosecute often depends on their findings. Experts called for the Defence, however, usually come into the picture much later; almost always after the Lower Court proceedings, and when Counsel is preparing his Defence for the final trial. If Legal Aid is involved this has to be asked for, the amount agreed, and granted, meaning more delay; and the Solicitor for the Defence has to find someone capable and willing to investigate the matter and to be called by his side.

Usually the hearing is imminent by then, and for the Defence expert days of work have to be crowded into hours, reports written at unorthodox times, and all this, of course, without the least sacrifice of accuracy and thoroughness. An additional time handicap is the fact that exhibits can be examined by the Defence expert only under supervision, and usually in a strange laboratory; and such a laboratory, however hospitable or well-equipped, is never the same as his own from a working point of view. The exhibits, too, are "secondhand," a fact that can prove a handicap in a number of ways. Thus, fibres of critical importance may be already mounted and stained in a way that the expert called by the Defence may feel does not show their true character. Scene-of-the-crime investigations are usually completely out of the question for the Defence expert.

In some cases, and this seems to apply specially to Courts in the provinces, this element of haste is carried to an extreme which is almost indecent. It is not uncommon in the writer's experience to have had to carry out experiments and produce a report overnight and to explain it to Counsel just before the Court sits, or even while it is sitting, in a consulting room or crowded Court corridor. The Defence expert witness must do his best in these circumstances, but it may not be as good a best as he would achieve if given reasonable time; and this could even affect the issue of the case. At the best, it is unrewarding in more senses than one.

There are several possible solutions to this problem. Firstly, an official register of expert witnesses to which solicitors can refer, and so place their instructions with less delay than at present. Secondly, and most important, would be freer access to exhibits by experts called for the Defence, whose integrity should be as acceptable as those of the expert called by the Prosecution, and of the police officer who is normally responsible for the care of the exhibits in the Case. The Case should, so far as possible, be heard at a time to be decided after the experts to be called by both sides have finished their work and made their reports. Variations in grants for Legal Aid for fees for expert witnesses as between one Court and another (for the same services) should be ironed out, so that the Defence expert knows where he stands at the outset, and is spared the undignified "bargaining" procedure which often results when his final account is sent in.

EQUIPMENT AND FACILITIES

The U.K. police laboratories are, and rightly so, the best of their kind probably anywhere in the world, and this applies both to staffing and to equipment. A mere admission of this fact in Court might well give the impression that no private expert witness could equal them in the latter respect, and, therefore, that the value of his evidence is diminished accordingly. This, too, has some bearing on the question of qualifications and competence mentioned above.

Such a deduction could be highly misleading. Most of the scientific investigations involved in forensic work can be carried out by what may be described as the classical methods and apparatus of science. Methods used in police laboratories may be more sophisticated and better adapted to carrying out a large number of tests of the same kind at the same time. Both types of method should give the same results, although approached in different ways and, perhaps, one may take longer than the other. Thus, the determination of alcohol in urine in traffic offences can conveniently be carried out by a chemical method. However, this cannot be used for alcohol in blood because the amount of blood taken for the purpose is not large enough, and the gas chromatograph must, therefore, be used. However, ordinary chemical analyses and microscopical examinations on which a great deal of forensic science evidence depends, can be carried out with equal accuracy in the two laboratories. As much or more depends on the experience of the operator, as distinct from the degree of sophistication of his instruments.

By the same token a private expert working in his own laboratory in his own way can often produce results of greater value than if he is suddenly transported into the better equipped police forensic science laboratory. In the latter he can even be at a disadvantage, because the more sophisticated type of apparatus (though familiar to him in principle) may be strange to him in practice; and using it for the first time can involve him in difficulties which would not otherwise be experienced. The Prosecution can and do always say with the utmost truth and sincerity that all their exhibits and facilities are available equally to the experts for the Prosecution and for the Defence. The writer has always found the utmost co-operation in cases of this kind, but the arguments set out above persist.

A solution to this particular problem has already been indicated above, namely, freer access to exhibits. The expert for the Defence should be afforded the same facilities as the expert called by the Prosecution in carrying out his work. The existence of his name on a suitable register should be sufficient indication and guarantee of his competence to do the work, and of his integrity in the handling of exhibits.

TRAINING

Forensic science is becoming so specialised that it is a sad reflection on the present position that no adequate system of organised training exists. It is encouraging to note, however, that in Scotland at the University of Strathclyde, first steps in this direction have recently been taken. As Secretary of the Society the writer frequently receives requests for information on, "How can I become a forensic scientist"? These usually come from teenagers who, no doubt, have been attracted by the glamour of the scientific detective as depicted on television. It is always difficult to reply to such requests because at present there is no training in the real sense of the word for such aspirants. Those without basic scientific qualifications must endeavour to obtain a post in a laboratory doing such work, and acquire experience as they go along. For the higher grades of work they must first obtain a conventional university degree and preferably also a post graduate degree, and then specialise in forensic science—again only by obtaining a post in a suitable laboratory. This means a laborious training over a period of years, which is not quite what most of the enquirers have in mind.

The number of posts of this kind that the police laboratories can offer is necessarily limited, although they are tending to increase; and the number of posts in the laboratories of private forensic scientists are even fewer. The position in the latter case is made more difficult by the fact that very few of these laboratories are occupied wholly and solely with forensic science. They have to cast their net widely to take in civil as well as criminal forensic work, to act as experts in industrial, commercial and patent cases, and on *ad hoc* problems in general. This is due very largely to the fact that the financial rewards of the private expert witness for the Defence are relatively low, and if he is to maintain his standards of staff, laboratory equipment and efficiency, they must be supplemented by the more profitable commercial work. This does not make him any the worse an expert witness, but reliance on private enterprise seems wrong in principle as a means of providing facilities for the Defence in cases where it is felt that an expert is necessary.

Here again the answer to the problem is not a clearcut one. Properly organised training courses for forensic scientists, with some kind of diploma as the ultimate objective, would be a tremendous step forward, and it is hoped that other universities, preferably in more central urban areas, will follow the example of the University of Strathclyde. One of the most important factors in developing training schemes of this kind will be to secure the right type of lecturers. Such a course would preferably be of a post-graduate type which means that the lecturers would have to be drawn from those practicing forensic science either in an official or non-official capacity at the present time. This would be the only way of ensuring the necessary case history and Court experience.

This is a matter to which organisations such as the Forensic Science Society, which deal with forensic science as a profession, could appropriately give their attention in the near future. Otherwise it may well happen that the private forensic scientist as such will become extinct; and the problem of the Defence expert will become that of finding him!

REFERENCE

Napley, D., 1968, *Medicine, Science and the Law*, **8**, 235.

FORENSIC SCIENCE IN CRIMINAL PROSECUTION

Joseph M. English

In recent years, the courts have subjected some of the classic methods of law enforcement to closer scrutiny than ever before. For centuries those methods used by enforcement agencies and the prosecution to solve crimes and to bring the perpetrators to justice, respectively, have depended upon: 1. confessions of guilt, 2. statements of witnesses to the crime, and 3. information derived from physical evidence, sometimes called "circumstantial" evidence.

DIRECT EVIDENCE

The first two—*i.e.*, confessions and witnesses—historically have been characterized as "direct evidence." The last, that is, physical or circumstantial evidence, has been called "indirect evidence," and because it is "indirect," there may have been a tendency to give it less weight than the "direct" evidence of the confession or the witness's statement.

After all, who should know better the details of what happened and the identity of the person who did the deed than the guilty party himself or those who saw the act committed?

Standing alone, free of the encumbrances of the real world, there would seem to be no more reliable premise upon which to base the quest for the truth of the matter and on which to base wise adjudication than the premise that the testimony of those who were present at the occurrence may be taken as dependable.

However, criminal justice is not administered in the rarefied air of pure thought and pure motives, but in a milieu of complex and sometimes conflicting information and, at times, considerably less than pure motives—a milieu in which those who administer justice must somehow sort out facts from fictions and, constantly testing the "facts," fit those which stand the test into place with such patience and skill that the true picture comes clear.

The world of the investigator and the jurist is one in which thought systems, therefore, loom importantly. True facts in inept though well-meaning hands can serve justice and injustice with an impartiality reminiscent of the roulette wheel. Cases come to mind in which, for sundry reasons, persons have seriously confused investigations by falsely confessing or by falsifying more or less essential details of the occurrence under investigation.

An extortionist, for fairly obvious purpose, in one case confessed to writing the threatening note which he had prevailed upon his young daughter to write for him. An airman falsely confessed, after several days of questioning, to murdering a young woman whom he probably had never even met. Two others had confessed to the same crime. However, a mistaken crime laboratory blood grouping misled the investigators, causing them to intensify their interrogation of the airman and to free the other suspects, one of whom it now appears committed the crime. After conviction and six years in prison, the airman was cleared by belatedly developed information brought to light by an energetic newspaper reporter, a dedicated private attorney, more careful crime laboratory work, and more accurate testimony than appears to have been used in the original investigation and trial. The attorney spent his own funds contacting widely dispersed witnesses and for other expenses. Over $3000 of these expenditures have not been reimbursed.

If some confessions are false, it hardly can be reasoned that all confessions are, therefore, unreliable and should be ignored as without evidential value. The problem may well lie elsewhere—*i.e.*, with the conditions under which the confession was obtained, emotional instability of the person under questioning, excess of zeal on the part of the interrogator, or other factors. When all necessary conditions are as they should be, a confession is as valid, trustworthy, and reliable a source of accurate information as probably any other.

There appears to be a widespread belief among the judiciary that fault too frequently may lie with the investigator through naiveté, zeal, or bias. This overworked public servant, the investigator, almost inherently is under pressure from the community and the news media, through his chief, to "solve" or to "close" cases. Usually he works without a system which provides less motivation to look behind a confession than to accept it at face value and thus to facilitate an increase in his department's statistical "accomplishments." That such a circumstance is a serious threat to objectivity cannot be gainsaid.

ERRORS IN EYEWITNESS TESTIMONY

Let us look at the evidential value of the testimony of eyewitnesses. For what might be considered very good reasons, this category of "direct" evidence is far less persuasive today than formerly. The fall from grace of eyewitness testimony has followed disquieting experience in cases in which sworn eyewitness testimony, like some confessions, has proved to be in error.

Cases can be cited in which convincing numbers of eyewitnesses have sworn that they observed persons, later proved to be innocent, in the act of committing a felony. Nine such eyewitnesses once swore in a court of law that two defendants on trial were seen by each of the witnesses in the act of committing a robbery and murder. Eight of the nine had picked the two defendants out of what appeared to have been a well-conducted lineup. During the course of the trial, in which the two defendants had all but abandoned hope of acquittal, an astute newsman, once again, led the police to the actual robbers. The culprits had disposed of the victimized concern's moneybags in the basement of the building in which the robbers lived. Each of the nine witnesses who previously had identified the two earlier defendants later identified the true robbers.

For some years, New York City banks were victimized by a check forger who regularly passed checks in very large amounts. One day a number of Wall Street banks were defrauded by this man of very large sums. Police were led to suspect a certain Mr. "A," an unexceptional suburbanite husband and father of two children. Mr. "A" happened to be present on the "Street" that day. Six persons who had had direct contact with the forger identified Mr. "A" as the person who had appeared at their banks and had negotiated the fraudulent instruments in their presence.

It was only after seven years in prison that Mr. "A" was exonerated and released as a result of the identification of the real forger through an FBI laboratory analysis of the handwriting on the checks. Mr. "A" died within a year of his release from prison.

Why was eyewitness testimony in error in these instances? The following may help to explain it.

When human society was younger, individuals in their daily lives numbered among their acquaintances much larger percentages of the populations of their communities than is possible today. As a consequence, when an event was witnessed in former times, it was a case of the witness's observing a friend or relative or someone whom the witness recognized. With increases in the numbers of people populating our cities and towns, a witness who sees a total stranger in the act of passing a fraudulent check, killing a merchant, or committing some other reprehensible act, too often cannot be relied upon to retain an accurate mental image of the criminal.

There is an old adage to the effect that "Murder will out!" It is a homely way of saying that the truth of the matter, regardless of how obscure it may be, will in time be clearly exposed for all to see. The real weaknesses of the classical methods, as was said earlier, would appear to lie largely in the imperfections in the circumstances of their use and from faulty understanding of the inherent weaknesses and strengths of the methods.

Now, admittedly, if it is a fact—and it seems to be a demonstrated one—that confessions and eyewitnesses are especially susceptible to abuse, then certainly the widespread negative judicial reaction is justified.

What is offered in their stead?

PHYSICAL EVIDENCE

As the courts rely more and more on scientific evaluation of physical evidence, what assurance is there that this kind of evidence will not also be misused? To avoid such misuse, there are several necessary conditions: There must, first and foremost, be an uncompromising dedication to finding the truth on the part of the examining scientist and everyone else involved in the investigation, prosecution, and adjudication processes. There must be a high level of sophistication on the part of the scientist, the laboratory administration, the prosecutor, and the presiding judge, not to mention the defense attorney. This would include a keen awareness of the state of the art and possible pitfalls of each of the many categories of physical evidence encountered.

But all of the sophistication and expertise which can be mustered can be brought to naught or worse in a climate in which those who play the crucial roles are wedded to one side or the other in the criminal justice process more firmly, perhaps than to the cause of justice itself. The adversary system in which any method for obtaining the facts of a case must be used with the resultant excesses of zeal sometimes observed indeed may well be the one single cause of the problems experienced with direct evidence. Who is to say that the courts will not have equally misleading results from biased "analyses" of physical evidence, results which will be the more heinous for their aura of "science?" A broader and firmer link with the Nation's universities may help this aspect of the situation. One shudders to contemplate what would be the likely quality of medicine if there were no medical schools, or if there were only as few universities providing the necessary support for education and research in medicine as now provide programs in the forensic sciences, as such.

MISUSE OF SCIENTIFIC EVIDENCE

That a misuse of the scientific analysis of physical evidence comparable to the misuse of confessions and witnesses is possible on a serious scale may be observed in a number of cases which have come to light in which misinterpretation of data obtained in the examination and evaluation of physical evidence has occurred.

These cases reveal serious defects in the professional preparation of investigators and of laboratory experts. Too often the cloak of expertise is gratuitously conferred on a poorly trained or untrained (in a scientific sense) police officer by a hard-pressed police administrator. The expert thus created by executive fiat has little time and few opportunities to upgrade his training.

The work loads of the Nation's crime laboratories are extremely heavy and are growing at a fast pace apparently due to the court decisions in *Miranda* and other cases. Present work loads predictably would be even larger if currently requested examinations could be conducted. Investigators soon learn that certain examinations cannot be handled. There is no point in repeating these requests.

Crime laboratory personnel can ill afford to take time from their case loads to acquaint themselves with the developments in the sciences or to obtain needed training even if enough adequate education and training programs were offered by the colleges and universities of the Nation.

These institutions of learning, with a few notable exceptions, have too long ignored society's needs in law enforcement education and training. High-quality educational programs in the disciplines of the crime laboratory, as such, are offered by even fewer institutions in the Nation's academic community. Little wonder that there is what appears to be a monumental failure of communication between the academic and law enforcement communities.

A contributing factor may be the innocence of much of the funding community. Foundations seem to be unaware that the forensic sciences constitute a valid academic area and that, in these sciences, there is enormous potential for addressing some of the more serious deficiencies of the criminal justice process and that this area is suffering, in its turn, from staggering problems due largely to chronic academic, governmental, and foundation community neglect.

STANDARDS ARE NEEDED

If we prescind from the foregoing and turn to an examination of the heart of the workings of physical evidence evaluation, we find that standards-setting is a major problem. There is little evidence of wide-spread agreement, for example, as to the extent of the qualitative and quantitative data extractable from soil evidence by the more advanced techniques which might safely be relied upon to provide the bases for source or origin determinations at useful levels of specificity. Identifying those acceptable and alternate laboratory procedures for obtaining data from each kind of evidence amenable to measurable data extraction may aid the courts in their efforts to exclude incompetent testimony. Standard reference materials to serve widely separated laboratories may speed the handling of cases and raise the quality of their examinations. Other needs are for:

1. A multidiscipline approach to a better understanding of the scholarly legitimacy of the "identification" process as a scientific procedure for determining with as high a level of specificity as possible the source of an item of questioned evidence in terms of comparable items of known source.

2. Programs of background sampling and data collection essential to the evaluation process in the determination of just how unique a questioned piece of evidence actually is.

3. Broad check sample programs which would serve to keep individual experts informed as to their true levels of expertise as compared with their fellows in a given area or with a given analytical method.

4. Programs to attract the better college graduates into the crime laboratory disciplines.

5. Professional education and training programs such as those which have brought medicine to the professional level it has achieved and would promote the continuing close rapport between the academic community and the professional practitioners in the crime laboratories.

6. Programs of public education to recognize the importance of competent examination and evaluation of physical evidence to the proper administration of justice.

7. Programs to alert the general public and the foundation community to the need to be informed in the Forensic Sciences.

8. Curricula improvement in our law schools to furnish those students who, in their professional lives, will be required to act on information furnished by scientific experts.

9. Curricula improvements in our medical and nursing schools for those who will be in positions to preserve or to destroy utterly, evidence which could lead to the identification of an assailant. (See also Rose, John C., M.D. "Medical Centers and Crime Laboratories," *Proceedings of The First Georgetown Conference on Surface Analysis,* October, 1969.) Many rapist have gone free to strike repeatedly because emergency room hospital personnel had no professional preparation to alert them to the importance of avoiding commingling of articles of the victim's clothing, and obtaining adequate and proper swab specimens while ensuring against evidential contamination and disturbance of chain of custody.

These are but a few of the problems the Nation faces in law enforcement and the preservation of a just order. They represent some of the more important problems which grow directly out of those of the Nation's crime laboratories.

Other problems exist in the state of research and the consequent state of the art in a number of the crime laboratory disciplines, in the state of expert qualification and certification standards, in legal education, and the continuing professional preparation of law students, lawyers, and judges in the sophisticated utilization of expert testimony.

What is most important is that informed Americans, especially scientists as well as all others who share a dedication to the improvement of the administration of justice and of the human condition be informed in this area, as in all others which are crucial to the well-being of society and its members.

TECHNICAL EVIDENCE–ITS AVAILABILITY

IN THE JUSTICE PROCESS

Ralph F. Turner

Today's preoccupation with crime and criminality, and our nation's concern with constitutional guarantees, has prompted writers and speakers of all types, including myself, to use the word justice in so many different ways, and at so many different times . . . that I sometimes wonder if we are aware of its proper significance? If to be just is to conform to divine or human laws and since at best we are able only to approach conformity to divine law, I think we can devote some of our attention to conformity to human law as it applies to justice.

This paper will concern itself with one small segment of the larger justice problem . . . that is, how well is our present day technological expertise integrated into the justice process? Most forensic scientists are quite familiar with the use of technology insofar as the solution of crime is concerned, but I direct your attention to an extension of this use, namely its availability and use by the defendant in the total justice process.

In addition to reading President Johnson's message to Congress of 6 February 1967, in which he dealt with crime in America, we have heard distinguished members of the National Crime Commission elaborate on the President's message. There is no question that this effort, mounted in 1965, represents the second and more complete concerted attack on crime and criminality that this nation has seen since its founding days. A careful reading of the President's message convinces us that the Crime Commission was, and is, concerned with the justice process. We read,

The system of criminal justice must itself be just and it must have the respect and cooperation of all citizens. . . . Make full use of advanced scientific methods in the courtroom, to reduce frustrating and unfair delays and to make available to the sentencing judge all necessary information about the defendant. (The President recommends) that the Safe Streets and Crime Control Act authorize the Attorney General to make research grants or contracts, of up to 100%, with public agencies, institutions of higher education projects of regional or national importance, establish national or regional institutes for research and education in law enforcement and criminal justice.(1)

Returning to the definition of justice, I have become concerned with an important omission in much that I have read and heard in recent months about a proposed national plan of action. The omission is the apparent absence of some specific recommendations to make our present, and yet-to-be-developed, criminalistic expertise available to defendants well in advance of the usual hectic few days before trial.

Upon the discovery and verification of a criminal offense, the usual investigative process begins. Turning specifically to physical evidence, if any is discovered, this evidence may be presented to some qualified expert for examination and interpretation. The expert usually must call upon the services of a local laboratory, or, in its absence, a state or federal laboratory. Under certain circumstances private experts may be retained. If the results of the examination are useful to the enforcement agency and the prosecution, these results can, and frequently are, introduced at the time of the trial. If one stops and considers for a moment the tremendous implications of this procedure, and then compares the prosecution's formidable array of potential talent with that available to the average defendant, one must ask whether the familiar scales of justice are anywhere near in balance. The resources in equipment and trained personnel represented by the combined talents of municipal, state and federal criminalistic laboratories are vast and are available to any duly constituted law enforcement agency. How do these resources compare with the resources available to the average defendant, much less the indigent defendant? If we acknowledge this disparity, how can it be reconciled with our sense of justice?

I do not wish to be labeled "anti-law enforcement, anti-police, etc." I testified in my first firearms identification case 28 years ago in a courtroom in northern Wisconsin, on behalf of the prosecution. Since then I have held but two positions, one in the laboratory of the Kansas City, Missouri, Police Department, and the other in the School of Police Administration and Public Safety at Michigan State University. My sympathies and biases have usually been with law enforcement agencies, but as a teacher, working with young men and women preparing for careers in law enforcement, I am forced by an adherence to the principle of academic integrity to deal with both sides of a criminal justice issue. Therefore, it seems appropriate at this time, when we are considering the establishment of such facilities as regional institutes for research and education in law enforcement and criminal justice, and when we are frequently being reminded of embarrassing unprofessional conduct by some of our colleagues, that we establish a procedure and a philosophy that will indeed do justice to our claims for wanting to improve the administration of justice process.

I have expressed some concern about the disparity between the resources available to the prosecution and to the defense. Perhaps the defense does quite well for itself if one only recalls the spectacular cases that have appeared in our national headlines recently. But these cases are the exceptions, rather than the rule. As I understand the justice process, there is no difference between the nature of proof and cross-examination; they are expected in the case of the celebrated defendant, as well as in the cases of hundreds of inconspicuous, unknown, and indigent defendants who appear in lower courts. Frequently, the convictions of the latter are abetted by forensic science testimony that goes unchallenged either because a defendant is not represented by an attorney, or an attorney is ill prepared to ask even the basic questions necessary to test the integrity of the scientific testimony. A discussion of the role of the public defender and the legal aid movement is beyond the scope of this paper, but I can recommend an article by Mr. Theodore Voorhees, immediate past president of the National Legal Aid and Defender Association, appearing in the *American Bar Association Journal* in January, 1967. The objectives of the Office of Economic Opportunity Legal Services Program described by Mr. Voorhees are compatible, I think, with the objectives of forensic scientists in improving our justice process.(2)

Recently a new group called the National Association of Police Laboratories was founded in New York State. Bernard Newman, a biochemist, was named temporary president at a recent meeting, and said:

> With the confession rulings and increasing presence of science in everyday life, there's never been a greater reliance by the prosecutor on physical evidence tested under the highest possible standards. There is a lot of sloppy lab work done in this country and our aim is to eliminate it, set high lab standards and keep up-to-date with the latest innovations.(3)

Acknowledging that poor lab work does occur, and knowing that many defense counsels are not prepared to cope with this kind of performance, what is this group planning to do to prevent a continuation of this imbalance in the justice process?

My proposal is a simple one, yet I am well aware of the political, practical, and philosophical difficulties that will be encountered if it is to be implemented. I would suggest that some consideration be given to establishing forensic science institutes, the primary purpose of which would be to serve the justice process, not simply the prosecution, nor the affluent or prominent defendant. As yet, no commitments have been made; innovation and experimentation are encouraged. Would it not be possible to establish at the state level, a forensic institute that would make its findings available at early, appropriate dates, to both presecution and defense? I view the criminal offense as not unlike a game wherein the criminal has the first opportunity to conceive, plan, and execute a crime. Upon discovery of the offense, the law enforcement system is obliged to act, and the forensic scientist in the proposed institute would be obligated to serve society by working with the enforcement agency, yet retaining his scientific objectivity and primary obligation to the justice process. Once the crime has been solved and the offender taken into custody and properly arraigned, the results of interpretation of the physical evidence would become the property of the *court* and would be available to defense counsel. Consequently, the defense would have an opportunity to examine the nature of scientific proof and prepare suitable cross-examination. That evidence would be available to the court, the prosecution, and the defense would probably insure that the enforcement agencies would amass proof beyond a reasonable doubt, would be meticulous in their case preparation, and would welcome effective, challenging cross-examination.

Processing evidence in this way would not impair the adversary system or the jury system. It would incorporate what appears to me to be some of the more desirable aspects of the Napoleonic Code procedure.

A second responsibility of the forensic institute would be to provide services to counsels when the request for examination of evidence did not originate as a result of a criminal investigation. Examples would be the examination of evidence not submitted by enforcement agencies in a criminal case, or interpretation of evidence connected with civil cases. As the courts today are expecting greater use of scientific interpretation of evidence, trial lawyers are having greater difficulty in securing the services of qualified experts. Members of the American Society of Questioned Document Examiners do make their services available to the justice process, but the same cannot be said for most other areas of forensic science except, possibly, forensic pathology. There are not enough services available.

It is necessary to mention an important possible danger in the creation of an elite group that could be viewed as the single source for answers to most questions raised in the courtroom. This potential must be avoided, and it would be, as long as the adversary and jury systems were retained. Erle Stanley Gardner estimated that trial judges and juries are right 90 per cent of the time, perhaps even 95 per cent.(4) His remark is significant, considering that it is based upon his experience with the Court of Last Resort, a group experience that is unique in the history of our justice process.

To summarize: 1. people concerned with crime and criminality have an opportunity to introduce a new ingredient into the justice process; 2. equal justice, with particular attention to the indigent defendant and the unprepared counsel, is not available to *all* insofar as the interpretation of technical evidence is concerned; 3. the establishment of a forensic institute has been proposed at a regional or state level, possibly associated with a university or private organization; 4. the services of this institute would be available to both parties of a litigation; and, 5. the integrity of the justice process under English common law would not be violated as long as the adversary and jury systems were retained.

NOTES

(1) Johnson, President Lyndon B., Message on Crime in America to the Congress of the United States, 6 February 1967.

(2) Voorhees, Theodore, The OEO Legal Services Program: Should the Bar Support It?, American Bar Association Journal, Vol. 53, Jan. 1967, pp. 23-28.

(3) Jones, Bethune, 321 Sunset Avenue, Asbury Park, New Jersey, *From the State Capitals*, a newsletter, February 6, 1967, p. 3.

(4) Morton, Charles W., The World of Erle Stanley Gardner, *The Atlantic*, Jan. 1967, pp. 79-91.

THE INDIGENT'S RIGHT TO AN ADEQUATE DEFENSE:

EXPERT AND INVESTIGATIONAL ASSISTANCE

IN CRIMINAL PROCEEDINGS

Craig Bowman

Many criminal cases find the prosecution and indigent defendant mismatched, with the indigent distinctly disadvantaged.(1) An indigent(2) charged with a serious crime is guaranteed court-appointed counsel to aid in his defense, and at one time this may have been sufficient to ensure the indigent's protection. Today, however, science, technology, and criminological specialization pervade the criminal process.(3) The state has an extensive arsenal of investigators and experts at its disposal, but the indigent defendant lacks similar resources. Without these additional services, the indigent is ill-equipped to meet the state's contentions.(4)

The inability of the indigent defendant to adequately develop a defense without expert and investigative aid is inconsistent with the exposed American fundamental of "equality before the law."(5) The government need not alleviate the accused's poverty, but neither should it allow poverty to create an imbalance in the administration of criminal justice.(6) To reduce the influence of poverty and ensure balance, the government should provide the indigent defendant with the services of investigators and experts to develop, prepare, and present his defense.

PRESENT STATUTORY AIDS TO INDIGENT DEFENDANTS

The Federal Criminal Justice Act,(7) enacted in 1964, is the first significant grant of federal aid to indigents for obtaining experts and investigation facilities.(8) Under section (e) of the Act,(9) the court may authorize counsel, upon request, to obtain necessary services on behalf of defendant at a cost not in excess of 300 dollars, exclusive of reasonable expenses, for each person rendering such services. The Criminal Justice Act has been praised for its strides in granting compensated counsel to indigent defendants(10) and has been relatively effective in this respect.(11) But the provisions of the Act dealing with additional services to indigents are relatively inadequate.(12)

The Act authorizes expenses only for services *"necessary"* to an adequate defense(13) and apparently distinguishes between services to develop and present existing defenses and services needed to ascertain whether other defenses are available.(14) The latter fall outside the statutory language. Furthermore, the federal courts have been unwilling to place aid in addition to counsel on the same constitutional plane as the right to counsel,(15) and most federal courts require that additional services be demonstrated *absolutely* necessary before they will grant a section (e) application.(16) A more definite standard should be delineated, comparable to the grant of counsel, that places the reasonably necessary services of experts and investigators within the indigent defendant's reach.

The 300-dollar limitation on the compensation available to each expert and investigator employed by the defense(17) also impairs the Act's effectiveness. The cost of such services may exceed this figure,(18) especially in proceedings involving extensive preparation or prolonged litigation.(19) Although statutory aid to the indigent must be limited by the reasonable bounds of practicality, rigid monetary limitations may unnecessarily hamper the indigent's ability to defend. It is ironic that additional aid is not approached with the same degree of flexibility as payment of court-appointed counsel,(20) which may exceed the stated limitations if litigation is protracted. Such an adjustment to section (e), coupled with a liberal interpretation of its provisions, would do much to increase the flexibility and effectiveness of its grant.

In most states the granting of aid is discretionary with the trial court.(21) Courts in some jurisdictions refuse to excercise their discretion on the ground that the payment of expert and investigative fees is a matter for legislative determination.(22) In jurisdictions in which courts exercise their discretion, additional assistance is often *seriously* considered only for capital offenses.(23) Even then, requests for assistance are not always granted;(24) some courts refuse defense requests for aid unless and until the prosecution calls or indicates its intention to call experts,(25) thus precluding defendants from determining whether possible defenses are available.

At least fourteen states have legislation providing some degree of additional aid to the indigent for his defense preparation.(26) Although most of these statutes were adopted in response to the Federal Criminal Justice Act, the federal principles were often modified in the transition, making, for example, expert and other services available only in "capital cases"(27) or only to persons "accused of murder."(28) Capital cases are not the only instances in which additional aid is needed,(29) and so limiting fund allotments excludes many needy defendants.(30) The most efficient state statutes granting services other than counsel are those modeled after section (e) of the Criminal Justice Act with least modification.(31) But the limitations encountered in these statutes are similar to those in the federal statute. Rigid monetary restrictions, for example, frustrate the statutes' purpose when need exceeds the statutory limit.

To meet these objections, several states have provided that the court may fix compensation for services rendered at an amount it deems reasonable.(32) These statutes avoid the problems of a statutory maximum, but they may work to deny defendant any allotment.(33) Moreover, inadequate financing may restrict the court's discretion. At present, funds are generally insufficient to finance even the cost of adequate representation programs.(34) Hence, states should move not only to enact effective additional aid legislation but should also make specific appropriations to ensure that reasonable requests for expert and investigative aid can be financed.(35)

CONSTITUTIONAL CONSIDERATIONS

At present the indigent defendant often lacks the tools to defend against the prosecution's contentions. When additional expert and investigative assistance are necessary to adequate representation and the opportunity to defend, such assistance may be constitutionally mandated.

Although the Supreme Court has not addressed the issue of auxiliary assistance on due process grounds, this question has been considered by several lower federal courts. In *McGarty v. O'Brien*,(36) the court held that it is not a violation of due process to deny an indigent defendant's application for expert witnesses when reports of the state's experts are available to both prosecution and defense.(37) Since the task of experts and investigators is to procure the evidence that most strongly bolsters their client's position, however, it seems that defendant should be given the opportunity to present his own evidence.(38)

Even if due process did not require that additional assistance be given an indigent in 1951 when *O'Brien* was decided, concepts of due process change.(39) "[A]s civilization progresses our ideas of fundamental fairness necessarily enlarge themselves."(40) More recent cases emphasizing the expanded notion of "fundamental fairness" in treatment of indigent defendants(41) suggest that federal courts would favor state-compensated experts and investigative services.(42) *Douglas v. California*,(43) although conceding that absolute equality was not required among all defendants, emphasized that due process demands that the concept of fair trial for indigents not be reduced to a "meaningless ritual."(44) Defendant's poverty may make his attempts at defense so ineffective that to deny him necessary additional assistance is to deny him the basic foundation of a fair and equitable proceeding.(45) In addition, an opportunity to prepare a defense is no less essential to the indigent defendant in many situations than is the opportunity to prepare an appeal,(46) which has been deemed an essential element of fundamental fairness.(47)

In *Griffin v. Illinois*,(48) the Supreme Court considered the impact of poverty on constitutional rights under the equal protection clause. The Court held that a state may not deprive indigent defendants of adequate review of alleged trial errors solely because of their inability to pay the cost of a necessary transcript.(49) There is no "rational relationship" between an individual's ability to pay costs and his guilt or innocence,(50) and discriminations based on poverty violate equal protection.(51)

On the reasoning of *Griffin* and its progeny, for the states to disallow necessary expert and investigative services to the indigent *as such* is a prohibited discrimination between "rich" and "poor" in the application of their laws. There is a blatant disparity in the consequences of state action for rich and poor when an indigent defendant, who would have been found innocent had he had the necessary funds to procure expert witnesses or investigative assistance, is found guilty.(52) The *Griffin-Douglas* doctrine, considered with respect to preparation of an adequate defense, seems to require at least that a state provide additional assistance at the trial level if that assistance is necessary to presenting a defense.(53)

The guarantee of additional services to indigent defendants may also be premised on the sixth amendment right to the assistance of counsel for one's defense.(54) The right to counsel requires the "effective assistance of counsel.(55) As early as 1932 the Supreme Court asserted that the duty to appoint counsel "is not discharged by an assignment at such a time or under such circumstances as to preclude the giving of effective aid in the preparation and trial of the case."(56) The word "effective" sets forth no concrete standard but rather connotes the state of being capable of bringing about an effect; *i.e.*, equipped and ready for service.(57) The defendant's attorney is incapable of giving effective aid unless many services available to the prosecution are also at his disposal.(58) The sixth amendment does not demand a favorably conclusive defense for the indigent, but effective assistance does require that each defense in the defendant's favor should be sought out, efficiently prepared, and adequately presented. If the "assistance" of the sixth amendment guarantee is emphasized in conjunction with the necessities of *effective* representation, the concomitant services of experts and investigators must be supplied.(59)

The sixth amendment further declares that the accused shall have "compulsory process for obtaining witnesses in his favor."(60) Initially, compulsory process to obtain witnesses may have meant merely the right to call directly involved laymen to the stand to testify for the defense. But as the science of criminology has developed, the state's contentions are increasingly founded on the testimony of skilled specialists.(61) If the defense is to meet such contentions, it must frequently call its own competent expert witnesses, who often require extensive pretrial efforts in order to arrive at their conclusions. Furthermore, investigators are frequently necessary to seek out lay individuals who are competent to testify on defendant's behalf. If the defense is unable to determine who its witnesses are, the right to call such individuals becomes of little value.

The compulsory process clause does not guarantee the favorable determination of possible defense contentions. In addition, there is an admitted difference between the right to call witnesses and the right to have the government pay for them. Expert witnesses and investigators, however, cannot be compelled to serve or testify without compensation.(62) If the indigent is without funds to compensate expert witnesses, investigators needed to find lay witnesses, or experts and investigators needed to make effective use of witnesses he has, the doctrine of compulsory process may be reduced to little more than the "sterile issuance of a paper."(63) Lack of funds could in reality prevent an indigent defendant from offering a defense. Although no Supreme Court decision has yet changed the rule to require state compensation of expert testimony or investigate evidence, *People v. Watson*(64) declared that production of compensated expert witnesses for indigents was constitutionally fundamental.(65) "[A]lthough the defendant is afforded the shadow of a right to call witnesses, he is deprived of the substance."(66) It is this substance that the indigent lacks. Funds for investigation to procure witnesses, for expert preparation, and for expert testimony must be deemed as realistically coming within the confines of a substantive theory of compulsory process.

The fundamental right of the accused "to be confronted by the witnesses against him"(67) guarantees not only the right of the accused to hear witnesses testify against him but also the right *effectively* to cross-examine them.(68) Cross-examination of lay witnesses is a valuable tool to defendant and can often separate hearsay from knowledge, error from truth, opinion from fact, and inference from recollection.(69) To become sufficiently familiar with the case to prepare an effective cross-examination, defense counsel may require investigative assistance.(70) Defense counsel must also be adequately prepared to examine adverse expert witnesses. This requires some knowledge of the potential subjects of expert evidence in the case. The attorney may extensively research the specialized areas of his case, but he often needs expert advice. The value of cross-examination is questionable if defense counsel is not armed with background material derived from pretrial investigations of the surrounding circumstances and expert consultation on the technical facets of these circumstances.(71) Expert assistance and investigative preparation therefore seem necessary to preserve "the defendant's . . . right to a fair trial as affected by his right *meaningfully* to cross-examine the witnesses against him."(72)

ADEQUATE DEFENSE SERVICES FOR INDIGENTS

Extending aid to indigent defendants to cover expert and investigative services is arguably required by constitutional doctrine; certainly the practical necessities of preparing an adequate defense at least justify such an extension.(73) Both the constitutional and the practical justifications for additional aid to indigents, however, may be opposed by arguments of "over-extension." But every principle of law that is carried as far as needed creates debate: "[W]here to draw the line . . . is the question in pretty much everything worth arguing in the law."(74)

The decision to implement various forms of additional-services aid must balance the cost to the state against the significance of the inequality affecting the indigent defendant's constitutional rights.(75) As the sums requested by the indigent for procuring additional services increase, some scale of priorities will have to be established to determine how much assistance must be made available. Several considerations will be pertinent in determining the degree of aid to be granted in a particular case. The complexity of the issues in the case should be evaluated in conjunction with the severity of the possible penalty, as should the likelihood of defendant's presenting a meaningful defense without the aid. What the prosecution is expending on the case and the range of expenditures made by defendants of means in like cases should also be relevant in determining the indigent's reasonable requirements for additional services.(76) Flexibility is an asset in a system of auxiliary services, and thus no exact line should be drawn. The most reasonable formula is to provide services and facilities at public expense to the extent that a refusal of funds in a particular case will work undue hardship on the defendant. The harm to the indigent caused by a denial of aid must outweigh the economic good to the state resulting from a refusal. If a crime is serious enough to require court appointment of an attorney, then it is serious enough to require provision that the appointment be effective.

The United States, which prides itself on notions of equality and progressiveness, lags behind other countries in providing funds for an indigent's effective defense. Great Britain provides nationwide payment of expenses for expert witnesses and investigation.(77) The Swiss mandate that "all are equal before the law" has resulted in a variety of services in addition to counsel being made available to all indigents.(78) The broadest programs of aid in criminal cases are those of the Scandinavian countries: in addition to receiving a court-appointed attorney, every criminal defendant, regardless of financial status, may make use of government laboratories, expert testimony, and investigation at government expense.(79) The Supreme Court should take note of these systems and expand its own constitutional mandate to include auxiliary aid to indigents.(80)

Even if directives are given by state or federal courts, effective assistance can be provided only by adequate state legislation. An excellent model is New Hampshire's statute, which provides that investigators, experts, and services necessary to an adequate defense may be obtained in any criminal case in which counsel has been appointed.(81) Upon application, the court will authorize counsel to obtain necessary services, but if timely procurement of services cannot await prior authorization, they may still be approved by the court after they have been obtained.(82) Court determination of reasonable compensation protects against excessive requests for funds. The court's determination is based upon a number of objective considerations, such as time expended, the nature of the services rendered, and the standard fees for similar services. And the maximum payment figure of 300 dollars exclusive of expenses reasonably incurred for each person rendering services may be increased when necessary.

The New Hampshire statute provides the indigent defendant with the tools needed to prepare and present an adequate defense. Substantive equality is the minimal condition that must exist to maintain the notion of fair and equitable trials, and the availability of experts and investigative aid is fundamental to that substantive equality. Only through comprehensive statutes such as New Hampshire's can these premises of our adversarial system be preserved.

NOTES

(1) Goldstein, *The State and the Accused: Balance of Advantage in Criminal Procedure*, 69 Yale L.J. 1149-50 (1960).

(2) Depending on the jurisdiction, an estimated 50% to 60% of all those charged with crime are classified as indigents. *See, e.g.,* Special Comm'n To Study Defender Systems, Equal Justice for the Accused 80, 134-35 (1959); E. Brownell, Legal Aid in the United States 83 (1951); Kennedy, *Judicial Administration: Fair and Equal Treatment to All Before the Law*, 28 Vital Speeches 706 (1962).

(3) *See* J. Maguire, J. Weinstein, J. Chadbourn & J. Mansfield. Cases on Evidence 250-51 (5th ed. 1965); Orfield, *Expert Witnesses in Federal Criminal Procedure*, 20 F.R.D. 317, 339-40 (1958). "[I] n countless suits tried every day in courts across the country, the outcome depends largely upon the testimony of an expert witness. . . ." N.Y. Times, Oct. 27, 1969, at 41, col. 1.

(4) In one case described to the author, the state presented expert witnesses employed by the FBI and the state bureau of investigation to identify blood samples, hair samples, and ballistics. Police officers from five sheriffs' offices also testified for the state, as did a pathologist and four psychiatrists. The state presented 60 witnesses in all. Since there was no preliminary hearing it was impossible for defense counsel either to interview or to investigate the background of all these witnesses; most of them were seen for the first time when they were called to testify. Letter from Jack W. Floyd to the *Cornell Law Review*, Nov. 10, 1969. The difficulty of preparing an adequate defense when expert and investigational services are unavailable is suggested by the continuing requests of Legal Aid and Defender Association offices for more such services. Letter from Lewis A. Wenzell, Assistant to the Director of Defender Services, National Legal Aid and Defender Association, Chicago, Illinois, to the *Cornell Law Review*, Nov. 25, 1969.

(5) *See* Chambers v. Florida, 309 U.S. 227, 241 (1940); Yick Wo v. Hopkins, 118 U.S. 356, 369 (1886).

(6) Report of Attorney General's Comm. On Poverty and the Administration of Federal Criminal Justice 6 (1963) [hereinafter cited as Allen Report, after the chairman of the committee, Francis A. Allen].

> It follows that insofar as the financial status of the accused impedes vigorous and proper challenges, it constitutes a threat to the viability of the adversarial system. . . . It is also clear that a situation in which persons are required to contest a serious accusation but are denied access to the tools of contest is offensive to fairness and equity.

Id. at 11. *See* the rational of the Federal Criminal Justice Act, in 1964 U.S. Code Congressional and Administrative News 2996. *See also* Note, *Right to Aid in Addition to Counsel for Indigent Criminal Defendants*, 47 Minn. L. Rev. 1054, 1068 (1963).

(7) 18 U.S.C. § 3006A (1964).

(8) Lewin, *Indigency—Informal and Formal Procedures to Provide Partisan Psychiatric Assistance to the Poor*, 52 Iowa L. Rev. 458, 464 (1966). *See* Kutak, *The Criminal Justice Act of 1964*, 44 Neb. L. Rev. 703, 704 (1965).

(9) 18 U.S.C. § 3006A(e) (1964):

Counsel for a defendant who is financially unable to obtain investigative, expert, or other services necessary to an adequate defense in his case may request them . . . . [A]fter appropriate inquiry . . . the court shall authorize counsel to obtain the services on behalf of the defendant. . . . The compensation to be paid to a person for such services rendered by him to a defendant . . . shall not exceed $300, exclusive of reimbursement of expenses reasonably incurred.

(10) *See, e.g.*, Kutak, *supra* note 8, at 703-04; Note, *Litigation Costs: The Hidden Barrier to the Indigent*, 56 Geo. L. J. 516 (1968).

(11) Since its passage in 1964, the Criminal Justice Act has provided over 300,000 indigent defendants with legal counsel. Note, *supra* note 10, at 516. *See also Editorial*, Trial Magazine, Aug.-Sept. 1967, at 3.

(12) Lewin, *supra* note 8, at 471, *citing* Letter from Daniel J. Freed, Acting Director, Office of Criminal Justice, to the Legislative Research Center, Univ. of Michigan School of Law, March 28, 1966:

The Department of Justice advised that in the entire country there were only 53 section (e) authorizations in the first eight months after the Act went into effect, with a total estimated cost of 13,000 dollars. Most of these authorizations were principally for factual investigations . . . .

(13) Note 9 *supra*.

(14) The court-appointed attorney for the accused must often go into the field in question and examine individuals possibly familiar with defendant's conduct and the crime committed, in order to learn what defenses, if any, are available. Not only is the attorney unskilled in investigative methods, but he lacks the time to expend in thorough investigation. For the problems that may arise when counsel attempts to act as his own investigator, see People v. Kennedy, 20 N.Y.2d 912, 233, N.E.2d 126, 286 N.Y.S.2d 32 (1967); Fish v. Commonwealth, 208 Va. 761, 160 S.E.2d 576 (1968).

(15) In Christian v. United States, 398 F.2d 517 (10th Cir. 1968), the court declared that, although every criminal defendant financially unable to obtain counsel is entitled to the appointment of counsel at government expense, not every similarly situated defendant is entitled to appointment of an investigator or other expert services. *See also* United States v. Bowe, 360 F2d 1 (2d Cir. 1966), in which the court held that no provision of the Criminal Justice Act authorizes a federal court to reimburse an indigent defendant's attorney for expenses incurred in preparing litigation.

Some commentators have suggested that in many cases the assistance of an expert is more important to effective representation than the assistance of counsel. *See* 1964-65 Comm. of the State Bar of Ga. on Compensated Counsel, *Assistance to the Indigent Person Charged With Crime*, 2 Ga. St. B.J. 197, 202 (1965). *See also* Special Comm'n To Study Defender Systems, *supra* note 2, at 58-70. For example, an indigent charged with breaking and entering may face conviction based solely on fingerprints left at the scene. In such a case, although the attorney for defendant may contest the state's allegations, only a defense fingerprint expert can establish that the prints were not defendant's.

(16) *E.g.*, Bradford v. United States, 413 F.2d 467 (5th Cir. 1969). In Ray v. United States, 367 F2d 258 (8th Cir. 1966), a forgery case, the prosecution called handwriting and fingerprint experts to testify on behalf of the state. Defendant was denied aid to obtain his own experts under § (e), on the ground that the Criminal Justice Act does not provide an indigent with any procedural

rights of discovery or defenses. Since § (e) is directed toward providing procedures by which the indigent may obtain services needed for his defense, the court's interpretation appears incorrect. *See* 1964 U.S. Code Congressional and Administrative News 2996.

(17) 18 U.S.C. § 3006A(e) (1964).

(18) The cost exclusive of expenses, may run as high as $2,300. Letter from James Cardona, Public Defender, Providence, R.I. to the *Cornell Law Review,* Nov. 25, 1969.

(19) *See, e.g.,* N.Y. Times, Oct. 27, 1969, at 41, cols. 1-4, citing fees of from $100 to $500 per day. Crowded court dockets, which often necessitate the expert's presence several times before the case is actually called, increase the fees. The expert must be reimbursed for his time even if his services are not used.

(20) 18 U.S.C. § 3006A(d) (1964):

> The court shall, in each instance, fix the compensation and reimbursement to be paid to the attorney . . . [T] he compensation to be paid . . . shall not exceed $500 in a case in which one or more felonies are charged, and $300 in a case in which only misdemeanors are charged. In extraordinary circumstances, *payment in excess of the limits stated herein may be made* if the district court certifies that such payment is necessary to provide fair compensation for protracted representation . . .
> (emphasis added).

(21) *E.g.,* People v. Thomas, 1 Mich. App. 118, 134 N.W.2d 352 (1965; Annot., 18 A.L.R.3d 1074, 1091-94 (1968).

(22) *See, e.g.,* People *ex rel.* Connecticut v. Randolph, 35 Ill. 2d 24, 219 N.E.2d 337 (1966); People v. Thomas, 1 Mich. App. 118, 134 N.W.2d 352 (1965). "Courts have generally refused to hold, in the absence of a statute authorizing it, that defense experts should be paid by the state. The approach has been a passive one which leaves the parties as before—mismatched." Goldstein & Fine, The Indigent Accused, The Psychiatrist, and the Insanity Defense, 110 U. Pa. L. Rev. 1061, 1080 (1962) (footnotes omitted).

(23) *See, e.g.,* State v. Horton, 34 N.J. 518, 170 A.2d 1 (1961). *But see* State v. Rush, 46 N.J. 399, 217 A.2d 441 (1966).

(24) *See, e.g.,* People v. Konono, 41 Misc. 2d 63, 245 NY.S.2d 105 (Sup. Ct. 1963) (services of a detective agency at the request of the attorney assigned to an indigent defendant charged with a capital crime are not payable from county funds). *See also* People v. Fernandez, 202 Misc. 190, 109 N.Y.S.2d 561 (Sup. Ct. 1951).

(25) *See, e.g.* People v. Scott, 17 Misc. 2d 134, 190 N.Y.S. 2d 461 (Sup. Ct. 1959).

(26) Cal. Evid. Code § § 730-31 (West 1966): Fla. Stat. § 932.30 (Supp. 1969); Ill. Rev. Stat. ch. 38, § 113-3 (1967); Iowa Code Ann. § 775.5 (1969); Minn. Stat. Ann. § 611.21 (Supp. 1969); N.H. Rev. Stat. Ann. § 604-A:6 (1965); N.Y. Code Crim. Proc. § 308 (McKinney Supp. 1969); N.C. Gen. Stat. § 15-5 (1966); Ohio Rev. Code Ann. § 2941.51 (Page Supp. 1968); Pa. Stat. tit. 19, § 784 (1964); R.I. Gen. Laws Ann. § 9-17-19 (1956); S.D. Compiled Laws Ann. § 23-2-3 (1969); Tex. Code Crim. Proc. art. 26.05 (1965); Utah Code Ann. § 77-64-1 (Supp. 1969).

Many other jurisdictions provide a court-appointed attorney with some compensation for his out-of-pocket expenses incurred in defending an indigent defendant. *See* Annot., 18 A.L.R.3d 1074, 1091 (1968).

(27) *E.g.,* Ill. Rev. Stat. ch. 38, § 113-3 (1967) (counsel and expert. witnesses).

(28) Pa. Stat. tit. 19, § 784 (1964).

(29) Although the defendant accused of a capital crime presents the most pressing case due to the possible punishment, there is no logic in withholding aid

from persons facing lesser degrees of official sanctions. The same rationale that led to granting counsel in a broad range of cases is applicable to additional assistance. *See* Gideon v. Wainwright, 372 U.S. 335 (1963).

(30) For restrictions other than the "capital" ones, see N.Y. Code Crim. Proc. § 308 (McKinney Supp. 1969) (funds for additional assistance available only in "relatively serious incidents"); S.D. Compiled Laws Ann. § 23-2-3 (1969) (additional aid restricted to post trial proceedings).

(31) *E.g.*, Minn. Stat. Ann. § 611.21 (Supp. 1969); Ohio Rev. Code Ann. § 2941.51 (Page Supp. 1968); Tex. Code Crim. Proc. art. 26.05 (1965).

(32) Cal. Evid. Code §§ 730-31 (West 1966); Fla. Stat. § 932.30 (Supp. 1969); N.C. Gen. Stat. § 15-5 (1966); R.I. Gen. Laws Ann. § 9-17-19 (1956).

(33) Letter from Jack W. Floyd, *supra* note 4.

(34) *E.g.*, Letter from Edward J. Reichert, Executive Director of the Tri-County Legal Services, Berlin, N.H., to the *Cornell Law Review*, Nov. 8, 1969. Mr. Reichert noted that the funds appropriated by the New Hampshire legislature for indigent defendants generally run out half-way through the fiscal year.

(35) A new provision of the New Hampshire statute adopted in 1969 states:
> Any defendant whose case is continued for sentence, or who receives a suspended sentence . . . may be ordered by the court to repay the state . . . all of the fees and expenses paid on his behalf on such terms as the court may order . . .

N.H. Rev. Stat. Ann. § 604-A:9 (1969). Such a provision may somewhat alleviate the financial burden on states that provide indigents with additional defense services.

(36) 188 F.2d 151 (1st Cir. 1951).

(37) *See also* United States *ex rel.* Smith v. Baldi, 192 F.2d 540 (3d Cir. 1951):
> The same argument that would entitle [defendant's lawyers] to psychiatric consultation would entitle them to consultation with ballistic experts, chemists, engineers, biologists, or any type of expert whose help in a particular case might be relevant. We do not think the requirements of due process go so far.

Id. at 547.

(38) Letter from William J. Ciolka, Public Defender of Poughkeepsie, N.Y., to the *Cornell Law Review*, Nov. 6, 1969. In a murder case in which defendant was represented by a court-appointed attorney, state police fingerprint experts testified that a latent print lifted from the crime's scene was defendant's by demonstrating 14 points of similarity. Defense was able to procure its own expert who proved three crucial points of dissimilarity. An acquittal followed. *Id.*

(39) "[W]e have never . . . restricted due process to a fixed catalogue of what was at a given time deemed to be the limits of fundamental rights." Harper v. Virginia Bd. of Elections, 383 U.S. 663, 669 (1969) (dictum).

(40) United States *ex rel.* Smith v. Baldi, 192 F.2d 540, 560 (3d Cir. 1951) (dissent of Biggs, C.J.). *See* Note, *supra* note 6, at 1070. This dissent in *Baldi* had previously pointed out that
> [t]he requirement[s] of due process . . . would not be met by the appointment of a layman as counsel. The appointment of counsel for a deaf mute would not constitute due process of law unless an interpreter also was available. Nor, in our opinion, would the appointment of counsel learned in the law fulfill the requirement of due process if that counsel required the assistance of a psychiatrist in order to prepare an insane client's defense.

192 F.2d at 559.

(41) Gideon v. Wainwright, 372 U.S. 335 (1963); Griffin v. Illinois, 351 U.S. 12 (1956). For an explanation of the fundamental fairness doctrine of due process, see Rochin v. California, 342 U.S. 165, 169 (1952). Due process of law is a constitutional guarantee respecting personal notions of fairness "so rooted in the traditions and conscience of our people as to be ranked as fundamental." Snyder v. Massachusetts, 291 U.S. 97, 105 (1935).

(42) In Bush v. Texas, 372 U.S. 586 (1963), the Supreme Court nearly had an opportunity to review the decision in *Baldi*, but the state decided to re-try the case. The Court's decision to re-examine its position after Griffin v. Illinois, 351 U.S. 12 (1956), and Gideon v. Wainwright, 372 U.S. 335 (1963), suggests that it might have granted additional services in *Bush*. For an indication of such an attitude, see United States v. Brodson, 241 F.2d 107, 111 (7th Cir. 1957) (dissent of Duffy, C.J.), in which the defense argued that expert accounting assistance was necessary for effective preparation. The assistance was denied, and the dissent argued that such denial "violates those canons of decency and fairness to which any defendant in a criminal case is entitled under the Fifth and Sixth Amendments of the Constitution . . . " *Id*, at 111-12. *But see* Feguer v. United States, 302 F.2d 214 (8th Cir. 1962), in which the court stated that, although the right to call expert witnesses was fundamental, "this right does not necessarily include the payment by the government of the expenses of witnesses." *Id.* at 241.

(43) 372 U.S. 353 (1963).

(44) *Id.* at 357. The Court stated that

[a]bsolute equality is not required; lines can be and are drawn and we often sustain them . . . But where the merits of *the one and only appeal* an indigent has of right are decided without benefit of counsel, we think an unconstitutional line has been drawn between rich and poor.

Id. (emphasis by the Court, citations omitted). *See also* Draper v. Washington, 372 U.S. 487 (1963), concerning state denial to an indigent defendant of a transcript on appeal. The Court declared that "the State must provide the indigent defendant with means of presenting his contentions to the appellate court which are as good as those available to a nonindigent defendant with similar contentions." *Id.* at 496.

(45) Allen Report, *supra* note 6, at 45-46. One of the assumptions of the adversary system is that defendant's attorney will have at his disposal the essential means and elements to conduct an effective defense. Failure to provide such services "may adversely affect the quality of the defense made or force a decision to plead guilty to a criminal charge in situations in which the charge might otherwise be properly contested." *Id.* at 46.

(46) *See* 32 Mo. L. Rev. 543, 549 (1967).

(47) *See* Douglas v. California, 372 U.S. 353 (1963).

(48) 351 U.S. 12 (1956). *See* Wilcox & Bloustein, *The Griffin Case—Poverty and the Fourteenth Amendment*, 43 Cornell L.Q. 1 (1957).

(49) "There can be no equal justice where the kind of trial a man gets depends on the amount of money he has." 351 U.S. at 19. *See*, however, the dissent of Justices Burton and Minton: "The Constitution requires the equal protection of the law, but it does not require the States to provide equal financial means for all defendants to avail themselves of such laws." *Id.* at 29.

(50) *Id.* at 17-18. The Court in *Griffin* stressed the theory of a "rational relationship:" "Plainly the ability to pay costs in advance bears no rational relationship to a defendant's guilt or innocence and could not be used as an excuse to deprive a defendant of a fair trial." *Id.*

(51) *Id.* at 17. *See also* Smith v. Bennett, 365 U.S. 708, 714 (1961), where the Supreme Court indicated that the policy of the equal protection clause is such that "the Fourteenth Amendment weighs the interests of rich and poor

criminals in equal scale, and its hand extends as far to each."

(52) Note, *Equal Protection and the Indigent Defendant: Griffin and Its Progeny,* 16 Stan. L. Rev. 394, 405 (1964).

(53) *See* Y. Kamisar, F. Inbau, & T. Arnold, Criminal Justice In Our Time 93 (1965). Providing this minimum assistance would not elevate the indigent defendant above others in the states' system of criminal procedure, but would merely place him on the level occupied by most individuals.

(54) For valuable commentary on the indigent's right to counsel, see W. Beany, The Right To Counsel In American Courts (1965); D. Fellman, The Defendant's Rights 112-17 (1958); Allen, *The Supreme Court, Federalism, and State Systems of Criminal Justice,* 8 DePaul L. Rev. 213 (1958); Kamisar, *The Right to Counsel and the Fourteenth Amendment: A Dialogue on "The Most Persuasive Right" of an Accused,* 30 U. Chi. L. Rev. 1 (1962); *The Right to Counsel: A Symposium,* 45 Minn. L. Rev. 693 (1961). Assistance of counsel in criminal proceedings is applicable to states under the fourteenth amendment. Gideon v. Wainright, 372 U.S. 335 (1963). *See* Note, *supra* note 6; 32 Mo. L. Rev. 543 (1967).

(55) "[T]he constitutional requirement of representation at trial is one of substance, not of form . . . Due Process does not require 'errorless counsel, and not counsel judged ineffective by hindsight, but counsel reasonably likely to render . . . reasonably effective assistance.' " Brubaker v. Dickson, 310 F.2d 30, 37 (9th Cir. 1962) (footnotes omitted), *quoting* Makenna v. Ellis, 280 F.2d 592, 599 (5th Cir. 1960), *modified,* 289 F.2d 928 (5th Cir. 1961).

(56) Powell v. Alabama, 287 U.S. 45, 71 (1932).

(57) For a general notion of what is meant by "effective counsel," see Waltz, *Inadequacy of Trial Defense Representation as a Ground for Post-Conviction Relief in Criminal Cases,* 59 Nw. U.L. Rev. 289 (1964); Note, *Effective Assistance of Counsel for the Indigent Defendant,* 78 Harv. L. Rev. 1434 (1965); Note, *Effective Assistance of Counsel,* 49 Va. L. Rev. 1531 (1963).

(58) *See, e.g.,* State v. Hancock, 164 N.W.2d 330 (Iowa 1969), where defendant was accused of forgery but was denied services of a handwriting expert, even though the state had given notice that its evidence consisted basically of similar expert testimony.

(59) *See* Note, *supra* note 6, at 1072.

(60) U.S. Const. amend. VI.

(61) *See* note 3 *supra.*

(62) *See* Annot., 77 A.L.R.2d 1182 (1961).

(63) 32 Mo. L. Rev. 543, 545 (1967).

(64) 36 Ill. 2d 228, 221 N.E.2d 645 (1966).

(65) *Id.* at 233, 221 N.E.2d at 648.

(66) *Id.*

(67) U.S. Const. amend. VI. This right is applicable to the states through the fourteenth amendment. Pointer v. Texas, 380 U.S. 400 (1965).

(68) *See* United States v. Barracota, 45 F. Supp. 38 (S.D.N.Y. 1942).

(69) Cross-examination is the tool by which the attorney can correctly ascertain the order of events, the time and place they occurred, and the attending circumstances. The Ottawa, 70 U.S.(3 Wall.) 268, 271 (1865). *See also* Alford v. United States, 282 U.S. 687 (1931):

> [Cross-examination's] permissible purposes, among others, are that the witness may be identified with his community so that independent testimony may be sought and offered of his reputation for veracity in his own neighborhood . . . ; that the jury may interpret his testimony in the light reflected upon it by knowledge of his environment . . . ; and that facts may be brought out tending to discredit the witness by showing that his testimony in chief was untrue or biased.

Id. at 691-92.

(70) Preparation for an effective cross-examining requires full knowledge of the case, the issues involved, and the witness's background, including his address and occupation, his interest in the case, his prejudice, if any, his relation to the parties and counsel, and, most particularly, all his prior statements and testimony concerning the case. Counsel should also know whether the witness has a criminal record, has a charge pending against him, or is involved in any pending civil litigation . . .

L. Friedman, Essentials of Cross-Examination 16 (1968).

(71) Allen Report, *supra* note 6, at 12-57.

(72) United States v. Wade, 388 U.S. 218, 227 (1967) (emphasis added).

(73) This need was well formulated in a letter from Lewis A. Wenzell, *supra* note 4. Responses to a questionnaire sent to all Defender Association member offices indicated that defender offices would use experts slightly over three times as often as they now use them were such services "readily available."

(74) Irwin v. Gavit, 268 U.S. 161, 168 (1925) (Holmes, J.).

(75) *See* W. McKechnie, Magna Carta: A Commentary On The Great Charter Of King John 395-96 (1914): "In the twentieth century, as in the thirteenth, justice cannot be had for nothing . . . "

(76) Note, *supra* note 52, at 414. *See also* sources cited in note 8 *supra*.

(77) *See* The English Legal Aid and Advice Act, 12 & 13 Geo. 6, c. 51 (1949) which makes possible state compensation for expert witnesses and investigation acquired in conjunction with an indigent defendant's trial preparation. The pauper selects counsel from a list of attorneys who have volunteered their names, and the attorney is paid 85% of the recommended fee out of a legal aid fund supported by Parliamentary appropriation. *See generally* Note, *Proceedings in Forma Pauperis*, 9 U. Fla. L. Rev. 65, 73 (1956); Note, *The British Legal Aid and Advice Bill*, 59 Yale L.J. 320 (1950).

(78) *See* Jacoby, *Legal Aid to the Poor*, 53 Harv. L. Rev. 940, 942-44 (1940) Note, *supra* note 52, at 413.

(79) *See* United States v. Johnson, 238 F.2d 565, 573 (2d Cir. 1956). *See also* comments on the Scandinavian practice in J. Frank & B. Frank, Not Guilty 87 (1957).

(80) The plan should provide for investigatory, expert, and other services necessary to an adequate defense. These should include not only those services and facilities needed for an effective defense at trial but also those that are required for effective defense participation in every phase of the process, including determinations on pretrial release, competency to stand trial and disposition following conviction.

ABA Project on Minimum Standards for Criminal Justice, standards relating to providing defense services 22 (approved draft, 1963).

(81) N.H. Rev. Stat. Ann. § 604-A:6 (1965).

(82) The difficulties that time limitations and deadlines impose can be detrimental to the indigent in need of additional trained services. *See, e.g.,* Letter from William J. Ciolka, *supra* note 38, noting that the defense has available neither government laboratories nor experts but must purchase expertise on the market place. If this must be done during the trial the defense is in difficulty, since good experts are booked well in advance. Further, the people's experts test fresh exhibits; if the defense must wait for additional services, the exhibits may be so old that it will be impossible to get sufficient reactions for a classification.

SELECTED BIBLIOGRAPHY

BOOKS

Benson, Walter R.; John E. Stacy, Jr.; and Michael L. Worley. *Systems Analysis of Criminalistics Operations.* LEAA Grant NI-044. Kansas City, Mo.: Midwest Research Institute, 1970.

Beveridge, W.I.B. *The Art of Scientific Investigation.* New York: Vintage Books, 1957.

Blumberg, Abraham S. *Criminal Justice.* Chicago: Quadrangle Books, 1967.

Bronowski, J. *The Common Sense of Science.* New York: Vintage Books, 1953.

Bugliosi, Vincent. *Helter Skelter.* New York: Norton, 1974.

Burd, David Q., ed. *Physical Evidence Manual.* Sacramento: Criminalistics Laboratory, State of California, Bureau of C. I. and I., 1970.

Clark, Ramsey. *Crime in America: Observations on its Nature, Causes, Prevention and Control.* New York: Simon and Schuster, 1970.

Cohn, S. I. and W. B. McMahon, eds. *Law Enforcement Science and Technology III.* U.S.A.: Port City Press, 1970.

Cray, Ed. *Burden of Proof: The Case of Juan Corona.* New York: Macmillan Publishing Co., Inc., 1973.

Crime Laboratory Division. *Criminal Investigation and Physical Evidence Handbook.* Madison, Wisc.: Department of Justice, 1968.

Eastman, George D., ed. *Municipal Police Administration.* Washington, D.C.:

International City Management Association, 1969.

Fox, Richard H., and Carl L. Cunningham. *Crime Scene Search and Physical Evidence Handbook.* Washington, D.C.: U.S. Government Printing Office, 1973.

Gerber, Samuel R., and Oliver Schroeder Jr., eds. *Criminal Investigation and Interrogation.* Cincinnati: The W. H. Anderson Co., 1962.

Germann, A. C.: Frank D. Day; and Robert P. Gallati. *Introduction to Law Enforcement and Criminal Justice.* Springfield, Ill.: Charles C. Thomas, 1968.

Greenwood, Peter W. *An Analysis of the Apprehension Activities of the New York City Police Department.* New York: The New York City Rand Institute, 1970.

Gross, Hans. *Criminal Investigation.* Fifth edition. Toronto: The Carswell Co. Ltd., 1962.

Heffron, Floyd N. *Evidence for the Patrolman.* Springfield, Ill.: Charles C. Thomas, 1958.

Joseph, Alexander. *Crime Laboratories—Three Study Reports.* OLEA Projects #013, #140 and #66-3. Washington, D.C.: U.S. Government Printing Office, 1968.

Kirk, Paul L. *Crime Investigation.* Second edition. New York: John Wiley and Sons, Inc., 1974.

Kirk, Paul L., and Lowell W. Bradford. *The Crime Laboratory: Organization and Operation.* Springfield, Ill.: Charles C. Thomas, 1965.

LaFave, Wayne R. *Arrest: The Decision to Take a Suspect into Custody.* Boston: Little, Brown and Co., 1965.

Lassers, Willard J. *Scapegoat Justice.* Bloomington: Indiana University Press, 1973.

Loth, David. *Crime Lab—Science Turns Detective.* New York: Julian Messner Inc., 1964.

Lundquist, Frank, and A. S. Curry. *Methods of Forensic Science.* Volumes 1-4. New York: Interscience Publishers, 1962-1965.

McIntyre, Donald M., Jr., and Daniel L. Rothenberg. *Detection of Crime.* Boston: Little, Brown and Co., 1967.

Marshall, James. *Law and Psychology in Conflict.* Garden City, N.Y.: Anchor Books, 1966.

Misner, Gordon E., and William F. McDonald. *Reduction of Robberies and Assaults of Bus Drivers, Volume II: The Scope of the Crime Problem and Its Resolution.* Berkeley: School of Criminology, University of California, 1970.

Moenssens, Andre; Ray Edward Moses; and Fred E. Inbau. *Scientific Evidence in Criminal Cases.* Mineola, N.Y.: The Foundation Press, Inc., 1973.

Morelend, Nigel. *Science in Crime Detection.* New York: Emerson Books, Inc., 1960.

National Advisory Commission on Criminal Justice Standards and Goals. *Police,* Standards 12.1 and 12.2. Washington, D.C.: U.S. Government Printing Office, 1973.

National Commission on Law Observance and Enforcement. *Report on Lawlessness in Law Enforcement*, No. 11. Washington, D.C.: U.S. Government Printing Office, 1931.

——————— *Report on Police*, No. 14. Washington, D.C.: U.S. Government Printing Office, 1931.

Niederhoffer, Arthur. *Behind the Shield: The Police in Urban Society*. Garden City, N.Y.: Anchor Books, 1969.

Niederhoffer, Arthur, and Abraham S. Blumberg, eds. *The Ambivalent Force*. Waltham, Mass.: Ginn and Co., 1970.

O'Hara, Charles E. *Fundamentals of Criminal Investigation*. Springfield, Ill.: Charles C. Thomas, 1956.

O'Hara, Charles E., and James W. Osterburg. *An Introduction to Criminalistics*. New York: The Macmillan Co., 1949.

Osterburg, James W. *The Crime Laboratory*. Bloomington, Ind.: Indiana University Press, 1968.

Parker, Brian. "The Scientific Assessment of Physical Evidence from Criminal Conduct." *Handbook of Criminology*. Daniel Glaser, ed. McNally College Publishing Co., 1974.

Parker, Brian, and Vonnie Gurgin. *Criminalistics in the World of the Future*. N.S.F. Grant GI-30011. Menlo Park, Calif.: Stanford Research Institute, 1972.

Parker, Brian, and Joseph Peterson. *Physical Evidence Utilization in the Administration of Criminal Justice*. LEAA Grant NI-032. Washington, D.C.: U.S. Government Printing Office, 1972.

Peterson, Joseph L. *Utilization of Criminalistics Services by the Police: An Analysis of the Physical Evidence Recovery Process*. Washington, D.C.: U.S. Government Printing Office, 1974.

President's Commission on Law Enforcement and Administration of Justice. *The Challenge of Crime in a Free Society*. Washington, D.C.: U.S. Government Printing Office, 1967.

——————————*Task Force Report: Science and Technology*. Washington, D.C.: U.S. Government Printing Office, 1967.

——————————*Task Force Report: The Police*. Washington, D.C.: U.S. Government Printing Office, 1967.

Rehling, C. J., and C. L. Rabren. *Alabama's Master Plan for a Crime Laboratory Delivery System*. Washington, D.C.: U.S. Government Printing Office, 1973.

Reiss, Albert J., Jr. *The Police and the Public*. New Haven: Yale University Press, 1971.

Richardson, James R. *Modern Scientific Evidence*. Second edition. Cincinnati: The W. H. Anderson Co., 1974.

Rosenthal, Paul. *Planning Study for Evaluation of Forensic Laboratory Services in Erie, Niagara and Wyoming Counties, New York*. Buffalo, N.Y.: Cornell Aeronautical Laboratory, Inc., 1969.

Schur, Edwin M. *Law and Society: A Sociological View*. New York: Random House, 1968.

Skolnick, Jerome H. *Justice Without Trial: Law Enforcement in Democratic Society*. New York: John Wiley and Sons, Inc., 1966.

Smith, Bruce, Sr. *Police Systems in the United States*. Second revised edition. New York: Harper and Brothers, 1960.

Soderman, Harry, and John J. O'Connell. *Modern Criminal Investigation*. Fifth edition. New York: Funk and Wagnalls, 1962.

Svensson, Arne, and Otto Wendel. *Techniques of Crime Scene Investigation*. New York: American Elsevier Publishing Co., Inc., 1965.

Thomas, William A. *Scientists in the Legal System*. Ann Arbor, Mich.: Ann Arbor Science Publishers, Inc., 1974.

Thorwald, Jurgen. *The Century of the Detective*. New York: Harcourt, Brace and World, Inc., 1965.

—————— *Crime and Science*. New York: Harcourt, Brace and World, Inc., 1967.

Turner, Ralph F. *Forensic Science and Laboratory Techniques*. Springfield, Ill.: Charles C. Thomas, 1949.

U.S. District Court, Northern District of Illinois, Eastern Division, *Report of the January 1970 Grand Jury*. Washington, D.C.: U.S. Government Printing Office, 1970. -

Walls, H.J. *Forensic Science*. Second edition. New York: Frederick A. Praeger, Inc., 1974.

Ward, Richard H. *Introduction to Criminal Investigation*. Reading, Mass.: Addison-Wesley Publishing Company, 1975.

Weihs, Frederick J. *Science Against Crime*. New York: Collier Books, 1964.

Weston, Paul B., and Kenneth Wells. *Criminal Investigation*. Second edition. Englewood Cliffs, N.J.: Prentice Hall, Inc., 1974.

Wilson, James Q. *Varieties of Police Behavior*. Cambridge, Mass.: Harvard University Press, 1968.

Wilson, O. W. *Police Administration*. Third edition. New York: McGraw-Hill Book Co., 1972.

Yefsky, S. A., ed. *Law Enforcement Science and Technology*. London: Academic Press, 1967.

ARTICLES

Baker, Norman F., and Fred E. Inbau, "The Scientific Detection of Crime." *Minnesota Law Review*, 17 (1933), 602-629.

Bonamarte, Michael F., Jr., and Andrew H. Principe. "Training a Task Force of Evidence Technicians." *Police Chief*, (June, 1970), 49-53.

Blumstein, Alfred. "Police Technology." *Science and Technology*, No. 72, (December, 1967), 42-50.

Ceccaldi, P.F. "From Crime to Evidence." *International Criminal Police Review*, 264, (January, 1973), 2-8.

Curry, Alan S. "Science Against Crime." *Science and Technology*, 47, (November, 1965), 39-48.

Flannery, Thomas A. "The Prosecutor and the Forensic Scientist." *Journal of the AOAC*, 55, No. 4, (1972), 860-865.

Guttenplan, Henry L. "The Role of the Laboratory in a Law Enforcement Agency." *Police*, 4, (March-April, 1967), 13-20.

Kingston, Charles R. "Forensic Science." *ASTM Standardization News*, 1, (April, 1973), 8-15.

Kingston, C. R. and J. L. Peterson, "Forensic Science and the Reduction of Crime." *Journal of Forensic Sciences*, 19, No. 3, (1974), 417-427.

Kirk, Paul. "Criminalistics at the Crossroads." *The Criminologist*, 4, No. 11, (February, 1969), 35-41.

——————— "The Ontogeny of Criminalistics." *Journal of Criminal Law, Criminology, and Police Science*, 54, No. 2, (1963), 235-238.

——————— "The Interrelationship of Law and Science." *Buffalo Law Review*, 13, No. 2, (Winter, 1964), 393-401.

Krendel, Ezra S., and R. Michael Dummer. "Evaluating and Planning of a Component in the Criminal Justice System." *Socio-Econ. Plan. Sci.*, 6, (1972), 217-226.

Loughrey, Leo C., and Herbert C. Friese, Jr. "Curriculum Development For a Police Science Program." *Journal of Criminal Law, Criminology and Police Science*, 60, No. 2, (June, 1969), 265-271.

Misner, Gordon E. "The Urban Police Mission." *Issues in Criminology*, 3, No. 1, (Summer, 1967), 35-46.

Moomaw, Joseph F. "Forensic Laboratory Services." *Laboratory Management*, 3, No. 1, (January, 1965), 30-33.

Parker, Brian P. "Scientific Proof." *Revista Juridica de la Universidad de P.R.*, XXXII, No. 2, (1963), 201-213.

Patterson, D. "Science and the Courts." *Journal of the Forensic Science Society*, 1, No. 1, (1960), 5-6.

Samen, Charles C. "Mini-Lab on Wheels." *FBI Law Enforcement Bulletin*, 38, (May, 1969), 12-15 and 23.

"Solving Crimes in the Laboratory." *Business Week*, April 20, 1968, 70-81.

Starrs, James E. "The Ethical Obligations of the Forensic Scientist in the Criminal Justice System." *Journal of the AOAC*, 54, (1971), 906-914.

Thomson, M. A. "Bias and Quality Control in Forensic Science: A Cause for Concern." *Journal of Forensic Sciences*, 19, No. 3, (July, 1974), 504-517.

INDEX

American Chemical Society, 292
Analytical methods of analysis, 120, 128, 276; in the FBI laboratory, 172-173
Asphyxia, 57, 60
Atomic absorption spectrometry, 131
Automated analyses, 143

Benson, W.R., (cont.) 261-288
Bertillon, Alphonse, 66
Blackstone, W., 24
Blood grouping, 138; electrophoretic techniques, 138; immunological methods, 139; statistical data, 204; as evidence in capital cases, 333
Blood-alcohol, determination of, 158-160
Borkenstein, Robert F., (cont.) 247-260
Bowman, Craig, (cont.) 415-427
Bullet comparisons, 79-80, 128
Bureau of Narcotics and Dangerous Drugs (BNDD), now the Drug Enforcement Administration (DEA), 166, 289
Burglaries, as a source of physical evidence, 361

California Association of Criminalists, 112, 373
California, University of, School of Criminology, 102, 167, 372
Capital crimes, 332
Cases per officer (CPO) concept, 263
Chicago: scientific crime detection laboratory, 73, 97-98
Chromatographic techniques, 115, 134-135, 154
Common origin, spatial, morphological and compositional, 113, 373; *see also* individualization
Communications, between the scientist and investigator, 96-97, 120; gap between scientists and attorneys, 385-386; with the layman, 125